THE
WALDORF
ASTORIA
BAR BOOK

THE
WALDORF
ASTORIA
BAR BOOK

FRANK
CAIAFA

PENGUIN BOOKS

PENGUIN BOOKS
An imprint of Penguin Random House LLC
375 Hudson Street
New York, New York 10014
penguin.com

The Old Waldorf-Astoria Bar Book by Albert Stevens Crockett
published by Dodd, Mead and Company 1934
This revised and expanded edition
published in Penguin Books 2016

Illustrations by Josie Portillo

ISBN 978-0-14-312480-1

Printed in the United States of America

1   3   5   7   9   10   8   6   4   2

Set in Basilia Com, Campton Book, and Vintage

Designed by Sabrina Bowers

CONTENTS

THE
WALDORF
ASTORIA
BAR BOOK

INTRODUCTION

I drink to the general joy o' the whole table.
—William Shakespeare, *Macbeth*

In the summer of 2005, I responded to an advertisement for a bar manager position. No mention was made of the venue, but when I made the short list, I discovered the restaurant was the newly renovated Peacock Alley, in the lobby of the Waldorf-Astoria. The opportunity to manage this iconic venue with such a long and storied history and many of New York City's brightest culinary stars was one I couldn't pass up. At the time, there weren't many beverage programs in NYC (or anywhere, for that matter, and certainly not in hotels) that concentrated on classic and seasonal cocktails along with a well-curated wine-by-the-glass program, prepared with care and meant to pair with the restaurant's cuisine. Though it had begun a few years prior in small bars and speakeasies, today's cocktail renaissance was really just getting under way, as the now classic NYC bars where we have come to expect this brand of service from were just opening.

Peacock Alley was an ideal showcase for ideas that had not fit the menu at my previous bars. I ran toward the challenge not only to offer such items but to execute them consistently and in an extremely high-volume arena. No easy task. After all, it would be the first time in its history that Peacock Alley would have a proper bar in the dining room and lounge. Previous incarnations did feature cocktail service, however drinks were prepared at a service bar to the side of what was then known as the Peacock Alley Café and Lounge or in the "back of the house" at a service bar far from the guests' views and then delivered to the dining room floor. Finally the lobby patrons of one of the most celebrated hotels in the world could congregate, imbibe, and see and be seen from a perch worthy of its history. More than thirty feet long, set in the center of the main lobby, this would represent the new beginning and the return of a proper bar worthy of its Fifth Avenue predecessor, which served its last historic drink at the onset of Prohibition. The new Peacock Alley would coexist with two iconic bars in the Bull and Bear Prime Steakhouse and Sir Harry's Bar. We would be players on an unparalleled stage. With an eye toward the future but fully aware of its storied past, we set out to accentuate the classic aesthetics of the Old Bar.

I grew up in a New York City much different from the one that exists today. When it came to bars in the 1970s and '80s, for instance, their open room-temperature vermouth bottles were a year old and spoiled. Further, a good portion of the fine folks who had been paying their rent working pridefully as bartenders probably couldn't tell you much more than that their Scotch was from Scotland and their beer from Milwaukee.

Today, vermouth has returned to its rightful place in the cocktail pecking order with varied choices, which include small-production brands and limited releases from larger houses. The skilled and well-trained bartenders behind the stick today not only can identify from where each whiskey hails but can probably describe the method of distillation and the master distiller to boot. It's a different world.

I recall going to the old Jimmy Day's Bar on West Fourth Street when I was sixteen or seventeen years old, having what I thought was the best pea soup in the world with a beer, hoping no one would card me. I watched as the older gentleman behind the bar, with his slightly soiled apron, muddled an orange wheel, a neon red cherry, and a spoonful of sugar in a double rocks glass (I don't recall the use of bitters, but I will give him the benefit of the doubt), pack it tightly with chipped ice, and glug in as much blended whiskey (usually Fleischmann's or Seagram's) as the glass could hold. Toss another cherry on top and a squirt of club soda from the soda gun and there was your Old Fashioned. Nearly every nonalcoholic item was dispensed from the soda gun, including overly sweetened and artificial sour mix and sometimes even "juice." Today, the use of a soda gun is not a sign of the coming apocalypse. Artisanal soda producers are creating cane-based syrups that can be used in that system. Even the old soda gun has evolved.

Those were not discerning times. Women frequently ordered Madrases (vodka, cranberry juice, and orange juice) and Melon Balls (vodka, Midori melon liqueur, and pineapple juice). Even the simple, fresh, and sometimes maligned Cosmopolitan (citrus vodka, triple sec, fresh lime juice, and a touch of cranberry) was still a few years away. Most men were drinking whiskey neat or in Highballs and mass-produced domestic beer, without any artisanal bitters in sight.

A catalyst for change was America's resurgent interest in all things culinary and the public's concern over what they served on their tables at home. Particularly here in New York, people went out for lunch and dinner, and beginning around the early 1980s or so it became the norm to identify a chef with his restaurant. Chefs became brands unto themselves. Word of mouth and unsolicited buzz began an interest in a component of the business previously reserved for the toniest of establishments. That begat the resurgence of television chefs, who really had not had a presence in the American home since the days of Julia Child and the Galloping Gourmet. It was inevitable that this kitchen culture (which never really went out of style in other countries) would turn its attention to the beverage portion of the meal. As palates were educated, people with increasingly selective tastes and expanding food vocabularies desired more from their predinner cocktail, choice of wine with dinner, and digestif.

Yet, as I stress with the team, not everyone wants an artisanal vermouth or a dissertation on the differences between Speyside and Islay Scotch whisky. Nor do they want a pre-Prohibition-style Old Fashioned, and yes, some people simply want a vodka tonic or a cold beer. It is really all about our guests. Our job is to provide them with what they want without a look down our collective noses. We are here to put smiles on people's faces and help create memories. If we procure that smile from an archival cocktail that was served in the Old Bar a hundred years ago, or from the finest Bay Breeze this particular guest has ever had, it doesn't matter in the least. To me, especially today, when everyone's time is at a premium, the more welcoming we can make our guests' experience, the better off everyone will be.

When the thought of updating two of the most iconic bar books of all time first came to me, I envisioned it for the novice bar enthusiast: one with an interest in cocktails and its modern culture but little or no experience preparing cocktails at home. In fact, that was the inspiration of this book. Years ago I found a 1960 *Calvert Party Encyclopedia*. These little guides were products of their time, sold inexpensively at the cash registers of liquor stores as a way to encourage brand support—and they were not ashamed to let you know it. (The more elaborate *Mr. Boston Official Bartender's Guide* is another example of this type of advertising.) If you wanted to know how to make a Martini, why, use Calvert gin! A Manhattan? You guessed it, Calvert whiskey! They also included jokes, party games, and limericks (all G-rated!). I thought that this kind of light-hearted touch would serve the Old Books well.

Alas, once I began the research, it became clear pretty quickly that the history of the Waldorf Astoria Hotel (henceforth referred to as the Hotel), although not without its light moments, would leave no room for limericks. Between the loose transcriptions of the two Waldorf Astoria bar books by Albert Stevens Crockett (*Old Waldorf Bar Days*, 1931, and *The Old Waldorf-Astoria Bar Book*, 1934) and the eighty-year gap of cocktail history between those books and the present day, I knew that there would be little space for party games.

That said, I did want to fill in as many holes as possible. My hope is that this book will appeal to not only the home cocktail enthusiast but the hotel guest, professional bartender, and anyone else who wants to make a few classic cocktails and be surprised at the sheer level of variety that the recipes offer, both old and new. Researching the recipes of the Old Books and the books of their era was like listening to scratchy recordings on well-worn vinyl. I felt like the modern audio engineer brought in to remaster old recordings, pulling away the hisses and scratches to reveal crystal clear sound and uncover the intended delicious cocktail beneath it all.

While trying to cover all of these bases, this book simply couldn't be a comprehensive guide to professional bartending. There was just too much ground to cover from the Old Books to include every essential cocktail or methodology from the end of Prohibition to the current day. I can say that every recipe that is included in the original two books is name-checked within. I also made room to include essential recipes that have remained popular or withstood trends, and even some that have made surprising comebacks. The Bloody Mary and the Hemingway Daiquiri both come to mind as recipes whose creations postdate the Old Books, but this anthology would not be complete without them. Just about every recipe that we created from the reconstruction of Peacock Alley in 2005 is also included. I like to think that these new recipes reflect the evolving tastes of the cocktail culture more than our foresight to include, for instance, a long-overlooked and challenging ingredient such as sherry. In other words, I may have had the idea for a sherry cocktail in 2005 and had the initiative to include it on the menu, but it would not have lasted long; the drinking guest was not quite ready for it. By 2010, it was a different story entirely.

In the case of nonalcoholic recipes, their sheer number excluded them. Having pages of different sodas with a variety of twists and bitters would have taken up much more space than I had room for. Although we have served plenty of interesting and fresh "mocktails" and the like throughout the years, they remain to be addressed in another forum.

While my main focus was revisiting, revising, and adapting every recipe in the Old Books, there are three other publications whose link to the Hotel made their inclusion necessary. The first was Jacques Straub's *Drinks* (1914). According to cocktail historian David Wondrich's preface to its latest edition, Jacques Straub was friends with Oscar Tschirky, the famous "Oscar of the Waldorf." Oscar was the maître d'hôtel from its opening until his semiretirement in 1943, and actually may have accompanied Mr. Straub to America from Switzerland. Mr. Tschirky does provide a brief preface to *Drinks* and in all likelihood allowed Mr. Straub a good look at the original, handwritten Waldorf-Astoria bar recipe book. Keeping Mr. Crockett's books the primary focus, I could not use Mr. Straub's book or any of the number of cocktail books that predated them as the root source for any particular recipe. In other words, I let common sense be my guide. Though this led me down many a rabbit hole, if a cocktail had variations that predated the Old Bar's and is widely recognized as the standard, I made sure to research it and, if necessary, include it in this book, allowing the Old Bar's version to lead the way. One such recipe is the classic Bijou cocktail. What is considered the standard recipe is found in most other books and differs greatly from the Waldorf Astoria version, so there was no way around including both. They each have their merits. I also used text to explain such differences in other recipes in an effort not to reprint every variation from every pre-Prohibition cocktail book. At the end of the day, I had to keep to the goal of updating the Waldorf Astoria recipes as they were, while recognizing the standards and describing the variations on the theme as concisely as possible.

Another important collection from which I made sure to glean any recipes credited to the Hotel was Ted Saucier's *Bottoms Up* (1951). Mr. Saucier was the director of publicity and public relations for the Hotel for twenty-one years, until 1950. He was also an integral part of the production of the classic film *Week-End at the Waldorf* (1945). He used his experience at Fox Film (where he broke into the PR field) to collaborate on the story and become the film's technical director for MGM. Besides being one the most used guidebooks for the savviest of bartenders during a time when cocktail books were not as commonplace as they are today, *Bottoms Up* is the first book to feature recipes that represented the "new" Waldorf-Astoria. It's also known for its risqué portraits of scantily clad women.

The final book whose link demanded inclusion in this volume was Oscar Tschirky's *100 Famous Cocktails* (1934). When I began researching this project, our archives remarkably did not hold a copy of this slim manual, so I was unaware of its existence until David Wondrich mentioned it to me very early in this book's gestation process. Though its contents mostly overlap with the Old Books, there are a couple of unique listings that I've adapted within.

For clarity's sake, I have added the recipe's origin next to the title of each entry that did not originate from the Waldorf Astoria. If I have not listed the origin, the recipe was included in either *Old Waldorf Bar Days* or *The Old Waldorf-Astoria Bar Book*, or both.

This is not to say that these were the only books that influenced the Old Bar or this book. Jerry Thomas's *Bartenders Guide* (1862), Harry Johnson's *Bartender's Manual* (1882), O. H. Byron's *Modern Bartenders' Guide* (1884), William Boothby's *American Bartender* (1891), William Schmidt's *The Flowing Bowl* (1891), George Kappeler's *Modern American Drinks* (1895), Tim Daly's *Bartenders' Encyclopedia* (1903), and Thomas Stuart's *Fancy Drinks and How to Mix Them* (1904) were among the first generation of books published that were geared for bartenders and the working bar, and renditions of their recipes comprise a good portion of the old Waldorf-Astoria bar books. Later books, which had an influence on the Old Bar (if not Mr. Crockett), included Jack Grohusko's *Jack's Manual* (1908), Tom Bullock's *The Ideal Bartender (1917),* and Hugo Ensslin's *Recipes for Mixed Drinks* (1917). Recipes from these books and others are mentioned as benchmarks in related Waldorf Astoria entries and make for appealing reads if your interest grows beyond this collection.

As for the original, legendary, handwritten bar book—which Joseph Taylor and the other bartenders at the Old Bar used to jot down recipes, ideas, and liquid combinations—it is, I'm afraid, lost to history. Mr. Crockett passed away in 1969; his papers are housed in the University of Wisconsin and this artifact is not among them. I also uncovered that in his later days, he was cared for by journalist friends Bob Considine (whose papers are held at Syracuse University) and Louis Lochner (Concordia Historical Institute). I've checked those in hopes that the book had been gifted to one of them by Mr. Crockett but to no avail. It is a fantasy of mine that upon publication of this book, someone whose great-grandfather might have been friends with Mr. Crockett will recall seeing an old box in the basement and decide to look for it, and realize he or she is in the possession of this bartending holy grail. What a thrill it would be to see even one page. My fantasy also includes this person forwarding the thing to me free of charge, of course. One can dream, can't one?

It took more than three years for me to taste and develop every cocktail contained in this book. Some entries were easier to adapt than others. Funnily enough, it was the ones that seemed simple on paper that took the longest to research and adjust. For recipes that are more than one hundred years old, so many of them surprised me with how well they managed to time travel and still be relevant. There are so many interesting, challenging, and delicious cocktails that could have easily been created today by any number of bartenders in the world's finest bars or restaurants. Another surprise was the amount of refreshing summertime Coolers and juice-based drinks that were included in the Old Books. At first glance the books can seem like one long list of Martini and Manhattan variations, but upon further review, plenty of seasonal variety can be found.

As for the cataloging of the recipes, I felt that the listing would be more accessible if I did not compartmentalize by genre. In other words, I did not want anyone to be scared off by a Martini (or Cocktail) chapter, with its booze-forward identity, and simply stick to the Sour or Highball section within their current comfort zone. I did not want to make reading through this book a job, and what's a "Fizz" or a "Smash," anyway? I felt you will be more apt to try something based on the lead spirit or maybe even its interesting story than disregard it because it has vermouth in it, for instance.

Another great by-product of researching and developing these old recipes is that some of them may wind up on the menus of existing establishments, giving these classic tipples a new lease on life in the twenty-first century. I can't wait to see which ones claim this type of attention.

When I finally landed on a rendition of a cocktail that I thought worthy of inclusion, I often imagined serving it to Oscar Tschirky, Albert Crockett, or the original bar staff. How wonderful it would be to see their faces as they tasted these cocktails, made with today's ingredients, with some brands that they would recognize and others they surely would not.

It is also interesting to note that I could not have even begun to attempt this undertaking ten years ago. I would have been unable to include many of the recipes, as there would have been too many unavailable ingredients. Most tellingly, for example, there was no Old Tom gin on the market when we reopened Peacock Alley, and in order to include kümmel in a recipe I had to make it myself from scratch.

Another goal of this book is to make home cocktail enthusiasts more adventurous and willing to take chances, expanding their palates and those of their guests. I know this will happen just by bearing witness to what transpires in bars today, with guests more than willing to have bartenders create cocktails for them based on a lead spirit or modifying ingredient of choice. Guests end up trying things they would never have dreamed of when they woke up that morning. Trying a mezcal- or grappa-based cocktail cannot be far behind. If the drinking public can take that kind of leap with a bartender whom they may not even know, I have to think that they will be able to trust themselves as they gain experience with the basic flavor profiles of most of the ingredients in this book.

This book is meant to be a launching pad, providing templates for you to tweak and enjoy as you would recipes in a cookbook. There are no hard-and-fast rules here; after all, that's how new cocktails are made. If you like a recipe that features bourbon in the lead role, try it the next time with rye whiskey or rum. Same goes for swapping lime juice for lemon. You will be surprised at how different it tastes and how the modifying ingredients react with the new lead spirit. You get the idea.

In 1893, George C. Boldt was selected by William Waldorf Astor to be the first manager of the Waldorf Hotel, which was located on Fifth Avenue and Thirty-third Street (where the Empire State Building stands today). In 1897, John Jacob Astor IV's adjoining Astoria hotel was opened. Boldt would come to direct both the Waldorf and the Astoria upon their merge, signified by the famous equal sign between the two entities. Once combined, the Waldorf=Astoria was the first hotel to feature electricity, private bathrooms, and telephones throughout its thousand-plus rooms. The glamorous, three-hundred-foot marble corridor that connected the two hotels came to be known as Peacock Alley, because of the well-dressed clientele who strutted the latest fashions in the great hall. An early supporter of women's equality, it was also the first hotel to employ female floor clerks, and it allowed women to smoke in public (which was a big deal at the time). Furthermore, the "ladies' entrance" of the Old Hotel was abolished, though it took until 1960 (in the "new" Hotel) to allow women into the Bull and Bear Prime Steakhouse when it replaced the Men's Bar. The new building's Men's Bar was on the corner of Forty-ninth Street and Park Avenue; Bull and Bear has been on the corner of Forty-ninth and Lexington since 1960. Oscar-winning actress Jessica Tandy cut the ribbon on opening day and her colleague Hermione Gingold was the first to cross the threshold. They were the first women served; however, women were allowed to enter only after three p.m., and then only with an escort.

Another of the Old Hotel's attractions was the installation of one of the first rooftop gardens, providing full service in the summer and an ice-skating rink in the winter. Its ballroom was the first of its size and gave the well-heeled of the day a place to host lavish balls and benefits that wouldn't fit in their own opulent homes.

The Waldorf-Astoria's Men's Bar opened in the Astoria Hotel in 1897 with its iconic four-sided bar, big brass rail, and bronze bull and bear (and baby lamb) statues. It was open from six a.m. to one a.m. (if not later) daily, and no less than ten bartenders were on hand, serving famous concoctions to crowds that grew to more than three deep during the hours between four p.m. and seven p.m. Nearly all major hotels at that time featured a lounge or bar, but listed above them all would have to be the bar at the old Waldorf-Astoria. It catered to all strata of society, from steel magnates to migrant construction workers and everyone in between, including publishers, ballplayers, beer barons, politicians, actors, and boxers. Anyone who wanted to be anyone made time to stop at this bar, which featured one of the first (if not the best) free lunch buffets in NYC and included a live fish pool where one's dinner was chosen and caught with a net. Cocktails were twenty cents, as were High-balls, and you helped yourself from the bottle! The cigar selection was second to none and top choices could be had for a dollar (a princely sum at the time). Much has been made about these innova-tions of the Old Hotel and Bar. Whether or not their origins can be verified, they all have iconic associations with the Waldorf Astoria legacy. The one that really knocks me out is that the red velvet rope outside an establishment to help form a queue is credited to Oscar Tschirky, who is better known for his culinary contributions, includ-ing the Waldorf salad, Eggs Benedict (a dish he modified and added to the menu when Lemuel Benedict, a Wall Street broker, requested the items in the dish as a hangover cure), Thousand Island dressing, Veal Oscar, and, of course, Red Velvet cake.

Albert Stevens Crockett was born in Solomons, Maryland, on June 19, 1873. He was an NYC newspaper columnist who served two separate stints in the 1920s as the Hotel's publicist. He was a col-umnist for the *Sun* (1909–1912), the *New York Herald,* and the *New York Times* (1912–1915). He also wrote a popular New York–based column, "Heard in Hotel Corridors," which was widely quoted at the time. He volunteered to work in Washington, D.C., during World War I for the U.S. Food Administration. After the war, he was vice president and general manager of the Bryant Advertising Company. He edited *World Traveler* and *Nomad* magazines from 1920 to 1929, which allowed him ample travel and helped broaden his palate during the Prohibition Era. During this period he also worked as the news editor for the Waldorf-Astoria (again) and he wrote several books: *Revelations of Louise* (1920), *When James Gordon Bennett Was Caliph of Bagdad* (1926), *Old Waldorf Bar Days* (1931), *Peacocks on Parade* (1931; a history of the Old Hotel), and a book of poetry, *Ditties from a Ditty Bag* (1922).

While he spent plenty of time at the Old Bar (and others like it),

Mr. Crockett was never a barman. His working knowledge of the bar came from his experiences in it and his relationships with the bar staff. With the onset of the Volstead Act on January 16, 1919 (Prohibition, to me and you), the Old Bar served its last drink. The bar staff took on other work, both in and out of the Hotel. One original bartender, Joseph Taylor, remained employed until the closing of the Hotel (May 3, 1929), and according to Mr.Crockett's recollection in *Old Waldorf Bar Days* (1931), Mr. Taylor gifted him "a leather-bound volume, its edges brown and its pages dog-eared from frequent use . . . a compendium of recipes for making all sorts of hard thirst-quenchers—a cyclopedia of directions for composing almost every kind of fancy drink served in the old Waldorf-Astoria Bar." He then attempted to "decode, rearrange and classify" the recipes, but because he was not a barman by trade, some of the subtleties were lost on him. Mr. Taylor's original listing was categorical by type of drink, rather than alphabetized, as in the first book (it seems that Mr. Crockett attempted to right this in the revised second book). On more than one occasion Crockett transcribed dashes of "gum" (a thickened sugar syrup containing gum arabic) as dashes of "gin." He transcribed cocktail titles incorrectly simply because he misread the handwritten entry. Some adjoining stories sit squarely in the realm of tall tale, but I'm okay with all of that. After all, *Old Waldorf Bar Days* was a book about "the history of the Old Waldorf Bar" whose only intention was posterity. Almost as an afterthought, it included 489 recipes, almost none of which could be made legally (much less properly) in the entire United States of America. Who could guess if or when that would change?

Well, things did change. On December 5, 1933, the Volstead Act was repealed and drinking in America began again with fervor. The book attracted plenty of attention, as it contained cocktail recipes of the bygone era, so much so that Mr. Crockett was asked by his publisher to revise *Old Waldorf Bar Days*. His journeys during the 1920s expanded his awareness of cocktails and concoctions from around the globe and he included recipes found in some of these faraway locales in his revised book, *The Old Waldorf-Astoria Bar Book*. (Notably, he credited the worldly hotel manager of the day, T. G. S. Hooke, for the forty-seven recipes included in the "Jamaican Jollifiers" chapter, though a good portion of their origins can be attributed elsewhere.) Originally released in 1934, with a second publication in 1935, *The Old Waldorf-Astoria Bar Book* went much lighter on the text and history of the Hotel and concentrated on the recipes, now totaling 625 in all. It is the version that most people who own an *Old Waldorf-Astoria Bar Book* have, as it has been reprinted throughout the years. *Old*

Waldorf Bar Days was never reprinted; that first silver pressing, with the small cartoon waiter on the cover, was the only version ever published.

The Waldorf Astoria Hotel that exists today nearly did not make it past being a grandiose vision. The contracts to begin construction on the project were signed on Monday, October 28, 1929, only one day prior to the stock market crash and the advent of the Great Depression. Had the signing been delayed by twelve hours, there certainly would not have been a new Waldorf-Astoria.

It took less than two years to build the new Waldorf-Astoria Hotel, a testament to the construction practices of the day. The Hotel opened on October 1, 1931 (just weeks before the George Washington Bridge). At the time of its opening, it was the largest and tallest hotel in the world. Its art deco take on the twentieth century included the Starlight Roof's original retractable ceiling, a four-story grand ballroom, air-conditioning in every room, twenty-four-hour room service, and the availability of nearly every amenity you could imagine, including a pharmacy, barber shop, a bank, and a haberdashery where guests could get custom-made clothing.

Every U.S. president since Herbert Hoover has called the Waldorf Astoria home when in New York City (Hoover and Dwight D. Eisenhower both actually lived at the Hotel after their presidencies). The three-bedroom, three-bathroom presidential suite on the thirty-fifth floor of the Towers was originally furnished in colonial style, but in 1969 it was remodeled with a Georgian motif in homage to the current White House. The suite also included the first electric kitchen, installed by General Electric.

As with the original Hotel, leaders in all areas of business, politics, sports, music, and movies continue to frequent the Waldorf Astoria as welcome guests and residents, and we don't expect that tradition to change anytime soon.

It took more than eighty years for the cocktail culture to begin to regain the heights of its pre-Prohibition glory, and we are lucky to be living during the second golden age today. But no matter how well versed you may become as a host and bartender, there is nothing quite like a cocktail (and a bite to eat) in your favorite bar or restaurant. It is special to be on the receiving end of great service and we hope to continue to provide it for you here at the Waldorf Astoria for many years to come.

THE HOME BAR

What makes a professional bartender, well, professional? Sure, there's the ability to mix drinks quickly and correctly, earning a sigh of pleasure or a nod of agreement at the quality of the cocktail in hand. But what is the defining skill that separates the professional from, say, a robot that can crank out cocktails and land them within the target of your cocktail napkin? For me, it is the ability to maintain a comfortable environment and provide proper hospitality, which is easier said than done. The best bartenders create a seamless, all-inclusive environment where guests immediately feel welcome. Remember, the bartender is never the star; the guests are. This is where you come in. This is the reason why people go to bars in the first place. If it was only to have a drink, they would stay at home and pour one themselves. We go out for the company of others, socializing and experiencing things that we could not at home. After all, the term *pub* is short for "public house."

While preparing for the daily operations of the commercial bar, we can anticipate a certain level of business flow, or at least we try to. But there are times when all the planning in the world will leave you unprepared and in mere moments you are "in the weeds."

By and large, these twists of circumstance won't happen to your planned event. Your guests are expecting a good time, and even if a few invitees decide to bring along some friends or an unforeseen incident keeps a few guests from attending, your party will proceed as planned. That's good news. Now it's just a matter of having the standard tools, supplies, and a bit of experience to host a gathering that will ensure a fun and successful event.

My first bit of advice, especially if you are completely new to hosting a bar and making consistent cocktails, is to start small and with a bit of practice. Prior to your event, prepare a stirred drink for yourself, using water at first to stand in for spirits. Become accustomed to holding a jigger, pouring a portion into it, adding the right type of ice, and then properly stirring or shaking, straining, and garnishing the "cocktail." Practice grating nutmeg and notice how much falls from the microplane with only one or two scrapes, or how much oil sprays out from a coin-size orange peel when it's snapped above the surface of the "cocktail." If you'd like to serve in another area of your home rather than where your preparation area or "bar" is located, place a few drinks on a tray and walk with them. It may seem a bit ridiculous now, but these few simple practice steps will give you confidence, even if your next step is to prepare a proper cocktail for yourself.

The goal is to familiarize yourself with your equipment and each tool's purpose. Don't worry, it won't take long for you to get the hang of it. After a few weekend barbecues or home cocktail hours, you will be on your way. As a result, you may also find a renewed appreciation for your local bartenders as you observe them ply their trade while maintaining light conversation, explaining menu items, and preparing for their next guest.

One of the things that you can do to guarantee success is limit the scope of your gathering. Building the event around a particular cuisine will help narrow your menu and ensure that you don't spend the majority of your time behind your bar. You can also "batch" a lower-alcohol punch for guests to enjoy throughout your party and individually prepare a more complicated cocktail to be served upon arrival. Just be sure to have plenty of water and nonalcoholic beverages available as well.

In the end, what really connects the pro bartender to the generous host and home bartender is the ability to provide the friendly and welcoming environment that allows guests to relax and have a good time.

BASIC TOOLS

The following list contains the basic tools you will need to assemble cocktails at home. It's not a bad idea to grow your inventory to include at least two sets of Boston shakers, jiggers, and bar spoons so your guests can pitch in. You can pass on your newfound knowledge while adding to the rich history and craft of bartending. I still have the same basic set of tools that I started bartending with more than twenty years ago, so your first set of most of these items could be your last. Quality versions will pay for themselves over time. Though there are many other items available to perform a variety of tasks, the following tools will get you through most recipes. You will probably have some of them in your kitchen already, but I recommend Cocktail Kingdom as a good place to start.

Boston shaker (one 28-oz. metal shaker, one tempered 16-oz. glass): Both are used for shaking; the glass is used for stirring.

Julep strainer: Perforated large, shell-like metal spoon, used for straining drinks from the glass half of the Boston shaker.

Hawthorne strainer: Larger, slotted metal strainer with coil attached, used for straining from the metal cup of the Boston shaker.

Fine strainer: Conical mesh strainer used to "double"-strain cocktails to eliminate pulp or ice shards.

Metal jigger (one with top 1 oz., bottom 2 oz.; one with top $3/4$ oz., bottom $1^1/2$ oz.): Some manufacturers make a 1- and 2-ounce jigger with markings on the inside denoting quarter, half, and three-quarter levels. This is the one I use. Avoid the layered plastic versions, as recognizing and reading the markings is close to impossible, especially if you're trying to move quickly in a low-light area.

Bar spoon: Long, thin spoon with twisted handle used for stirring drinks and measuring very small amounts of liquid. Some may have flat tops for swizzling drinks with crushed ice.

Muddler: Although other kitchen items may be used in a

pinch, once you use a well-made, dedicated muddler you won't go back.

Citrus hand press: These come in different sizes for various fruits and are important when preparing only a few drinks.

Horizontal, or "Y," vegetable peeler: For your standard peel garnish.

Paring knives: I recommend having two kinds: a flat edge and a serrated version.

Cutting board: Used for cutting and preparing garnishes.

Wine key (corkscrew): Preferably one with a double hinge that allows you to pull the cork from a bottle in two incremental moves; makes opening a corked bottle a breeze.

Bottle opener: Having more than one is essential, especially in summertime. Your wine key will probably have one.

Microplane: Essential for zesting citrus and grating chocolate and nutmeg.

Pitchers: You can't have too many glass and sealable plastic pitchers, both for service and to store fresh juices and other mixers. I also recommend one made of aluminum. I use mine constantly during the summer, building drinks (such as Margaritas and the pitchers in the "Large Cups and Punches" chapter) directly in it.

Ice buckets: Ideally one for each type of ice you'll be using.

Ice tongs and scoops: It is proper etiquette not to touch your ice directly with your hands. Also, never use a glass to scoop ice. It's dangerous and will definitely put a wrinkle in your event if it includes a trip to the emergency room.

Coasters or cocktail napkins: Often overlooked but essential for stain-free service.

Biodegradable or metal straws: Essential for Juleps and drinks that use crushed ice.

Skewers: A necessity for garnishes that would otherwise sink to the bottom of the glass.

Pour spouts: Preferably stainless steel; they make measuring a breeze, but be sure to save your bottle caps to recap at the party's end to avoid flies or ants getting in and enjoying your goods.

Lewis bag and mallet: A canvas bag and wooden mallet used to crush ice by hand—just like they did it at the Old Bar.

Electric blender: The closer you can get to commercial grade, the better.

GLASSWARE

In general, glassware was much smaller during the time of the Old Bar. You can easily find historically accurate duplications today, but I've opted to meet in the middle here and go with modern industry standards where I can.

Though you may not need all of these, the importance of having and using the proper glassware cannot be overstated. Nothing is worse than trying to enjoy a Highball from a wineglass (unless you're enjoying a gin and tonic in Spain). You don't need a million types of glasses, but the right glass for the right drink will make all the difference. That said, I would start with what you use the most and build from there. Do you enjoy Highballs but don't typically partake in after-dinner cordials? Then there's no need to purchase cordial glasses right away. Give your glassware collection (and your palate) time to grow. As for service, when serving a chilled cocktail, it is imperative that the glass it is being presented in is properly chilled. You can place your glass in the freezer for a few minutes or you can fill it with ice and water as you build your cocktail in your mixing glass. By the time your drink is prepared, your glass will be ready to go. Just be sure that all water is removed prior to filling.

Champagne flute: Champagne coupes are optional, though I prefer them for larger parties, as they add a decided air of elegance. Wine purists most always prefer standard wineglasses to best appreciate the aromatics, but it's a party, not a tasting. Let's have fun.

Cocktail glass or coupe: The V-shaped (post-Prohibition) or coupes are perfect for your classic cocktails, but I also enjoy the rounded "Nick and Nora" style as well.

Old Fashioned or rocks glass: Reliable vessel made to hold mixed cocktails and spirits served both neat and on the rocks.

Collins or highball glass: Tall 10- to 12-ounce glass for "Coolers" of all types.

Small Collins or Fizz glass: Smaller, 6- to 8-ounce glasses for Fizzes and Fixes.

Tumbler: A shorter, 6- to 8-ounce catchall glass that works for Punches as well.

Footed Sour: A 4- to 6-ounce glass with small stem and base. For Sours of all types. If unavailable, a cocktail glass will do fine.

Julep cup: Pewter or silver cup for Juleps of all varieties.

Hoffman House goblet: Though they're not in use much today, I like these thicker-walled 10- to 12-ounce glasses. They're perfect accompaniments to the old-style Punches and mixers found throughout this book. They're also great beer glasses and I consider their use one of my guilty pleasures.

Wineglass: If you're choosing only one, the smaller, Bordeaux-styled glass is much more adaptable for a wider array of uses, such as Sours and cream-based drinks.

Sherry glass: A smaller wineglass, typically about 3 to 6 ounces, used for sherry, port, and even some cocktails.

Cordial glass: Delicate, stemmed, and flared 3- to 4-ounce glass used for liqueurs and digestifs, such as grappa and amaro.

Pony glass: Now hard to find, the smallest of the stemmed glasses holds about 1 ounce each. If you come across the old 1¼-ounce variety, get those.

Brandy snifter: Armagnac, brandy, calvados, and cognac can all find a home here. If you enjoy the ceremony of the swirl, extra añejo tequila expresses itself well here too. You could also substitute your Bordeaux-style wine glass. It's what we use to taste new products and works just fine. I don't care for snifters as the bulbous shape and small opening tend to accentuate mostly the alcohol portion of even the finest brandies.

BASIC TECHNIQUE

▌ Stirring and Shaking

Although addressed throughout this book, there is a basic rule to adhere to that will make your home bartending life much easier: any recipe that contains juice, dairy, or muddled herbs (think food items) gets shaken and any that doesn't (consisting only of spirits, liqueurs, and wines) should be stirred. This holds true 95 percent of the time, with the main exception being those drinks in which a small amount of fresh juice is used for balance as a bittering agent and/or for its acidic properties. In this instance, the cocktail would be stirred.

I pour all ingredients into the mixing glass without ice. This helps you prepare the cocktail without splashing your ingredients atop the ice cubes, which results in an unbalanced cocktail and a messy work area. Mostly, however, it prevents an over-diluted cocktail because it is not sitting on melting ice as you build it. It's a good idea to get yourself into the habit of following some kind of order when building a drink. Starting with bitters, then modifiers, ending with the main spirit, or you could reverse the order, starting with the lead spirit. Either way, this will help you memorize recipes and get a feel for the reason of inclusion for each ingredient.

If I had to say only one thing about ice it would be this: try as you might, you can never, ever have enough of it! In a home bar environment, you really only need one type of ice: $1^1/_4$- to $1^1/_2$-inch cubes. You can repurpose those for most any kind of presentation. You can crack your standard cubes with your bar spoon and crush your ice in your canvas Lewis bag (mallet optional). I also like a few two-inch cubes or spheres (the molds are easily found online) for chilling whiskey without fear of over-dilution.

With recipes requiring stirring, I've directed up to 30 seconds in this book. This is based on using standard, uncracked, "dry" $1^1/_4$- to $1^1/_2$-inch cubes. If using cracked ice or smaller cubes, stir for about 20 seconds. I recommend a mix of both types of ice for best results. At the end of the day, you want a properly chilled and diluted cocktail. Either way, you should be exercising about 50–60 revolutions in that time span. Be sure to fill the mixing glass about three-quarters with ice and stir evenly, using the momentum of the ice to push the contents around the inside of the glass and not just plunging your spoon into and out of the ice, aerating the contents and making a racket in the process. The reason for stirring is to ensure your cocktail has a smooth and weighty trip across the palate. When done stirring, use the Julep strainer to pour from the mixing glass.

Shaken drinks should begin in the same fashion as stirred recipes. When ingredients and ice are both in the mixing glass, you place the metal shaker over the top of the glass with enough force to form a seal. If it's done correctly, a vacuum will form and keep both attached to each other. Clasping both ends of the shaker, you should shake hard and with a rhythm, moving the contents from one end of the cylinder to the other, for at least eight to twelve seconds, depending on the size of your ice and whether the drink will be served up or on ice. If it's to be served over fresh ice, shake less; if it's served up, shake it slightly more. Over time you will be able to adjust the amount of time by intuition, taking into account all of these variables. Don't overthink it. Remember, we are only serving drinks here. When done, allow the cocktail to settle into the bottom shaker for a moment prior to breaking the seal, which is best done by using the heel of your free hand at the lower point of contact. Use the Hawthorne strainer to pour the cocktail from the shaker end.

Finally, if you are completely uncomfortable using a Boston shaker, you can begin with a cobbler shaker. This three-part contraption includes the shaker bottom, a top with a built-in strainer, and a cap to secure it. I recommend skipping this entirely and moving directly to the standard-use, two-piece shaker and spend the bit of time getting the hang of it rather than spending your night trying to remove the top of the frozen cobbler strainer.

▌ "Dry" Shaking

This method is used primarily when the recipe includes egg whites. Thoroughly shaking the egg white prior to adding ice will ensure proper emulsification. Some bartenders opt to preshake the egg white only, then add other ingredients, but it's not really necessary. You can dry-shake the entire contents, as this better incorporates the egg white instead of simply coating the shakers. A better option, especially if preparing for more than one cocktail, would be to dry-shake and emulsify the whites of several eggs and then pour into a measuring cup or small squeeze bottle. Then just measure about a half ounce of egg white per cocktail. This entirely negates the need to dry-shake. Just be sure to keep the whites refrigerated or on ice.

▌ Rolling

This is just pouring the contents of a drink from shaker to shaker (or mixing glass) three or four times and then into the serving glass. This is practiced in recipes in which standard shaking would result in over-dilution. The White Russian and Bloody Mary come to mind as perfect examples of "rolled" recipes.

▌ Muddling

This classic procedure is used for releasing the essence of an ingredient by pressing down on it at the bottom of the mixing glass with a pestle (a rolling pin or a wooden spoon can do the job if you don't have a dedicated muddler on hand). This does not mean that we are to smash all items to a pulp. The level of muddling should be adjusted to the delicacy of the ingredient. Prewashed mint and other herbs should only be tapped or pressed a few times to release their oils. Citrus wedges can take a good press or three to extract the oils from their skins.

▌ Straining

Traditionally, stirred cocktails should be strained with a Julep strainer from the mixing glass portion of the Boston shaker, and shaken drinks from the metal portion using the Hawthorne strainer, though the Hawthorne strainer will work just fine for stirred drinks as well. Most cocktails should be strained onto fresh ice unless the (rare) recipe specifies otherwise. You may also choose to "fine" or "double" strain, holding a fine mesh strainer above the glass when straining from the mixing glass or shaker, ensuring that any unwanted pulp or ice shards are not poured into the cocktail.

STOCKING YOUR HOME BAR

▌ Basic Ingredients

There are several items that should be staples in your home bar, especially if you plan on making the recipes in this book. This is not like your basic home bar—getting these recipes off the ground will require a bit more of a "back bar" as well. Once you have them, they will be the foundation for many cocktails to follow.

Throughout this book, I lean on recommended brands because they work for the recipes at hand and are pretty widely available. It's no different here; the items listed are the ones I feel best represent your typical home bar needs. Feel free to experiment within the categories to find your own personal favorites. See the "House-Made Recipes" chapter for more information regarding usage of the following ingredients.

Bitters

Angostura bitters, Regans' Orange Bitters No. 6, and Peychaud's bitters are the essentials, although there are many other alternatives, including recipes for homemade.

Vermouth, Aromatized, Sherry, and Port Wines

For the dry (French) vermouth, I recommend Noilly Prat extra dry or Dolin dry. For the sweet (Italian) vermouth, I would opt for two. The first and standard style would include Martini & Rossi, Dolin Rouge, Cinzano, and Cocchi Vermouth di Torino (the last two if a slightly more robust version is more your taste, though all fit the classic profile). Second, I would also consider Punt e Mes, Carpano Antica, or Martini Gran Lusso for variety's sake, when more body, spice, and botanicals are the call, though these are not going to be your standard-use items.

When you're looking to expand this category a bit more, the clear and sweet bianco vermouth is your next logical step. Most brands that produce dry and sweet vermouth also make a bianco. Dolin and Carpano make interesting renditions. In general, smaller-production, artisanal brands are also worth investigating when looking for bolder flavors.

For the majority of recipes in this book, other aromatized wines would also fill out your bar nicely and go a long way in allowing you to sample them in all their pre-Prohibition glory. Quinquina, such as the white wine–based Cocchi Americano or Lillet Blanc, can do the job, along with lighter red wine and infused aperitifs such as Maurin Quina and Byrrh. The other extension is the darker chinchona- and gentian-root-based aperitifs such as Bonal Quinquina

Aperitif and Cocchi Barolo Chinato. Just be sure that once opened, they are all stored in your refrigerator for an extended shelf life.

Finally, **sherry, port,** and **Madeira wines** played a prominent role in the era of the Old Bar and their inclusion in cocktails has returned. A basic dry fino style such as Tio Pepe or La Ina and a richer oloroso style such as Lustau Don Nuño will fill many a recipe herein and expand the palates of your guests. The sweet red ruby port would have been the style most used during the time of the Old Bar, but in several recipes I found the more complex and aged tawny style to work wonders. You'll just have to try both and see for yourself.

Liqueurs and Absinthe

Curaçao of some kind is listed throughout this book. Traditionally, this would mean something along the lines of a brandy-based version such as Grand Marnier. Marie Brizard's version works as well. Clear triple secs such as Combier and Cointreau can fill your top shelf though Luxardo and Bols fill in admirably in all recipes. The recently released dry curaçao from the cognac house of Pierre Ferrand plays the middle; we have used it in many of Peacock Alley's recipes since its release in 2012.

Maraschino liqueur is a classic, clear cherry-based liqueur used very liberally at the time of the Old Bar. By the time we reopened Peacock Alley in 2005, its availability was inconsistent, but it is readily available today. There are several on the market, though Luxardo's is the standard.

Absinthe is another essential to fill out a basic bar centered on classic cocktails. For traditional methods of service, there is no replacing the real thing, though if you're only looking to rinse glasses with it or add a dash or two, a good anise-based liqueur such as Herbsaint, Granier, or Henri Bardouin can do the job. Start with a classic absinthe such as Émile Pernot Vieux Pontarlier, Pernod Original Recipe, or the domestic St. George Absinthe Verte if you are only going to keep one of these on hand.

Now that you have the basics, I thought it would be fun to list a few home bar suggestions. As you weave your way through this book, you will find yourself adding to your bar organically to match your evolving palate. The following lists are meant as simple starting points. Feel free to add to your home bar in the order that you see fit for yourself and your guests.

Spirits

1. THE "LET'S GET STARTED" BAR	2. THE "NEXT STEP" BAR	3. THE "NO SENSE IN GOING OUT" BAR
London dry gin	Applejack (bonded) or calvados	Irish whiskey
Old Tom gin	Apricot liqueur	Rhum agricole (aged)
Genever	Amber rum	Tequila blanco
White rum	Dark rum	Tequila reposado
Rye whiskey	Bourbon whiskey	Mezcal
Cognac (VSOP preferred)	Plymouth gin	Vodka
	Scotch whisky (blended)	Bénédictine
		Campari
		Chartreuse (green)
		Crème de cacao (white)
		Crème de menthe (white)

Mixers

As for soda and other mixers, this is another area where it pays to upgrade. Purchase sodas sweetened only with pure cane sugar and not high-fructose corn syrup. These are much less cloying and will allow the spirit and other ingredients to shine through. Be sure to chill all of your mixers prior to using. The refreshing gin and tonic that you were looking forward to will just be a watery and flavorless mess in a minute if you pour warm tonic water over your gin and ice, not to mention the loss of bubbles, as much of the carbonation will foam up and be lost. Once you put this small but important tip into practice, you will never use warm mixers again, and you will know when someone offers you a drink and they did. But you will be happy to pass on your newfound expertise and improve their life as well.

HOUSE-MADE RECIPES

BITTERS

For years, bitters were an afterthought to the preparation in a cocktail, or at best, the cocktail's forgotten friend. Sure, there was a trusty bottle of Angostura underneath the bar, its iconic paper label peeling off because of age and too many spills, ready to win a residency competition against the vermouths that had been there so long they would not even be fit to cook with (we'll get to those).

Every once in a while, a customer would call for some bitters in club soda with plenty of lemon for hiccups or indigestion, or a more refined guest might insist on a drop in his or her over-boozed Manhattan or punchy Old Fashioned, but that was about it. Fortunately, all of that has changed. First came the commercial release of orange bitters from cocktail writer (and lifelong barman extraordinaire) Gary "Gaz" Regan. Then came the resurgence in popularity of New Orleans–style, anise-forward Peychaud's bitters. I will stop here and say that if you only have room for three bitters in your home bar, these two, along with Angostura, constitute your medal stand. Ninety-five percent of all cocktails can be made using these three styles.

The Old Bar used bitters of all varieties, some no longer made, some barely remembered. There is plenty of history regarding the production and use of bitters for "medicinal purposes" as well as use in alcohol-based drinks and punches dating back to the early 1700s. Most important, they are also a key ingredient in the first known mention of the cocktail. Along with spirit, sugar, and water, they help define the category. Besides several pre-Prohibition bar books, Mark Bitterman's *Field Guide to Bitters and Amari* (2015), Brad Thomas Parsons's book, *Bitters (2011)*, and Darcy O'Neil's *Fix the Pumps* (2009) are excellent catchalls on the subject. *Fix the Pumps* also includes recipes for many of the elixirs available at the time of the Old Bar. If you want to become a bitters expert, start with those fine books.

What is most important to know is that bitters are just a flavoring agent in cocktails. Like a bay leaf or other spices added to a stock, they are something that you may not initially taste but that have been layered in to provide complexity to the finished product.

We have made our own bitters at Peacock Alley since the reconstruction in 2005. Our aromatic bitters are used in most cocktails calling for Angostura bitters, and are most notably featured in our popular *1860 Manhattan*, a riff on cocktails dating back to the mid-1800s. We do, of course, stock plenty of Angostura bitters, as it is a classic and there really is no substitute, but there's nothing like being able to offer our guests a unique, house-made ingredient that can only be enjoyed here at Peacock Alley. Coming in a close second would be our house-made *Citrus Bitters*. We make them throughout the year, and often feature them in cocktails, especially in the summertime.

In an effort to keep things simple I have limited the bitters component to the three main styles and brands previously listed. There is room for plenty of experimentation by using other brands (see below), and if there is a need for another flavor or brand of bitters, they are listed in the recipes themselves by name. The idea is to be adventurous, but my goal is to keep things approachable. A recipe isn't un-makeable because you didn't happen to have rhubarb bitters in the cupboard. It will surprise most that the same cocktail made with different bitters will have a different flavor profile, so much so that by just altering the bitter component of a Manhattan you can technically have a different one every night, though it is essentially the same cocktail.

You will notice that I use the standard "dash" for servings. This does not mean to squeeze out one lone drop or two. By "dashes" I mean "stabs," a significant amount. As a point of reference, two dashes should equal about a twelfth of an ounce. You can adjust for your own personal taste, of course, but one hard shake should be the starting point. If you are using a full bottle of bitters, you will have to adjust your stab, as less liquid will be released from the bottle; more will exit if your bottle is less than half-full.

The following recipes represent the varieties that we have used and made over the years. There are commercially made versions of nearly all of them, so feel free to purchase and use those. Our house recipes are here for those wanting to make their own and maybe, with experience, create a personal stamp for their own favorite cocktail. There are more rapid ways to produce bitters without the long infusion time, but we prepare ours in an old-fashioned way and I think that they are worth the wait.

We make the aromatic bitters, in one-gallon batches; believe it or not, a batch lasts only about four months. Needless to say, that's a lot of bitters. However, it is a labor of love, as they are an essential part of our guests' experience when they enjoy a unique and memorable cocktail at Peacock Alley, in the center of the iconic lobby of the Waldorf Astoria.

AB/INTHE BITTER/

3 oz. Peychaud's bitters
3 oz. Émile Pernot Vieux Pontarlier absinthe

Add ingredients to glass jar and stir to integrate. Funnel into bitters bottle. Lasts indefinitely.

We have been using this recipe since the reopening of Peacock Alley in 2005. This simple homemade ingredient is a great alternative for whatever drink calls for either item. It is fitting that it is the first item listed in this chapter, as it is a simple stepping-stone into the world of homemade ingredients.

AROMATIC BITTERS

PEEL RIND OF
THE FOLLOWING:

- 1 grapefruit
- 2 oranges
- 4 lemons
- 4 limes

- ⅛ c. allspice berries
- ⅛ c. caraway
- ⅛ c. cardamom pods
- ⅛ c. celery seed
- ⅛ c. coriander seed

- ⅛ c. fennel seed
- ⅛ c. juniper berries
- ⅛ c. peppercorns
- 1 cinnamon stick
- 2 whole nutmeg seeds
- 12 cloves
- 1 star anise
- 1 vanilla bean, split
- 750 ml. Wray & Nephew overproof rum

Place citrus rinds on baking sheet and bake for approximately 30 minutes at 200 degrees, or until about 60 percent dry. I do not recommend drying them out completely at this temperature, as they will not have much flavor left to add. You can skip this process entirely and use fresh rinds for a different taste. We have used both to pleasing results.

Add all ingredients to an airtight glass jar. Let sit for 2 to 3 months and then strain twice, first through fine mesh, then through a coffee filter. Funnel into a bitters bottle. Lasts indefinitely.

CITRUS BITTERS

PEEL RIND OF
THE FOLLOWING:

- 1 grapefruit
- 2 oranges
- 4 lemons
- 4 limes

- ⅛ c. caraway
- ⅛ c. cardamom
- ⅛ c. celery seed
- ⅛ c. coriander seed
- 2 whole nutmeg seeds
- 1 vanilla bean, split
- 750 ml. Wray & Nephew overproof rum

Place citrus rinds on baking sheet and bake for approximately 30 minutes at 200 degrees, or until about 60 percent dry. I do not recommend drying out completely at this temperature, as, again, they will not have much flavor left. As with the aromatic bitters, you can skip this process and use fresh rinds for a brighter result.

Add all ingredients to an airtight glass jar. Let sit for 2 to 3 months and strain twice, first through fine mesh, then through a coffee filter. Funnel into a bitters bottle. Lasts indefinitely.

You can make this recipe strictly orange bitters by omitting the other citrus ingredients, but I wouldn't (you could include the rinds of eight oranges and omit the remaining citrus). In my opinion, using only orange peels leaves you with a one-trick pony. In fact, if orange bitters is your goal, I suggest making the citrus bitters as directed, then placing them back in a fresh infusion jar with the rind of an orange or two for another couple of weeks. This will leave you with an orange-forward product that retains the depth of the full-palate citrus variation. This process can also be performed with commercial orange bitters to ramp up the orange component.

■ ■ ■

I have always used Wray & Nephew's overproof rum as the base for all of our bitters in lieu of a neutral grain spirit or vodka, as the rum adds its own rustic quality. It's like starting a baseball game with a runner on first base.

As for the other ingredients, by definition most bitters recipes call for exotic roots and bittering agents, which commonly include angelica root, cinchona bark, and gentian root, among others. Although most of these can be procured online easily enough, I prefer not to use them if I can help it, mainly as an aesthetic choice. All commercial bitters rely quite heavily on these ingredients as the thread that links them, resulting in a certain uniformity from brand to brand. Because our bitters lean on the spice end of the spectrum, I think the outcome is unique, fresher, and much more aromatic.

We do, however, prepare a separate gentian root mix, of which I can add a small amount to a particular finished product if it needs some balance. A little goes a long way and you will want to add in tiny increments. Although many classic bitters recipes include the use of raisins or other dried fruit, I think that they were included to mask some of the harshness of the available hooch at the time. By and large, today's spirits are very well made and require no such enhancements. There are also many more ingredients available today that add a sugar component to a cocktail. Adding dried fruit would limit their usage, or at the very least require making two versions.

We also are not completely averse to leaving some pith on our citrus peels, which acts as a natural bittering agent. Using more of the exotic roots would eliminate the need to rest our bitters as long as we do, but I believe that the extra period of integration gives the spices ample time to coalesce, and it is that profile that has become the identity of our bitters.

There are plenty of blogs and books that will guide you through making specific bitters from scratch, but what I do both at the Hotel and at home is try to find a happy medium, adding a homemade touch to a well-made commercial product if creating completely from scratch proves to be excessive. In the end, you want unique items with your own personal stamp on them. Using the recipes below as a template, you will be able to use your imagination to accentuate your home bar.

GENTIAN ROOT INFUSION

1 tbsp. dried gentian root
8 oz. Wray & Nephew overproof rum

Carefully place gentian in airtight glass jar. Add rum and infuse for at least 1 month. Fine-strain and funnel into bitters bottle. Lasts indefinitely.

Add a small amount to any bitters recipe to give it an additional bitter note.

CINNAMON BITTERS

1 cinnamon stick
8 oz. house-made Aromatic Bitters or Angostura bitters

Add ingredients to airtight glass jar and let sit for 1 week. Strain twice, first through fine mesh, then through a coffee filter. Funnel into a bitters bottle. Lasts indefinitely.

This simple, ramped-up cinnamon blast will get the most use in the autumn and winter months, but it's quite versatile. Use in Daiquiri variations or add to your favorite tea for an instant flavor spike.

COCOA BITTERS

8 oz. house-made Citrus Bitters or Regans' Orange Bitters No. 6
4 oz. Noel cocoa nibs

Add ingredients to airtight glass jar. Stir to integrate and let infuse for at least 3 weeks, stirring occasionally. Strain twice, first through fine mesh, then through a coffee filter. Funnel into a bitters bottle. Lasts indefinitely.

Perfect for summer Sours, among others, cocoa bitters adds the coveted "What is that?" quality to almost any cocktail and pairs extremely well with tequila. Be adventurous—try adding it to your favorite cocktails and prepare for new favorites in your repertoire.

COFFEE BITTERS

8 oz. house-made Citrus Bitters or Regans' Orange Bitters No. 6
⅓ c. whole espresso or French roast coffee beans

Add ingredients to airtight glass jar. Stir to integrate and let infuse for 2 weeks. Strain twice, first through fine mesh, then through a coffee filter. Funnel into a bitters bottle. Lasts indefinitely.

A unique addition to most any of your classic cocktails, to be used when you're in an adventurous mood. Adds a unique twist to Old Fashioneds and Sazeracs, among many others.

CRANBERRY BITTERS

2 oz. house-made Citrus Bitters or Regans' Orange Bitters No. 6
6 oz. Wray & Nephew overproof rum
1 c. fresh or frozen cranberries
1 rind of whole orange

Add all ingredients to airtight glass jar. Stir to integrate. Let rest for at least 2 weeks. Strain twice, first through fine mesh, then through a coffee filter. Funnel into a bitters bottle. Best if used within 6 months.

Originally created for use in Champagne cocktails, these versatile bitters can also be used quite creatively. Add a few dashes to a Collins or a gin and tonic.

PEACH BITTERS

8 oz. house-made Citrus Bitters or Regans' Orange Bitters No. 6
1–2 fresh, ripe peaches, pitted and cubed
½ oz. Combier Pêche de Vigne peach liqueur (optional)

Add peach to airtight glass jar. Add bitters and infuse for two weeks. Strain through sieve, extracting as much liquid from fruit as possible. Strain through coffee filter. Add peach liqueur if necessary.

This simple recipe results in a tangy, peachy enhancement with nearly unlimited uses. Try in a summertime Old Fashioned or a Julep for surprising results. The addition of the peach liqueur is a way to prop up less than ripe peaches. Add in quarter-ounce increments if needed only. If peach bitters are unavailable, use orange bitters as an alternate.

PEPSIN BITTERS

12 oz. Dr Pepper soda reduced to 4 oz.
2 oz. house-made Citrus Bitters or Regans' Orange Bitters No. 6

Place Dr Pepper in a saucepan over low to medium heat. Reduce to about 4 oz. (about 10 minutes). Let cool and funnel into small, clean bitters bottle. Add Citrus Bitters and shake to integrate. Best used within 6 months.

These bitters appear in a few recipes in this book. As pepsin bitters are no longer produced, I think this is a good facsimile. History claims they were the basis for Pepsi and Dr Pepper soda. Whether this is true is not really important, as no sample of or usable recipe for pepsin bitters survives today. If not technically correct, it is easily made and close enough to get the job done. Have some fun with it. Try a dash or two in an entry-level rum or bourbon on the rocks.

▌ Other Commercially Available Bitters

It seems that new bitters enter the marketplace monthly. This isn't a bad thing; it allows for us to add unique tools to our box and results in new and interesting cocktails. Most of the following brands are easily available and offer a wide array of flavors, from the spicy to the sweet, including prepared versions of the preceding recipes.

Abbott's

This brand was discontinued in the 1950s and has recently been brought back. Mentioned in more than a few cocktails herein, these unique vanilla, mint, and citrus bitters brighten as they intensify.

The Bitter Truth

This brand's extensive line includes Jerry Thomas's Own Decanter bitters, which are based on recipes found in Thomas's nineteenth-century books. Other interesting offerings include lemon, peach, and tonic bitters.

Bittermens

Made in New Orleans, these unique bitters and shrubs bring a sense of individuality to each cocktail. Everything from celery to habanero peppers are in their well-curated arsenal.

Dale Degroff's Pimento Aromatic Bitters

Led by its cinnamon, nutmeg, and allspice core, this offering from one of the planet's premier barmen and quite possibly the person who is single-handedly responsible for the return of the well-crafted cocktail is quite the versatile item. Try it in Tiki-style cocktails and wintertime Manhattans.

Dr. Adam Elmegirab's Bitters

These small-production, historically accurate items (including Falernum and orgeat syrups) also include a version of Boker's bitters to help tie up many pre-Prohibition recipes.

Fee Brothers

In business since the 1800s, this New York state company has been a leader in product introduction and offerings, including brines, syrups, and flavorings. Some recommended types include black walnut, celery, rhubarb (great in a gin and tonic) and whiskey-barrel-aged bitters. Though mostly glycerin-based, which some purists scoff at (though some do contain alcohol) the first leap from the three standard bitters usually begins here. The alcohol-free bitters can bring complexity and spice to "mocktails," for those who are serious about avoiding even a few drops of alcohol.

JUICES

Being able to make drinks at home on a regular basis requires having fresh fruit on hand; there is no way around it. Your gin and tonic will not reach its quenching potential without the squeeze of a fresh lime wedge. There is no such thing as a classic Daiquiri made with a commercial lime cordial (well, there is, but you won't want to drink it). A proper Bronx cannot be raised to its pre-Prohibition heights with pasteurized orange juice. There is no substitute for fresh juice.

Today's fruit is selectively bred to be much larger and thus yield more juice than the produce available at the time of the Old Bar. Recipes calling for the "juice of half a lime" would be overwhelmingly tart if you followed the rest of the listed ingredients. No small part of my goal in deciphering all of the recipes in the Old Books was ensuring that the original intention of the finished product was reached. Following the recipes as listed would've resulted in less than potable cocktails and left our hard-earned clientele wondering what all the fuss was about.

Though it is best to incorporate your juice immediately, there are a few differences when it comes to optimal usage from time of extraction. Lemon and lime juice actually peak a few hours after squeezing and, along with grapefruits, can be used up to a full day later. Oranges, however, begin to decline immediately and are only truly usable for no more than an hour or so post-juicing.

There are exceptions. Pineapple, carrot, and tomato juice come to mind. As I've said, there is no substitute for fresh juice, but fresh pineapple may be unavailable or out of season, or it just may not make sense to pull out your juicer for one or two drinks. If that is the case, I often recommend frozen purees, but as a complementary ingredient, canned product can be used if necessary for satisfactory results (as long as it's not from concentrate). If you're choosing a cocktail in which the pineapple is the star; you may want to wait for the appropriate season or number of guests and enjoy it in all its intended glory. There are plenty of locally sourced and pressed carrot juices that can be utilized for the handful of cocktails that call for it. Unless you have an electric juicer on your kitchen counter, the bottled product works just fine. As for tomato juice, especially in a Bloody Mary, it is trumpeted in many a book and blog that roasting fresh tomatoes or using canned (the same ones we use for pasta sauce) leaves the classic seasoned product in the dust. You may find that to be true, but it just isn't the same item we have come to enjoy on weekend brunches since its creation eighty or so years ago. Ultimately, if you are looking to add diversity to your rotation, by all means experiment, but expect unique results. For the recipes in this book, if something other than fresh can work, it is listed in that particular recipe.

As a guideline for your menu planning here are the average yields for citrus juices.

Fresh Fruit Juice Yields

> 1 lime yields 1 oz. juice
>
> 1 lemon yields $1^{1}/_{2}$ oz. juice
>
> 1 orange yields $2^{1}/_{2}$ oz. juice
>
> 1 grapefruit yields 5 oz. juice

For citrus fruits, hand presses in different sizes are easy to find and simple to use. However, I've found that a good tabletop mechanical press is just as easily cleaned and transfers between fruit sizes much easier, as there will be no need to cut larger fruit into quarters. In the end, it takes the same amount of work to clean the removable parts.

Pro Tip: Fine-strain all juices prior to use to eliminate the need for fine-straining most cocktails at time of preparation. This will make it necessary to fine-strain only when ice shards will cause further dilution or interrupt an otherwise smooth trip across the palate.

PUREES

We often use high-quality commercially available purees such as those produced by Les vergers Boiron, Perfect Purée, or Ravifruit in our cocktails for consistency's sake. If you're preparing cocktails for a small gathering, it will definitely be worth the effort to puree fresh fruit. If you're hosting a large party, frozen is obviously the easier option, depending on the fruit that is needed and the size of your event.

There is no need to heat or break down fresh fruit. Blending it will maintain the freshness and true flavor. Put it in a food processor or blender and process to a fine puree.

I usually add a touch of simple syrup to taste (depending on seasonality and ripeness of fruit) and half an ounce of lemon juice for every cup or so of puree. The lemon juice will help balance the final result and delay oxidation and the natural change in color of the fruit over time.

GARNISHES

Working in the bar business for many years, I have prepared and created cocktail lists for bars and restaurants around the world. Every once in a while I will chance upon someone with an investment in a project who has plenty of business acumen and success in their field but very little food and beverage experience. It invariably happens that I will present them with a cocktail at a preopening tasting and even before they lift their glass, they inquire about the garnish. They think the cocktail would be more appealing if somehow I could serve it on fire or include moving parts. I am exaggerating, of course, but not by much. I am a big fan of function over form; there should be a reason for every component of a cocktail. I love the look of an elaborate garnish that some of the world's finest cocktail bars specialize in, whether it involves a vessel or edible portion, but for the home bar, especially if you are inexperienced, it's best to concentrate on the quality of the cocktail rather than the wow factor of a smoke globe or edible container.

A cocktail does go through a transformation when properly garnished. Like your gin and tonic with its lime wedge, your Martini will only be truly complete with a slice of fresh lemon peel twisted above the rim of the glass to release its flavorful and aromatic oils, and nothing anticipates the coming meal like the briny and savory notes in the bite of a Queen Anne olive. A few of our most popular cocktails were garnished with edible flowers, baby rose petals, and a variety of herbs. As for the Old Books, if most of the cocktails did include garnishes, they weren't uniformly listed by Mr. Crockett. I took liberties in this area, letting tradition and common practice act as my guide as to whether a particular cocktail needed a particular garnish. In other words, I went with what made sense. You'll notice that the garnish itself is not listed with the cocktail ingredients, and is instead in the methodology of each recipe.

DRIED APPLE CHIPS

1 Granny Smith apple, cored and thinly sliced
1 c. Simple Syrup

Place syrup in container and steep apple slices in it for a few minutes. Remove slices from syrup and place on baking tray lined with parchment paper or Silpat nonstick mat. Dry in 180-degree oven for about 1 hour and 15 minutes. Wrap in plastic and store in airtight container for up to a week.

▮ Citrus Peel

Tool: Horizontal or Y Peeler

First, rinse all fruit well. The width of the peel can make all the difference. A broader swath of peel will be much easier to manipulate and render the most oils onto the surface of the cocktail. You will want to be able to nearly fold the peel horizontally and "snap" the oils from it, directing them downward toward the drink. Then run the shiny side (not the bitter pith side) of the peel around the rim of the glass to leave its mark on every new sip. You may want to begin with a coin-size peel cut with a paring knife, as it can be snapped with two fingers and its oils more easily directed to the surface of the cocktail.

At the Hotel, we include the peel in the cocktails, if only to help distinguish them from one another at the service station. At home, there is no real need to include the garnish, as the peel has already performed its duty by the time you toss it into the pool, but that choice remains yours.

This type of garnish is also used for the Brandy Crusta, encircling the entire lemon or orange peel with the peeler in one long run, then placing it in a small wineglass or goblet. Another purpose includes the "flaming" of citrus peels. This is a relatively simple process that, with a bit of practice, will impress your guests not only with the flash of light caused by the oils within the skin but, more important, with the smoky flavor it will leave on top of the cocktail. As for the act itself, just squeeze a coin-size peel through the flame of a lit match and down onto the surface of the cocktail. Just be sure to let the sulfur burn away from the match before pressing the oils onto the flame. After the "fireworks," discard the match, run the peel around the rim of the glass, and garnish as usual. Don't get carried away, though, as the singed oils have a distinct flavor that is not suitable for every cocktail.

Tool: Channel Knife

This tool is used to carve a long, thin "string" of peel for garnishes that lean toward the decorative side but do little in regard to flavor or scent enhancement unless the fruit is held above the drink while the channel knife is drawn through the fruit. This is true when using a peeler or paring knife as well. It is worth your time to learn how to handle one, as it also makes a unique and decorative garnish in punch bowls. Though once common practice in daily bar operations, they are rarely used today. One example of a cocktail included herein that does is the Alley Cat.

Tool: Paring Knife

Wheels and wedges of citrus fruit are cut with a paring knife. The best and easiest way to cut a wedge is to cut the ends off the fruit and split it lengthwise, then cut a slit across the center of each half before cutting into wedges. This will allow you to place the wedge on the rim of a Collins glass to adorn a gin and tonic, for example.

Wheels are cut in quarter-inch slices with a small notch cut in from the outer edge to allow you to stand it upright on the rim of an Old Fashioned glass for a Margarita, for example. You might wish to cut them thinner for simple decoration in a punch bowl or coupe, to float on the surface of the drink for presentation purposes.

■ Herbs

We often use fresh herbs as ingredients and garnishes in our cocktails. We save the imperfect leaves and sprigs for infusing or muddling and use the more visually appealing ones for garnish, creating the final touch for both the eyes and the nose. When using fresh herbs, such as mint, rosemary, or thyme, it is important that you wake up the essence of the herb by slapping the sprig against the palm of your hand prior to placing it on top of the drink. This will release its bouquet and elevate the experience to exemplary heights.

RIMMED GARNISHES

When utilizing a rimmed garnish (kosher salt for a *Margarita*, sugar for a *Sidecar*) we only rim one side of the glass. Guests may not want the flavor of the prepared rim with every sip so by only using half of the glass you give them the choice of whether to taste the rimmed garnish or not.

To properly rim a glass, simply moisten the glass with a lemon or lime wedge halfway around the top of the glass and about a half inch to an inch vertically. Then roll onto a plate with about half an inch of salt, sugar, or spice with the stem perpendicular to the plate's surface to avoid sugar or salt on the inner rim. Tap away any excess powder and fill to serve.

CORIANDER AND PINK PEPPERCORN RIM

4 oz. coriander seeds

2 oz. pink peppercorns

1 oz. kosher salt

Add coriander and peppercorns to electric spice grinder and grind until fine. Add kosher salt and pulse once or twice to integrate. Place on small plate.

We use this spice combination for our Bloody Bunny, a Bloody Mary variation made with carrot juice, but you can use it with a standard Bloody Mary as well.

LARGE BATCHES

BLOODY MARY MIX

1 46 oz. can Sacramento tomato juice (chilled)

1 tbsp. freshly ground pepper

1 tbsp. celery seed (or dried celery flakes)

2 rounded tbsp. white horseradish

1 tsp. kosher salt (optional)

12 dashes Lea & Perrins Worcestershire sauce

8 dashes Tabasco sauce

1 tsp. brown sugar

Add all ingredients to large, sealable container. Shake well.

Best if used next day. See *Bloody Mary* recipe for serving suggestions.

HOT (COLD) COCOA MIX

4 oz. heavy cream

8 oz. whole milk

3–4 oz. Manjari chocolate pistoles, 64% cocoa

Bring the cream and milk just to a boil over medium heat, remove from heat, and add the chocolate. Let sit for 2 minutes, then whisk until fully blended.

▪ *Yield: About 16 oz.*

This is used in our *Chocolatini* and served warm as our hot cocoa in the wintertime. You can tweak the amount of chocolate in it if you prefer a thinner or thicker texture. If you prefer it a bit sweeter, adding an ounce or so of simple syrup to the end product will do the trick.

WHITE COCOA MIX

4 oz. heavy cream
8 oz. whole milk
6 oz. Valrhona white chocolate pistoles

Bring the cream and milk just to a boil over medium heat, remove from heat, and add the white chocolate. Let sit for 2 minutes, then whisk until fully blended.

▪ *Yield: About 18 oz.*

This is included in our *Biscotti and Cream* cocktail but can also be served warm as a decadent and rich hot cocoa alternative in the winter months, though it is best served in small portions.

▪ Sour Mix

We make a sour mix daily at Peacock Alley. Without it, we would not be able to serve our many guests in the timely fashion that they have come to expect. When making drinks at home, a premade mix is not necessary unless you're serving a large group. Lemon juice, simple syrup, and a bit of egg white included in the build of the cocktail will do the job. It's how I've listed it in the methodology of each cocktail in this book. When making more than a few, or hosting an event where Sours or Collinses will be featured, a prebatched container is easy enough to prepare and will be a welcome assist when the festivities commence.

Technically, a sour mix would not contain egg white, but I think a couple in a large batch is just enough to create a nice froth. You can omit it if you feel strongly one way or the other.

One of my goals over the years has been to offer our guests items that they could not easily get at home or at other establishments. When the mix is completed, we add some orange rinds and a cinnamon stick to finish it and to add our own stamp. Their influence is nearly imperceptible, but I maintain that these small additions complement the soul of the cocktails that the mix completes.

There are a couple of ways to prepare a sour mix. We do it the "long" way daily at Peacock Alley (in double the portions that are listed in the following recipe). It includes whisking the whites to a meringue and is an old-fashioned approach, which we take pride in, but in no way is it necessary. The short way will more than do the trick. I prefer a little less syrup, so this recipe is not your classic 1:1 ratio of juice to syrup, but you can adjust for personal taste.

ƒOUR MIX

2 egg whites
12 oz. freshly squeezed lemon juice (fine-strained)
10 oz. Simple Syrup

Add egg whites and half of the syrup to an airtight container and shake well for 10 seconds. Add remaining ingredients and continue to shake well for 10 seconds. Funnel into glass bottle, refrigerate, and use as needed. Best if used within 48 hours.

SHRUBS

These ancient combinations of fruit, sugar, and vinegar were very much a part of the beverage lexicon of the nineteenth century and prior, though none made it into Mr. Crockett's books. Older versions, as in *Jerry Thomas' Bartenders Guide* (1862), adds brandy and would be served as is. The elementary recipe that follows allows you to add your spirit of choice. I could dedicate a whole chapter explaining the origin, usage, disappearance, and finally the resurgence of these elixirs, and although I have used them in many recipes, only one in this book contains a shrub (*Gardening at Night,* in the Champagne Cocktail entry). If you want to know more, *Shrubs,* by Michael Dietsch (2014), will have you raiding your local farmers market in no time.

There are, of course, traditional methods for creating shrubs, but as with everything else, we opt for simplicity whenever we can, and since you would ostensibly have raspberry syrup already on hand, the recipe below will more than get the job done. The Raspberry Shrub can also be added to club soda for a seasonal treat with a bit of a (non-alcoholic) kick. The following recipe is a fine template for most any fruit shrub, but feel free to adjust for your personal taste.

RASPBERRY SHRUB (Basic)

2 parts house-made Raspberry Syrup
1 part apple cider vinegar

Add ingredients to clean glass container and stir to combine. Store in the refrigerator for up to 6 months.

SYRUPS

Some recipes in the Old Books call for "gum" or "gomme" syrup. This is sugar in liquid form enhanced with gum arabic (a natural thickener). As far as the old recipes go, all other instances requiring sugar called for just that: sugar in granulated form. In the era of the Old Bar, you would most commonly find an unrefined or "loaf" sugar, chipped off blocks. Today, a simple syrup will do. There are times when I prefer granulated sugar—like when preparing a Caipirinha, for instance, as the abrasive sugar will break down the lime wedges, helping to release the oils from the rinds or an Old Fashioned, when I err on the side of tradition.

Storage of syrups, even refrigerated, is not indefinite. Some will start to get moldy after about two weeks, so be sure to prepare the right amount to use within that window of time.

You may also add about an ounce of unflavored vodka for every 16 to 20 ounces of syrup to extend its shelf life, but as a general rule of thumb, when your syrups become cloudy, it's time to make a new batch.

SIMPLE SYRUP (Basic)

8 oz. granulated sugar
8 oz. water

Add ingredients to saucepan and stir over medium heat until sugar is dissolved (about 3 minutes). Remove from heat, let cool, and store in clean glass bottle. Lasts in the refrigerator for up to 1 month. For a richer syrup, cut the amount of water in half (refrigerated shelf life: about three months).

GUM SYRUP

STEP 1

2 oz. gum arabic powder
2 oz. room-temperature water

Add ingredients to a medium-size, nonreactive bowl and whisk for a couple of minutes to integrate. Cover and let rest for at least an hour or until all gum arabic powder has been absorbed by the water.

STEP 2

4 oz. water
12 oz. superfine sugar

In a saucepan, combine sugar and water. Heat until sugar dissolves (about 3 minutes). Add gum arabic mixture and stir to integrate. Remove from heat immediately and allow to cool. Let rest for at least an hour. A white foam should form on the top. Fine-strain through conical strainer into glass bottle or plastic squeeze bottle and refrigerate.

You can also take this to another level by adding chunks of fresh pineapple to the finished gum syrup overnight. This is perfect for use in classic Punches (both the fruit and the syrup) including *Pisco Punch*, which was all the rage in the late nineteenth century. Lasts in the refrigerator for about 3 months.

DEMERARA SYRUP

12 oz. demerara sugar
6 oz. water

Add ingredients to saucepan and stir over medium heat until sugar is dissolved. Remove from heat, let cool, and store in clean glass bottle. Refrigerated shelf life is about 2 months.

This recipe yields a richer and thicker syrup, though you could prepare it with a 1:1 ratio. Just be sure to adjust the amount accordingly within recipes.

AGAVE SYRUP

4 oz. organic agave nectar
4 oz. hot water

Mix ingredients in a medium bowl. Whisk until combined, then store in a glass jar. Refrigerated shelf life is about 2 months.

BERRY SYRUP *(Raspberries, Strawberries, Etc.)*

8 oz. water
1 c. sugar
1½ c. fresh berries of choice (about 12 oz.)
1 oz. vodka (optional)

▌ *Yield: Approximately 16 oz.*

Add water and sugar to saucepan. Stir over medium heat until integrated, about 3 minutes. Add fruit and simmer over low heat for 3 to 5 minutes, breaking up the fruit a bit with a spoon. Larger and denser fruit, such as strawberries, may have to simmer for a couple of minutes longer. Do not boil. Remove from heat and allow to steep for 15 minutes, then strain through fine mesh strainer, gently pressing down on the fruit. Continue to cool to room temperature, then funnel into clean glass bottle. Refrigerate for up to 3 weeks. Add vodka to extend shelf life up to 6 weeks.

Though commonly used today in most every bar, these syrups go back to the earliest of recipes. Raspberry and strawberry syrups are included in many of the Old Bar's cocktails. You can also swap in other berries for your own original recipes.

The best part about these syrups is that they can be used for more than just cocktails. As previously mentioned, they can be used to make shrubs for both alcoholic and nonalcoholic recipes. Enhance your breakfast oatmeal with some instead of sugar or maple syrup, or add to club soda for a bright nonalcoholic drink at lunchtime. Stir some into hot tea for a unique twist. The sky is the limit.

FALERNUM (Caribbean Simple Syrup)

16 oz. Wray & Nephew overproof rum
Rinds from 5 large limes
10 cloves
¼ oz. almond extract
½ c. peeled and chopped gingerroot
½ split vanilla bean
2 star anise
1 cinnamon stick
Simple Syrup

Combine all ingredients except the simple syrup, infuse for at least 10 days, then fine-strain. Add 4 oz. simple syrup to every 1 oz. Falernum base. Place in a glass jar and shake to combine. Falernum base lasts indefinitely; Falernum syrup, up to 6 weeks.

Falernum is a Caribbean spiced syrup used primarily in rum-based, Tiki-style drinks such as Planter's Punch and Zombies, though adventurous bartenders find unique ways to incorporate it into other recipes as well. Try it as the sugar component for your next Tom Collins. In the preceding recipe, keeping the base separate from the simple syrup until ready to serve will allow you to have your home-made Falernum syrup ready to go at a moment's notice, as the infused rum will last indefinitely. It yields about 64 ounces of syrup, so obviously a little goes a long way. You can tweak this recipe by adding your own favorite spices such as nutmeg or allspice, or even coconut. If you do plan on experimenting, I recommend pouring off three or four ounces of the basic Falernum infusion and adding your twist to that and infusing it for a week to see if it works for you. You may not enjoy it as much as you thought, and this will save you from having to discard your whole batch. It is traditionally prepared by adding fresh almonds to the mix, but you can forgo that. The almond extract more than does the job (and keeps the cost down).

You may adjust how much of the flavor profile you want to give over to the assertive flavors of the infusion. I like the 4:1 ratio of simple syrup to Falernum base as listed, but 3:1 can work as well. Just be sure to taste for adjustments. In my opinion, although some brands make for practical ingredients, this is yet another item that no commercial product can duplicate.

GRENADINE

12 oz. pomegranate juice (Pom Wonderful brand works just fine)
12 oz. demerara sugar
Peel of two oranges

Add all ingredients to saucepan. Heat and remove as soon as boiling begins. Leave peels in for 3 to 5 minutes, then remove. Let cool, strain into glass container, and refrigerate. Add 1 oz. unflavored vodka to preserve for up to 1 month (optional).

Once you prepare your own grenadine, there will be no going back. Its depth of flavor will bring the wow factor to every recipe that includes it, even your Shirley Temple (omit the vodka preservative if serving to children).

I have prepared this two ways over the years. The alternate version uses standard white granulated sugar, reduces the syrup by about one-fourth and omits the orange peel, using orange flower water instead. This makes for a deeper end result. The recipe above represents a more versatile rendition. Please do try both.

For the juice, I recommend commercially available brands, but fresh pomegranate juice can be used for a more laborious preparation, if you don't mind it. Just be sure to strain it well prior to use.

HONEY SYRUP

4 oz. honey
4 oz. hot water

Add ingredients to saucepan and stir over medium heat until honey is dissolved. Remove from heat, let cool, and store in clean glass bottle. Refrigerate up to 2 months.

Different honeys yield unique flavor profiles. Please feel free to experiment. You might want to adjust the water to honey ratio slightly to showcase the particular profile of your honey.

HONEY AND GINGER SYRUP

½ c. peeled and chopped gingerroot
8 oz. honey
4 oz. water

Add honey and water to saucepan and bring to a boil. Add chopped ginger and allow to simmer over low heat for 10 minutes. Remove from heat and let steep for 30 minutes. Strain and refrigerate for up to 2 months.

MINT OR HERBAL SYRUP

8 oz. water
8 oz. granulated sugar
1 c. fresh mint or fresh basil leaves or
½ c. fresh rosemary leaves

Stir together water and sugar in a saucepan and heat to integrate. Bring to a boil and remove from heat. Add herb of choice and let steep for 5 minutes. Strain through fine mesh sieve. Best if used within 1 week.

Be mindful that regardless of the base, all herb steeps are like tea: anything more than five minutes and you run the risk of a bitter result. Not only are these flavorful syrups great additions to cocktails, they also make interesting additions to lemonade and iced tea. The three herbs listed in this recipe are just some examples. Please note that the amount of rosemary is cut in half, as the flavor profile of that particular herb is very strong.

PINEAPPLE SYRUP

2 c. granulated sugar
16 oz. water
1 fresh pineapple, peeled, cored, and cubed

Add sugar and water to saucepan and stir over medium heat until sugar is dissolved. Remove from heat and pour into heatproof bowl. Add prepared pineapple. Allow to cool, and refrigerate overnight.

Strain pineapple from syrup using a mesh strainer, pressing down on fruit to draw out as much syrup as possible. Fine-strain again and funnel into clean glass bottle. Add 2 oz. unflavored vodka as a preservative and refrigerate. Lasts 4 to 6 weeks.

Pineapple syrup is an integral part of summertime cocktails and definitely worth the trouble of preparing. The trick is to add the pineapple to the hot syrup to jump-start the flavor extraction.

INFUSIONS

CINNAMON VODKA *(or Spirit of Choice)*

Place one 750 ml. bottle of unflavored vodka and 2 cinnamon sticks in airtight glass container and stir every other day for a week. Strain and funnel back into bottle. Lasts indefinitely. Do not add cinnamon sticks directly to liquor bottle, as they will expand and you will not be able to remove them, which will leave you with an overly bitter product. Used in *Cinful*, *Fallen Apples*, *Fezziwig's Recline*, *Gingerbread Man*, *Pie on the Sill*, and *Rabbit's Dilemma*.

PREPARED LIQUEUR

PEACH BRANDY *(Homemade Substitute)*

4 oz. Laird's bonded applejack
2 oz. Combier Pêche de Vigne peach liqueur
1 oz. Alexander grappa di Cabernet (optional)

Place all ingredients in glass bottle and gently shake to combine. Lasts indefinitely.

Used in *Fish House Punch*, *Julep/Smash*, and *Punch*.

To date, only a few small, independent distillers make true peach brandy, which is a barrel-aged peach eau-de-vie. If you're unable to secure some, cocktail historian David Wondrich recommends a 2:1 ratio of Laird's bonded applejack and a good imported peach liqueur. I'll take it a step further and recommend adding a half portion of decent grappa or other eau-de-vie—I think it brings a touch of the rustic note that genuine peach brandy possesses. Be aware that this mix will add a bit of sweetness to the finished product, so you might want to slightly reduce the other sugar component in recipes that call for it.

RECIPES

A TO Z

ABSINTHE COCKTAIL

1½ oz. Pernod Original Recipe absinthe
1 oz. cold water
¼ oz. Simple Syrup or Gum Syrup
2 dashes Angostura bitters

Add all ingredients to mixing glass. Add ice and stir for 30 seconds. Strain into chilled cocktail glass. Garnish with lemon peel.

This cocktail technically belongs under the **Cocktail (Basic Recipe)** entry, as it is simply a cocktail (spirit, sugar, water, bitters) with absinthe in the leading role instead of whiskey. It would've been traditionally called for in this manner ("I'll have an Absinthe Cocktail," . . . "a Whiskey Cocktail," etc.). I decided to grant it its own entry because many pre-Prohibition bar books feature interpretations of this cocktail. Both versions of Mr. Crockett's books include this classic presentation (though his omits bitters). Others include splitting the amount of absinthe with anisette. If you opt to go in this direction, I would forego the use of simple syrup. An equal amount of anisette makes for an overly sweet drink. Other interpretations add a bit of orgeat to that as well; feel free to give it a try, though only after trying the example presented here.

Incidentally, this is a recipe in which Mr. Crockett included "two dashes of gin." Odds are, the original recipe read "gum" (for gomme," meaning sugar syrup with the stabilizer gum arabic added—see page 43) and he misinterpreted the entry.

ABSINTHE DRIP

1½ oz. Émile Pernot Vieux Pontarlier absinthe
1 sugar cube
4 oz. cold water

Place slotted spoon on rim of glass. Place sugar cube on slotted spoon. Slowly pour ice cold water over sugar cube to dissolve. Stir with spoon.

The classic and ornate absinthe fountain has one simple purpose: to drip ice cold water very slowly onto a single sugar cube supported on a slotted spoon until the cube dissolves into the absinthe in the glass below. Once the sugar is dissolved, use the spoon to integrate a bit further and enjoy. Made for slow summer afternoons, as the tradition and ceremony of the act adds to the allure. Knowing that some of the greatest artistic minds have also participated in this timeless ritual surely adds to the appeal. The fountain has either two or four spouts so you can prepare for your guests simultaneously. If you don't have an absinthe fountain, slowly pour ice cold water from a small water pitcher over the top of the sugar cube and into the glass for the same result.

ABSINTHE FIZZ (Suissesse Fizz)

1½ oz. chilled club soda
1½ oz. Kübler absinthe
½ oz. Marie Brizard anisette
½ egg white

Add chilled club soda to small chilled Fizz or Collins glass. Add remaining ingredients to mixing glass. Dry-shake for 5 seconds. Add ice and shake for 10 seconds. Strain into Fizz or Collins glass. Stir briefly with bar spoon to integrate. No garnish.

This simple absinthe-based Fizz is listed as the **Suissesse** in the Old Books. In keeping with its roots, I chose a Swiss absinthe, though any will do. Some similar recipes call for sugar or syrup to sweeten it up. I would just add another quarter ounce of anisette.

In the Old Bar's recipe, they skip the egg whites, but other books of the era did utilize them. You can easily omit them for a straight

Fizz, but I'd try it both ways. The frothy version makes it the Bracer that it was meant to be. See *Fizz* for variations.

ABSINTHE FRAPPÉ *(Blended)*

2 oz. Vieux Carré absinthe
½ oz. Simple Syrup
4 large ice cubes
2 oz. cold water

Add all ingredients to blender. Blend until smooth. Pour into small wineglass or footed tumbler (traditional absinthe glass).

This one works best at home, and we love these in the backyard on a hot summer day. Well before the rum, fruit, and sugar make their appearance to appease your thirsty and less demanding crowd, try this one with your early arrivals as the coals are heating up. You will not be disappointed (and neither will they). For best results, double the ingredients and serve for two.

ABSINTHE FRAPPÉ *(California and New York Versions)*

1½ oz. Pacifique absinthe
Simple Syrup, 1 bar spoon to ½ oz. (optional)

Add ingredients to mixing glass. Add ice and stir for 30 seconds. Strain into coupe glass filled with crushed or pellet ice for New York version. Strain into small water or Fizz glass without ice and add 3 oz. chilled club soda for California version.

Both of these variations appear in the 1934 book. Note that there is no sugar added; anything from a bar spoon to a half ounce of simple syrup remains optional. Traditional recipes would direct you to shake to prepare, but it's not necessary. I've chosen a domestic (Washington state) and herb-forward absinthe to take the lead to keep with the "stately" theme, though any will do. See *Ojen* for variation.

ABSINTHE FRAPPÉ *(New Orleans Version)*

1½ oz. St. George Absinthe Verte
8–10 mint leaves
½ oz. Simple Syrup
2 oz. chilled club soda

Add all ingredients except club soda to mixing glass. Add ice and shake well. Fine-strain into Old Fashioned glass filled with crushed or shaved ice. Top with club soda. Garnish with a mint leaf.

There is no need to muddle the mint here, as shaking the cocktail will more than do the job. It bears noting that Tom Bullock, author of *The Ideal Bartender* (1917), of the famous Pendennis Club in Louisville, Kentucky, omitted the mint but topped his Frappé with a bar spoon of Bénédictine. For his Italian version, he added a bar spoon of maraschino. Both variations are fine alternatives. I've included this one to round out the map.

ACROSS THE BORDER ∎ *Peacock Alley*

1½ oz. Sombra mezcal (or Astral tequila)
½ oz. Averna amaro
¾ oz. fresh grapefruit juice
⅓ oz. fresh lime juice
2 oz. Fever-Tree or Q ginger beer

Add all ingredients except ginger beer to mixing glass. Add ice and shake well. Strain into Collins glass filled with large ice cubes. Add ginger beer and stir briefly to integrate. Garnish with lime wedge.

Looking for a unique way to present mezcal (or tequila) in the cooler months of the year, I felt its smoky notes would pair well with ginger beer, but the drink did not truly come together until the amaro was added. It lent body and a pleasing level of herbaceousness. It's a complex but enjoyable mix. Use tequila if you need a gateway to the slightly more demanding mezcal version.

ADMIRAL SCHLEY PUNCH

¾ oz. fresh lime juice plus rind of 1 whole lime
1½ oz. Knob Creek straight rye whiskey
¾ oz. Smith & Cross navy-strength rum
⅓ oz. house-made Demerara Syrup
1½ oz. chilled club soda

Using a hand press, juice the lime directly into mixing glass, then add used rind. Add all ingredients except club soda to mixing glass. Add ice and shake well. Strain into Collins glass filled with large ice cubes. Add club soda and stir briefly to integrate. Garnish with orange peel.

"Named after Commodore Winfield Scott Schley, of Spanish-American War fame," according to Mr. Crockett, this Punch survived Prohibition, as it was included in Charles H. Baker's popular *The Gentleman's Companion* cocktail/travel book in 1939.

The original recipe called for a tamer St. Croix rum; I opted for the fuller-flavored Smith & Cross navy-strength, as it has no problem standing up to the double portion of rye whiskey, not to mention the spritz. The lime rind adds a noticeable and welcome spicy note. The Old Bar presented this strained into a tumbler with no ice—passable, though not the best. Other recipes serve this cocktail up and omit the soda. Or you can use the large ice cubes, as you would any Punch. Either way, this is a nicely balanced (and strong) late-afternoon summertime treat if there ever was one.

ADONIS

1½ oz. Lustau La Ina fino sherry
1½ oz. Martini Gran Lusso sweet vermouth
2 dashes Regans' Orange Bitters No. 6

Add all ingredients to mixing glass. Add ice and stir for 15 seconds to integrate. Strain into chilled cocktail glass. Garnish with orange peel.

BAMBOO

1½ oz. Lustau La Ina fino sherry
1½ oz. Noilly Prat extra dry vermouth or Carpano bianco vermouth
1 dash Angostura bitters
2 dashes Regans' Orange Bitters No. 6

Add all ingredients to mixing glass. Add ice and stir for 15 seconds to integrate. Strain into chilled cocktail glass. Garnish with lemon peel.

The *Adonis* was named for the longest-running Broadway musical of its era, produced back in 1884. This classic aperitif makes the perfect predinner cocktail for those wanting to avoid the wallop of a Martini. In order to offset and accompany the full-flavored sweet vermouth, you should utilize a bone-dry sherry, but feel free to use a Manzanilla or an amontillado for a rounder finish. This recipe is also listed as ***Armour*** in the Old Books.

The *Bamboo* variation uses either dry vermouth or the sweet yet clear bianco vermouth and adds Angostura bitters. Old recipes simply list it as "French," defined as "dry," but using a bianco vermouth will add a bit of sweetness and viscosity without being cloying. Carpano's bianco is in a slightly drier style and naturally meets in the middle. Try both—these are low-alcohol cocktails, after all. You could also try a newly popular amber vermouth. If that's unavailable, try a perfect *Bamboo* by splitting the vermouth portion equally between the standard sweet and dry variations.

The *Bamboo* claims more than a few origin stories. The most common theory is credited to German-born San Francisco–based bartender Louis Eppinger. Lore has it that he created the *Bamboo* at the Yokohama Grand Hotel in the late 1800s. They continue to serve it, and variations, with pride today.

As with any low-alcohol recipe, please be sure not to dilute by over-stirring. Storing your ingredients in the refrigerator will allow you to add ice for a brief stir for integration purposes and present the drink quickly, yet ice cold. These delicious, low-impact cocktails are all now standards in restaurants operating without a full liquor license (a full license extends beyond wine and beer). Try them and you'll be glad that they have survived the ages, and you will have survived the night with a clearer head.

2 oz. Hayman's Old Tom gin or Beefeater London dry gin
½ oz. yellow Chartreuse
2 dashes Regans' Orange Bitters No. 6

Add all ingredients to mixing glass. Add ice and stir for 30 seconds. Strain into chilled cocktail glass. Garnish with lemon peel.

ALLEY CAT ▮ *Peacock Alley*

2 oz. Citadelle gin
½ oz. Bénédictine liqueur
2 dashes Regans' Orange Bitters No. 6

Add all ingredients to mixing glass. Add ice and stir for 30 seconds. Strain into chilled cocktail glass. Garnish with orange peel: using a channel knife, peel one whole orange once around, cut the peel long and thin, and hang it to mimic a cat's tail over the side of the glass.

When experiencing certain cocktails for the first time, you sometimes realize that they are products of their era. The *Alaska* is one such cocktail that can be best enjoyed as a well-chilled after-dinner potable. Different styles of gin (barrel-aged Old Tom, London dry, etc.) were used with varying results before finally settling on the original Old Tom, which is the one called for in the Old Books. Though harmonious, it doesn't challenge the Chartreuse. The London dry–style gin does add contrast and a bit of spiciness that you may also enjoy. I recommend trying both.

As for the *Alley Cat*, this was one of the first cocktails that I created for the restoration and reopening of Peacock Alley in 2005. It was inspired by the simple, boozy concoctions found in the Old Books. I used the same portions here for simplicity's sake, but you can pull back or slightly increase either ingredient. The finish on this one has a wonderful creaminess that makes for an exceptional summertime after-dinner drink. Gary "Gaz" Regan included this recipe in his *Bartender's Gin Compendium* (2009).

Coincidentally, there is yet another similar, proprietary cocktail called the **Rose**, which placed Grand Marnier where the other liqueurs sit. It's a fine alternative that also comes alive with a simple lemon twist.

ALEXANDER

1½ oz. Plymouth gin
1 oz. Marie Brizard white crème de cacao
1 oz. heavy cream (or half and half)

Add all ingredients to mixing glass. Add ice and shake well. Fine-strain into chilled cocktail glass.

*Alternate: Add brandy or cognac in lieu of gin and garnish with freshly grated nutmeg or dark chocolate shavings.

Although it was first found in print in 1916, I still like the legend regarding the origin of this concoction that has it being made in honor of the great baseball pitcher Grover Cleveland Alexander during the 1915 World Series. Whatever its inspiration, this gin version came first, made with a London dry style; however, I think that the less herbal Plymouth works best or the sweeter Old Tom if going that way. The more popular **Brandy Alexander** can now be made era appropriate with overproof cognacs (Royer Force 53 and Pierre Ferrand 1840 are both recommended), which makes the decadent richness (and calorie count) of this cocktail well worth it. You can pull back the base spirit by half an ounce if you require something sweet but less strong. If you do, you may want to use half and half in lieu of the heavy cream for a more balanced trip across the palate. My grandmother added the slightest drop of real vanilla extract to hers. There you go. See **Alphonse**, **Boston Milk Punch**, and **1915** for variations.

ALL RIGHT

2 oz. New York Distilling Company Dorothy Parker dry gin
½ oz. Martini Gran Lusso sweet vermouth

Add ingredients to mixing glass. Add ice and stir for 30 seconds. Strain into chilled cocktail glass. Garnish with orange peel.

Tom Bullock Version ∎ *Classic*

2¼ oz. Rittenhouse bonded rye whiskey
¾ oz. Pierre Ferrand dry curaçao or Grand Marnier
2 dashes Angostura bitters

Add all ingredients to mixing glass. Add ice and stir for 30 seconds. Strain into chilled cocktail glass. Garnish with orange peel.

In the 1931 book, Mr. Crockett writes that this was "popular among those who wanted quick results." Of that you can be sure; this complex cocktail will definitely allow you to disconnect from the daily grind in a hurry. The inclusion of an assertive vermouth makes for a more memorable cocktail. If you cannot obtain the newly resurrected Nicholson gin, which was named in the original recipe but not yet imported to the United States at the time of printing, your favorite London dry–style gin will work fine here. The twist of orange oil from the peel is essential. See *Martini "Easy—Enhanced"* for variation.

The lack of bitters and its connection to a well-known cocktail by legendary bartender Tom Bullock, of the Pendennis Club in Louisville, are the reasons that this is not under the *Martini* entry in this book. Mr. Bullock included this whiskey version in *The Ideal Bartender* (1917), I've included two different styles of orange curaçao, so you can try both. Each yields a different yet tasty result.

Almost All Grape ∎ *Peacock Alley*

2 oz. Ciroc vodka or G'Vine Floraison gin
1 small apricot, pitted and cubed
2 wedges fresh peach, cubed
1 dash Regans' Orange Bitters No. 6
1 oz. Wölffer rosé wine (Long Island), or any Provence style
¾ oz. Inniskillin ice wine (or Sauternes, if unavailable)

Add fruit and bitters to mixing glass and muddle. Add remaining ingredients. Add ice and shake well. Fine-strain into chilled cocktail glass. Garnish with orange peel.

In an effort to incorporate the grape in all of its incarnations (Ciroc vodka is grape based), I tried just muddling it as the fruit component, but it left something lacking. Surprisingly, the fresh apricot and peach made all the difference here. The rosé wine tempers the fruit and sweeter components, pulling them all in line. If you're trying a gin version, the grape-based, French G'Vine Floraison gin will keep with the theme. Either way, this was a guest favorite during the reopening days of Peacock Alley. A fine summertime treat.

ALPHONSE

¾ oz. Bombay London dry gin
¾ oz. Tempus Fugit dark crème de cacao
¼ oz. heavy cream (for float)

Add gin and crème de cacao to mixing glass. Add ice and stir for 20 seconds. Strain into chilled sherry glass. Slowly float heavy cream on the top by pouring it over the back of a spoon.

Named for a nineteenth-century French-influenced comic strip and one of its characters, this delicate after-dinner drink will do the trick every time. Although it's not quite a Pousse-Café, you may want to attempt to impress your guests by displaying your ability to float the heavy cream, or you can just place a small dollop of whipped cream on top for an easier and slightly more vertical presentation. See **Alexander** for variation.

AMALFI COASTAL ▮ *Peacock Alley*

1½ oz. Tanqueray No. Ten gin
1 oz. Toschi limoncello
1½ oz. fresh blood orange juice or puree

Add all ingredients to mixing glass. Add ice and shake well. Strain into chilled cocktail glass. Garnish with lemon peel.

Using the Amalfi coast as inspiration, this treat will have you whisked away to the villa of your dreams. If you would like to enjoy it in the summer (when blood oranges are out of season), I recommend a well-made frozen product such as Les vergers Boiron blood orange puree. You can also substitute a few ounces of San Pellegrino Aranciata Rossa (blood orange soda) and serve on the rocks to create one of the world's best Highballs. Gaz Regan included this recipe in *The Bartender's Gin Compendium*.

AMPERſAND

1 oz. Castarède Selection Armagnac (or Pierre Ferrand Ambre cognac)
1 oz. Ransom Old Tom gin (or Hayman's Old Tom gin)
1 oz. Martini & Rossi sweet vermouth
⅓ oz. Pierre Ferrand dry curaçao (or Grand Marnier)
2 dashes Bittermens Orange Cream Citrate (or Regans' Orange Bitters No. 6)

Add all ingredients to mixing glass. Add ice and stir for 30 seconds. Strain into chilled cocktail glass. Garnish with lemon peel.

Our adapted version takes advantage of small-production ingredients and some slightly outside-the-box substitutions. Please feel free to sweeten the pot by using the ingredients included in parentheses for the Old Bar's more traditional method. Either way, this will surely become one of your wintertime cocktail hour staples.

ARCTIC/ARDſLEY

1½ oz. Plymouth sloe gin
1½ oz. Bonal Quinquina Aperitif or Cocchi Barolo Chinato
2 dashes Regans' Orange Bitters No. 6

Add all ingredients to mixing glass. Add ice and stir for 30 seconds. Strain into chilled cocktail glass. Garnish with orange and lemon peels.

ARCTIC/ARDſLEY (IMPROVED) ∎ *Peacock Alley*

1 oz. Plymouth gin
1 oz. Plymouth sloe gin
1 oz. Bonal Quinquina Aperitif or Cocchi Barolo Chinato
2 dashes Regans' Orange Bitters No. 6

Add all ingredients to mixing glass. Add ice and stir for 30 seconds. Strain into chilled cocktail glass. Garnish with orange and lemon peels.

The *Arctic*, created to celebrate Rear Admiral Robert Peary's (near) discovery of the North Pole, was originally served without a base spirit and was (to me) a one-trick pony, all sugar and no spine. The *Ardsley* version is apparently the same drink but named for the well-to-do North Hudson town, whose residents were regulars at the Old Bar.

With gin supplying the backbone, it can once again enter your cocktail rotation (not just for after dinner anymore). Try both, but I find the gin-fortified version much more appealing and I think you will too.

The "Red Calisaya" called for in the original recipe (in the quin-quina slot) was a generic term for liqueurs, bitters, or aromatized wines that contained calisaya bark, cinchona bark, and quinine, among other spices and herbs, and is included in ten recipes of the Old Books, as they were just being introduced at the time of the Old Hotel. Bonal and Cocchi Barolo Chinato are two such commercially available products that are similar, though there are others that are mentioned throughout this book. Feel free to alternate between them; they each have their own unique stamp. There was a Spanish product branded Calisaya, which is no longer exported, but there is a fine domestic version being produced in Oregon today that also may be appropriate for some recipes. I alternate between the two examples, going with what I think works best for each recipe. In the end, the choice is yours. See **Futurity** for variations.

ARRIVEDERCI ∎ *Peacock Alley*

- 1 oz. Candolini Ruta grappa
- 1 oz. Averell Damson gin
- 2 oz. fresh blood orange juice or 2 rounded tsp. blood orange sorbet
- 1 oz. Nino Franco Rustico prosecco

Add all ingredients except prosecco to mixing glass. Add ice and shake well. Strain into chilled Champagne coupe. Float 1 oz. prosecco. No garnish.

This summertime refresher will impress your guests and make your cocktail the center of any outdoor gathering. Like the **Amalfi Coastal** cocktail, this was also inspired by ocean-side summers in southern Italy. Candolini Ruta grappa is a delicate (and beautifully packaged) offering, infused with genuine rue flowers, which are left in the bottle. If you'd like a drier version, substitute San Pellegrino sparkling water for the prosecco. When fresh blood oranges are unavailable, blood orange sorbet will provide a creamy alternative. Be sure to try both. You might be surprised to know that sorbet has been used in cocktails since the time of the Old Bar and even prior. Everything old is new again.

ASTOR

1½ oz. Bombay London dry gin
1 oz. Kronan Swedish punsch
¼ oz. fresh lemon juice
¼ oz. fresh orange juice
1 dash Angostura bitters

Add all ingredients to mixing glass. Add ice and stir for 30 seconds. Strain into chilled cocktail glass. Garnish with brandied cherry.

DOCTOR ▮ *(Peacock Alley Adaptation)*

1½ oz. Kronan Swedish punsch
1 oz. Smith & Cross navy-strength rum
½ oz. fresh lemon juice
½ oz. fresh lime juice
½ oz. fresh orange juice

Add all ingredients to mixing glass. Add ice and shake well. Strain into chilled cocktail glass. Garnish with brandied cherry.

This recipe was adapted from *Old Waldorf Bar Days*, in which Mr. Crockett writes, "Perhaps [named] after John Jacob of that name; perhaps after William Waldorf, his cousin; however, chances are, it was originated either at the old Astor House or the Astor Hotel, and took its name from its bar of nativity." It's also one of the rare drinks (though there are a few in this book) in which citrus is added less as an ingredient and more as a vehicle for tannin and acidity. This is why I recommend stirring when preparing, as I would think they did at the Old Bar. I also took the liberty of adding a touch of aromatic bitters for some complexity. In the summer I often add another quarter ounce of each ingredient and shake it for a lighter, refreshing variation that can be served on the rocks. Try them both.

Swedish punsch can connect its lineage to its base, Batavia arrack (a rum relative) and to the eighteenth century. Its sweet and spicy flavor profile makes a nice addition to many cocktails. I like to float a small amount on the top of a standard Collins or Daiquiri, though you may be as adventurous as you like. The traditional recipe for the **Doctor** recorded equal parts Swedish punsch and lime juice. That was it. I feel that there is certainly room for improvement there. After sampling a dozen or so variations, and numerous degrees of lime, lemon, and orange juice, I think the recipe above represents a fine evolution of this drink. The higher proof Smith & Cross rum is the perfect pairing here, though any good Jamaican rum will bring the desired flavor profile.

ASTORIA

2 oz. Noilly Prat extra dry vermouth
1 oz. Hayman's Old Tom gin

Add ingredients to mixing glass. Add ice and stir for 30 seconds. Strain into chilled cocktail glass. Garnish with orange peel.

The *Astoria* is a great addition to your summertime predinner ritual —a reverse Martini, if you will. It's light enough for warm weather but with just the right amount of impact to displace a white wine on your go-to list. As Mr. Crockett wrote: "[Named] after the big annex to the old Waldorf, which at its opening, in 1897, became the main part of the establishment." I've included a standard Old Tom gin here but unique variations would also be worthy of inclusion. If you're feeling adventurous, barrel-aged Ransom or Greenhook Ginsmiths add some intriguing complexity for a drier finish. I would not be surprised if this cocktail sees a comeback in light of all the new artisan vermouths being produced today. This would make a great platform for them. If you use sweet vermouth in the dry slot you would have what the Old Books referred to as a **Black**. The newly released Tanqueray Old Tom gin holds up nicely to the full-flavored Punt e Mes vermouth (which also helps make this drink stand by its name). If using a lighter vermouth, a dash or two of aromatic bitters will help make up the difference. See **Chanler**, for variation.

AU PEAR ∎ *Peacock Alley*

1½ oz. homemade pear-infused spirit
½ oz. Dolin de Chambery sweet vermouth
**½ oz. dried-fruit-infused Alexander
grappa di Cabernet**
1½ oz. Les vergers Boiron pear puree
¼ oz. fresh lemon juice
1 dash Angostura bitters

Add all ingredients to mixing glass. Add
ice and shake well. Strain into chilled
cocktail glass. Garnish with fresh mint
leaf sprig.

Pear-Infused Spirit

Rinse, peel, and core 4 to 6 Bosc pears,
then cut into cubes. Place into airtight glass container along with
one liter of the spirit of your choice and infuse for 7 to 10 days,
stirring occasionally. Fine-strain and funnel back into bottle. Best if
used within 3 months.

Dried Fruit–Infused Grappa

750 ml. bottle Alexander grappa di Cabernet
½ c. dried white raisins
½ c. dried figs, halved (about 5)
1 split vanilla bean

Add all ingredients to airtight glass container. Infuse for at least 2
weeks, stirring every few days. Fine-strain and funnel back into
grappa bottle. Best if used within 6 months.

The *Au Pear*, which made its debut in 2006, has spent many a fall and
holiday season on our cocktail list. It's a perennial guest favorite—
many consider it an essential part of any visit during that time of year.

I recommend preparing the homemade infused spirit instead of
purchasing a flavored product. We originally used a strong, unflavored
vodka, though white rum would make a more flavorful foundation.
This is a wonderful seasonal treat that can be enjoyed up or on the
rocks.

You could blend a couple of cored Bosc pears if preparing a serving or two, but for bar use, we like to opt for consistency and use a commercially available puree. It's easily produced and presented either way. We also don't fine-strain this viscous cocktail, as the pear's grittiness adds to its freshness and authenticity. Finally, I prefer to include a "neutral" vermouth here to allow the pear flavors to come through. If you use a full-flavored vermouth, it makes for a more complex cocktail but tends to emphasize the dried-fruit-infused grappa, which, when served neat, makes for a fine wintertime dram.

AUTOMOBILE (Collins Version)

8 mint leaves (about 2 sprigs)
2 dashes Regans' Orange Bitters No. 6
¾ oz. lemon juice
2 oz. Greenhook Ginsmiths American dry gin
4 oz. Boylan ginger ale (or Fever-Tree ginger beer) or any cane-based ginger ale

Add mint and bitters to Collins glass and briefly muddle to bruise and release essence. Then add lemon juice and gin. Fill with ice and add ginger ale. Stir to integrate.

AUTOMOBILE (Jacques Straub Version) ▮ Classic

1 oz. Hayman's Old Tom gin
1 oz. Compass Box Great King St. blended Scotch whisky
1 oz. Martini & Rossi sweet vermouth
2 dashes Regans' Orange Bitters No. 6

Add all ingredients to mixing glass. Add ice and stir for 30 seconds. Strain into chilled cocktail glass. Garnish with lemon peel.

The *Automobile* cocktail apparently came in many models. There was even a simply enhanced Champagne cocktail making the rounds at the time of the Old Hotel (with dashes of bitters, curacao, and Crème Yvette). The one attached to the history of the hotel was Collins in style, quickly made with the ice cubes bruising the mint, with the rest of the ingredients added and served. The Old Bar's version included the choice of lemon or lime juice. I went with lemon because it added a certain freshness and separated itself from other recipes. I can recommend replacing the standard ginger ale with ginger beer for a spicier version. Either way, it's a refresher for sure.

The other version with a tie to the hotel is a rendition that first appeared in print in 1914, in Jacques Straub's *Drinks*. Mr. Straub's version, somewhere between a Rob Roy and a Martini, probably best represents its time. I modified the ingredients to tone down the more traditional bases, using Old Tom for London dry gin and a modern light-bodied, blended Scotch as a fill-in for a more conventional and fuller style. A spray of a lemon twist makes a nice addition to a forgotten classic, now found.

AUTUMN SOLSTICE ▮ *Peacock Alley*

2 oz. Banks 7 Golden Age dark rum
¾ oz. Meletti amaro
¼ oz. fresh lemon juice
3 dashes house-made Cinnamon Bitters

Add all ingredients to mixing glass. Add ice and stir for 30 seconds. Strain into chilled cocktail glass. Garnish with orange peel.

These ingredients combine to make an appealing autumnal libation, best enjoyed during the cool days between Halloween and Thanksgiving. I kept whittling this concoction, which originally contained fig puree and even fig jam, down to its most essential parts. The lemon juice is included here for its acidic properties and should be viewed as a bitter component, which is why you would stir this. The *Cinnamon Bitters* pair extremely well with the rum and amaro, but if you don't have some handy, **Cinnamon Vodka** (used for other recipes in this book) will yield the desired result.

AVIATION ▮ *Classic*

2 oz. Beefeater London dry gin
¾ oz. fresh lemon juice
½ oz. Luxardo maraschino liqueur
¼ oz. Rothman & Winter crème de violette

Strain into chilled cocktail glass. Garnish with brandied cherry.

The *Aviation* has become one of the most popular cocktails recently resurrected from the pre-Prohibition era. Though no mention of this cocktail is made in either of Mr. Crockett's books, I think it's safe to say that any bartender at the Old Bar would have had it in his repertoire. Our genever variation, **Uptown Aviation**, substitutes Bols genever for London dry gin and was adapted for one of the annual Rock and Roll Hall of Fame induction ceremonies that the hotel has long had the pleasure of hosting. Some early recipes omit the crème de violette. I recommend at least a touch, but you can adjust from there. If you do decide to leave the violette out, share the lemon juice portion with orange juice and you will have a **Gypsy Serenade**. This alternate was, according to ex-Waldorf publicist Ted Saucier, created by Mischa "Maestro" Barton, a Waldorf-Astoria bartender who held court in the 1940s.

A **Doctor Cook** omits the violette and adds half of an egg white for a lighter and leaner variation. Try today's American-styled gins here to display their floral notes. See **Blue Moon** and **First Class** for additional variations.

BACARDI APERITIF

1½ oz. Bacardi gold rum
1½ oz. Dubonnet Rouge or Bonal Quinquina aperitif
½ oz. fresh lime juice
¼ oz. house-made Grenadine

Add all ingredients to mixing glass. Add ice and shake well. Strain into Old Fashioned glass or Champagne coupe filled with crushed or shaved ice. Garnish with orange peel. Serve with small (metal) straw.

In *The Old Waldorf Bar Book* the title of this cocktail is **Bacardi Dubonnet**, in the "Cuban Concoctions" chapter. Because it's not quite the same product as was available during the time of the Old Bar, Dubonnet can also be substituted with sweet vermouth or Bonal aperitif. Its deeper flavor profile makes this cocktail a keeper and I think most closely resembles the original intention. Bacardi gold rum steps in for the original white rum, which complements the vermouth component as opposed to being masked by it. I've chosen to include the house-made *Grenadine,* but you can omit or pour it over as a finishing touch as per your taste. Be sure to release the orange oil from the peel on top of the drink to add some pop for a rediscovered summer sipper.

Another variation exists in the same chapter of the old book: the **Havana Opera**, which utilizes the same ingredients but uses a dash of lemon juice (I would use a third of an ounce) in lieu of the lime juice listed here. I would stir this and serve it up in a cocktail glass. The original recipe omits the grenadine, but you can include it if you like. It's a pleasing predinner cocktail either way.

BACARDI COCKTAIL

2 oz. Bacardi y Cia Heritage white rum
¾ oz. fresh lime juice
½ oz. house-made Grenadine

Add all ingredients to mixing glass. Add ice and shake well. Strain into chilled cocktail glass. Garnish with lime wheel.

BACARDI COCKTAIL NO. 2

2 oz. Bacardi y Cia Heritage white rum
1 oz. fresh lime juice
½ oz. fresh pineapple juice
½ oz. Simple Syrup

Add all ingredients to mixing glass. Add ice and shake well. Strain into coupe glass filled with shaved or pellet ice. Garnish with lime wheel.

(HARRY'S) BACARDI COCKTAIL NO. 3 ▮ *Classic*

2 oz. Bacardi y Cia Heritage white rum
1 oz. G'Vine Floraison gin
¾ oz. fresh lime juice
½ oz. Simple Syrup
¼ oz. house-made Grenadine

Add all ingredients to mixing glass. Add ice and shake well. Strain into chilled cocktail glass. Garnish with lime wheel.

Bacardi rum is of Cuban origin and was the most popular brand during the heyday of the Old Bar. The only issue with that is the Bacardi product available during the days of the Old Bar bears little resemblance to the current offering. Although today's Bacardi will do just fine when preparing these cocktails, I would recommend the Bacardi y Cia Heritage if you can get your hands on it. It's bottled at 89 proof and is a nice improvement over the standard offering. If it's unavailable, add a dash of orange bitters to your standard white rum. It will provide a more complex flavor profile and will get you closer to the intent of the original recipe.

The first simple Daiquiri became known as the ***Bacardi Cocktail*** in America. The addition of grenadine ensured a life of its own. *Old Waldorf Bar Days* includes two versions, though others appear with different titles. The first was known as **Peg o' My Heart** (named for the Broadway play), and is identical except that it pulls back on the grenadine a bit. It's unbalanced to me, though completists are free to try it. The Grenadine cocktail is simply a *Peg O' My Heart* served Frappé-style, on shaved or crushed ice. The original recipe had a teaspoon of the namesake grenadine. I find it interesting that the original **Grenade** (see **Country Club**) was mostly composed of grenadine but this cocktail, with barely a touch, wound up with the identifying ingredient in its title. I wouldn't be surprised if they were transposed by Mr. Crockett in error. Either way, I left them as history would have them.

To branch out a bit, add half an egg white to the *Bacardi Cocktail* and you'll have a **September Morn** (supposedly named for a painting of the same title). Try it with a Jamaican rum for a more complex twist. For another adaptation, add ¾ oz. fresh orange juice and pull back the grenadine by half, you will have a **Raleigh**. Again, adding a dash of orange bitters to this one will result in a more complex profile. The *Bacardi Cocktail No. 2* includes pineapple juice in place of grenadine.

The third recipe here is an adaptation of Harry MacElhone's 1919 version in *Harry's ABC of Mixing Cocktails*, from his New York Bar, in Paris, which adds gin as an accompanying base ingredient. If we are to deviate from the classic, we may as well go all the way. The softer, floral profile of France's G'Vine Floraison gin slides right into its slot, honing the rum and unifying the cocktail. If this is unavailable, you could substitute with Hayman's Old Tom gin.

In 1936, the New York State Supreme Court ruled that in order for this drink to use "Bacardi" in its name, it can only be made with this specific rum. See **Cuban Rose**, **Daiquiri**, and **Flamingo** (listed under **Cuban Sunshine**) for variations.

BACARDI PLUS

2 oz. Bacardi Superior white rum
¾ oz. Tempus Fugit crème de cacao
¼ oz. Varnelli l'Anice Secco Speciale anisette

Add all ingredients to mixing glass. Add ice and stir for 30 seconds. Strain into chilled cocktail glass. Garnish with orange peel.

This overlooked cocktail should have made it out of the pre-Prohibition era. One of the great qualities of a recipe like this is that it bears tweaking according to personal taste. Do you like the licorice profile of anisette? Use a half-ounce portion of the two liqueurs. An egg white would add another dimension, as would an amber rum. The original recipe did not include a garnish, but I feel that an orange twist makes this beauty sing.

BACARDI VERMOUTH (Dry or Sweet)

1½ oz. Bacardi Superior white rum
1½ oz. Dolin de Chambery dry vermouth or 1½ oz. Cinzano Rosso sweet vermouth

Add ingredients to mixing glass. Add ice and stir for 30 seconds. Strain into chilled cocktail glass. Garnish with orange peel.

While developing these recipes, I realized quite quickly that they could find a place at a contemporary bar. Unbelievably easy to make, they over-deliver in their simplicity. Don't go crazy with these. If you don't want to enjoy them up, they work on the rocks as well, even with a splash of soda. Subbing in other rums for variety's sake is a great idea, though I would avoid the spiced variety. Be adventurous. I also tried an array of bitters and found that they may overwhelm the drinks. If you feel they could use a nudge, go ahead, but I recommend a light touch. If I had to choose a garnish, a nice spray of fresh orange or lemon peel livens all three. I would also offer an improved version by using the fine aperitif *Cocchi Americano* in the vermouth slot, a variation I've adapted that begged for inclusion. It's best on a summer afternoon. A "Perfect Bacardi Vermouth" (equal parts rum and sweet and dry vermouth) is called **Four Dollars** in the Old Books. Another variation of the Bacardi Vermouth Sweet from the "Cuban Concoctions" chapter is the **Havana Smile**, which adds a quarter ounce each of lime juice and simple syrup for an interesting alternative, as they nudge this a bit closer to **Daiquiri** territory in flavor—but please don't shake it. The citrus is there for balance, not as a fruit component. I would recommend a fuller vermouth such as Carpano Antica, which stands up to the citrus and also improves the balance of the cocktail while giving it a singular identity. See **Country Club** for variation.

BACO

2 dashes Regans' Orange Bitters No. 6
1½ oz. Bombay London dry gin
¾ oz. Noilly Prat extra dry vermouth
¾ oz. Cinzano Rosso sweet vermouth

Twist orange peel over Old Fashioned glass to release oils, then place in glass. Add bitters and muddle briefly. Add gin and vermouth to same glass. Add ice and stir to integrate. Garnish with additional orange peel.

I.D.K.

2 oz. Nicholson London dry gin or Plymouth gin
1 oz. Carpano Antica sweet vermouth

Place large ice cubes into Old Fashioned glass. Add ingredients and stir briefly to integrate. Garnish with orange peel.

MONTAUK

1½ oz. New York Distilling Company Dorothy Parker dry gin
¾ oz. Noilly Prat extra dry vermouth
¾ oz. Cinzano Rosso sweet vermouth
3 dashes Peychaud's bitters

Add all ingredients to mixing glass. Add ice and stir for 15 seconds to integrate. Strain into Old Fashioned glass filled with large ice cubes or sphere. Garnish with lemon peel.

ST. JOHN

1½ oz. Greenhook Ginsmiths Old Tom gin or Ransom Old Tom gin
1½ oz. Martini & Rossi sweet vermouth
2 dashes Regans' Orange Bitters No. 6

Add all ingredients to mixing glass. Add ice and stir for 15 seconds to integrate. Strain into Old Fashioned glass filled with large ice cubes or sphere. Garnish with lemon peel.

These can be viewed as "one-glass cocktails," simply prepared but complex enough to be enjoyed on a regular basis. The *Baco* was traditionally built in the glass, twisting the peels to extract their essence, and though I found that sufficient, I would suggest muddling the bitters and orange peel first for a more thorough extraction. Adding a lemon peel is a nice twist as well. Feel free to expand within the gin category to your personal preference; this recipe can take it. Also listed as **Halsey** in the Old Books (named for a stockbroker patron of the Old Bar).

The *I.D.K.* is nearly the same cocktail as the *Baco* save for the bitters and dry vermouth. Mr. Crockett noted that bartender Johnnie Solan did not know who or what these initials represented. I'd like to think that Solan might have been pulling his leg, alluding to the fact that the letters may have stood for "I Don't Know." You can just call this drink—quickly prepared in the serving glass—what it is: a sweet Martini on the rocks. Plymouth gin does a fine job if the Nicholson brand is hard to find. *See* **Cooperstown** for *I.D.K. No. 2*.

As for the *Montauk,* it's the Peychaud's bitters that save the day. The anise note makes for a most interesting summertime sipper. You can prepare this directly in the glass, but like the Negroni, the integration makes for a more complete trip across the palate. Try with a bianco vermouth instead of the dry for a slightly sweeter sundown cocktail.

Propped up by the full-flavored, barrel-aged Old Tom gin, the *St. John* is an assertive predinner **Martini** or **Manhattan** alternative that brings a lot to the table. There is a lasting cola note on the finish that makes this more than worthwhile. The lemon twist tempers the sweet side just enough. A good one.

BAGPIPER ∎ *Peacock Alley*

1½ oz. clove-infused Monkey Shoulder blended Scotch whisky
1 oz. Pama pomegranate liqueur
1½ oz. fresh orange juice
3 cloves

Add all ingredients to mixing glass. Add ice and shake well. Strain into chilled cocktail glass. Garnish with brandied cherry.

Clove-Infused Scotch

Add 15 whole cloves to 750 ml. of Scotch whisky for two weeks. Fine-strain and funnel back into bottle.

In an effort to make Scotch whisky more accessible to the drinker who might be intimidated by even the mention of it, the *Bagpiper* found its way in the world. Pama's purpose here is to help the Scotch "down the stairs," and it certainly achieves that! Be certain to count the cloves, as too many will overpower the cocktail's balance. I love this perennial autumnal and winter favorite for the unique flavor profile. It was a finalist in the 2014 inaugural Pama "Are You Indispensable?" cocktail competition. See **Big Country** for variation.

BALLANTINE

2 oz. Plymouth gin
1 oz. Noilly Prat extra dry vermouth
¼ oz. Pernod Original Recipe absinthe
2 dashes Regans' Orange Bitters No. 6

Add all ingredients to mixing glass. Add ice and stir for 30 seconds. Strain into chilled cocktail glass. Garnish with lemon peel.

The original recipe called for equal parts Plymouth gin and dry vermouth, but I found it a bit bland and unbalanced. If you do choose to go that route, I would recommend a heartier London dry–style gin, whose profile will be strong enough to stand up to the vermouth. If you omit the absinthe when preparing this "fifty-fifty" version of the cocktail and only add it as drops on top as a finish, you will have an ***Opal***.

This is also the type of recipe that would call for the absinthe to be "rinsed," (by placing about a quarter ounce of absinthe in a glass, swirling to coat, and then discarding it), but I found that if I included it in the mix, it helped make for its own identity. For a more concrete measurement, two good dashes equals about an eighth of an ounce.

Post-Crockett, public relations officer Ted Saucier included a drier version of this cocktail in his 1951 book *Bottoms Up* named ***La Liberté***. He credits the resident manager at the time, Edwin K. Hastings, with its creation in honor of a newly rechristened ocean liner.

The two differences in the recipes are the use of London dry gin called for in the *La Liberté* (Beefeater would work) and the omission of the orange bitters. Refer to both of these as classic Martinis all dressed up for Saturday night and enjoy them as such.

Yet another variation is named for the tough interrogation practices of the early twentieth century. The **Third Degree** presents itself as a 7:1 bone-dry Plymouth Martini with the added absinthe (originally without bitters, but you may add the orange variety). This one is certainly worth a try on braver days.

Lastly there is the **Fourth Degree**. This "mirrored" version slides sweet vermouth in the dry slot. This enhanced original **Martini**, to which Mr. Crockett credits the patrons of the Old Bar and their relation to an unnamed secret society (Masons? Oddfellows? Even barkeep Johnnie Solan did not know) was first found in print in Straub's *Drinks* (1914). It differed from the Old Books version, as his included equal parts of all ingredients. It was way too much of everything. I prefer to believe that the more-than-capable guys at the Old Bar had their own rendition that is immensely more drinkable (a lemon twist is my idea). Bitters were not included, but I think it brightens the final show up a bit. Every once in a while I will feature this for a reception and guests will be wowed, even more so when informed that this simple recipe is over one hundred years old.

BALTIMORE BRACER FIZZ

2 oz. chilled club soda
1½ oz. Courvoisier VSOP cognac
1 oz. Marie Brizard anisette
½ egg white

Add chilled club soda to small Collins or Fizz glass. Add remaining ingredients to mixing glass. Dry-shake for 5 seconds. Add ice and shake for 10 seconds. Strain into Fizz glass. Stir briefly to integrate. No garnish.

Bracers were traditionally taken soon after waking in an effort to nullify the prior evening's overindulgence, until the Internet and the never-ending workday took over. I have modified the portions to lean on the brandy here as opposed to the original equal amounts of spirits, and the result is a noticeable improvement. See **Fizz** for variations.

BAYARD BEAUTY FIZZ

2 oz. club soda
2 oz. Hayman's Old Tom gin
¾ oz. fresh lemon juice
½ oz. Luxardo maraschino liqueur
½ oz. house-made Raspberry Syrup
½ egg white

Add chilled club soda to small Collins or Fizz glass. Add remaining ingredients to mixing glass. Dry-shake for 5 seconds. Add ice and shake for 10 seconds. Strain into Fizz glass. Stir briefly to integrate. No garnish.

Firmly planted in the Bracer category, this delicate item was probably most enjoyed before and throughout lunch at the turn of the twentieth century. The dashes of maraschino and raspberry syrup and just a spoon of lemon juice served as enhancers to the gin. I have ramped these up a bit, which helps round it all out, especially if you prefer to replace the Old Tom with London dry gin. See **Clover Club** for variations.

BEE'S KNEES ▪ *Classic*

2 oz. Citadelle gin
¾ oz. house-made Honey Syrup
¾ oz. fresh lemon juice

Add all ingredients to mixing glass. Add ice and shake well. Strain into chilled cocktail glass. Garnish with lemon twist.

LEAVES OF GRASS ▪ *Peacock Alley*

2 oz. Zubrowka bison grass vodka
¾ oz. Quinta de Noval 10 Year Old tawny port
½ oz. house-made Honey Syrup
¼ oz. fresh lemon juice

Add ingredients to mixing glass. Add ice and shake well. Strain into chilled cocktail glass. Garnish with one blade of bison grass.

This cocktail emerged during the Prohibition years. It was most likely created to mask the unappealing qualities of the "bathtub" gin of the time. The honey syrup adds not only a depth of flavor but a noticeable viscosity on the palate as well. It's a classic that has survived with good reason and is the inspiration for the **Wax Poetic**, a simple twist that uses Zubrowka bison grass vodka, in the gin slot. With its unique lavender and coconut flavor profile and nose, it makes for a completely different profile and one that has turned into a warm-weather guest favorite. For our honey syrup, we use honey harvested from our rooftop bee hives, which were installed by Director of Culinary David Garcelon in 2012. We garnish the finished cocktail with a single blade of actual Polish bison grass (which is happily supplied from Poland by Zubrowka), yet another step away from the *Bee's Knees* is the *Leaves of Grass*. The floral nose that is inherent to bison grass vodka pairs surprisingly well with the complex, slight toffee profile of the ten-year-old port. The lemon brings just enough zip, and the honey adds a tactile weight to the entire offering. Although only incorporating a mere quarter ounce of lemon juice, a stirred variation left something lacking on the finish, so shake away. It's versatile enough to be served year round, though we serve it in the fall and winter at Peacock Alley.

BELLINI ∎ *Classic*

1 oz. peach puree
¾ oz. Combier Pêche de Vigne liqueur
5 oz. Nino Franco Rustico prosecco

Chill all ingredients. This will help prevent spillage during preparation, along with ensuring that it is served at the correct and most enjoyable temperature.

Pour peach puree into mixing glass, then add peach liqueur. Using bar spoon to mix with one hand, slowly add prosecco to glass with your other hand. Be careful not to "break" the prosecco by mixing too quickly and causing it to lose its effervescence. Strain into Champagne flute.

This classic cocktail goes back to 1945, when it was created by Giuseppe Cipriani at Harry's Bar in Venice, Italy, and named for the Renaissance painter Giovanni Bellini. This is one of our most popular offerings at Peacock Alley because our bar happens to open at eleven thirty a.m. daily. We also routinely pour well over 150 of these each Sunday during our famous brunch season. In the summer, I highly recommend fresh peach puree, using ripe white peaches if they can be had. We use a commercial puree (Les vergers Boiron) for consistency's sake. A more refreshing quaff and head clearer is nearly impossible to find. See **Champagne Cocktail** for variations.

BERMUDA HIGHBALL

1 oz. Château de Montifaud VSOP cognac
1 oz. Plymouth gin
1 oz. Contratto bianco vermouth
2 dashes Regans' Orange Bitters No. 6
3 oz. club soda

Add spirits and bitters to Collins glass. Add large ice cubes and fill with club soda. Garnish with orange peel (or lemon peel).

After various attempts with different brands of dry vermouth, the winner turned out to be a restrained bianco vermouth. It added the herbal and slightly sweet note that brings out the best qualities of the gin and especially the cognac. The difference may make this as popular as I think it was when it was served at the Old Bar. Initially, some may be taken aback from the combination of brandy and gin, but with the addition of the bianco vermouth (Contratto is a nineteenth-century brand that peaked in the 1930s but has recently returned with its original recipe), there seems to be a fusion at the molecular level that makes this quite the refresher. Later recipes substitute ginger ale for the club soda, but I stand by the Waldorf-Astoria original, though the orange bitters and a twist of peel does ratchet it up with a welcome brightness.

BERRY

2 oz. Santa Teresa 1796 Ron Antiguo de Solera rum
¾ oz. fresh orange juice
½ oz. fresh pineapple juice
½ oz. fresh lemon juice
¼ oz. house-made Grenadine
2 dashes Dale DeGroff's pimento aromatic bitters

Add all ingredients to mixing glass. Add ice and shake well. Strain into chilled cocktail glass. No garnish.

This largely unknown rum-based cocktail does not appear in *Old Waldorf Bar Days,* but makes its first appearance in the "Cuban Concoctions" chapter of the second *Old Waldorf-Astoria Bar Book.* The rum used, of course, was Bacardi, but I took this opportunity to imagine a different flavor profile and use an aged rum at its base. I also modified the juices to include lemon, which was not in the original recipe at all; it helps temper the sugar level of the original. I've added pimento bitters for backbone and complexity. This has become a new Peacock Alley summertime favorite. As for the namesake ingredient, your guess is as good as mine, though feel free to garnish with one.

BERRY BREEZE ∎ *Peacock Alley*

2 oz. Farmer's botanical small batch organic gin infused with fresh raspberries, strawberries, and blueberries
¾ oz. Luxardo Triplum orange liqueur
1 oz. fresh lime juice
3 fresh basil leaves
2 oz. club soda

Add all ingredients except club soda to mixing glass. Add ice and shake well. Fine-strain into Collins glass filled with ice cubes. Top with club soda. Garnish with fresh berries.

BLUEBERRY AND BASIL SMASH ∎ *Peacock Alley*

2 oz. Farmer's botanical small batch organic gin infused with frozen blueberries
1 oz. fresh lemon juice
½ oz. Simple Syrup
½ egg white
4 fresh basil leaves

Add all ingredients to mixing glass and dry-shake for 5 seconds. Add ice and shake well for 10 seconds. Fine-strain into Old Fashioned glass filled with ice cubes. Garnish with basil leaf.

Infused Gin

½ cup each of fresh raspberries, strawberries, and blueberries (for Berry Breeze)
1 liter bottle 80 proof gin
Or
1½ cups frozen blueberries (for Blueberry and Basil Smash)

Add fruit and gin to airtight glass container and let sit for 7 to 10 days. Fine-strain and funnel back into bottle. Best if used within 3 months.

The *Berry Breeze* is a favorite of our summertime guests and for good reason: the freshness of the summer produce in concert with the basil (which from 2012 onward has been grown in our rooftop garden) completely and triumphantly represents the season. Gaz Regan included this recipe in *The Bartender's Gin Compendium*.

Another simple but ultra-refreshing summertime Cooler is the *Blueberry and Basil Smash*. Basil, an iconic representative of summer, pairs extremely well with its fellow ingredients here. For the blueberry gin, I settled on using frozen blueberries in lieu of fresh for the infusion because they are more concentrated and yield a much more consistent result. Be sure to use a gin that is lower in alcohol (80 proof), as the real enjoyment of this one lies in the second serving. Each modified gin can be used in either recipe for excellent results.

BIG COUNTRY ▮ *Peacock Alley*

2 oz. clove-infused Monkey Shoulder blended Scotch whisky
1 oz. Wölffer rosé wine or any Provence-style rosé
⅓ oz. house-made Honey-Ginger Syrup
Pinch of paprika

Add all ingredients except paprika to mixing glass. Add ice and stir for 30 seconds. Strain into chilled cocktail glass. Add pinch of paprika to top of cocktail to finish.

SCOTTISH HIGHLANDS, HERE WE COME ∎ *Peacock Alley*

2 oz. clove-infused Monkey Shoulder blended Scotch whisky
¾ oz. house-made Honey-Ginger Syrup
¼ oz. fresh lemon juice

Add all ingredients to mixing glass. Add ice and stir for 30 seconds. Strain into chilled cocktail glass. Garnish with lemon peel.

Clove-Infused Scotch

Add 15 whole cloves in 750 ml. bottle of Scotch whisky and let sit for 2 weeks. Fine-strain and funnel back into bottle.

The complex *Big Country* cocktail was created for our annual Battle of the Bees honey-tasting contest in 2014. It has become one of the Hotel's more high-profile media events, promoting rooftop beehives around New York City. The charity-focused (and good-natured) competition has been judged by such culinary notables as Chef Eric Ripert, of Le Bernardin, among others. A great time was had by all and our honey came out on top!

Scottish Highlands was created for a guest's special request for a warm-weather Scotch whisky cocktail. Again, we use our rooftop honey.

Preparation tip: If you don't have the time to prepare the **Honey-Ginger Syrup**, you can just chop and muddle a one-inch piece of fresh ginger with **Honey Syrup** and then proceed as directed. See **Bagpiper** for variation.

BIJOU *(Old Bar Variation)*

1½ oz. Grand Marnier
1½ oz. Noilly Prat extra dry vermouth
1 dash Angostura bitters
1 dash Regans' Orange Bitters No. 6

Add all ingredients to mixing glass. Add ice and stir for 30 seconds. Strain into chilled cocktail glass. Garnish with lemon peel.

Adapted Waldorf Astoria Variation

1½ oz. Plymouth gin
¾ oz. Pierre Ferrand dry curaçao
¾ oz. Noilly Prat extra dry vermouth
2 dashes Regans' Orange Bitters No. 6

Add all ingredients to mixing glass. Add ice and stir for 30 seconds.
Strain into chilled cocktail glass. Garnish with orange peel.

Savoy Variation

1½ oz. Beefeater London dry gin
1 oz. Martini & Rossi sweet vermouth
½ oz. green Chartreuse
2 dashes Regans' Orange Bitters No. 6

Add all ingredients to mixing glass. Add ice and stir for 30 seconds.
Strain into chilled cocktail glass. Garnish with brandied cherry and
lemon twist.

The Waldorf Astoria version of this cocktail, named for a Broadway
theater of the day, is one of the few recipes that appear in all five
Waldorf Astoria–related cocktail books, including Jacques Straub's
Drinks, Ted Saucier's *Bottoms Up,* and Oscar Tschirky's *100 Famous
Cocktails.* Orange bitters are the choice of Mr. Crockett's books,
while both Tschirky and Saucier use aromatic. I recommend the
more robust aromatic bitters, as they
temper the sugar quotient of the Grand
Marnier, though I've listed one dash of
each in the Old Bar variation. Ultimately,
it's your call. Another slight adjustment
will also make a great lower-alcohol cocktail by transposing to a 2:1 vermouth to
Grand Marnier ratio—also a must-try.

The Adapted Waldorf Astoria Variation
included here is a riff on Christopher
Lawlor's version in *The Mixicologist* (1895).
This twist adds gin as a component but uses
equal amounts of all ingredients. Sweet but
potable, the drink is improved by upping the
gin (stick with lower-alcohol and less aro-

matic gins, as they tend to blend best with the other ingredients here). I swapped the Grand Marnier for dry curaçao and the difference is a notable upgrade in complexity and drinkability.

Neither of these is to be confused with Harry Craddock's cocktail, made famous in *The Savoy Cocktail Book* (and in *Straub's Drinks*) and what you will most likely get if you call for this cocktail around the world today. Based on Harry Johnson's 1882 *Bartenders' Manual* Frappé (served over crushed or shaved ice), it too called for equal parts of all ingredients. The obvious difference between the Waldorf and these notable variations is the use of sweet vermouth and green Chartreuse, which makes the drinks potable but cloying. I have adjusted and adapted ingredient amounts and style of gin to appeal to a modern palate in hopes that you could enjoy a second one. All told, I think that all of these cocktails can take to personal adjustments and that a bit of citrus peel sprites all of them up tremendously.

BIRD

2 oz. Cointreau
1 oz. Pierre Ferrand 1840 cognac

Twist two large orange peels into Old Fashioned glass or tumbler. Fill with crushed or shaved ice. Add ingredients. Twist two additional orange peels for garnish. Serve with small metal straw.

The end result of this uniquely presented offering is ever so appealing. Research points to this old-timer being an indigenous special of the Old Bar. The ceremony of the preparation is sure to impress your guests, and this would be great for user participation as well. You can use equal amounts of spirits here, but I think it's best to let the curaçao do the heavy lifting, as was the original intention. Try with dry curaçao or Grand Marnier leading the way in the cooler months. Either way, I heartily recommend this as an after-dinner sipper.

BISCOTTI AND CREAM ∎ *Peacock Alley*

1¼ oz. Faretti biscotti liqueur
1¼ oz. Boulard Grand Solage VSOP calvados
1½ oz. house-made White Cocoa Mix

Add all ingredients to mixing glass. Add ice and shake well. Fine-strain into chilled cocktail glass. Place thin chocolate biscotti across top of glass.

This dessert in a glass was created with our wintertime post-theater guest in mind. Faretti biscotti liqueur is an almond biscotti in a bottle. It's very concentrated but balanced with notes of cocoa and vanilla, which somehow pair extremely well with the apple-forward profile of the calvados. Along with the *White Cocoa Mix,* the chocolate biscotti garnish is provided by executive pastry chef Charlie Romano and his world–class pastry team.

BISHOP

2 oz. 86 Co. Caña Brava white rum
1 oz. pinot noir
½ oz. fresh lime juice
½ oz. house-made Demerara Syrup
2 dashes Dale DeGroff's pimento bitters (or allspice dram)

Add all ingredients to mixing glass. Add ice and shake well. Strain into chilled cocktail glass. Garnish with orange peel.

Adapted to celebrate the one hundredth anniversary of the completion of the Panama Canal and the signing of the treaty that took place in the Old Hotel in 1914, this should not be confused with the *Sangaree* or *Punch* of the same name. The original Waldorf-Astoria recipe called for white rum, so I used an aged Panamanian rum here along with pimento bitters. This quencher was served until the start of Prohibition in 1920.

The demerara syrup adds a bit of viscosity and weight to the finish. I would suggest not using your best or heaviest grape in the wine slot. I settled on pinot noir, as it's delicate enough not to overpower the other ingredients yet assertive enough to add tannin and grip, which makes this cocktail unique.

BISHOP POKER

1 oz. Plymouth gin
1 oz. Martini & Rossi sweet vermouth
1 oz. Noilly Prat dry vermouth
⅓ oz. Bigallet "China-China" Amer liqueur

Add all ingredients to mixing glass. Add ice and stir for 30 seconds. Strain into chilled cocktail glass. Garnish with orange peel.

BISHOP POTTER (JACQUES STRAUB VERSION)

1½ oz. Plymouth gin
¾ oz. Martini & Rossi sweet vermouth
¾ oz. Noilly Prat extra dry vermouth
⅓ oz. Calisaya liqueur
2 dashes Regan's Orange Bitters

Add all ingredients to mixing glass. Add ice and stir for 30 seconds. Strain into chilled cocktail glass. Garnish with orange peel.

NEWMAN

1½ oz. Plymouth gin
1½ oz. Noilly Prat extra dry vermouth
⅓ oz. Bigallet China-China Amer liqueur

Add ingredients to mixing glass. Add ice and stir for 30 seconds. Strain into chilled cocktail glass. Garnish with lemon peel.

LIEUTENANT COLONEL

2½ oz. Carpano dry vermouth
½ oz. Bigallet China-China Amer liqueur

Add ingredients to mixing glass. Add ice and stir for 30 seconds. Strain into chilled cocktail glass. Garnish with lemon and orange peel.

Okay, here's one that gets the "chicken or the egg" award. Jacques Straub's 1914 recipe book, *Drinks,* which at the very least was influenced by *The Old Waldorf Astoria Bar Book* (he was probably given access to the actual book by Oscar Tschirky; it predates

Straub's publication by seventeen years), cites calisaya and orange bitters as the accoutrements to its *Bishop Potter*. They allow the gin to take the lead. (I enjoy using Calisaya liqueur here, as it adds a bit of body.) Mr. Crockett somehow comes to a completely different name by possibly misinterpreting the title (Bishop Poker) and story of origin, dedicating a whole paragraph to its questionable beginnings while utilizing equal portions of ingredients. Either way, I've tried every combination and decided to include the Straub version here because it was first in print and the ingredients in Mr. Crockett's recipe are represented several times over in the other recipes.

I personally prefer the drier *Newman variation,* which was named for a frequenter of the Old Bar who owned a resort near the Old Hotel. I can easily see this becoming a mainstay on the cocktail list at Peacock Alley. If you split the portion of vermouth between sweet and dry, you will have what the Old Books called a **Milliken** (I prefer mine with an orange twist).

The **Coxey** subs in sweet vermouth in the dry slot of the *Newman*. It was named for Ohioan Jacob Coxey's famous 1894 march on Washington, D.C., where he led unemployed protesters known as Coxey's Army in an effort to gain employment during the worst U.S. economic depression known until that point. He caused quite the ruckus. Whether Mr. Coxey knew that his influence reached as far as the east side of Midtown Manhattan will probably remain unknown. A very close relative of this drink, but unrelated to the oldest printed recipe of the same name (William Schmidt, *The Flowing Bowl*, 1891), the **Fin de Siècle**, is also included in the Old Books. It leans on the Plymouth with a 2:1 ratio to vermouth and includes orange bitters. If including the bitters, I would pull back the Amer to a quarter ounce. It's very much worth a try.

The *Lieutenant Colonel* was a fifty-fifty dry vermouth and Amer hybrid, a nonstarter for me no matter how I played it. I adapted this one by leaning on the fuller-flavored vermouth to carry this easy, predinner aperitif. I used the two twists because I couldn't really settle on either, as they both worked exceptionally well. You can fiddle with the ratio to your personal taste. This will remain in my rotation for a long time to come.

BISMARCK FIZZ

3 oz. chilled club soda
2½ oz. German Riesling (trocken or other dry style preferred)
1 oz. house-made Raspberry Syrup
¾ oz. fresh lemon juice

Add chilled club soda to small Collins glass. Add remaining ingredients to mixing glass. Add ice and shake well. Strain into Collins glass. Stir briefly to integrate. No garnish.

This easy-drinking Fizz (true to its German roots, as the popular spritzer began there) is most likely named for the nineteenth-century first Chancellor of Germany, Otto von Bismarck (hence the wine component). Although the original recipes suggest a sweet version of German wine, I feel the drier, contrasting trocken-style's acidity adds complexity. Shake with a few mint leaves (and fine-strain) for a pleasing seasonal variation.

BLACK CHERRY SODA ▮ *Peacock Alley*

2 oz. Black Cherry Infusion Absolut vodka (recipe follows)
4 oz. club soda
¼ oz. house-made Grenadine (for float)

Add infused vodka to chilled Collins glass. Add large ice cubes and fill with club soda. Top with grenadine. Garnish with lemon peel and brandied cherry.

Black Cherry Infusion

1 c. fresh black cherries, split
1 liter Absolut vodka

Place all ingredients in airtight glass container for 7 days. Fine-strain and funnel back into bottle. Best if used within 3 months.

This refreshing summer Cooler is a perennial guest favorite. Using fresh cherries for the infusion makes for a drier and slightly tart Highball. I prefer preparing this in season and using fresh cherries, as the dried variety makes for a much sweeter result. You can utilize most any clear spirit as the base (white rum, Old Tom gin, pisco, etc.) but in this case I think that the vodka delivers the subtle fruit in its purest form. Expect this to be a hit at your next barbecue.

BLACKJACK

- **1 oz. Etter Zuger kirsch cherry brandy**
- **½ oz. Hardy VSOP cognac**
- **½ oz. Luxardo maraschino liqueur**
- **1 oz. French roast coffee (strongly brewed and cooled to room temperature or chilled)**

Add all ingredients to mixing glass. Add ice and stir for 30 seconds. Strain into chilled cocktail glass. No garnish.

This cocktail is named for the leather-covered lead hand weapon of nineteenth- and twentieth-century criminals, and mandatory equipment for police departments of the era. The original had this shaken with equal parts kirschwasser and coffee and only a dash of brandy. That variation sorely needed some viscosity as well as a touch of sweetness for balance. After developing about a dozen models, I settled on this one. The maraschino makes for the perfect sweetness and pairing to the ramped-up portion of brandy that adds body. A find as an after-dinner cocktail. See **Café Kirsch** for variation.

BLACK STRIPE (BLACKSTRAP)

- **¾ oz. cold water**
- **⅓ oz. Plantation blackstrap molasses**
- **2 oz. Pusser's British Navy rum**

Add water and molasses to Old Fashioned glass and stir to combine. Add rum and stir to combine. Fill with crushed or pellet ice. Garnish with freshly grated nutmeg.

This ancient Toddy template dates back a few centuries, and is not for the faint of heart; blackstrap molasses can curl some toes. This old-timer can be adapted to a hot beverage and is much more palatable that way. Just replace the cold water with a couple of ounces of hot water. Honey is often mentioned as an ingredient in other recipes and would make for an easier-drinking example, but you won't earn your pirate stripes that way. See "Hot Drinks" chapter for variation.

BLOOD AND SAND ▮ *Classic*

1½ oz. Chivas Regal 12 Year Old blended Scotch whisky
1 oz. blood orange juice (Valencia or Naval orange can be
substituted)
¾ oz. Heering cherry liqueur
¾ oz. Punt e Mes vermouth

Add all ingredients to mixing glass. Add ice and shake well. Strain into chilled cocktail glass. Garnish with flamed orange coin (optional) and brandied cherry.

Named for the 1922 Rudolph Valentino film of the same name, this often-overlooked cocktail is nonetheless frequently ordered at Peacock Alley. I have adjusted the portions of each ingredient to reflect the taste of the modern drinker's palate (and mine) by ramping up the amount of Scotch, transforming it into a base ingredient. The original recipes call for equal amounts of each item, but I found it a bit cloying and muddy. The bitter orange notes of the Punt e Mes vermouth were a nice surprise. The beauty of most of the best cocktails is that they take well to a bit of tinkering.

BLOODY BUNNY ▮ *Peacock Alley*

2 dashes Lea & Perrins Worcestershire sauce
1 dash Tabasco sauce
Pinch kosher salt

Pinch coarse black pepper
Pinch celery seed
2 oz. Tito's Handmade vodka
4 oz. fresh carrot juice (Bolthouse Farms or
other commercially available, if necessary)
Toasted coriander powder, pink peppercorn,
and kosher salt rim

FOR RIM:
¼ c. coriander powder
⅛ c. fine-ground pink peppercorns
2 tbsp. kosher salt

Add all ingredients to airtight sealable plastic container and shake to combine. Place on shallow plate. Using fresh lemon wedge, moisten half of rim of glass and roll rim through the mixture. Fill with large ice cubes.

FOR DRINK PREPARATION:

   Add all ingredients to mixing glass in order listed. Add large ice cubes and roll between mixing glass and shaker 3 to 5 times. Strain into prepared Collins glass. Garnish with ⅓ celery stalk and thin coin of carrot, notched to sit on nonrimmed side of glass.

This brunch-inspired concoction was devised for a guest's special event and I've been featuring it every Sunday since. Chef Cedric Tovar helped create the coriander and pink peppercorn rim and it makes all the difference. We originally toasted the spices in a hot dry pan for a minute or so prior to grinding, which is recommended when you want to elevate the result even more. I have also enjoyed a bay leaf–infused vodka here. Just place three or four dried bay leaves in a bottle of (un-flavored) vodka of your choice for two weeks and you are ready to go (works great with standard Bloody Mary as well).

BLOODY MARY ▮ *Classic*

½ oz. fresh lemon juice
2 dashes Lea & Perrins Worcestershire sauce
2 dashes Tabasco sauce
½ bar spoon of freshly grated horseradish (jarred works, if fresh is unavailable)
Pinch kosher salt
Pinch coarse black pepper
Pinch celery seed (omit kosher salt if using celery salt)
Pinch light brown sugar
4 oz. chilled Sacramento tomato juice
2 oz. Tito's Handmade vodka
(Or 5 oz. house-made Bloody Mary Mix)

Add all ingredients to mixing glass in order listed. Add large ice cubes and roll between mixing glass and shaker 3 to 5 times and transfer to chilled Collins glass. Place lemon wedge on side of glass. Garnish with ⅓ celery stalk. Optional garnish: prepare skewer with Peppadew (sweet pepper), cornichon (small French pickle), cocktail onion, and Queen Anne olive and place across top of glass.

This drink's tomato juice base is best prepared the night before you plan on using it (do not add spirit or lemon juice), as the integration of ingredients makes a big difference. Try it for yourself and compare. We make this by the batch at Peacock Alley and even more during our brunch season, as Bloody Marys are ordered by the tray.

The base recipe can be adjusted to taste: add more Tabasco or substitute your personal favorite hot sauce (smoked or chipotle variations work well), celery salt, dried celery flakes (my wife Margaret's preference), etc. You can omit the brown sugar for the classic version, but I have been adding it for years, though you should never taste its presence. It's there to only provide background contrast, especially as spicier *Bloody Marys* have become the norm lately.

Early on, we attempted using freshly blended tomatoes and juice, and though it's a unique and tasty variation, it just did not hold a candle to the canned version, especially when it came to viscosity.

There are conflicting stories as to the origin of the Bloody Mary. Some cite actor George Jessel, who, in the 1920s, supposedly combined vodka and tomato juice as tonic for his hangovers. The other name that comes up is St. Regis barman, the Frenchman Fernand Petiot. Yet another story offers an archaeological answer in a nonalcoholic version called the *Oyster Cocktail*, from the Manhattan nightlife of the late 1800s. One thing is for certain: the Bloody Mary has survived for a reason. Its cold, savory, and spicy profile provides the morning tide to wash away even the most persistent "night befores."

As for classic spirit variations, the **Red Snapper** substitutes London dry gin for the vodka and is a New York staple, most known for being the signature cocktail at the King Cole Bar in the St. Regis Hotel. The **Bloody Maria** features tequila as the base spirit (preferably blanco 100 percent agave, but a good mezcal works as well). You may want to sub in fresh lime juice for the lemon, but other than that, it's the same drink. The **Bloody Caesar**, popularized in the late 1960s at Calgary, Canada's Westin Hotel's Owl's Nest Bar, is a *Bloody Mary* that includes Clamato, a clam juice and tomato juice hybrid. This version is best with raw or cold seafood. Finally, the **Bloody Bull** shares base ingredient duties by adding beef stock in equal parts to the tomato juice. It's thinner on the palate, but the stock adds a richness and a savory drinkability some may prefer.

It's an absolute necessity to roll this cocktail. Shaking will severely dilute the tomato juice, and it will lose its signature thickness. Straining over fresh ice is not necessary as long as the ice cubes you are using are still around an inch and a quarter in size, post-roll. Incidentally, it's become common practice for bars and restaurants to rim the top of the serving glass with a myriad of salts and spices. I typically don't partake in this practice at Peacock Alley (the **Bloody Bunny** notwithstanding), as I feel it gets in the way of the already complex drink, but if you do, I would pull back on the hot sauce in the base mix a bit and allow the rim to add the heat. I like a spicy Hungarian paprika and salt mix here. Garnishes have also come to represent the host bar's identity, but I think less is more. Other than your preference of pickled vegetables (green bean, asparagus, carrot, etc.), I would steer clear of adding any other food items to this or any other cocktail. Shrimp, bacon, and the like belong on a plate and not in a cocktail or drink. Would you believe there exist hamburger slider on a skewer and whole Cornish hen on a skewer versions? If I hadn't seen it for myself, I wouldn't either.

BLUE MOON ▮ *Oscar Tschirky's Variation*

2 oz. Nolet's Silver dry gin or Hendrick's gin
½ oz. crème Yvette

Add ingredients to mixing glass. Add ice and stir for 30 seconds. Strain into chilled cocktail glass. Garnish with lemon peel.

Though not mentioned in either of Mr. Crockett's books, this cocktail can be found in Oscar Tschirky's *100 Famous Cocktails*, published in 1934. His recipe (which added red wine!), was a take on an earlier version published in *Recipes for Mixed Drinks* (1917), by Hugo R. Ensslin, in which I would add two-thirds of an ounce of dry vermouth and a dash of orange bitters to the recipe above, to meet his intention. A fine rendering. Oscar's base ingredient was Old Tom gin, but I found it left the recipe leaning too heavily on the crème Yvette and made it unbalanced. I've also tried several London dry styles of varying proofs and they all performed serviceably, though they did not help the end result rise above the field. However, if your tastes remain undaring, it will yield the traditional and intended result.

I chose the unique floral qualities of both Nolet's Silver dry gin and Hendrick's gin to pair with the crème Yvette, led by Nolet's saffron note, which gives the *Blue Moon* its own identity. Either way, it worked for me. There is a "juiced" and probably more popular version (first found in 1941's *Crosby Gaige's Cocktail Guide)* listed as an **Aviation** variation that did not contain any maraschino liqueur. It simply added a half ounce of fresh lemon juice to Oscar's recipe and is shaken, of course. In the summer months this version will end the day with a swirl. Top off with a touch of club soda, if you're opting to serve it on ice. See **Aviation** for variation.

BORDELAI/E

2 oz. Trimbach Framboise Grande Reserve raspberry brandy
¾ oz. house-made Raspberry Syrup
¾ oz. fresh lemon juice
4 oz. chilled club soda

Add ingredients to Collins glass. Add ice and stir briefly to integrate. Garnish with lemon peel.

You're right, bordelaise sauce does not include berries of any kind. This tweaked Rickey presentation does find its way into both of the Old Books and is quite the Cooler. The original required a kirsch (cherry) eau-de-vie. I replaced the kirsch with framboise (raspberry) to match the syrup. A real summer winner.

BOWMAN BACARDI

1 oz. Bacardi Superior white rum
1 oz. Bacardi 8 Year Old dark rum
1 oz. fresh orange juice
¼ oz. Simple Syrup
6 mint leaves
2 dashes Dale DeGroff's pimento bitters

Add all ingredients to mixing glass. Add ice and shake well. Fine-strain into chilled cocktail glass. Garnish with 1 mint leaf.

According to Mr. Crockett, it's named for nineteenth-century hotelier John McEntee Bowman, who introduced modern hotel management to Havana, Cuba. Once there, he apparently fell in love with its native spirit (Bacardi rum), and he became the product's unofficial ambassador. The original called for Bacardi white rum, but I felt it could take a step up in flavor, so I split it with the full-flavored Bacardi 8 Year Old dark and it makes all the difference. The use of mint is here to complement the other ingredients, so be sure not to overdo it. The addition of the pimento bitters brings it all home, though Angostura will do in a pinch. Double-straining ensures a clean presentation.

BRADLEY-MARTIN

1½ oz. Tempus Fugit crème de menthe
1 oz. Tempus Fugit crème de cacao

Add ingredients to Old Fashioned glass with cubed or crushed ice. Stir briefly to integrate.

This cocktail is named for society leaders of the day who hosted a poorly timed, much ballyhooed, and opulent ball on February 10, 1897, at the Old Hotel. Condemned by local and even the world press, the Bradley-Martins went ahead as planned with their ball, as unemployment rates soared and the country was in the worst economic era of its history to that point. The tally amounted to more than $350,000 for the one-night grand ballroom event (about $10 million today). Public dissatisfaction ran so high that there were rumors of bombs being placed at the home of the Bradley-Martins.

Though the memory of the controversy wanes over time, its namesake survivor is an inoffensive after-dinner drink if there ever was one. Simply presented here with superior ingredients, it can be loosely translated as a Grasshopper without the cream. It's surprisingly unfancy.

BRAMBLE ∎ *Classic*

2 oz. Spencerfield Spirit Edinburgh gin
1 oz. fresh lemon juice
½ oz. Simple Syrup
½ oz. Giffard crème de mûre

Add all ingredients except crème de mûre to mixing glass. Add ice and shake well. Strain into Old Fashioned glass filled with crushed or pellet ice. Top with crème de mûre. Garnish with one fresh blackberry on a skewer.

Rooftop Ramble ▮ *Peacock Alley*

2 oz. Nolet's Silver gin
1 oz. fresh lemon juice
½ oz. Simple Syrup
½ egg white
4 fresh basil leaves (cleaned and stemmed)
2 oz. chilled club soda
½ oz. Combier Crème de Fruits rouges

Add all ingredients except basil, Combier, and club soda to mixing glass and dry-shake for 5 seconds. Add basil and ice and shake well for 10 seconds. Fine-strain into Old Fashioned glass filled with large ice cubes. Add club soda and stir briefly to integrate. Float Crème de Fruits Rouges over top. No garnish.

Created in the 1980s in London's Soho neighborhood by Dick Bradsell, the *Bramble* became a modern-day classic. There's no reason to overthink this one, but if you like, try muddling six midsummer blackberries in lieu of the blackberry liqueur float (or use just a touch of the liqueur in the muddling process) for a drier and fresher result (just be sure to fine-strain).

The Peacock Alley variation is known as the *Rooftop Ramble*. I used Nolet's Silver gin (a uniquely flavored spirit with a perfumed finish that pairs nicely with citrus) in the lead role and added the touch of egg white. I like the way it tempers all the ingredients and takes a bit of edge off. The crème de fruits rouges is a five-berry blend liqueur that also fits snuggly into its slot. I added a few fresh basil leaves from our rooftop garden (hence the title) shaken in for a nice outcome. You could omit the club soda but it keeps it light (and another step away from the *Bramble*).

BRANDY CHAMPERELLE COCKTAIL

2 oz. Courvoisier VSOP cognac
½ oz. Luxardo Triplum triple sec
½ oz. Angostura bitters

Add all ingredients to mixing glass. Add ice and stir for 30 seconds. Strain into chilled cocktail glass. Garnish with lemon peel.

BRANDY CHAMPERELLE POUSSE-CAFÉ

⅓ oz. Luxardo Triplum triple sec
¼ oz. Dr. Adam Elmegirab's Boker's bitters or Angostura bitters
⅓ oz. Courvoisier VSOP cognac (or Lustau Don Nuño oloroso sherry)

Add all ingredients, in order listed, to pony or small sherry glass. No garnish.

Different versions of this mid-nineteenth-century creation appear in each of the Old Books.

The 1931 book (*Old Waldorf Bar Days*) includes sherry as the identifying ingredient and serves it in a pony glass, à la the Pousse-Café (see "Historical Concoctions" chapter).

The 1934 *Old Waldorf-Astoria Bar Book* lists brandy in the sherry slot; this is also how it first appeared in print in *Jerry Thomas' Bartenders Guide* (1862). Other previous recipes list maraschino liqueur in the curaçao or triple sec slot, which is also worth a try.

I did happen across a recipe in William Terrington's *Cooling Cups and Dainty Drinks* (1869) that presented these ingredients as a cocktail, and since it's from the same era as the other versions and is a serious upgrade from the digestif serving, I feel it is worthy of inclusion here. Although Mr. Terrington specified bitters as a main ingredient, he could have meant an aromatized wine such as Bonal (which would've been referred to as a bitter; you can try it that way). I used the unusual portion of Angostura bitters and it lent an amaro-like flavor profile and viscosity to the finished product and proved too tempting a result to pass up (cutting to the chase with an actual amaro works too). I think this delivers a unique after-dinner offering either way.

BRANDY COCKTAIL NO. 2

**1½ oz. Royer Force 53 cognac or Boulard Grand Solage VSOP
calvados**
1½ oz. Dolin de Chambery dry vermouth
1 dash Regans' Orange Bitters No. 6
1 dash Angostura bitters

Add all ingredients to mixing glass. Add ice and stir for 30 seconds.
Strain into chilled cocktail glass. Garnish with lemon peel.

After experimentation with an applejack and calvados for base ingredients as listed in the original recipes, it was the cognac variation, with its fuller body and finish, that took the title. Both have
merit, but I prefer the cognac version.

I've added a dash of orange and aromatic bitters, but if you omit
one, make it the aromatic, especially with the calvados-based version. Either way, a snap of a lemon peel adds zip for lovers of dry
yet flavorful cocktails.

BRANDY CRUSTA

2 oz. Kelt VSOP cognac
½ oz. Cointreau
¼ oz. house-made Demerara Syrup
¼ oz. fresh lemon juice
1 dash Angostura bitters
1 dash Peychaud's bitters

Prior to building this cocktail, moisten rim of small goblet or
wineglass with lemon wedge (about ½ inch down), then carefully
dab and roll in superfine sugar on a small plate.

Peel a lemon in one long swath (or if you prefer orange, this
works as well and is slightly easier to peel in the called-for fashion).
Carefully place in glass by curling peel around the inside.

Add all ingredients to mixing glass. Add ice and stir for 30
seconds. Strain into prepared glass.

Originating in New Orleans in the 1850s from creative Italian barman
Joseph Santini, and debuting in print courtesy of Jerry Thomas a
short time later, the *Brandy Crusta* is a true "big bang" cocktail,
named for the sugar crust applied to both citrus rind and glass. It's

undeniably linked to its direct descendant, the Sidecar (and by asso-ciation, the Margarita, in the evolutionary cocktail chain). One must be cognizant not to overdo this first-generation classic. All of the accompanying accoutrements are only there to adorn the main in-gredient. In fact, I have included a very good cognac and brought just about every modifying ingredient to its absolute limit to ensure that any personal adjustments be made by subtraction.

One ingredient found in later versions is maraschino liqueur. If so inclined, feel free to add a quarter ounce of Luxardo maraschino, substituting it for Cointreau. A nice orange alternate to the Cointreau is Grand Marnier or event Pierre Ferrand's dry curaçao. Although it's not included in the Old Books, I would also consider a dash of Peychaud's bitters, as an homage to its New Orleans roots; it adds a bit to the nose and tannin on the palate as well. The Old Books include a **Rum Crusta** variation. Just use a dark and flavorful vari-ety in the brandy slot.

From my personal experience, preparing this drink in the pres-ence of an intended loved one can't help but impress. Just try it once or twice beforehand, to work out the kinks.

BRANDY FLOAT

2 oz. chilled club soda
1½ oz. Royer VSOP cognac

Add three large ice cubes or sphere to rocks glass. Add club soda. Float cognac on top. Twist orange peel to release oils, then discard.

Yes, it's as simple as it sounds, but simplicity has its merits. It's a great post-dinner treat, especially in the summertime when the thought of a neat cognac might be a bit overwhelming. I've added a spray of an orange peel that was not included in the original recipe just to brighten it up a bit.

BRANDY PUNCH

2 oz. Royer Force 53 cognac
¾ oz. fresh lemon juice
¾ oz. Simple Syrup
½ oz. cold water

Add all ingredients to mixing glass. Add large ice cubes, roll between mixing glass and shaker 3 to 5 times, and transfer to Old Fashioned glass or Hoffman House goblet. Garnish with fresh, seasonal fruit.

Derived from one of the earliest (large format) Punch recipes, *Brandy Punch* was first found in print in 1695. Punches of that era leaned on limes for their citrus profile, as lemon did not come into favor until the mid-nineteenth century. By the time the Old Bar got around to serving these, lemons were the choice, as Mr. Crockett noted in both books. This evolved to be the made-to-order version of a classic Punch. Presentation counts here, so look to adorn with berries and an orange wheel, if possible.

BRONX ∎ *Modern*

1½ oz. Beefeater London dry gin
½ oz. Cinzano Rosso sweet vermouth
½ oz. Noilly Prat extra dry vermouth
1 oz. fresh orange juice
1 dash Regans' Orange Bitters No. 6 (optional)

Add all ingredients to mixing glass. Add ice and shake well. Strain into chilled cocktail glass. No garnish.

BRONX ∎ *Old Waldorf Bar Days Variation*

1½ oz. Plymouth gin
¾ oz. Martini & Rossi sweet vermouth
¾ oz. Noilly Prat extra dry vermouth
2 orange peels (two 1-by-2-inch peels, snapped to release oils, then added to mixing glass)
1 dash Regans' Orange Bitters No. 6

Add all ingredients to mixing glass. Add ice and stir for 30 seconds. Strain into chilled cocktail glass. Garnish with orange peel.

Of all the cocktails associated with or attributed to the Hotel, not one—not even the venerable Rob Roy—was as popular as the *Bronx*. Sometimes referred to as the **Cosmopolitan** of its day, it was one of the most requested cocktails prior to Prohibition.

Despite plenty of controversy over the truth about its origins, I would like to think that one of the Waldorf's fine bartenders was responsible for creating this cocktail. In *Old Waldorf Bar Days*, Mr. Crockett devotes a whole chapter to the subject, quoting Waldorf barman Johnnie Solan at length (though newspaper articles of the day cite another house barman, John "Curley" O'Connor, as its creator). Solan explains that it was based on another popular cocktail, the **Duplex**. As the legend goes, he had just finished preparing one when a waiter challenged him to create a new quencher on the spot. He basically added gin and orange juice to the *Duplex* and the *Bronx* was born—supposedly named for rowdy guests who reminded him of a recent trip to the zoo. It met with the waiter's approval and became the lunchtime special. Interestingly, Solan's story tells of going from using a dozen oranges a day to several cases. I love to imagine a time when rivers of gin and juice were consumed before three p.m. Those were the days.

If you believe that the *Bronx* is indeed an evolution of the *Duplex*, it stands to reason that a fair amount of vermouth would have remained and would not have diminished to bar-spoon levels, and that by ramping up the juice, you get the originally intended refresher that was a staple of the lunchtime bar. You can tinker all you want with brands of vermouth, levels of potency, styles of gin and genever, even varieties of oranges, but what's most essential for me, in the end, is a dash of orange bitters, as it adds a bit of spice and backbone that orange juice lacks.

That said, some of the controversy over this cocktail should be addressed. The first time the *Bronx* appears in book form is in William "Cocktail" Boothby's *World Drinks and How to Mix Them*, 1908 edition. In Boothby's book, as well as in Jacques Straub's *Drinks* (1914) and Mr. Crockett's first *Old Waldorf Bar Days* (1931), the *Bronx* is a true cocktail, a Perfect Martini accented by either an orange peel or a bar spoon of juice, stirred, and served with an orange twist. Now, whether Mr. Solan's real contribution to the *Bronx* was not in adding gin and juice to the Duplex, but in adding more juice to the already existing cocktail that was the

Bronx, will never be known. Either way, it seems that the boys of the Old Bar had that covered anyway—later in the book the *Jazz* appears, whose listing reads: "Same as *Bronx*, with plenty of orange juice." The Old Bar's original *Bronx* is transformed into the modern *Bronx* recipe by following this directive. *Old Waldorf Bar Days* mentions that there were already plenty of variations around, and also includes Johnnie Solan's rendition.

As for the *Jazz*, I would separate this from the previous two recipes by adding another ounce of juice—perfect to serve at your next jazz brunch, on the rocks, as a refined head clearer.

A **Cuban Bronx** uses Bacardi white rum as the base ingredient, though in my view the amber variety brings a more heightened result.

Making a **Dry Bronx** by omitting the sweet vermouth and doubling the portion of dry vermouth, as in the modern recipe, will give you what the Old Books called a **Passipe**. It's not for everyone, but if your tastes lean toward the dry side of things, it's more than worth a try.

If you do the opposite, making sweet vermouth the star and omitting the dry, you will have a **Widow**, which is more of a crowd-pleaser, but decidedly much less balanced, in my opinion.

The Old Books list a recipe for the **Cooperstown** as "a *Bronx* shaken with fresh mint." Although this works pretty well, other printed recipes omit the orange juice and present it as a stirred cocktail. See **Cooperstown** for variation. The last namesake recipe is the **Waldorf Bronx**, which appears, strangely enough, within the Manhattan-like **Waldorf** cocktail entry in *Old Waldorf Bar Days*. Mr. Crockett notes that it was never entered into the actual Bar Book but was a popular order by those who "sometimes tired of the ordinary 'Bronx.'" He cites Johnnie Solan again, offering that "it was composed of two-thirds gin, one-third orange juice and two slices of fresh pineapple." It is, at its heart, a pineapple-enhanced **Orange Blossom No. 2**.

The **Orange Blossom**, with its own signature controversy, warrants its own lengthy entry later in this book.

Another related title can be found in Mr. Straub's *Drinks* under **Chantecler**, in which he claims that drink to be a "*Bronx* with four dashes of grenadine syrup." You can try it if you want, but don't go out of your way. See **Chanticleer** for the Waldorf Astoria variant.

A cocktail surprisingly missing from the Old Books but namechecked in other books of the era is the **Silver Bronx**, which has the good sense to include half an egg white prior to shaking (as anything silver would imply). It works like a charm for those who would prefer their *Bronx* with a bit of froth; I would add another quarter ounce of sweet vermouth to recalibrate its balance.

QUEENS

1 dash Regan's Orange Bitters
2 wedges fresh pineapple (or ½ oz. pineapple juice, if unavailable)
1½ oz. Tanqueray No. Ten gin
¾ oz. Noilly Prat extra dry vermouth
¾ oz. Cinzano Rosso sweet vermouth

Add bitters and one pineapple wedge to mixing glass and muddle briefly. Add remaining ingredients. Add ice and shake well. Fine-strain into chilled cocktail glass. Garnish with one pineapple wedge.

The listed recipe calls for equal amounts of liquid ingredients, but I've opted to lean on the gin here for a bit of gas, as the bar staff at the newly opened Park Avenue Waldorf-Astoria did in the mid-twentieth century. Ted Saucier credited this cocktail to them, calling it a **New Waldorf** in *Bottoms Up* (1951). Some older recipes include a slice of orange in the muddling process, but it's not necessary, as it pulls closer to the *Bronx* in flavor. This recipe bounced around some famous haunts but never made the transition to a classic cocktail. It's a charming crowd-pleaser and another one that you can present to those who claim an aversion to gin. Ultimately, I think it was a failed attempt to attach a modified *Bronx* cocktail recipe to its sister borough. See **Orange Blossom** for variation and **Thompson** for a whiskey-based variation.

SATAN'S WHISKERS ❚ *Classic*

1 oz. Beefeater London dry gin
¾ oz. Noilly Prat extra dry vermouth
¾ oz. Cinzano Rosso sweet vermouth
½ oz. Cointreau (Straight) or Grand Marnier (Curled) or Pierre Ferrand dry curaçao (Pencil) (see below)
1 oz. fresh orange juice
1 dash Regans' Orange Bitters No. 6 (or Angostura bitters)

Add all ingredients to mixing glass. Add ice and shake well. Strain into chilled cocktail glass. No garnish.

Lastly, although not included in either of the Old Books, there is *Satan's Whiskers*. First appearing in print in Harry Craddock's *The Savoy Cocktail Book* (1930), this enhanced *Bronx* earns its inclusion here by taking the *Bronx* up one notch with the addition of an orange liqueur. According to Craddock, if you use Grand Marnier (or its like) you would have a **Curled Whisker**, and by using a triple sec (such as Cointreau) you would have a **Straight Whisker**. Each has its merits. Using Pierre Ferrand dry curaçao meets in the middle (I'll go out on a limb here and call it the **Pencil Whisker**).

The original called for equal parts of all ingredients except for the orange element, which was taken down by half. Using today's products, I feel it could use an adjustment, hence the methodology noted. I would also recommend using aromatic bitters in lieu of orange for a nice contrast. Try all variations and adjust to your personal taste; it's one of those kinds of cocktails. See **Marble Hill** and **Marmalade** for variations.

BROOKLYN   ▮ *Classic*

> **2 oz. Wild Turkey 101 rye whiskey**
> **1 oz. Noilly Prat extra dry vermouth**
> **¼ oz. Bigallet China-China Amer**
> **¼ oz. Luxardo maraschino liqueur**
>
> Add all ingredients to mixing glass. Add ice and stir for 30 seconds. Strain into chilled cocktail glass. Garnish with lemon peel.

Though no representation of the classic *Brooklyn* cocktail exists in either edition of the Old Books, it does appear in Jacques Straub's *Drinks*. It was a popular **Manhattan** variation in its day, and has recently enjoyed a comeback (it first appeared in print in 1908). An oft-used cocktail ingredient at the time was Amer Picon, which is no longer imported to the United States. Bigallet's is a fine replacement (made since 1875). If you had to replicate without either, I would combine one-half portion each of orange bitters and Ramazzotti amaro, integrate, and use that. As for the vermouth, the original recipe in *Jack's Manual* (1908) used sweet vermouth (and was also referred to as a **Creole** cocktail—not to be confused with the other namesake cocktail; see **New Orleans**). I prefer this one, as the dry vermouth gives it an identity and is not just a **Martinez** variation. Onetime Peacock Alley manager Orion Berge suggested a delicious autumnal variation, utilizing Laird's bonded applejack in the rye spot (though a good calvados would make for a nice treat); we called it **An Apple Tree Grows in Brooklyn**. See **Liberal** for variation.

BRUT

1½ oz. Foro extra dry organic vermouth
1½ oz. Cocchi Barolo Chinato or Bonal quinquina aperitif
1 dash Pacifique absinthe
2 dashes Regans' Orange Bitters No. 6

Add all ingredients to mixing glass. Add ice and stir for 15 seconds. Strain into chilled cocktail glass. Garnish with lemon peel.

BRUT (PEACOCK ALLEY VARIATION)

2 oz. Foro extra dry organic vermouth
½ oz. Calisaya liqueur
½ oz. Rittenhouse bonded rye whiskey
2 dashes Pernod Original Recipe absinthe
2 dashes Regans' Orange Bitters No. 6

Add all ingredients to mixing glass. Add ice and stir for 30 seconds. Strain into chilled cocktail glass. Garnish with lemon peel.

This cocktail, originally made with equal parts of quinquina and dry vermouth, is a fine predinner sipper when you're in the mood for something lighter. In the process of working with these ingredients, I took the liberty of creating something with just a touch more alcohol. It's better served as an aperitif cocktail with the vermouth taking the lead. Here, I have cut back on the quinquina and added a bit of Calisaya liqueur for some viscosity. I have also added some rye whiskey, which is included as an ingredient in a few other similarly named recipes of the era—and after inclusion, I found out why. Now it's a quintessential predinner cocktail; a summer respite, for sure. For a cocktail in which a **Calisaya** takes the lead, see its own, self-titled entry. As for the first, lighter rendition, your ingredients should be prechilled, which makes for the shorter time on ice to avoid over-dilution.

BUCK/RICKEY (Basic Recipe)

½ oz. fresh lime or lemon juice

2 oz. spirit of choice (brandy, bourbon, gin, rum, rye, Scotch, tequila, etc.)

4 oz. cane-based ginger ale or ginger beer (Boylan, Fever-Tree, or Q) or club soda

Squeeze citrus of choice into Collins glass and add shell (optional). Add ice. Add spirit and fill with ginger ale or ginger beer.

This classic refresher dates back to the mid-nineteenth century and there are plenty of variations. *Buck* is a category of drink, one in which the base ingredient can be exchanged for many a spirit, but the key is the citrus and ginger ale or ginger beer, which separates it from the rest of the Highballs. More often than not, I prefer the use of ginger beer. It probably more closely resembles the "imported ginger ale" called for in some of the old recipes, though a quality, cane syrup–based, domestic ginger ale works just fine in more subtle variations.

As for the choice of base spirit, use vodka, lime, and ginger beer and you'll have the famous **Moscow Mule**; gin and lemon and the result is a **Gin Buck**. Gin and lime begets the **Foghorn**. Old Tom gin and lime begets the **Marguerite** (there also exists a cocktail version by the same name herein). Use bourbon and you have a **Jim Renwick** (for the architect of the same name). Use Scotch whisky and lime and you have a **Mamie Taylor** (named for the opera singer). Add a couple of dashes of absinthe to a *Mamie Taylor* and you'll have the **Robert E. Lee**. *The Old Waldorf-Astoria Bar Book* features a **Bacardi Buck**, though I would recommend an aged variety for a richer drink. Probably the most popular of them all would be the **Dark and Stormy**, which uses Goslings Black Seal rum at its base, with lime juice and ginger beer. I modified that classic a bit to come up with the **Stormy Monday**. It adds a half ounce of Domaine de Canton ginger liqueur, which we infused directly in the bottle with fresh julienned ginger (you should do this anyway and just leave it on your shelf). You can sub in club soda for a more balanced result, but it works either way. It also takes nicely to a bit of freshly grated nutmeg as a "throwback" garnish. It's definitely worth a try.

Rickeys are typically *Bucks* with club soda in lieu of ginger ale. With gin, lime, and club soda, you have the classic **Gin Rickey** (named for "Colonel" Joe Rickey, though in practice he preferred whiskey at the base of his—that's called a **Single Standard**, by the way) and there is, of course, the **Bacardi Rickey**. If you use a Jamaican rum, you will then have a **Rum Rickey**. If you use sloe gin as the base, you will of course have the **Sloe Gin Rickey**. If you top it with a touch of grenadine, you'll have what the Old Book called a **Porto Rico**. Use Scotch whisky and lime and a couple of dashes of aromatic bitters and you'll be enjoying a **Mamie Gilroy** (named for the stage actress).

And finally, to confuse things a bit, there's the **Boston Cooler** (which, with its inclusion of lemon juice, makes it a *Buck*). It includes Medford rum, a product that was indigenous to New England, went dormant for about a hundred years, and is now once again available; try the flavorful and rustic GrandTen Distilling's version, or see if you can get your hands on Berkshire Mountain Distillers' Ragged Mountain rum. If not, use any dark Appleton Estate rum, add a half ounce of fresh lemon juice and a touch of simple syrup and top with club soda. See **Cooler** and **Mojito** for variations.

THE BUMBLED BEE ▮ *Peacock Alley*

1½ oz. New York Distilling Company Ragtime Rye whiskey
¾ oz. Salers Gentiane aperitif
½ oz. Noilly Prat extra dry vermouth
¼ oz. house-made Honey Syrup
2 dashes Angostura bitters
1 dash Regans' Orange Bitters No. 6

Add all ingredients to mixing glass. Add ice and stir for 30 seconds. Strain into chilled cocktail glass. Garnish with lemon peel.

This one represented the Waldorf Astoria as our 2015 entry in the annual Battle of the Bees charity event with other New York City businesses and restaurants that have beehives on their property. I used a local rye whiskey to keep with the local theme. To my palate, rye makes for a more balanced result (an entry-level Armagnac does the trick as well), though if you use bourbon, it may be a more winning crowd-pleaser. Do try all. This was originally conceived as a gin-based vehicle for the first harvest of our honey in 2013, and the **First Night** proved to be quite versatile. Simply omit the dry vermouth and Angostura bitters and add a full ounce of Salers and an additional ounce of freshly squeezed orange juice and finish with an orange peel twist. Best served as a refreshing rendition in the warmer months, with a London dry gin at its base.

BUNYAN

2½ oz. Anchor Distilling Co. Junipero gin

Add to mixing glass. Add ice and stir for 30 seconds. Strain into chilled cocktail glass. Garnish with Queen Anne olive.

Let me introduce you to one of the first versions of what many now refer to as a Martini. This, the driest of all dry Martinis, contains no vermouth (or bitters) at all, which gives this its own identity. It was named for the popular folklore character of the early 1900s, Paul Bunyan (as you would have to be quite brawny to drink one). I advise adhering to the stirring time and making sure to use some ice to temper the gin and make it more palatable. Though not mentioned in the Old Books, the addition of a lemon twist here is fantastic. As per the original recipe, be sure to serve with a glass of chilled club soda on the side.

Other slightly enhanced but like-minded cocktails from the Old Books are the **Holland Gin Cocktail** (genever as the ingredient) and the **Old Tom Gin Cocktail**, both prepared as the *Bunyan* but including a dash or two of orange bitters. If you add a dash of Angostura bitters (along with the orange bitters) to the *Old Tom* version, you'll have a version of the **Turf** cocktail (from *Modern American Drinks*, 1895). If you add orange bitters to the Bunyan, you are enjoying a **Jockey Club**. In addition, if you use Plymouth gin and add orange bitters, prepare that as in the recipe and top with two dashes of Angostura bitters, you'll have the uniquely presented **Howard** cocktail. See **Ruby** for yet one more, slightly off-kilter variation.

CAFÉ KIRSCH

½ egg white
½ oz. Simple Syrup
1 oz. Lustau Solera Gran Reserva brandy
1 oz. Trimbach Grande Reserve kirsch cherry brandy
1 oz. French roast coffee, chilled

Add egg white and simple syrup to mixing glass. Dry-shake ice for 5 seconds. Add remaining ingredients to mixing glass. Add ice and shake for 10 seconds. Fine-strain into chilled cocktail glass or small wineglass.

This is one of my favorite discoveries from the Old Books. A more complex yet perfectly balanced and enjoyable coffee cocktail—or for that matter, any cocktail—would be difficult to find. The sweet and spiced notes of the Solera brandy pair so well with the coffee and with the kirsch running a line right through it all, this drink leaves the palate dazzled. The airy body, thanks to the egg white, will have you looking forward to your second before your first is done. The other classic presentation omits the egg. Stir the remaining ingredients and then serve over crushed ice as an after-dinner drink. I would not turn that one down either. See ***Blackjack*** for variation.

CAIPIRINHA ▎Classic

½ lime, quartered
1 tsp. demerara sugar or 2 demerara sugar cubes
2 oz. Avuá Amburana cachaça

Add lime and sugar to mixing glass. Muddle to release oils and juice from lime. Add cachaça and ice. Shake well and pour into Old Fashioned glass.

This Brazilian import is a summertime favorite and there's a reason: it's cold, tart, and sweet, with the limes and sugar pairing extremely well with the slightly rustic characteristic of cachaça. If you prefer, you can alternate a barrel-aged version, which lends some pretty complex notes to the flavor profile. This is highly recommended when you want to treat yourself to something out of the ordinary. One thing: I do not recommend substituting sugar syrup for the granular or cubed sugar. The abrasive quality of the sugar will get the most out of your limes. For best results, top with an ounce or so of chilled club soda that you used to rinse your mixing glass.

CALISAYA

3 oz. Bonal quinquina aperitif or Calisaya liqueur (2 oz.)
2 dashes Regans' Orange Bitters No. 6

Add ingredients to mixing glass. Add ice and stir for 15 seconds. Strain into chilled cocktail glass. Garnish with lemon peel.

George Kappeler Variation

2 oz. Bulleit rye whiskey
1 oz. Cocchi Barolo Chinato quinquina aperitif or Calisaya liqueur
1 dash Angostura bitters (optional)

Add ingredients to mixing glass. Add ice and stir for 30 seconds. Strain into small cocktail glass. Garnish with lemon peel.

This cocktail, which was presented and served up, made for a simple predinner aperitif. You could also build it directly in an Old Fashioned glass, add ice and stir for a simple alternate take.

Research led to George Kappeler's *Modern American Drinks* (1895), in which he split the aromatized wine with rye whiskey for an off-center Manhattan alternate. After trying it in equal portions, I felt it was best served as a whiskey-forward cocktail, with rye whiskey propping up the foundation. Whether Joseph Taylor and the other bartenders transitioned the whiskey out of the recipe or they just served the aperitif neat may never be known. In any case, this cocktail is worth a try and will take to personal adjustments. See **Arctic/Ardsley** for more information on Calisaya and its like. See **Riding Club** for another variation of this entry.

CAMPFIRE STORY ■ *Peacock Alley*

1½ oz. High West Campfire whiskey
½ oz. Bigallet China-China Amer
½ oz. Pierre Ferrand dry curaçao
1½ oz. fresh orange juice
Pinch Himalayan fine pink salt

Add all ingredients except salt to mixing glass. Add ice and shake well. Fine-strain into chilled cocktail glass. Top with pinch of salt.

Amer Picon is no longer imported to the United States, but Bigallet China-China (made since 1872) is, and it makes this unique flavor profile possible. The High West Campfire is also a special product, a combination of corn, rye, and barley grains, and it incorporates the taste profiles of bourbon, rye, and Scotch whiskies. The inclusion of Ferrand dry curaçao adds to the complexity. Orange juice is often overlooked in modern cocktail recipes, but if it's used in combination with the right partners, it adds not only a touch of acidity but brightness as well (for a boozier rendition and a version that allows the whiskey to shine, cut the orange juice by half an ounce).

The Himalayan salt is not high in salinity but adds a savory note that attaches itself to the cocktail and somehow completes the story—kind of like what happens when you combine prosciutto and melon.

CHAMPAGNE COCKTAIL *(Basic Recipe)*

1 sugar cube

2 dashes Angostura bitters

5 oz. Laurent-Perrier brut Champagne nonvintage (Tours-sur-Marne)

Place sugar cube on small plate and douse with bitters. Place into Champagne flute, then fill flute with Champagne. Twist lemon peel to release oils, then discard.

One of the "big bang" cocktails, this indulgent sipper has lasted for a reason. It's a splurge—an exercise in decadence and a fine treat. I would stop short of including vintage Champagne, and if a nonvintage remains out of the question (especially if you're in a group setting), a refined, dry Spanish cava will do the trick.

If you use the recently rereleased Abbott's bitters in the Angostura slot and an orange twist, you will have the **Monopole**, a favorite of Oscar Tschirky. I would also recommend trying the classic **Death in the Afternoon**, created by Ernest Hemingway, which is simply 1½ oz. absinthe (preferably from the freezer) and 4 oz. of Champagne. If you must, you may stray from Mr. Hemingway's recipe by reducing the absinthe by a half an ounce, especially if planning on having more than one. A personal favorite.

CHAMPAGNE COCKTAIL ▮ *Peacock Alley*

**1 oz. chilled Galliano liqueur infused with strawberries and pink
peppercorns (recipe follows)**
5 oz. Veuve Clicquot brut Champagne nonvintage (Reims)

Pour chilled, infused Galliano into Champagne flute. Fill with
Champagne.

Galliano Infusion

1 lb. fresh, ripe strawberries (rinsed, cored, and halved)
1 750 ml. bottle Galliano
3 tbsp. pink peppercorns

Add ingredients to airtight, glass container and let infuse for 7 to
10 days. Fine-strain, then funnel back into bottle.

For this cocktail, created at our relaunching of Peacock Alley in
2005, I was inspired by some of the core flavors of former executive
chef John Doherty's favorite dishes. His inventive use of strawberries and peppercorns, in both savory and sweet dishes, was always
a revelation and found a perfect pairing in the complex Galliano liqueur. Try with black peppercorns if your tastes run on the spicier
side (these fill the role that bitters would in the classic version).
This popular crowd-pleaser remains on our menu to this day.

CHAMPAGNE COCKTAIL BY PHILIPPE OF THE WALDORF ▮ *Ted Saucier's* Bottoms Up

⅓ oz. green Chartreuse
¼ oz. Etter Zuger kirschwasser
4 oz. Drappier brut Champagne nonvintage (Reims)

Add champagne to flute or coupe. Add first two ingredients to
mixing glass. Add ice and stir briefly to integrate and chill. Slowly
strain into flute or coupe.

This cocktail is from Ted Saucier's *Bottoms Up* and he credits it to
Claude C. Philippe, host of the Waldorf-Astoria. Philippe served as
Oscar Tschirky's assistant until Tschirky's retirement in 1943. He
took over the position of maître d'hôtel until 1959, and in some cir-
cles his colorful personality was nearly as popular.

The recipe originally called for the now-defunct Vieille Cure liqueur (there were two, probably made in the vein of Chartreuse, as there were both green and yellow varieties). The kirsch thins it out to surprisingly tasty results. Do try this unique offering.

CLEOPATRA CHAMPAGNE COCKTAIL ▮ *Classic*

4 oz. Gosset brut Champagne nonvintage (Ay)
¾ oz. Boulard Grand Solage VSOP calvados or Laird's 7½ Year Old apple brandy (chilled)
¼ oz. Bénédictine
¼ oz. Grand Marnier
1 bar spoon (or ⅛ oz.) Campari

Add Champagne to flute or coupe. Add all other ingredients to mixing glass. Add ice and stir briefly to integrate and chill. Slowly strain into prepared flute or coupe. Twist lemon peel to release oils, then discard.

This is a complex cocktail often attributed to the Old Hotel, though this recipe does not appear in either book. Either way, I can recommend trying this when looking for something special to celebrate with. It's worth the trouble and inclusion of the high-tone ingredients.

GARDENING AT NIGHT ▮ *Peacock Alley*

4 oz. Sparkling Pointe Méthode Champenoise (North Fork)
¾ oz. Żubrówka bison grass vodka (chilled)
¾ oz. house-made Raspberry Shrub (chilled)

Add sparkling wine to flute or coupe. Add all other ingredients to mixing glass. Add ice and stir briefly to integrate and chill. Slowly strain into prepared flute or coupe. Twist lemon peel to release oils, then discard.

Originally created for a Waldorf Astoria rooftop garden event, this summertime Champagne cocktail has become one of our most requested cocktails.

Easily made but deceptively complex, this will surely become one of your backyard staples. Expect to serve this year-round once your guests try it. You will probably be forced to give them this recipe, if only so they will stop arriving at your house every week-end expecting it in copious amounts. This can be easily scaled up and served as a Punch in a bowl for a larger gathering.

ROOFTOP SUNSET **▪** *Peacock Alley*

5 oz. Sparkling Pointe Méthode Champenoise (North Fork)
.75 oz. house-made Honey Syrup (chilled)
1 or 2 dashes Peychaud's bitters

Add sparkling wine to flute or coupe. Add honey syrup to mixing glass. Add ice and stir briefly to integrate and chill. Slowly strain into prepared Champagne flute or coupe. Carefully stab in the bitters. A pinkish cloud will form.

This cocktail was created for our inaugaural Battle of the Bees in 2013, an event in which the Hotel invites other NYC businesses that produce their own honey to a blind tasting with some of the city's top chefs and culinary personalities. Proceeds go to local charities and everyone has a grand time. This easily made yet complex cocktail is best served outdoors, during long summer sunsets.

SPRINGTIME **▪** *Peacock Alley*

5 oz. Vranken Demoiselle brut rose Champagne nonvintage
(Reims)
¾ oz. Esprit de June liqueur (chilled)
4 dashes house-made Cranberry Bitters

Add Champagne to flute or coupe. Add June liqueur and two dashes of cranberry bitters to mixing glass. Add ice and stir briefly to integrate and chill. Strain into prepared Champagne flute or coupe. Top with two more dashes of cranberry bitters. Garnish with brandied cherry.

I created this cocktail spontaneously at my initial tasting of Esprit de June liqueur. Made from the vine flowers of several wine grapes, this clear and delicate liqueur pairs wonderfully with rose sparkling wine. Our house-made cranberry bitters add an important level of tannin that completes this treat.

TUSCAN TERRACE ▮ *Peacock Alley*

5 oz. Nino Franco Rustico prosecco (Valdobbiadene)
¾ oz. Tuaca liqueur (chilled)
⅓ oz. Allegrini grappa di Amarone

Add prosecco to flute or coupe. Add all other ingredients to mixing glass. Add ice and stir briefly to integrate and chill. Slowly strain into prepared Champagne flute or coupe. Garnish with brandied cherry.

Prior to the Cocktail Terrace's physical removal for the restoration of the lobby's landmark status specifications in 2012, this cocktail was created for the guests who preferred not to participate in the revered high tea service but wanted a midafternoon Champagne cocktail instead. It was quite the success and occasionally still gets requested by loyal guests.

VELVET

5 oz. Nino Franco Rustico prosecco (Valdobbiadene)
2 oz. Guinness Irish stout

Add sparkling wine to small, chilled Bordeaux glass or large champagne flute. Using back of spoon, slowly pour the beer onto the spoon and down the side of glass to float.

Often called a **Black Velvet**, the Old Bar's recipe denoted equal parts of both Champagne and stout and was presented in a large-format serving. This variation uses the slightly bitter stout to temper a fruit-forward sparkling wine. Using actual Champagne here is unnecessary, as it's best saved for enjoying on its own merit. A nice touch to a "black and white" party.

CHANLER

2 oz. Ransom Old Tom gin or Hayman's Old Tom gin
1 oz. Carpano Antica sweet vermouth

Add ingredients to mixing glass. Add ice and stir briefly to integrate. Strain into Old Fashioned glass with two or three large ice cubes or sphere. Garnish with lemon peel.

Having the unique, barrel-aged Ransom Old Tom gin available made for a nice competition between the two styles. Both are fine cocktails, especially in summer, as this should be served on the rocks. Though the Old Books made not a mention of bitters, you can add a dash of your choice if you like, especially if using a less robust vermouth. As for the gin, I recommend the Hayman's version before dinner and the Ransom after.

This offering is named for the artist Robert Winthrop Chanler, whose marriage to opera star Lina Cavalieri caused quite a stir in the newspapers of the day. "Sherriff Bob" was a regular at the Old Bar and as Johnnie Solan pointed out, "Bob knew all the Waldorf bartenders by their first names." Please take a moment to investigate Mr. Chanler's expressive art, especially his glassworks. See **Astoria** for variations.

CHANTICLEER

1½ oz. house-made Orange Gin (recipe follows) or Hayman's Old Tom gin

1 oz. Noilly Prat extra dry vermouth

½ egg white

½ oz. Luxardo Triplum orange liqueur (optional, if not using orange gin)

Add all ingredients to mixing glass. Dry-shake for 5 seconds. Add ice and shake for 10 seconds. Fine-strain into chilled cocktail glass. Garnish with orange peel.

Orange Gin

20 oz. Hayman's Old Tom gin
5 oz. Luxardo Triplum orange liqueur
1 peel of whole orange (with no pith)
3 whole cloves

Add all ingredients to airtight container and infuse for two weeks, stirring occasionally. Fine-strain and funnel back into bottle. Best used within 6 months.

This libation is named for the *Cyrano de Bergerac* writer Edmond Rostand's 1910 play, *Chantecler*, a barnyard fable in which the main character, a rooster, believes his morning crowing causes the sun to rise. At the Old Bar, they served the cocktail garnished with an actual cock's comb. The original recipe called for orange gin, a commercially available and popular orange-flavored, sweetened gin product of the time. Occasionally, one or two pop onto the market, but I wouldn't recommend them. I've included an easy enough work-around that more than does the job.

Alex Nicol, founder of Spencerfield Spirit, in Edinburgh, Scotland, who began his career at Beefeater and Plymouth and now produces Edinburgh gin and many fine whiskies, confided in me that our approximation would be an accurate one. He offered that it is similar in profile "to one of the bestselling orange gins of the 1950s, Crabbie's, as the recipe for orange was through infusion and not distilling."

The *Chanticleer* can also be strained and topped with club soda as a Fizz for a fine summer refresher.

CHARLIE CHAPLIN

1 oz. Rothman & Winter orchard apricot liqueur
1 oz. Plymouth sloe gin
1 oz. fresh lime juice

Add all ingredients to mixing glass. Add ice and shake well. Strain into chilled cocktail glass. No garnish.

DOUGLAS FAIRBANKS

1½ oz. Plymouth gin
¾ oz. Rothman & Winter orchard apricot liqueur
¾ oz. lime juice
½ egg white

Add all ingredients to mixing glass and dry shake for five seconds. Add ice and shake well. Strain into chilled cocktail glass. No garnish.

THREE-TO-ONE

2 oz. Portobello Road No. 171 London dry gin
1 oz. Combier Abricot apricot liqueur
¾ oz. fresh lime juice
2 dashes house-made Peach Bitters or The Bitter Truth Peach Bitters

Add all ingredients to mixing glass. Add ice and shake well. Fine-strain into chilled cocktail glass. No garnish.

The original recipe for the *Charlie Chaplin,* named for the comedic star of early film, did not include gin of any sort. An adapted **Peacock Alley Variation** is occasionally featured on our cocktail list and is often requested by returning guests. The additional ounce of gin adds a bit of backbone and balances the sweeter notes, making for a nice alternative to the **Cosmopolitan** and our current signature **Peacock** cocktail.

The *Douglas Fairbanks* is another cocktail named for an actor and, along with the **Dorothy Gish** and the **Mary Pickford**, it finds its roots firmly planted in Havana, as Cuba was quite the getaway for celebrities of the era.

In the case of the *Three-to-One,* the addition of another stone fruit, peach bitters in this case, added the bit of zip that this recipe lacked, but orange bitters will certainly do the job. This can also be served to astounding success as a summertime Cooler, on the rocks and topped with a bit of club soda. Incidentally, this was named for the horse players who frequented the Old Bar. Apparently they preferred a favorite set of odds. Finally, if you replace the gin with tequila (a good blanco) in the *Three-to-One,* you will have the classic **Toreador** cocktail. Although not listed in the Old Books, it is another very rare tequila-based cocktail (and a fine **Margarita** alternate) from the first half of the twentieth century that was too good not to include. See **Hop Toad** for variation.

CHARLIE ROSE

2 oz. Château de Montifaud VSOP cognac

Peel large swath or two of lemon and twist over rocks glass or tumbler. Rub peel on inside of rim, then discard. Add cognac. Garnish with a twist of lemon peel.

The printed recipe clearly stated "no ice" with just a lone twist of lemon to adorn a pony glass of brandy. What fun is that? Now that this old-timer is seeing the light of day again, we may as well push its original intention to the limit. Though no tangible information remains regarding its origin, I imagine some perennial patron of the Old Bar called this his own.

CHAUNCEY

¾ oz. Hayman's Old Tom gin

¾ oz. Russell's Reserve 6 Year Old rye whiskey (or Maker's Mark bourbon whiskey)

¾ oz. Pierre Ferrand 1840 cognac

¾ oz. Dolin de Chambery sweet vermouth

2 dashes Regans' Orange Bitters No. 6

Add all ingredients to mixing glass. Add ice and stir for 30 seconds. Strain into chilled cocktail glass. Garnish with lemon peel (orange peel, for bourbon version).

As Mr. Crockett alluded to, this complex cocktail, apparently named for a regular, "a famous orator and wit," should find a resurgence. This is the complete original recipe, spirit-wise, except for the inclusion of bourbon as an alternative to spicier rye whiskey. Comparing both versions, the wheated, sweeter bourbon really made for a palate-coating mouthfeel and had a longer finish to boot. Either way, it's a winner, but it's up to your personal taste (and that's one of the things that makes this a great cocktail).

I poured a lot of whiskey down the sink experimenting with different gins and brandies before finally settling here. If you're looking to jazz it up a bit more, use the venerable Carpano Antica in the sweet vermouth slot, and it all still holds up (especially in the rye version, which boasts a toasted marshmallow finish).

Though not included in the original recipe, the citrus twist is essential. Sometime in the 1940s, a published rendition of this cocktail pulled back on the vermouth and cognac, allowing the gin to take the lead and resulting in a crowd-pleasing, if less complex, cocktail. It may have been popular, but it's not a *Chauncey*.

CHICAGO ∎ *Classic*

2 oz. Frapin VSOP cognac

½ oz. Cointreau

2 dashes Angostura bitters

1½ oz. Laurent-Perrier brut NV Champagne

Prepare the glass by rubbing a lemon wedge around one half of chilled cocktail glass and about ½ inch down. Then roll the moistened half in superfine sugar. Add all ingredients except champagne to mixing glass. Add ice and stir for 30 seconds. Strain into prepared cocktail glass. Top with Champagne.

I find it hard to believe that this era-appropriate classic did not see time at the Old Bar. It is an elegant and "imperial" (so called because of the added Champagne) **Brandy Cocktail** and it should be poised for a comeback any day now. Enjoy with your favorite dry cava if you prefer your Champagne unaccompanied.

CHICAGO FIZZ

2 oz. chilled club soda
½ egg white
½ oz. Simple Syrup
1 oz. Smith & Cross navy-strength rum
1 oz. Graham's ruby port
½ oz. fresh lemon juice

Add chilled club soda to small Collins or Fizz glass. Add egg white and simple syrup to mixing glass. Dry-shake for 5 seconds. Add remaining ingredients to mixing glass. Add ice and shake for 10 seconds. Fine-strain into Fizz glass. Stir briefly with bar spoon to integrate.

This cocktail reportedly made its way over from the Windy City, becoming a favorite at the Old Bar. It's pretty much taken as is from the Old Books, except for the use of navy-strength rum standing in for a standard Jamaican rum. I figured that if you are only using one ounce of spirit, the recipe can take the bump. And it does, wonderfully so.

CHINEſE

2 oz. Appleton Estate 12 Year Old Rum (1 oz. each of cognac and aged rhum agricole)
¼ oz. Pierre Ferrand dry curaçao
¼ oz. Luxardo maraschino liqueur (or Crème de Noyaux)
¼ oz. house-made Grenadine (or Simple Syrup)
2 dashes Angostura bitters

Add all ingredients to mixing glass. Add ice and stir for 30 seconds. Strain into chilled cocktail glass. Garnish with brandied cherry and lemon peel (twisted and discarded).

A version of this cocktail dates back to the late nineteenth century and is first found in a French cocktail book, *Bariana*, by Louis Fouquet, published in 1896. It must've been quite popular, as it finds its way into most of the major books of the early twentieth century. The Old Books forgo the use of simple syrup and crème de noyaux (almond liqueur), which some recipes include, but adds maraschino and grenadine instead. It works either way—just don't use them all at once. If adapting the French variation and you don't have crème de noyaux handy, amaretto or even orgeat syrup work fine here. You can also split the lead spirit between an aged rhum agricole and cognac as the original recipe did. In any case, going generally light on the liqueurs makes for a much more pleasant drink, which leads me to believe that this archival cocktail may be another on the verge of making a comeback.

CHOCOLATE

1¼ oz. yellow Chartreuse
1¼ oz. Luxardo maraschino liqueur
1 egg yolk

Add all ingredients to mixing glass. Add ice and shake well. Fine-strain into small cocktail wineglass. No garnish.

Chocolate (Savoy Adaptation)

1½ oz. Graham's 10 Year tawny port
¾ oz. yellow Chartreuse
¾ oz. Luxardo maraschino liqueur
¾ oz. chocolate mix (see below)
1 egg yolk

PREPARATION NO. 1:
Add 1 heaping teaspoon Ghirardelli unsweetened cocoa powder to measuring cup or glass. Add 1 oz. water. Mix with spoon to combine. Yield is for two cocktails. As an alternate, you can just use chilled **Hot (Cold) Cocoa Mix**.

PREPARATION NO.2:
Add all ingredients to separate mixing glass. Dry-shake for 5 seconds. Add ice and shake for 10 seconds. Fine-strain into chilled cocktail glass. Garnish with grated nutmeg.

First found in print in Christopher Lawlor's *The Mixicologist (*1895), which called for equal amounts of yellow Chartreuse and maraschino liqueur along with a whole egg, it is a wonder how this became associated with anything chocolate in the first place. As you'll see, the same could also be said of the **Coffee Cocktail**. The Old Books version is practically identical to the 1895 version except the whole egg was reduced to just the yolk portion, which is preferable. Interestingly, other ingredients found in Chocolate drinks of the era range from port wine (most mentioned) to blackberry brandy (least), along with, get this: chocolate powder!

I have included an adaptation of the two *Savoy Cocktail Book* offerings for the recipe simply because it took the original and modified by adding actual cocoa. One rendition added cocoa powder and the other took that and swapped the maraschino for port wine. I am pretty sure they used a ruby port, but I liked the more complex tawny here. Either way, it's a time-machine, after-dinner Flip that you can wow your guests with. Just be sure to double-strain to remove any ice chips. See **Flip** for variations.

CHOCOLATINI ▮ *Peacock Alley*

1½ oz. Van Gogh Dutch chocolate vodka
½ oz. Pierre Ferrand dry curaçao (or Grand Marnier liqueur)
2 oz. chilled house-made Hot (Cold) Cocoa Mix

Add all ingredients to mixing glass. Add ice and shake well. Strain into chilled cocktail glass. Garnish with dark chocolate curls or shavings.

Although given a bad name of late, "dessert" cocktails do have their place. Made with care and quality ingredients, they can be surprisingly complex. This is one of our most popular post-theater cocktails; the chocolate ganache, made by our heralded pastry kitchen, brings a luxurious viscosity to this dessert-in-a-glass. As for the name, the staff and I kept kiddingly referring to this offering as the *Chocolatini* as we developed it and promised to arrive at a better name. It never happened.

The menus had to be printed and I let the first round go out like that. It has remained ever since, and I don't care. It's another cocktail that simply cannot be removed from the cocktail list at Peacock Alley, It's quite possibly the best spiked liquid dessert on the planet.

CHOCOLATE CREAM PHO/PHATE FIZZ

2 oz. chilled club soda
1 egg yolk
¾ oz. Simple Syrup
1½ oz. Etter Zuger kirsch cherry brandy
1 oz. heavy cream
3 dashes Horsford's acid phosphate

Add chilled club soda to small Collins or Fizz glass. Add egg yolk and simple syrup to mixing glass. Dry-shake for 5 seconds. Add remaining ingredients to mixing glass. Add ice and shake for 10 seconds. Fine-strain into Fizz glass. Stir briefly with bar spoon to integrate.

Although quite the mouthful title-wise, this is aesthetically similar to the **Chocolate**, as it also does not contain any of its namesake ingredients. Another notable aspect of this cocktail is the appearance of the once-popular acid phosphate. This liquid ingredient is added to impart a sour note, as would result if you used citrus, but without the flavor of it. Use sparingly; a little goes a long way, though you will find plenty of uses for it both within this book and outside it.

As for this rare recipe, a nonalcoholic, creamless Egg Cream (with actual chocolate syrup, acid phosphate, and soda water) would be the standard fountain offering. Whether or not Mr. Crockett managed to misinterpret the entry for this one will probably never be known, as a correlating recipe could not be found. Nevertheless, it's quite satisfying and retains its relation to the *Chocolate*.

CHOCOLATE /OLDIER

1½ oz. Plymouth gin or Nicholson London dry gin
1½ oz. Bonal Quinquina aperitif or Dubonnet
¼ oz. fresh lime juice

Add all ingredients to mixing glass. Add ice and stir for 30 seconds. Strain into chilled cocktail glass. Garnish with brandied cherry.

As was the tradition of the day, this was named for the successful Broadway production that debuted in 1909. The original recipe called for a 2:1 ratio of gin to Dubonnet, but the winey taste profile of the current version of the aperitif was unbalanced, so I substituted Bonal, which is probably more in line with the originally intended taste profile of Dubonnet anyway.

Now produced in New Zealand from the original recipe, Nicholson London dry gin appeared quite often in the Old Books. Its flavor profile is less herbal than a traditional London dry and takes to mixing quite well. Finally, I distributed the amounts of ingredients evenly and stirred it despite the inclusion of juice. Citrus, when used in a small amount, takes the place of bitters as an enhancement and when stirred, it maintains a more leaden mouthfeel, retaining the recipe's intended complexity. It's worthy of a resurgence, for sure.

CINFUL ∎ *Peacock Alley*

1 oz. Schönauer Apfel liqueur
¾ oz. Appleton Estate Reserve rum
¾ oz. house-made Cinnamon Vodka
¾ oz. fresh apple cider
¼ oz. fresh lemon juice
2 dashes Angostura bitters

Add all ingredients to mixing glass. Add ice and shake well. Fine-strain into chilled cocktail glass. Garnish with freshly grated nutmeg and dried apple slice.

PIE ON THE SILL ∎ *Peacock Alley*

1½ oz. Laird's bonded applejack
½ oz. fresh lemon juice
½ oz. house-made Demerara Syrup
½ oz. house-made Cinnamon Vodka
1 dash Angostura bitters
2 heaping bar spoons house-made Apple Compote (recipe follows)
or
1 heaping bar spoon Medford Farms apple butter
(If using apple butter with sugar added, omit Demerara Syrup)

Add all ingredients to mixing glass. Add ice and shake well. Fine-strain into chilled cocktail glass. Garnish with freshly grated nutmeg and house-made **Dried Apple Chip**.

Apple Compote

1 c. water
¼ c. demerara sugar
½ vanilla bean, split in half lengthwise
2 oz. Laird's bonded applejack
⅛ tsp. ground cinnamon
⅛ tsp. ground cloves
⅛ tsp. ground nutmeg
2 oz. fresh lemon juice
1 pinch salt
4 large Golden Delicious apples (or other sweet apple), cored and cubed

In a saucepan, combine all ingredients except apples and bring to a boil. Simmer until the sugar is dissolved and the mixture thickens slightly, about 5 minutes. Add the apples and return to a boil. Lower the heat and simmer, stirring occasionally, until the apples are very tender and the mixture thickens, about 30 minutes.

Remove from heat and remove the vanilla bean pods. Let cool to room temperature before serving (mixture will thicken as it cools). Place in plastic container and refrigerate for later use.

The *Cinful* is a seasonal favorite of our guests, and is requested as soon as the weather turns cooler. The Jamaican rum adds a nice contrast to the fruit and spice components. This is certainly one you will find yourself preparing annually from Halloween through the end of the year.

Pie on the Sill is another autumnal specialty and can be made successfully using either the apple compote or the apple butter. There are many uses for the homemade apple compote (I like mine in warm oatmeal), so don't be concerned about preparing it, it will be used.

CLARET PUNCH *(Claret Cup)*

3 oz. dry red wine of choice (Bordeaux Supérieur is recommended)
½ oz. fresh lemon juice
⅓ oz. Simple Syrup

Add all ingredients to mixing glass. Add large ice cubes and roll from mixing glass to shaker 3 or 4 times. Pour into chilled goblet or Hoffman House glass (a Collins glass works as well). Garnish with citrus wheels.

This one goes back to old England and was one of the most popular drinks up until the time of the Old Waldorf-Astoria. The most ancient recipes include only slices of lemon, but I went with the evolved recipe of the Old Bar. Obviously granulated sugar would have been used but the syrup integrates easier. A simple preparation that can be served on long afternoons in a large format as well. It is sure to become another new favorite. See **Sangaree** for variations.

CLIQUET

1½ oz. Jim Beam rye
½ oz. Cruzan aged dark rum
2 oz. fresh orange juice
1 dash Regans' Orange Bitters No. 6

Add all ingredients to Old Fashioned glass. Add large ice cubes and stir briefly to integrate. Garnish with orange wheel.

This indigenous creation of the Old Bar can be thought of as a "whiskey Screwdriver." You can substitute bourbon for the rye, if you choose. The original recipe called for dashes of St. Croix rum, hence the Cruzan, though I've taken the liberty of adding just enough to make it noticeable. Please take note that lower-proof whiskey works best here, as you will most likely be having more than one. As previously mentioned, there is no substitute for fresh juice.

Named for the writers of the old *New York Herald* newspaper who frequented the Old Bar, it was also listed in *Old Waldorf Bar Days* as the **Herald Punch**; just add a half ounce of demerara syrup, sub Wild Turkey 101 rye (or other overproof whiskey) in the whiskey slot, and shake and strain onto fresh ice, and that's what you will have.

CLOVER CLUB

½ egg white
½ oz. house-made Raspberry Syrup
2 oz. Bombay London dry gin
½ oz. fresh lemon juice
½ oz. Carpano dry vermouth (optional)

Add egg white and syrup to mixing glass. Dry-shake for 5 seconds. Add remaining ingredients and ice and shake for 10 seconds. Fine-strain into chilled cocktail glass. Twist lemon peel over drink, then discard. Garnish with one fresh raspberry on skewer.

This recently resuscitated number originated at the old Bellevue-Stratford Hotel, in Philadelphia, where the high-society Clover Club held its meetings. It was the hotel's manager, George C. Boldt, who went on to become the first owner/operator of the Waldorf, and it's a good bet that he was the one responsible for this cocktail's appearance in the Old Bar in the first place. It's also perfect for guests who claim an aversion to gin. The first printed recipe (1909) included dry vermouth and I can certainly recommend trying this version, as it adds a discernible depth and length of flavor. The recipe here represents a modern take on the Old Bar recipe. Feel free to pull back a half ounce of gin if you're having more than one.

The famed poet William Butler Yeats certainly had more than one when he was served a **Clover Club** at a luncheon in his honor. Mr. Crockett noted he enjoyed them "all the way through his meal." I always appreciated Yeats's quote: "The problem with some people is that when they aren't drunk, they're sober."

Jacques Straub's *Drinks* (1914) utilizes Old Tom gin and lime juice, along with grenadine as the sweetener for the **Sunshine**. Just be sure to include the dry vermouth. A slight deviation that deserves a try. A **September Morn No. 2** replaces the gin with a flavorful white rum. Plantation 3 Stars or Caña Brava work well here. A **Cuban Clover Club** subs lime juice for the lemon and also utilizes white rum.

This recipe, listed in the text portion of Old Waldorf Bar Days, is recalled as a **Christ** cocktail (not to be confused with the **Christ**, a Martini variation of the same name; see **Martini**). Whether it was an editing error or confusion on the part of Mr. Crockett will never be known, but he did cleverly believe that the name of that drink came from a guest who wanted something spiritual but settled for something spirituous. I think that his theory still fits this satisfying survivor, regardless of the title.

Gloom Lifter

1½ oz. Bushmills Irish whiskey
½ oz. Cardenal Mendoza Solera Gran Reserva brandy
½ oz. fresh lemon juice
¼ oz. house-made Raspberry Syrup
¼ oz. house-made Grenadine
½ egg white

Add all ingredients to mixing glass. Dry-shake for 5 seconds. Add ice and shake for 10 seconds. Fine-strain into chilled cocktail glass. Garnish with brandied cherry.

This whiskey take on the *Clover Club* makes for an interesting alternative and takes to tinkering pretty well. I settled on Spanish brandy (the original recipe called for "one-half teaspoon"); its spicy yet musty profile made itself known without the need to add more. If using a cognac, you may split the starring role with the Irish whiskey. Handing over the sweet spot to either syrup makes for a nice alternative as well.

This cocktail is listed as the **Waldorf Gloom Lifter** in *The Old Waldorf-Astoria Bar Book*.

Cora Middleton

1½ oz. Appleton Estate Extra rum
½ oz. Bols genever
¾ oz. fresh lemon juice
½ oz. house-made Grenadine
½ egg white
5 drops Regans' Orange Bitters No. 6

Add all ingredients except bitters to mixing glass. Dry-shake for 5 seconds. Add ice and shake for 10 seconds. Fine-strain into chilled cocktail glass. Top with drops of bitters and twist orange peel to release oils, then discard.

Yet another variation on the *Clover Club,* the rum-based *Cora Middleton* made its debut at the Old Bar. I prefer using house-made grenadine as the sugar component to give it a separate identity from the parent cocktail. Other recipes of the day sub in lime juice in the lemon spot. Feel free to try that if you'd like.

For a Repeal Day event a few years ago, the theme was twists on obscure cocktails, and **Cora's Daughter** was born. Place a flavorful and slightly smoky blended Scotch whisky in the rum slot (I like Spencerfield Spirit "Pig's Nose" or Black Grouse) and use Peychaud's bitters instead of orange for the garnish. Though chaotic on paper, all of the ingredients are quite harmonious. I like this one a lot.

CLUB COCKTAIL NO. 2 ∎ *William Schmidt version*

2 oz. Plymouth gin
1 oz. Martini & Rossi sweet vermouth
¼ oz. green Chartreuse
2 dashes Regans' Orange Bitters No. 6

Add all ingredients to mixing glass. Add ice and stir for 30 seconds. Strain into chilled cocktail glass. Garnish with lemon peel.

The Old Bar version of this cocktail uses a couple of dashes of Angostura bitters in lieu of green Chartreuse for a "spiced" Martini. It's a fine rendition, but I've opted to list this recipe in its standard form. It first materializes in William Schmidt's *The Flowing Bowl* (1891). I adapted it to let the green Chartreuse define what the cocktail could be and separated it from the pack. Its luxurious finish surprised both my wife and me with its complexity. Try both. See **Martini** for **Club Cocktail**.

COBBLER *(Basic Recipe)*

2½ oz. spirit of choice or
4 oz. wine or sherry of choice
½ oz. Simple Syrup (or 1 tsp. superfine sugar, for traditional method)
2 orange and lemon wheels

TRADITIONAL PREPARATION:
Add all ingredients to mixing glass. Add ice and shake well. Pour unstrained into a tumbler or Collins glass. Garnish with additional citrus wheels and seasonal berries and fruit. Serve with metal straw.

MODERN PREPARATION:

Add all ingredients to mixing glass. Add ice and shake well. Fine-strain into goblet or Hoffman House goblet filled with crushed or pellet ice. Garnish with additional citrus wheels and seasonal berries and fruit. Serve with metal straw.

By the time the Old Bar was at its peak of popularity, the *Cobbler* had already seen its best days, though based on the number of recipes in the Old Books, it was more than holding its own. It was the first to feature a straw (a new invention of the mid-nineteenth century), and it freely exploited the availability of ice (also a new amenity at that time). Variations mostly consisted of wine or liquor, which was another source of popularity. This recipe got the job done.

The first appearance in *The Old Waldorf Bar Book* is the **Brandy Cobbler**. This strong sipper included a couple of dashes of maraschino. You may even want to substitute the maraschino for the simple syrup entirely, There is the **Claret Cobbler**, which utilizes your favorite dry red wine. The oldest and most popular of all is the **Sherry Cobbler**. I recommend an amontillado or oloroso sherry, as it is flavorful enough to take the sugar and fruit while still retaining its identity. Please adjust sugar accordingly if using a bone-dry fino. If going with a port or a Pedro Ximénez, the sweetest sherry, pull back on the sugar, or better yet, omit it entirely.

As for the whole shake-and-strain thing, traditionally the barman would shake this in preparation and serve as is, unstrained. I find this rustic and visually unappealing; I prefer to strain it into a goblet with fresh pellet ice. Then I add fresh fruit for garnish prior to serving.

Although the *Cobbler* is traditionally served in a thick water-type tumbler, I think it's best served in something slightly fancier. Hoffman House goblets work well here. The origin of these large goblets can be traced back to the famous but now extinct Hoffman House Hotel, on Broadway and Twenty-fifth Street in NYC (which, by the way, had its own influential bar books). See **Julep/Smash**, **Peachy Peacock Cobbler** and **Tea Cobbler** for variations.

(WHI/KEY) COCKTAIL *(Basic Recipe)*

2½ oz. spirit of choice (bourbon, brandy, gin [genever, Old Tom],
rum, rye, Scotch, etc.)
¼ oz. Simple Syrup or Gum Syrup
2 dashes bitters of choice

Add all ingredients to mixing glass. Add ice and stir for 30 seconds.
Strain into chilled cocktail glass. Garnish with lemon or orange peel.

So here you have another genre of drink—one, that like the Buck
or Sling, is identified by its base ingredient. That's also how it would
have been called for in its day ("I'll have a Whiskey Cocktail"). The
recipe remains the same, though over time, other modifications, or
"improvements," such as curaçao, maraschino liqueur, and absinthe, were added for variety. This is the recipe that represents
your Old Fashioned.

As for the bitters, everything works here. The Bitter Truth produces one based on Jerry Thomas's recipe that pairs extremely well
with all of the gin variations. If you are a tequila lover, chocolate
bitters would make a reposado tequila version shine.

As for the twist, it's essential. I lean toward lemon in most, but
orange does brighten things up a bit and pairs exceptionally well
with bourbon (and tequila). As always, it's your call.

This Cocktail entry is not to be confused with anything called a
"Martini." For a modern definition, I'll let the addition of vermouth
be the identifying ingredient there.

The original recipe in both Old Books (as well as Oscar's) all
mistakenly list "dash of gin" in lieu of "dash of gum" (a recurring
misinterpretation of Mr. Crockett's). Have no fear, I have tried it
with gin and the appropriate intention is listed here.

The Old Books also include a recipe that omits sugar (don't) and
uses rye whiskey as the base ingredient. If you go that route, you
are enjoying a **Ewing** cocktail. See **Old Fashioned** for variations.

COFFEE COCKTAIL

1 whole egg
1 tsp. superfine sugar
2 oz. Quinta de Noval 10 Year Old tawny port
1 oz. Lustau Solera Gran Reserva brandy

Add egg and sugar to mixing glass. Dry-shake for 5 seconds. Add remaining ingredients to mixing glass. Add ice and shake for 10 seconds. Fine-strain into chilled cocktail glass. Garnish with freshly grated nutmeg.

The intriguingly obvious missing component of this drink (which is technically a Flip and not a cocktail) is its namesake. It does date back to the mid-nineteenth century and probably got its name from those who drank it in lieu of coffee as a morning-after cure-all. Although no preference is noted in the Old Books, other recipes of the era (of which there are many in print) call for ruby-style port when one is being used. Younger, sweeter, and more winey than its brother tawny port, it definitely brings those characteristics to the show. I personally prefer the tawny port here, as it blends more harmoniously with the excellent Spanish brandy from one of Spain's finest sherry houses.

In an effort to be era-appropriate, I prefer the use of actual granulated sugar for this old-timer, though you can use syrup if you like. Go easy on the nutmeg; a little goes a long way. The double-strain is essential for a smooth trip across the palate. For a version that actually contains coffee, see **Espresso Cocktail**. See **Flip** for variations.

COLE PORTER ▮ *Peacock Alley*

1½ oz. Willett Family Estate straight rye whiskey
1 oz. Lustau Don Nuño oloroso sherry
¾ oz. fresh lemon juice
½ oz. Simple Syrup
¼ egg white

Add all ingredients to mixing glass and dry-shake for 5 seconds. Add ice and shake for 10 seconds. Fine-strain into Collins glass filled with fresh ice cubes. Garnish with orange peel and brandied cherry.

This charmingly enhanced Whiskey Sour was created to celebrate one of the hotel's most notable past residents, whose piano our guests have the pleasure of listening to every evening at Peacock Alley. I imagine Mr. Porter ordering a couple of these up to his room, maybe on the verge of his next big hit. It's the top!

COLLINS *(Basic Recipe)*

2 oz. Hayman's Old Tom gin
¾ oz. fresh lemon juice
½ oz. Simple Syrup
2 oz. chilled club soda

Add all ingredients except club soda to mixing glass. Add ice and shake well. Strain into Collins glass filled with large ice cubes. Top with chilled club soda and stir briefly to integrate. Garnish with brandied cherry and/or citrus peel or slice (optional).

First served by John Collins (famous for his gin Punch) at London's Limmer's Hotel in the early nineteenth century, this "big bang" concoction made it to the United States in time to be included in Jerry Thomas's 1876 edition of *The Bartenders Guide*. A number of renditions are included in the Old books and the recipe's adaptability must've been a boon to the boys behind the Waldorf bar. Variations of this recipe abound, namely the listed **Fizz**. In fact, they have identical ingredients; what separates the two is the way in which they are served. A Collins is served on ice, while a Fizz is strained into a smaller glass, meant to be consumed more quickly. There is also room for garnish in a Collins, whereas the Fizz does not have any. This is another instance in which our prebatched fresh **Sour Mix** would be used when preparing for a group of guests (see "House-Made Recipes" chapter).

As for the drink itself, it is a victim of what is probably one of the most famous examples of the game of "telephone" the world has ever known: how the recipe listed here became the Tom Collins, as opposed to the correctly named John Collins. John Collins did get a version, using genever at its base, named after him. There is also a **Brandy Collins**, in which I'd use a VS cognac at its foundation. The **Durkee** (named for the sandwich condiment family) incorporates Jamaican rum. The apparently popular **Bacardi Collins** obviously uses rum at its root, but substitutes lime in the juice slot. I would do the same if going the tequila route, if that is your fancy. In recent times, making a **John Collins** often means using a whiskey base, which is also fine. Included in the Old Books is a **Fin de Siècle** (Sour), which incorporates grenadine and/or raspberry syrup in lieu of simple syrup with the standard gin base. It's a fine alternate.

I would add another ounce of club soda if having more than one, but that's just me. This classic's elasticity lends itself to any base spirit, which is probably the main reason it has survived the ages.

Though I personally would never succumb to vodka; that would just be lazy.

COMMODORE *(Cocktail Adaptation)* ❘ *Peacock Alley*

2 oz. Diplomático Blanco Reserve rum
¼ oz. house-made Grenadine
¼ oz. house-made Raspberry Syrup
¼ oz. fresh lemon juice
1 dash Regans' Orange Bitters No. 6

Add all ingredients to mixing glass. Add ice and stir for 30 seconds. Strain into chilled cocktail glass. Garnish with lemon peel and brandied cherry.

According to opening Waldorf-Astoria bartender Johnnie Solan, this was named for a ranking officer of a local yacht club. For the cocktail variation, I made an effort to give these ingredients their own identity. The small amount of lemon juice makes this cocktail unique and is what led me to believe that this was another example in which the juice component was meant as an enhancement and not a full-on ingredient. I also omitted the "white of one egg" and the added white sugar. This somewhat adventurous reading, with added bitters and prepared by stirring, resulted in this simple but satisfying summer sipper. Following the directions of the Old Books to the letter left me with a pretty bland, rum-based *Clover Club* derivative, which already exists anyway. If you must try it for yourself, just add half of an egg white and a quarter ounce of simple syrup to the listed recipe and shake very well. Do yourself a favor and leave in the bitters, or even add another dash. They do help out immensely.

COMMODORE NO. 2

1½ oz. Basil Hayden's bourbon
1 oz. Tempus Fugit crème de cacao
¾ oz. fresh lemon juice
¼ oz. house-made Grenadine

Add all ingredients to mixing glass. Add ice and shake well. Strain into chilled cocktail glass. Garnish with lemon peel and brandied cherry.

This creation of the Old Bar originally called for equal portions of all ingredients (excluding grenadine), but I've made the whiskey take the lead here. It props up the rest of the cocktail along with the complex cocoa liqueur. You can use this recipe, with its uncommon combination of ingredients, to surprise and satisfy your guests.

COOLER/HIGHBALL (Basic Recipe)

2 oz. spirit of choice (brandy, bourbon, gin, rum, rye, Scotch, tequila, etc.)
4 oz. club soda, ginger ale or ginger beer, tonic, etc.

Add spirit of choice to Collins glass. Add large ice cubes and fill with ginger ale or other carbonated option. Stir briefly to integrate and serve.

Pulling back on the amount of citrus (if any) to a squeeze of a wedge (to separate it from the more citrus-forward Buck or Rickey), these tall drinks, meant for enjoyment on a hot summer day but great anytime, are as versatile as it gets. I would not get too tied up as to the difference between a Cooler and a Highball—it traditionally rested on the amount of ice used, with the cooler containing more. These days, the difference probably lies in the use of an aromatic wine in a Cooler, resulting in a lower-proof beverage, though traditional versions, such as those found in the Old Books, show no such disparity.

Some notable Coolers referred to in the Old Books include the **Bacardi Cooler**, which was made with white rum and ginger ale and garnished with a bit of fresh mint. Another is the **Hilly Croft**, which includes Old Tom gin, ginger ale, and a lemon twist. Make this with club soda and it becomes a **Remsen Cooler**. The **Seawanhaka Yacht Club** is made with rye whiskey, ginger ale, and a lemon twist. A **Narragansett** includes bourbon, ginger ale, and an orange wedge. Substitute rye whiskey and you have the **Hawaii** and quite outrageously, a **Klondike** as well. Also name-checked in the Old Books are the **Brandy and Ginger Ale Frappé** (prepared like the *Cooler*, served with an orange peel for garnish) and **Brandy and Soda** (do the same). The **Jamaica Highball** is prepared with Jamaican dark rum and club soda. An orange twist here is glorious.

Both *100 Famous Cocktails* and *Bottoms Up* credit the **Starlight Roof Garden Cooler** to the "New Waldorf-Astoria." It's simply a dry vermouth *Cooler* enhanced by a sugar cube doused with Angostura bitters and a touch of lime juice, topped with ginger ale. Enjoyable for those who prefer things on the drier side.

The **Highball** hails from England, where they thoroughly enjoy their Scotch and sodas. The name's origin, though, is a different story, and breaking from my usual response when it comes to these matters, I'm willing to go with almost all of them here.

For one, New York City–based, UK-born barman Patrick Gavin Duffy (*The Official Mixer's Manual*) is credited with the naming of the genre, though it did not see print until 1934. What actual Highball he named it after falls into three categories: The first was the railroad analogy, likening the "lump of ice" to the boiler pressure gauge on the steam engines of the day. When it reached optimum capacity it was considered "highballing." The second is baseball based, and of course most likely pairs itself to the "chin music" pitch, in which the pitcher throws high and inside to the batter in an effort to back him off the plate. He would be "highballing." The third, and the one I believe works best, is the simple, old-school moniker for a whiskey shot, otherwise known as a "ball"; and when served in a Collins-type glass, with a "lump of ice" and club soda, it was a "high ball."

To me, what separates a Highball from a Buck or Rickey is its sheer simplicity. It's just spirit and soda, maybe a twist or wedge, and that's it—anything more and you technically have something else. But at the end of the day it really doesn't matter; they are all simple spirits with mixers served on ice in a tall glass.

One recommendation I'd like to make is to stay adventurous and use these types of drinks as opportunities to sample base spirits that you would usually try to avoid. They may provide the entry to expanding your palate. See **Buck/Rickey** for variations.

COOPER*S*TOWN *(Adapted Waldorf Astoria Version)*

1½ oz. Tanqueray London dry gin
½ oz. Dolin de Chambery sweet vermouth
½ oz. Dolin de Chambery dry vermouth
1 oz. fresh orange juice
1 dash Regans' Orange Bitters No. 6 (optional)
12 fresh mint leaves

Add all ingredients to mixing glass. Add ice and shake well. Fine-strain into chilled cocktail glass. No garnish.

I.D.K. No. 2 (IMPROVED)

2½ oz. Plymouth gin (or Nicholson London dry gin)
½ oz. Carpano Antica sweet vermouth
12 mint leaves
3 dashes house-made Chocolate Bitters or Fee Brothers Aztec chocolate bitters

Add all ingredients to mixing glass. Add ice and shake well. Fine-strain into chilled cocktail glass. Garnish with orange peel (optional).

HUGO EN*SS*LIN VER*S*ION

1 oz. Plymouth gin
1 oz. Dolin de Chambery sweet vermouth
1 oz. Dolin de Chambery dry vermouth
1 dash Regans' Orange Bitters No. 6
8 fresh mint leaves

Add all ingredients to mixing glass. Add ice and shake well. Fine-strain into chilled cocktail glass. Garnish with orange peel (optional).

The Old Bar entry for the *Cooperstown* is dedicated to one Craig Wadsworth and the "young sportsmen" from "the richest and prettiest town up-State." The recipe's simple direction: "Bronx, with Mint." The adapted recipe here is exactly that: our *Bronx, with mint.*

The *I.D.K. No. 2* is a mint-enhanced, spirit-forward rendition, which, when developed, fell far short of expectations. The original recipe is simply 4:1 gin to sweet vermouth with a "sprig of mint." This improved version gives each ingredient a reason for being there. Both of these recipes originally called for Nicholson London dry gin, which is currently being produced in New Zealand. It is lighter in style but Plymouth will stand in just fine.

Carpano Antica or other full-flavored vermouth is essential in order to keep the original heady intention intact. The chocolate bitters bring a nice complexity and natural partner to the mint, but if it's unavailable, any aromatic bitters will do. Now it's an adult mint chocolate–tinged cocktail served up, which makes it the first of its distinctive kind. See *Baco* for *I.D.K.*

A similar recipe under the title of *Cooperstown* that also omits the orange juice can be found in Tom Bullock's *The Ideal Bartender;* just use a 2:1 ratio of Old Tom gin to sweet vermouth and orange bitters (along with the mint) for a lighter and sweeter rendition.

Hugo Ensslin, whose 1917 *Recipes for Mixed Drinks* was, along with *The Ideal Bartender*, one of the last cocktail books published prior to Prohibition. Ensslin's equal-measure variant is a tasty, lower-proof cocktail. It's just enough to easily make it through the seventh-inning stretch.

Finally, from just prior to the release of the Old Books, Harry MacElhone's *Barflies and Cocktails* (1927) included a dry version. The original called for gin; I'm going to assume a London dry. You can go that route, but the Old Tom gin added some extra body and a slightly sweet back note while still allowing this to land firmly in the dry camp. Just sub in dry vermouth for the sweet in Tom Bullock's version and you'll have the one that Harry served in his New York Bar in Paris.

All of these cocktails are best when your mint is in season. I also think the orange twist is an essential component for each of them, but I will leave the pairing with mint to your personal preference. See *Bronx* for variation.

CORONATION

1 oz. Laird's bonded applejack or Boulard Grand Solage VSOP calvados

1 oz. Noilly Prat sweet vermouth

1 oz. Noilly Prat extra dry vermouth

¼ oz. Marie Brizard Apry apricot liqueur

Add all ingredients to mixing glass. Add ice and stir for 30 seconds. Strain into chilled cocktail glass. Garnish with lemon peel.

The first known rendition is from Jacques Straub's *Drinks* (1914) and is simply equal parts London dry gin, dry vermouth, and Dubonnet (nothing to write home about there). The other of note is from the *Savoy* book (1930) and is an improvement with equal parts oloroso sherry and dry vermouth, enhanced with dashes of maraschino liqueur and orange bitters. This one, served at the Old Bar, was named in honor of the 1911 ceremony of King George V. I attempted a version that ramped up the applejack to Manhattan proportions, but this original outshone it. Calvados can be substituted for the Laird's, of course. Either way, this is sure to become one of your autumn staples.

The **Cuban Coronation** is an alternate that switched out the applejack for rum, subbed in Dubonnet for the sweet vermouth, and omitted the apricot liqueur. After much testing and tasting, I came to the conclusion the *Cuban Coronation* would be best served in the same manner as the original here, only substituting a dark, flavorful rum of your choice for the applejack.

CORPƧE REVIVER NO. 1 ∎ *Classic*

1½ oz. Courvoisier VSOP cognac
¾ oz. Boulard Grand Solage VSOP calvados
¾ oz. Carpano Antica sweet vermouth
1 dash Regan's Orange Bitters No. 6

Add all ingredients to mixing glass. Add ice and stir for 30 seconds. Strain into chilled cocktail glass. Garnish with orange peel.

CORPƧE REVIVER NO. 2 ∎ *Classic*

1 oz. Tanqueray No. Ten gin
1 oz. Cocchi Americano
1 oz. Cointreau
1 oz. fresh lemon juice
2 dashes Pernod Original Recipe absinthe

Add all ingredients to mixing glass. Add ice and shake well. Strain into chilled cocktail glass. No garnish.

Though neither of these cocktails appear in the Old Books, the *No. 2* has regained its popularity and is often requested at Peacock Alley. Rest assured, the Corpse Reviver No. 1 makes for a terrible "eye opener," but it is one heck of a post-dinner **Manhattan** alternate.

The popular—and more worthy of its name—*No. 2* is the appropriate noontime crowd-pleaser. We use Cocchi Americano in lieu of the originally called-for Lillet, as the Cocchi's bittersweet profile is more in line with the classic Kina Lillet, which would have been used at the time of this cocktail's origin but is no longer produced. It's a classic for a reason. And yes, I did not "rinse" the glass with absinthe as usually called for. I think that its inclusion makes for a finer drink. I also personally prefer to cut the Cointreau by half, but that's just me.

COSMOPOLITAN **I** *Classic*

2 oz. Absolut Citron vodka
1 oz. Combier Liqueur d'Orange
¾ oz. fresh lime juice
½ oz. Northland cranberry Juice

Add all ingredients to mixing glass. Add ice and shake well. Strain into chilled cocktail glass. Garnish with orange peel.

This classic 1980s NYC survivor was still going strong when we re-opened Peacock Alley in 2005. It was so popular that we decided to model our new signature cocktail on it, and *The Peacock* was born. Please do your best to secure the more natural-flavored Northland brand of cranberry Juice. It makes a discernible difference. See **The Peacock** for variation.

COUNTRY CLUB

1½ oz. Plantation 3 Stars white rum
1 oz. Sacred extra dry vermouth
½ oz. Pierre Ferrand dry curaçao
1 dash Regans' Orange Bitters No. 6

Add all ingredients to mixing glass. Add ice and stir for 30 seconds. Strain into chilled cocktail glass. Garnish with lemon peel.

FLAPPER

1½ oz. Appleton Estate Reserve rum
1½ oz. Noilly Prat extra dry vermouth
½ oz. house-made Demerara Syrup
2 dashes Angostura bitters

Add all ingredients to mixing glass. Add ice and stir for 30 seconds. Strain into chilled cocktail glass. Garnish with lemon peel and brandied cherry.

With the same base as the **Bacardi Vermouth Dry**, the *Country Club* is a more complex rendition and is one of my personal favorites in the entire book. My take is that if you are going to have a cocktail, especially today, when distilleries are creating complex and complete spirits that satisfy on their own, all parts must not only make themselves known but also be harmonious and end with a lingering flourish—like your all-time favorite pop song if it was condensed to only fifteen seconds. The nose, palate, and most important, the finish are what make classic cocktails . . . classic.

Be sure to use a white rum whose flavor profile has a character of its own. The original recipe called for an even ratio of rum to vermouth, but this recipe best fits the modern palate. It also had the curaçao down to a dash, but leaning on the orange-forward liqueur a bit added a viscosity that helped define this cocktail's identity. You can use Grand Marnier or even Cointreau for equal but unique results. You can also try a "sweet" adaptation, utilizing Carpano Antica sweet vermouth in place of the dry. Both are worthwhile tipples.

Named for the independent women of the Jazz Age, the *Flapper* is an unassuming, easy drinker that makes for an appetizing pre-dinner cocktail. Substitute grenadine for the demerara syrup and you'll have what the boys at the Old Bar called a **Grenade**. They leaned hard on the grenadine; the original recipe called for 2:1 grenadine to remaining ingredients. I considered this a misinterpretation, hence its adapted and much more pleasing inclusion here.

CREAM PUFF FIZZ

3 oz. chilled club soda
2 oz. Cruzan aged dark rum
¾ oz. Simple Syrup
1 oz. heavy cream

Add chilled club soda to small Collins or Fizz glass. Add remaining ingredients to mixing glass. Add ice and shake well. Strain into serving glass. Stir briefly to integrate. No garnish.

Taking it all the way back to the soda fountain days, this super Fizz (and extremely pleasing Bracer) will be sure to have your guests lining up. The choice of rum plays an important part here. The original recipe called for St. Croix rum, so I went with the aged Cruzan. It works just fine, but you can plug in your rum of choice—just try to steer clear of the superdark varieties here. Please remember that this is a Fizz—once it's strained there is no additional ice used, so be sure your soda water is well chilled. This may be one of the single best (adult) Egg Creams of all time.

CREOLE LADY

1 oz. Four Roses small-batch bourbon
1 oz. Sandeman Fine Rich Madeira
½ oz. Luxardo maraschino liqueur

Add all ingredients to small white wineglass (Bordeaux-style). Stir to integrate. Garnish with brandied cherry on a skewer.

"A no-ice cocktail?" you say. Well, prepare to be surprised. It's quite the after-dinner cordial or accompaniment to a fine cigar.

See **Rees** for similar presentation.

CREOLE LADY ▮ *Peacock Alley Cocktail Adaptation*

1½ oz. Four Roses small-batch bourbon
1 oz. Sandeman Fine Rich Madeira or Lustau Don Nuño oloroso sherry
½ oz. Luxardo maraschino liqueur
2 dashes Peychaud's bitters

Add all ingredients to mixing glass. Add ice and stir for 30 seconds. Strain into chilled cocktail glass. Garnish with brandied cherry and lemon peel.

The Peychaud's bitters add another dimension to its New Orleans roots. My preferred variation subs oloroso sherry for the Madeira, securing this as a personal favorite. See **French Quarter** for variation.

CUBA LIBRE

1 lime
2 oz. Bacardi gold rum
4 oz. Coca-Cola or other cane-based cola

Cut lime into quarters. Squeeze one wedge into chilled Collins glass and discard. Squeeze another and drop into glass. Add rum and ice. Add Coca-Cola and stir briefly to integrate. Reserve the other half of lime for the next serving.

"Free Cuba" was the rallying cry at the end of the Spanish-American war at the turn of the twentieth century. Since the creation of this drink in Cuba by U.S. soldiers, Americans have made it their adopted national Cooler. Not even the *Mojito* has enjoyed the unwavering popularity that this drink has. I would recommend finding the sugar cane–based (not corn syrup), Mexican-made Coca-Cola or other cane sugar–based cola, for best results.

CUBAN ROSE

2 oz. Bacardi y Cia Heritage white rum
1 oz. fresh orange juice
¼ oz. house-made Grenadine
1 dash Regans' Orange Bitters No. 6

Add all ingredients to mixing glass. Add ice and shake well. Strain into chilled cocktail glass. Garnish with orange peel.

In this Prohibition-era add-on of Mr. Crockett, the freshly squeezed juice and homemade grenadine are essential. I went with the more potent version of Bacardi rum here, but you can experiment with other styles as well. Finally, there was no mention of bitters in the original recipe, but as with most cocktails that include orange juice, after trying one with a good stab of bitters added, there was no going back.

Although there are cocktails of the era named **Santiago**, they are simply mistitled *Bacardi Cocktails*. The best and proper *Santiago* is a *Cuban Rose* with equal parts rum and orange juice. The result is a lighter, midday tipple that can also be served on the rocks as a brunch treat. If you have some handy (and you should) it can take a couple of dashes of Horsford's acid phosphate prior to shaking to add some tannin without adding another citrus element or bitters. Amber rums make a nice pairing with orange juice if you want to try a more serious adaptation.

CUBAN SUNSHINE

2 oz. Caña Brava white rum
1 oz. Noilly Prat extra dry vermouth
¾ oz. fresh pineapple juice or puree
¼ oz. house-made Grenadine
1 dash Regans' Orange Bitters No. 6

Add all ingredients to mixing glass. Add ice and shake well. Fine-strain into chilled cocktail glass. No garnish.

FLAMINGO ▪ *Classic*

2 oz. Caña Brava white rum or Rhum J.M agricole white rhum (80 proof)
1 oz. fresh pineapple juice or puree
¾ oz. fresh lime juice
¼ oz. house-made Grenadine
1 dash Peychaud's bitters

Add all ingredients to mixing glass (except bitters). Add ice and shake well. Strain into chilled cocktail glass. Garnish with one long dash of Peychaud's bitters across the top of drink.

Originally listed with equal parts in the "Cuban Concoctions" chapter of the Old Books, this adaptation brings the recipe more in line with the modern palate, ensuring that all ingredients keep their own identities. Once again, bitters were not included, but to prepare this without them would be a major disservice. A new summertime staple.

The simple **Flamingo** is, if not a descendant of the **(Cuban) Sunshine**, certainly related to it. It first appears in Ted Saucier's

Bottom's Up (1951) and I have served this crowd-pleaser at numerous events ever since I began bartending.

Though the original recipe called for a "Cuban rum," through the years I have adapted it to include the white rhum agricole, which is a bit malty and changes a rum cocktail in a way that genever would a gin cocktail. (I use genever here too and call it a **Soho Flamingo**.) I also tacked on a long dash of Peychaud's bitters across the top to add the "what is that" quality that we all enjoy and make it a bit more appealing to the eye as well. See **Clover Club** for variations.

CUCUMBER RHUMBA ▮ *Peacock Alley*

4 quarter-inch round slices of fresh cucumber
3 dashes Fee Brothers rhubarb bitters
2 oz. Hendricks gin
¾ oz. Cocchi Americano
¾ oz. fresh orange juice

Place cucumber slices into mixing glass. Add rhubarb bitters and muddle thoroughly. Add remaining ingredients. Add ice and shake well. Fine-strain into chilled cocktail glass. Twist an orange peel to release oils, then discard (optional). Garnish with cucumber slice placed vertically on rim of glass.

In my never-ending quest to keep with Hotel tradition and incorporate orange juice as a proper ingredient, I was inspired to fill a request for a summer cocktail "on the fly," and I came up with this one. The cucumber and Hendricks are a natural pairing and the Cocchi Americano and orange juice bring the grip that really sends this home. Without a doubt, your guests will drink these faster than you can make them, so you may want to consider batching them.

As an alternate preparation, infusing a bottle of Hendricks with a sliced cucumber for a few days will eliminate the need for muddling at the time of your event. Just place in airtight glass jar, stirring every other day. Fine-strain back into bottle and prepare as directed, post-muddle. See **Emerald Isle** for variation.

DAIQUIRI ∎ *Classic*

2 oz. Bacardi y Cia Heritage white rum
¾ oz. fresh lime juice
½ oz. Simple Syrup

Add all ingredients to mixing glass. Add ice and shake well. Strain into chilled cocktail glass. Garnish with lime wheel.

HEMINGWAY DAIQUIRI ∎ *Classic*

2 oz. 86 Co. Caña Brava white rum
¾ oz. fresh lime juice
½ oz. fresh grapefruit juice
½ oz. Luxardo maraschino liqueur

Add all ingredients to mixing glass. Add ice and shake well. Strain into chilled Old Fashioned glass filled with crushed or pebble ice. Garnish with lime wheel.

Strawberry and Cardamom Infusion for
Strawberry and Spice Daiquiri

Rinse, hull, and halve one pound of fresh strawberries and add to airtight glass container. Add 10 crushed cardamom pods and 32 oz. of rum. Infuse for 7 days, stirring occasionally. Fine-strain and funnel back into bottle.

Listed in the Old Bar book as a **Bacardi Sour**, this is your classic *Daiquiri*, for sure. I would take advantage of today's large variety of flavorful white rums and go from there. The recipe here reflects a modern build, but feel free to pull back on the sugar to make something more like the old, drier Cuban presentation (substitute a bar spoon of superfine sugar for the syrup and serve Frappé style, over crushed ice).

A related recipe is the **Jamaican Punch**, which features that island's rum in the starring role. One version that shows its heritage and delivers is the **Maree**, which includes Jamaican rum and a dash of Angostura bitters, garnished with grated nutmeg. This one is very much worth a try.

At Peacock Alley, we have featured the **Strawberry and Spice Daiquiri**, in which we use the Strawberry and Cardamom Infusion as the base ingredient. A more popular crowd-pleaser is hard to find, and it's a nice twist that's worth the time, especially if you're hosting a special summertime soirée. See **Bacardi Cocktail** and **Islands in the Stream** for variations.

One of the most famous writers of the twentieth century, Ernest Hemingway was a regular at the Floridita Bar in Havana, where he enjoyed this namesake concoction frozen, with the ingredient portions doubled and blended with ice (the **Papa Doble**). To enjoy these even more like Papa did, reduce the amount of grapefruit juice and maraschino by half, as his aversion to sugar dictated. Of course, it can also be served up. I have been featuring a *Hemingway Daiquiri* on my menus for many years, as it is a favorite of mine. In recent times it has taken on a life of its own, with guests now calling for it quite regularly. See **World Cup** for variation.

A **Bacardi Planter's Punch** is also included in the Old Books. Though it differs from what we now know as a *Planter's Punch*, it is essentially a standard *Daiquiri* served on shaved ice and dressed with fruit, for a fine alternate—if misnamed—presentation.

GRAPEFRUIT BLOSSOM

2 oz. Diplomático Blanco Reserve rum
1 oz. fresh grapefruit juice
¼ oz. Luxardo maraschino liqueur

Strain into chilled cocktail glass. Garnish with grapefruit peel and brandied cherry.

Finally, we have the *Grapefruit Blossom*. Like its brother the *Orange Blossom*, this Prohibition-era staple can take to some tinkering, but ultimately use your most flavorful white rum for best results. This simply assembled but refreshing quaff will end your search for your new brunch treat. For the record, I tried it with grapefruit bitters and it was overkill. Stick with orange or even aromatic bitters for unique results. If you sub in simple syrup for the maraschino, you'll have the **Isle of Pines**, which is also listed in the "Cuban Concoctions" chapter of *The Old Waldorf-Astoria Bar Book*.

DAISY *(Basic Recipe)*

2 oz. spirit of choice (brandy, gin, rum, tequila, whiskey, etc.)
¾ oz. fresh lemon or fresh lime juice
½ oz. curaçao, maraschino, or other liqueur
¼ oz. house-made Grenadine, Gum Syrup, or Simple Syrup (optional)

Add all ingredients to mixing glass. Add ice and shake well. Strain into chilled goblet or cocktail glass. Garnish with fresh mint and seasonal fruit.

RUM DAISY

2 oz. Bacardi y Cia Heritage white rum or Appleton Estate Reserve rum
¾ oz. fresh lime juice
½ oz. yellow Chartreuse
¼ oz. house-made Grenadine (optional)

Add all ingredients to mixing glass. Add ice and shake well. Strain into chilled goblet or cocktail glass. Garnish with fresh mint and seasonal fruit.

BRANDY DAISY

2 oz. Hine VSOP cognac
½ oz. fresh lemon juice
¼ oz. Grand Marnier
¼ oz. Simple Syrup
½ oz. chilled club soda

Add all ingredients except club soda to mixing glass. Add ice and shake well. Strain into chilled goblet or cocktail glass. Top with club soda. No garnish.

The *Daisy* family of cocktails can be loosely described as a *Sour* sweetened by a liqueur. These refreshing, first-generation concoctions date back to the mid-1800s. In most cases, the added liqueur is enough of a sugar component to do the job, though you can add a touch of syrup or grenadine to suit your personal taste. And that's what is most important: finding what it is about the recipe that you like, and have that come through. After all, you are the one drinking it!

By the turn of the twentieth century, grenadine and raspberry syrup had grown to be popular choices as sugaring agents, and breaking from the tradition of granulated sugar, it was what the guys at the Old Bar used.

As for lemon and lime combinations, it's usually a safe bet to pair lemon with brown spirits and lime with clear, though exceptions can be happily made based on personal preference. I don't believe there should be hard-and-fast rules when it comes to these types of things.

The renditions that get their own recipes by name in the Old Books are pretty standard. The *Bacardi Daisy* and *Rum Daisy* are almost identical, save for the base rums and use of liqueur, so I've combined them here. The *Brandy Daisy* recipe (in which you could sub in gin, rum, etc.) was topped with a charge of club soda, which was the other traditional presentation. It was a holdover from the old days; by the turn of the twentieth century and certainly by the peak of the Old Bar, Daisies were beginning to be served with no soda. And finally, for a recognizable point of reference, the most famous and popular *Daisy* of them all is the **Margarita** (which means "daisy" in Spanish).

DOLORES

- 1½ oz. Lustau Don Nuño oloroso sherry
- ¾ oz. Appleton Estate Reserve rum
- ½ oz. Bonal Quinquina aperitif
- ½ oz. fresh orange juice
- Pink peppercorns

Add all ingredients except peppercorns to mixing glass. Add ice and shake well. Fine-strain into chilled cocktail glass. Garnish with one coarse grind of pink peppercorns.

This unique survivor makes for quite the tippler. The combination of sherry and Jamaican rum works surprisingly well for the base. The recipe originally called for Dubonnet, but I chose the fuller-flavored Bonal, as I think it adds more to the spine. The dry sherry results in a predictably arid result, but the sweetened profile of the Bonal and fresh orange juice balance it out. I envision this as a sunset summer sipper, so I tried to keep it light, but if you'd like a bit more of a punch, you can add Smith & Cross navy-strength rum as a sub for the Appleton. As for the pepper component, the original called for "dash of Aromatic Pepper" and here I chose a coarse grind of pink peppercorn as opposed to the slightly overpowering black variety. The floral quality of the pink pepper does the job on nose without overpowering the ingredients. If going with a sweeter sherry, you can use black pepper.

DORFLINGER

2 oz. Plymouth gin
¾ oz. St. George Absinthe Verte
¼ oz. Simple Syrup (or Gum Syrup, preferred)
2 dashes Regans' Orange Bitters No. 6

Add all ingredients to mixing glass. Add ice and stir for 30 seconds. Strain into chilled cocktail glass. Garnish with lemon peel.

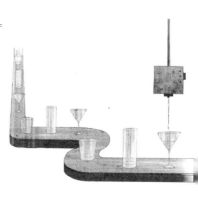

The absinthe really hides itself well in this heightened cocktail. The original recipe did not include simple syrup, but I think a touch improves not only the taste profile but the texture and tactile weight as well. If you have gum syrup prepared, use that for optimal results. Christian Dorflinger was a master glassmaker at the time of the Old Bar whose company provided the lead cut crystal that graced the Hotel's tables. His family's company also provided the glass sculptures for the back bar of the refurbished Peacock Alley in 2005.

DOROTHY GISH

2 oz. Plantation 3 Stars white rum
½ oz. fresh orange juice
½ oz. fresh pineapple juice
¼ oz. Combier Abricot apricot liqueur

Add all ingredients to mixing glass. Add ice and shake well. Strain into chilled cocktail glass. Garnish with brandied cherry.

NACIONAL

1½ oz. Bacardi gold rum
1½ oz. pineapple juice
¼ oz. fresh lemon juice
¼ oz. Rothman & Winter apricot liqueur

Add all ingredients to mixing glass. Add ice and shake well. Fine-strain into chilled cocktail glass. Garnish with brandied cherry.

The *Dorothy Gish*, named for the famous actress of the era, was created (along with the **Presidente**, **Mary Pickford**, and **Douglas Fairbanks**) by Havana's Hotel Sevilla bartenders and was originally made with the full-flavored Bacardi of its day. The Plantation rum is a good alternative. Pineapple puree or even canned (if not from concentrate) is a more than acceptable substitute, especially if you are not preparing for a group. I have also made a variation of this cocktail with a dry, dark rum (Don Q añejo is recommended and so is an aged rhum agricole) and the result is a unique and delicious alternative. For an even drier and lighter variation, split the rum portion of the recipe with dry vermouth and you have the excellent and dangerous **Menendez**. Another namesake cocktail is the **Mary Pickford**, named for the silent film star. This cocktail was created for Pickford during Prohibition in Havana while she was visiting with Charlie Chaplin and Douglas Fairbanks. It relies entirely on pineapple in the juice slot of the *Dorothy Gish* and omits the apricot liqueur for a half ounce of grenadine. Add a dash of orange bitters to temper its sweet side. Other known variations include a couple of dashes of maraschino liqueur. Try this modification if your tastes run on the even sweeter side. If so, consider serving on ice.

Then there is the **High-Stepper**, a variation that takes the *Dorothy Gish* and leans entirely on the orange juice and omits pineapple altogether. I would just add an extra quarter ounce of apricot liqueur and a couple of dashes of orange bitters to bring it all home. An aged amber rum would work as well. As for orange juice, which the Old Bar seemed to love, I personally don't mind it as an ingredient. Though it doesn't have the bracing tartness of lemon or lime, this can be easily remedied by a couple of dashes of bitters or acid phosphate to retain the distinctive brightness and fruit that orange juice brings to the palate.

Will P. Taylor was once the manager of the Hotel Nacional in Cuba and went on to become the last resident manager of the Old Waldorf-Astoria. He took the *Nacional* with him to the Hotel. Another rendition, found in Charles M. Baker's *The Gentleman's Companion* (1939), included lime juice to provide the balancing note (and a bit more at that) in lieu of the lemon suggested above. Believe it or not, the lemon is superior in this cocktail. If your tastes run on the drier side, pull back on the pineapple juice by a half ounce. I chose Rothman & Winter apricot liqueur as it leans to the dry side but imparts a natural, slightly bitter note to the finish, though any apricot liqueur will do the job.

DOUBLE-STANDARD SOUR

1 oz. Old Overholt rye whiskey
1 oz. Hayman's Old Tom gin
¾ oz. fresh lime juice
½ oz. house-made Raspberry Syrup
¼ oz. Simple Syrup

Add all ingredients to mixing glass. Add ice and shake well. Strain into chilled cocktail glass. Garnish with orange peel.

Resisting the temptation to gentrify this one by subbing out the lime for lemon juice, I made it a personal goal to attempt to keep to the original intention whenever possible. I tried more robust rye whiskeys, but I prefer the softer and lower proof profile (80 proof) of the Old Overholt. I also tried an aromatic, modern gin or two, but they tried to steal the show. As always, the sugar component can be adjusted for personal taste. The orange peel is essential. The name of this cocktail originates from the 1890s political argument over the use of both a gold and silver standard of currency. Mr. Crockett made sure to note that it had nothing to do with masculine or feminine conduct.

DUKE

2½ oz. Noilly Prat extra dry vermouth
¼ oz. Pacifique absinthe
¼ oz. Marie Brizard anisette
2 dashes Regans' Orange Bitters No. 6

Add all ingredients to mixing glass. Add ice and stir for 30 seconds. Strain into chilled cocktail glass. Garnish with lemon peel.

This simply adorned, aromatized wine–based cocktail is the perfect premeal summertime treat. It pairs amazingly well with freshly shucked oysters. See **Pick Me Up** for variations.

DUPLEX

2 oz. Noilly Prat extra dry vermouth
2 oz. Carpano Antica sweet vermouth
2 dashes Regans' Orange Bitters No. 6

Add all ingredients to mixing glass. Add ice and stir for 30 seconds. Strain into chilled cocktail glass. Garnish with lemon peel.

This is the concoction that Johnnie Solan claimed he modified to create the **Bronx**. It's a wine-based, deceptively complex quaff that really delivers, especially when you're in the mood for something on the lighter side. Be adventurous with your aromatic wines for additionally unique and interesting results. Also listed in the Old Books as a **Neudine**.

EGGNOG *(Basic Recipe)*

1 whole egg
½ oz. Simple Syrup
2 oz. Royer Force 53 cognac or Pierre Ferrand 1840 cognac or
2 oz. Brugal 1888 Gran Reserva rum or Ron Zacapa Gran Reserva Solera 23 rum or
2 oz. Baker's 107 proof bourbon or Henry McKenna 10 Year Old bourbon
1 oz. heavy cream (or half and half)
2 drops pure vanilla extract (optional)

Crack egg and place in mixing glass. Add syrup and dry-shake for 5 seconds. Add remaining ingredients and ice and shake well for at least 10 seconds. Fine-strain into small wineglass or chilled cocktail glass. Garnish with freshly grated nutmeg.

SABBATH CALM

1 whole egg
½ oz. Simple Syrup
¾ oz. Cardenal Mendoza Solera Gran Reserva brandy
¾ oz. port wine
¾ oz. French roast coffee (chilled)
¾ oz. heavy cream (or half and half)

Crack egg and place in mixing glass. Add syrup and dry-shake for 5 seconds. Add remaining ingredients and ice and shake well for at least 10 seconds. Fine-strain into small wineglass or chilled cocktail glass. Garnish with freshly grated nutmeg.

Dating back to the 1700s and a favorite of the upper classes, *Eggnog* had evolved to become a winter holiday specialty by the time of the Old Bar, with both warm and cold versions basking in a fair level of popularity. The Old Books listed recipes for no less than six of them (not counting nonalcoholic varieties). I have included a basic recipe that can be tempered for personal taste and mood and will also help facilitate preparing the other variations.

I personally prefer the base spirit to have a bit of grip so the other ingredients will render it anonymous. I know for some that is the purpose of the nog, but I think it's better served if consumed with the brakes on. That said, I prefer overproof cognacs here. Lustau Gran Solera Spanish brandy and Cardenal Mendoza Solera Gran Reserva (which adds a traditional sherry note) are fine regular-strength alternatives in the Spanish brandy category.

I tried plenty of rums and arrived at the same conclusion: you want something with a bit of sweetness but also one that can leave its mark. The two recommended in this recipe worked very well, but in the end, use what you prefer (try Smith & Cross navy-strength when feeling adventurous). I even sampled a round made with a good spiced rum (the lightly spiced rum Eldorado proved tasty without going overboard) and I would not stop you from trying one. I recommend the homemade rendition in the **High Thread Count** entry.

As for whiskey, I prefer a higher-proof variety, as it's both sweet and strong enough to retain its identity. The bourbon paired very well with the sugar and cream components of the nog, but a high-proof rye whiskey would make for a nice contrast.

The other ingredients are not without room for personal interpretation as well. Most old recipes cite milk, some call for cream, and as the recipe is a shrunken Punch I can see why. When making the single serving listed here, I prefer the cream for its richness, but if you're planning on enjoying more than one, half and half works well enough. Milk remains a bit thin for me but is recommended when making a larger portion.

Dry shaking is a necessity to emulsify the entire egg. Anyway, your guests will be thoroughly impressed as you prepare and complete this recipe in two stages. The double-strain is essential for removing any ice chips. This will ensure the luxurious flavor, which is what makes this classic worth the calories. I like a touch of vanilla extract, but try the first one without and make your own call.

Because of its variety and sum of ingredients, I've included the full recipe for the *Sabbath Calm*, a must-try mocha lover's new favorite treat. Of course there would be a **Bacardi Eggnog**. White rum gets lost in the nog for me, but is mentioned here for completion's sake. Prepare it with a good dark rum for best results. If you split the rum portion with port wine, you'll have the **Morning Star** (I would use a tawny here, though I'm pretty sure ruby would have been used at the Old Bar). The classic **Baltimore Eggnog**, from *Jerry Thomas' Bartenders Guide* (1862), incorporates Jamaican rum and Madeira wine. Appleton Estate 12 Year Old is worth the splurge. Blandy's 5 Year Old Madeira does the job as well. The **Jamaica Eggnog** loses the Madeira and goes soley with Jamaican rum. Then there is the **Myers's Eggnog**. There's Myers's rum in there, but it splits the bill with brandy. It's another winner. The last of the rum variations is the **Cuban Milk Punch**, which, although it's listed as such in the Old Books, is essentially identical to *Bacardi Eggnog* (just be sure to include the vanilla extract). The funnily named **Sherry Chicken** is a nog with sherry at the base. I recommend trying both dry and sweet varieties here.

ELIXIR

2 oz. house-made Bacardi Elixir Cordial (recipe follows)
1 oz. Bacardi y Cia Heritage white rum
½ oz. fresh lime juice
⅓ oz. house-made Demerara Syrup

Add all ingredients to mixing glass. Add ice and stir for 30 seconds. Strain into chilled cocktail glass. No garnish.

Bacardi Elixir Cordial

2 c. prunes (halved)
20 oz. Bacardi y Cia Heritage white rum
6 oz. Bacardi 8 Year Old dark rum
4 oz. Carpano Antica sweet vermouth
2 oz. house-made Demerara Syrup

Add prunes to airtight container, cover with both rums, and let rest for 2 weeks, stirring once or twice a week. Strain to remove prunes. Add vermouth and syrup. Stir to integrate and funnel into bottle.

According to legend, Don Facundo Bacardi created this elixir during his company's earliest days (1862), and it was made until the distillery departed Cuba in 1960. Initially it was given to Bacardi employees at Christmastime. While the company no longer produces this product, its flavor profile was described to me based on a recipe developed for a special event in 2013. Cocoa, port wine, and rich vermouth were all included in the tasting notes. Sadly, no bottles remain at the distillery and there are no plans to release it commercially, so it is hard to come by, though in the meantime you can enjoy this slightly ramped-up Daiquiri adaptation.

The original item was closer to cordial level in strength, but I believe that since I am not in the cordial-making business, it was best to try to approximate the flavor profile in a simple manner. The higher alcohol level will help preserve it as well. During the winter, you can serve the liqueur neat, as originally intended. In the summer, it makes for an interesting float on a standard Daiquiri in lieu of making it the main ingredient as in the *Elixir*.

EMERALD ISLE ▮ *Peacock Alley*

3 cucumber slices
10 fresh tarragon leaves
1½ oz. Dingle Irish pot still gin
½ oz. Bushmills Black Bush Irish whiskey
¾ oz. Cocchi Americano aperitif
1 oz. grapefruit juice

Add cucumber and tarragon to mixing glass and muddle well. Add remaining ingredients. Add ice and shake well. Fine-strain into chilled cocktail glass. No garnish.

Created to incorporate the seasonally grown herbs from our rooftop garden, this unique cocktail is one of my summertime favorites. The pot still Irish gin has a soft and floral profile, so if you're unable to procure it, I would go with one of the recently released lower-alcohol gins of your choice, steering clear of juniper-heavy renditions. The ingredients complement each other so well, you can't help but taste something distinctive and different in every sip. It's a must-try. See **Cucumber Rhumba** for variation.

EMERSON

1½ oz. Greenhook Ginsmiths Old Tom gin or Ransom Old Tom gin
1 oz. Carpano Antica sweet vermouth
¼ oz. Luxardo maraschino liqueur
¼ oz. fresh lime juice
1 dash Regans' Orange Bitters No. 6

Add all ingredients to mixing glass. Add ice and stir for 30 seconds. Strain into chilled cocktail glass. Garnish with brandied cherry.

This **Martinez** variation was named for a Baltimore pharmacist who frequented the Old Bar, whose story and newfangled fizzled hangover cure (presumably some form of sodium bicarbonate) merited nearly two pages of print in *Old Waldorf Bar Days*. The limited use of lime here is like that of bitters, included to add a bit of tannin and spine rather than a citrus note.

This is another recipe whose first appearance is in Jacques Straub's *Drinks* (1914). Our somewhat bold use of a barrel-aged gin makes for a fine year-round cocktail. It also makes using a full-flavored vermouth an easy call. Feel free to utilize unaged Old Tom gin and a less complex vermouth for a more restrained result.

ESPRESSO COCKTAIL ▮ *Peacock Alley*

2½ oz. Coffee Bean–Infused Vodka (recipe follows)
¾ oz. Simple Syrup
¼ oz. Varnelli l'Anice Secco Speciale anisette (optional)

Add all ingredients to mixing glass. Add ice and stir for 30 seconds. Strain into chilled cocktail glass. Garnish with lemon peel (optional).

Coffee Bean–Infused Vodka

Add 1 c. Italian espresso beans and 1 c. French roast coffee beans to airtight glass jar. Add 32 oz. unflavored vodka and infuse for no more than 7 days. Fine-strain and funnel back into bottle. Lasts at least 6 months.

As you may have recognized, this is not the sticky sweet or creamy cocktail of 1980s lore. I have been preparing this version of the

Espresso Cocktail for as long as I can remember; it may have been my first infused offering. The infused vodka incorporates the coffee into its DNA, making this simply assembled cocktail enjoyable even to those who claim an aversion to coffee.

You may adjust the sugar content for personal preference, especially if opting for the touch of anisette. You could omit the anisette and add a couple of dashes of chocolate bitters for a mocha-like profile. The lemon twist is a nod to the days when coffee may have been poorly roasted, sourced, or generally not as well made as it is today and imbibers would cut their bitter espresso with it. Today's premium coffee offers no such imperfections, but you can err on the side of tradition if you like.

FAƧCINATION

2 oz. Kübler absinthe
1 oz. Cointreau
2 oz. chilled club soda or Champagne

Add all ingredients except club soda or Champagne to mixing glass. Add ice and stir for 30 seconds. Strain into chilled Old Fashioned glass with large ice cubes or sphere. Add chilled club soda or champagne and stir briefly to incorporate. Garnish with orange peel.

This recipe, originally served in a Champagne coupe, called for one ice cube, a strange presentation, for sure. I would just add a few ice cubes to an Old Fashioned glass for best results. After all, I don't want ice cubes sliding around my coupe, as that would make balancing skills a requirement, not to mention them colliding with your teeth. You could sub in a sparkling wine for the club soda, but I prefer keeping it on the light side with the club soda (and the orange twist made for a bright lift to the nose).

FALL IN A GLAƧƧ **❚** *Peacock Alley*

2 oz. Don Q añejo rum
1 oz. Lustau Don Nuño oloroso sherry
¾ oz. fresh orange juice
¼ oz. grade A maple syrup
2 dashes Angostura bitters

Add all ingredients to mixing glass. Add ice and shake well. Fine-strain into chilled cocktail glass. Garnish with freshly grated nutmeg.

This popular seasonal cocktail has been reappearing on our list for years. I recommend rums that run on the dry side. Another such alternative is a dark rhum agricole, which can really help balance this cocktail's flavor profile to tightrope levels.

FALLEN APPLE∫ ∎ Peacock Alley

- 2 oz. Père Magloire Fine VS calvados
- ½ oz. house-made Cinnamon Vodka
- ½ oz. Lustau Don Nuño oloroso sherry
- ¾ oz. fresh lemon juice
- 1 bar spoon Stonewall Kitchen cinnamon apple jelly or Sarabeth's chunky apple preserves
- 1 dash Angostura bitters
- 1½ oz. Doc's Draft hard apple cider (NY) or Orchard Hill hard apple cider (NY)

Add all ingredients except cider to mixing glass. Add ice and shake well. Fine-strain into Old Fashioned glass filled with large ice cubes or sphere. Top with cider. Garnish with freshly grated nutmeg.

This seasonal item was created at the request of a magazine for an autumnal Punch. The great thing about it is that although it includes many ingredients, it can take to tinkering quite well. Feel free to tone down the calvados and ramp up the sherry a bit for a different take; just be sure to keep the cider on the dry side. I would also recommend batching this out the night before a holiday party so serving consists simply of chilling and topping with cider and nutmeg (omit the jam). A new (adult) family gathering favorite.

FANCIULLI

- 1½ oz. Rittenhouse bonded rye whiskey
- ¾ oz. Martini & Rossi sweet vermouth
- ¾ oz. Fernet-Branca liqueur

Add all ingredients to mixing glass. Add ice and stir for 30 seconds. Strain into chilled cocktail glass. Garnish with orange peel and brandied cherry.

LARCENY AND OLD LACE ▎ *Peacock Alley*

1½ oz. Larceny bourbon
¾ oz. Carpano Antica sweet vermouth
¾ oz. Cynar liqueur
1 dash Regans' Orange Bitters No. 6

Add all ingredients to mixing glass. Add ice and stir for 30 seconds. Strain into chilled cocktail glass. Garnish with lemon peel and brandied cherry.

Francesco Fanciulli (1853–1915) replaced John Philip Sousa as leader of the United States Marine Band. He immigrated to New York City and wound up calling it home for most of his life after his bumpy tenure in the service. His namesake cocktail, in *Old Waldorf Bar Days,* is a masterful play on the Manhattan. The addition of Fernet-Branca to the rye whiskey makes this truly an Italian Manhattan. Its spicy and racy profile makes for an interesting sipper, geared toward post–steak meal time (preferably paired with a cigar). Although there's a lot to like, I felt that there was room for some tempering to create a stepping-stone version for those unfamiliar.

Our *Larceny and Old Lace* exchanges the full-flavored fernet for Cynar (an artichoke-based liqueur). The "wheated" bourbon, in lieu of the rye whiskey, adds a weight and slight sweetness that accompanies Cynar nicely. The fuller-flavored vermouth helps keep the cocktail balanced, adding to the long and complex finish.

FEZZIWIG'S RECLINE (Holiday
Cocktail) ▌ Peacock Alley

> 1½ oz. Old Forester 86 proof bourbon
> 1 oz. Carpano Antica sweet vermouth
> ½ oz. Pierre Ferrand dry curaçao
> ¼ oz. house-made Cinnamon Vodka
> ¼ oz. St. Elizabeth allspice dram or The Bitter Truth pimento dram
> 1 dash Angostura bitters
>
> Add all ingredients to mixing glass. Add ice and stir for 30 seconds. Strain into chilled cocktail glass. Garnish with orange peel.

I named this for the character in Charles Dickens's *A Christmas Carol*. This seasonally tweaked **Manhattan** alternate has become a favorite of our guests and will most likely be one of your December post-dinner pleasures for years to come.

FIRST CLASS ▌ Peacock Alley

> ½ oz. fresh lime juice
> 4 fresh sage leaves
> 1 lime wedge
> 2½ oz. G-Vine Floraison gin
> ¾ oz. Luxardo maraschino liqueur
>
> Add lime juice, sage, and lime wedge to mixing glass and muddle. Add ice and remaining ingredients and shake well. Fine-strain into chilled cocktail glass. Garnish with one turn of freshly ground black pepper.

This cocktail was chosen by Gaz Regan for his book *101 Best New Cocktails of 2011*. I suggest serving it to **Aviation** fans as a unique deviation.

FISH HOUSE PUNCH

1 oz. Royer Force 53 VSOP cognac
1 oz. Appleton Estate Reserve rum
½ oz. Dutch's Spirits peach brandy (or house-made Peach Brandy)
¾ oz. fresh lemon juice
½ oz. house-made Demerara Syrup

Add all ingredients to mixing glass. Add ice and shake well. Fine-strain into Old Fashioned glass or Hoffman House goblet filled with large ice cubes or sphere. Garnish with freshly grated nutmeg.

This eighteenth-century survivor is making a comeback and is now a regular feature on cocktail menus across the country. Named for the Schuylkill Fishing Company, which was founded in 1732 and known as the "Fish House," on the Schuylkill ("Skookill") River, this Punch has witnessed more than a few notables partaking: none other than George Washington was a fan, and since the club is still operating today, I think it's safe to say that our first president is not alone in his admiration.

Traditionally made in large format and appropriately diluted, this recipe is on the strong side, and although it's a single serving, it does its best to replicate the Punch experience. The large version would be made with an oleo saccharum, which adds a unique depth of flavor (see "Large Cups and Punches" chapter). Using a demerara syrup with the lemon juice here will help you come close. As for the peach aspect, the Old Books did without it but most other recipes of the era included peach brandy, which was a peach-based eau-de-vie aged in oak barrels. Though it's currently produced by a few small distilleries, I have included a good substitute. If going with a peach liqueur (which is also fine), just cut the sugar component by half. You may also want to add an ounce of chilled water prior to shaking, especially if having more than one. Punches are meant to be enjoyed over long stretches of time and would traditionally have a lower alcohol content.

Lastly, bucking convention, I think a dash of allspice dram or pimento bitters on top adds a bit of backbone to the whole thing and is a pleasing alternate presentation. If going that way, you can omit the nutmeg if you like.

FIX *(Basic Recipe)*

2 oz. spirit of choice (brandy, gin, rum, whiskey, etc.)
¼ oz. Simple Syrup
⅓ oz. fresh lemon juice

Add all ingredients to mixing glass. Shake well and strain into rocks glass or tumbler filled with crushed or pellet ice. Garnish with citrus peel and/or seasonal fruit.

One of the oldest categories in the modern history of mixed drinks, these shrunken Punch descendants (along with the Sour) were immensely popular in the mid-nineteenth century. As with the *(Whiskey) Cocktail,* a guest would belly up to the Old Bar and order these by the base ingredient. Whether your choice was brandy, genever, rum, or another spirit, the recipe was the same, with the called-for liquor taking the lead.

I would let the use of ice be the defining element between the Fix and the Sour. Think of it as enhancing the base ingredient, then fancying it up a bit with seasonal fruit and berries for garnish. Traditional recipes would have you use water and sugar, but you can just cut to the chase by using simple syrup for an easier preparation and a more consistent drink. Although the Old Books omit any flavor enhancements, other variations of the day included fruit syrups (pineapple was very popular) or liqueurs such as orange curaçao as the sugar component, which added another dimension to this classic.

FIZZ *(Basic Recipe)*

1½ oz. chilled club soda
2 oz. Beefeater London dry gin or Tanqueray Old Tom gin
1 oz. fresh lemon juice
¾ oz. Simple Syrup

Add chilled club soda to small Collins glass or tumbler. Add remaining ingredients to mixing glass. Add ice and shake well. Fine-strain into small Collins glass. No garnish.

The Old Bar was world famous for its Fizzes. This entry reflects the basic recipe for a *Gin Fizz* and is the basis for the many variations in the Old books. When the recipe calls for egg whites, it's best to use half; today's eggs are larger than those at the time of the Old Bar. You're looking for about a half ounce total unless directed otherwise. Just dry-shake the egg white, then split between two glasses. The identifying profile of a Fizz is that once prepared, it contains no additional ice when served.

The Old Bar featured many renditions, so here goes:

A **Silver Fizz** adds half an egg white to the preceding recipe. A **Golden Fizz** adds the yolk only. For the **Royal Fizz**, add the entire egg. The **Murdock Fizz** is prepared as the standard *Fizz*, with rye whiskey in the gin slot. The **Japanese Fizz** is prepared with an ounce each of rye whiskey and ruby port wine and an egg white (finish with a snap of orange peel and discard—there are no garnishes when it comes to the *Fizz*). *The classic* **Diamond Fizz** subs Champagne for the club soda, kind of like a reverse *French 75*(!). A **Horton Fizz** has you shake a basic *Gin Fizz* with a sprig or two of fresh mint (a Derby Day alternative for those with an aversion to whiskey). Speaking of whiskey, if you use it as the base ingredient, you have the overly obvious **Whiskey Fizz** (the same goes for the **Brandy Fizz**—use a VS cognac). I prefer the drier rye variation in the *Whiskey Fizz*, as it takes to the sugar component better than the naturally sweeter bourbon version. A **Strawberry Fizz** subs in strawberry syrup for the standard white sugar simple syrup; a **Raspberry Fizz** would work as well. Although fresh fruits are not listed as ingredients, you can forgo the fruit syrups and just muddle a few fresh berries with a touch of simple syrup for a more seasonal alternate. Just be sure to double-strain.

Since almost every style of cocktail from the Old Bar has a Bacardi iteration, there is of course the **Bacardi Fizz**. Again, I would recommend the Bacardi y Cia Heritage for better results. If you split the citrus between lemon and orange juices in the *Bacardi Fizz* and add half an egg white, you'll have the pleasing **Sunshine Fizz**. There were two other variations with that title, placing lime juice in the lemon slot. The others led with gin (Old Tom makes it a must-try) and whiskey (although rye was used in the time of the Old Bar, I would sub in a slightly sweet, "wheated" bourbon such as Larceny or Maker's Mark for a more balanced result and a natural pair to the orange component).

Finally, there is the famous **Sloe Gin Fizz**. These were prepared haphazardly throughout the twentieth century, often with poorly made sloe gin masquerading as the real thing. With today's available sloe gins, you can experience one as they would've at the Old Bar (The Bitter Truth sloeberry blue gin, Greenhook Ginsmiths beach plum gin liqueur, as well as the classic Plymouth sloe gin will all result in fine specimens). As usual, you can adjust the lemon and sugar levels as you see fit for maximum enjoyment.

Although against convention, I wouldn't squawk at the idea of the snap of a lemon peel on top of any of these to release the oils of the rind (as long as you discard it afterward). The result will delight the nose as well as the palate.

There are other unique variations on the Fizz that merit their own entries in this book, but be sure to look up the **Ramos Gin Fizz** for the most famous.

FLIP (Basic Recipe)

2 oz. spirit or fortified wine of choice
1 whole egg
½ oz. Simple Syrup

Add whole egg and syrup to mixing glass. Dry-shake for 5 seconds. Add spirit or wine of choice and ice. Shake well for 10 seconds. Fine-strain into small wineglass or goblet. Garnish with freshly grated nutmeg.

Like Eggnog and Punch, these types of drinks were originally made in a large format and by the time of the Old Bar, they had seen their best days and had been largely relegated to New Year's celebrations. After revisiting the category over the years, mostly for special events and requests, I see no reason why they cannot become, at the very least, a more common dessert substitute during the colder months. They are fairly simple to make and are much lighter than cheesecake.

In the **Sherry Flip**, I like an oloroso sherry; it becomes quickly apparent why this is a classic. For the **Kruger Special**, strain the Sherry Flip into a small Collins glass filled with a couple of ounces of club soda and top with a few dashes of grenadine (It veers close to a Fizz, but I will let lack of citrus define it.)

The **Whiskey Flip** is just that (lean on naturally sweeter bourbon here; rye proves to be a bit too grassy). The **Brandy Flip** (Spanish brandy works great) and **Rum Flip** (I prefer dark rums here) are both worth a try. The **Bacardi Flip** is what it sounds like, but other white rums can work as well. An **Orange Juice Flip** is a Bacardi Flip with an ounce of fresh OJ added. It's a very nice item, especially as an "eye opener" for brunch. I personally take to a **Tawny Port Flip**, using a 10 Year version to excellent results.

Be sure to look up the **Chocolate**, **Chocolate Cream Phosphate Fizz**, and **Coffee** entries, as they are actually fancied-up Flips and should definitely be sampled.

FLOATER

1½ oz. Courvoisier VSOP cognac
¾ oz. Combier kümmel liqueur

Fill Old Fashioned glass with crushed ice and spirits in order listed. Garnish with lemon peel (optional).

LUCKY GEORGE ∎ *Peacock Alley*

2 oz. Bushmills Black Bush Irish whiskey
1 oz. Giffard Banane du Brésil

Add ingredients to chilled Old Fashioned glass. Add large ice cubes or sphere and stir to integrate. Garnish with dried banana chip (optional).

Mr. Crockett included not one, but two stories concerning this old time Toddy. One involved legendary tycoon racehorse owner and breeder James R. Keene (six-time Belmont Stakes winner!) and horses named Voter, Ballot Box, and possibly Floater. Which brings us to origin story two: a "floater" was a citizen who "floated" from district to district, voting early and often, or one who floated more slowly and with more purpose, moving his residence from district to district, applying his political affiliation where it was needed most.

In the bar business, a float is a smaller portion of liquor poured on top of a base liquor to enhance its profile. An example of this would be the **Rusty Nail** (blended Scotch with a float of Drambuie). Typically, large ice cubes or a sphere would be used, not the crushed ice featured above.

As for this recipe, it was originally proportioned in reverse order, with the kümmel doing the heavy lifting and the cognac as the "floater," but the liqueur proved too much for even the sturdiest of cognacs and brandies. After several variations, it became clear that the kümmel had to take the title role.

After I sampled the newly imported line of Giffard cordials and syrups, it was immediately apparent how well made they are. One of the standouts is their crème de banana. Made with Brazilian bananas and a touch of cognac for body, it really has to be tasted. You can cut it back to a half ounce but you won't want to. The signature "canned peach" flavor profile and durable backbone of the Black Bush Irish whiskey seems to be a perfect pairing for yet another take on the classic *Rusty Nail*. The "Luck" is for the Irish; "George" is an homage to the "curious" one.

Besides the *Lucky George,* we have featured a couple more variations through the years. One favorite was the **Trade Wind**. We used a 2:1 ratio of house barrel-aged rum to Tuaca liqueur (vanilla and orange leads its taste profile). We aged our own white rum in a used bourbon barrel for eighteen months until it was a fine amber color (and had picked up a bit of the sweeter notes of the bourbon cask). If you're trying at home, a drier rum such as Don Q añejo would work marvelously. All worth trying as quickly prepared after-dinner drinks. Oh, and a lemon peel twist works wonders on all of them. See **Robin** for variation.

FLORADORA

1½ oz. 86 Co. Fords London dry gin

½ oz. fresh lime juice

½ oz. house-made Raspberry Syrup

4 oz. Boylan's ginger ale or other sugar cane–based ginger ale (chilled)

Add all ingredients except ginger ale to chilled Collins glass. Fill with ice cubes. Stir briefly to integrate. Add ginger ale. Stir with bar spoon from bottom until integrated. Garnish with lime wheel.

Named for the 1900 play of the same name, a risqué, lighthearted musical centered on six beautiful young women known as the Floradora Sextette. At an after-show party, one of the girls challenged the barkeep to come up with something new and this enhanced Buck was born. For a **Floradora Imperial Style**, sub in cognac for the gin and champagne for the ginger ale. It's a royal treatment, for sure.

FLORIDA

2½ oz. Cinzano Rosso sweet vermouth
1½ oz. fresh orange juice
2 dashes Regans' Orange Bitters No. 6

Add all ingredients to mixing glass. Add ice and shake well. Strain into chilled cocktail glass. Garnish with orange peel.

This is a medium-bodied, low-alcohol, warm-weather sipper from another era. Freshly squeezed juice is essential. Experimenting with vermouths is encouraged though adjust the bitters accordingly. Don't overthink it; just enjoy it.

FLYING SHAMROCK ▮ *Peacock Alley*

¾ oz. Bushmills Black Bush Irish whiskey
¾ oz. Irish Mist liqueur
1½ oz. Baileys Irish cream
1 sprig mint

Add all ingredients to mixing glass. Add ice and shake well. Fine-strain into chilled cocktail glass. Garnish with mint leaf.

Created for a guest's St. Patrick's Day event, this crowd-pleaser is a (high-octane) dessert in a glass; it will surely become a holiday tradition at your home. For an alternate presentation, you could serve this on ice. As always when using fresh herbs, be sure to give the mint sprig a good smack against the palm of your hand to help release its essence prior to placing it in the drink.

FOG CUTTER ▮ *Classic*

1½ oz. Don Q añejo rum
1 oz. Courvoisier VSOP cognac
½ oz. Beefeater London dry gin
½ oz. Torani or Giffard orgeat syrup
1½ oz. fresh lemon juice
1 oz. fresh orange juice
½ oz. fresh lime juice
½ oz. Lustau Don Nuño oloroso sherry

Add all ingredients except sherry to mixing glass. Add ice and shake well. Strain into Collins glass or tiki mug filled with ice. Float sherry. Garnish with brandied cherry and orange slice on skewer.

This potent classic, created by "Trader Vic" Bergeron in 1947 along with the Mai Tai, are both "tiki" drinks that we have served for events at Peacock Alley. We typically pre-batch the ingredients, ensuring that they will be completely integrated and to guarantee timely service. You can do the same if preparing for a barbecue or event. Just batch the juices and spirits separately and combine them when it's time to serve. The original included no lime juice, but I think a touch offsets the intense lemon profile and dries it out a bit while adding another layer of depth. You can also split the juice duties between the lemon and orange for another variation. As for the float, I prefer oloroso sherry, but you can sub in a drier or sweeter version if you like. In summer, there is almost nothing better to beat the heat.

FRAGILE   ∎ Peacock Alley

1½ oz. Pisco 100 Acholado pisco (Peru)
1½ oz. Maurin quina aperitif
¼ oz. Combier kümmel liqueur

Add all ingredients to mixing glass. Add ice and stir for 30 seconds. Strain into chilled cocktail glass. Garnish with orange peel.

More often than not, it's the change of seasons that inspires the creation of cocktails for me and looking for a way to feature spirits that are usually associated with summertime in the fall or winter, I wound up pairing Maurin quina aperitif with kümmel to bring a new dimension to pisco, the South American brandy. This is one of the rare instances when vodka works like a charm in the starring role, if you happen not to have pisco handy. It was featured in this form in Peacock Alley during the 2014 Winter Olympics as a nod to host country Russia.

FREE SILVER FIZZ

2 oz. chilled club soda
1½ oz. Tanqueray Old Tom gin
1 oz. GrandTen Distilling Medford rum or
Berkshire Mountain Distillers Ragged Mountain rum
½ oz. fresh lemon juice
½ oz. Simple Syrup
½ oz. half and half

Add chilled club soda to small Collins glass. Add remaining ingredients to mixing glass. Add ice and shake well. Fine-strain into Collins glass. No garnish.

Like the ***Double-Standard Sour***, this concoction is attributed to the controversial debate about gold or silver standard. The country was in a depression in the last years of the nineteenth century, and debates ensued as to how best to rescue the economy. Some pundits, including Secretary of State William Jennings Bryan, advocated "free silver" and a separation from the gold standard, which would have essentially sent inflation skyrocketing. Cooler heads prevailed and eventually the Greenbacks won out in 1913 with the Federal Reserve Act and the advent of the dollar.

The combination of gin and rum is really the only distinction that separates this from your workaday Fizz, but since the result is so different, it is more than worthy of its own entry. The Medford rums of the Northeastern United States would have been very much in use at the Old Bar. Substitute with Appleton dark rum if the recently released labels are unavailable.

FRENCH 75 ∎ *Classic*

1½ oz. Citadelle gin
½ oz. fresh lemon juice
½ oz. Simple Syrup
3 oz. Moët & Chandon brut NV champagne

Add all ingredients except Champagne to mixing glass. Add ice and shake well. Strain into chilled champagne flute. Add Champagne. Twist lemon peel to release oils, then discard.

Named after the WWI-era 75mm Howitzer artillery gun, this powerful classic packs quite the punch. We serve more than a few of these daily at Peacock Alley, where their popularity has never waned. Some guests prefer the *New Orleans* variation, which subs in cognac for the gin (I like a VS or the on-the-sweet-side Rémy Martin 1738 Accord Royal). If you're going the New Orleans route, I would pull back the simple syrup by a quarter ounce, as most brandies are sweet enough to get the job done. More than likely, you will be enjoying more than one, so a little less sugar will make that a bit more possible. A treat most any time of day or night.

FRENCH QUARTER *(No. 1, 2, and 3)* ▌ *Peacock Alley*

1½ oz. Royer Force 53 cognac
1 oz. Lustau Don Nuño oloroso sherry (No. 1) or
1 oz. Quinta do Noval 10 Year Old tawny port (No. 2) or
1 oz. Bordeaux Supérieur red wine (No. 3)
¼ oz. Luxardo maraschino liqueur
2 dashes Peychaud's bitters

Add all ingredients to mixing glass. Add ice and stir for 30 seconds. Strain into chilled Martini glass. Garnish with orange peel.

This cocktail was inspired by another of the Old Bar, the *Creole Lady*. Although typically served up, this fine libation would shine with a couple of large ice cubes or large sphere. Either way, the finish remains long and luxurious. Try all three variations, as they all yield interesting and unique results (just don't do it all on the same night). The overproof cognac helps keep the balance sturdy. The drier the sherry, the better; madeira wine will work as well. Finally, if you're keeping score at home, out of all the versions, the *No. 3* has spent the most time on our cocktail list (if for no other reason than I yielded to our über-palated bar staff, who prefer the table wine version).

FRIDA ▌ *Peacock Alley*

1½ oz. Espolòn blanco tequila
½ oz. green Chartreuse
½ oz. fresh lime juice
½ oz. fresh grapefruit juice
½ oz. house-made Raspberry Syrup

Add ingredients to mixing glass. Add ice and shake well. Strain into Old Fashioned glass filled with pellet or crushed ice. Garnish with grapefruit twist.

Created for a 2010 Cinco de Mayo event (and named for the famed Mexican artist Frida Kahlo), this crowd-pleaser is surprisingly not as sweet as it sounds, though it does hit on all cylinders. It's a great example for those who claim an aversion to tequila. You can also serve this up as a summertime predinner tipple.

FRUITS DE ROUGES *(Valentine's Day)* ∎ *Peacock Alley*

1¼ oz. Etter Zuger framboise eau-de-vie (raspberry brandy)
1 oz. Combier Crème de Fruits Rouges liqueur
¾ oz. fresh lemon juice
½ egg white

Add all ingredients to mixing glass and dry-shake for 5 seconds. Add ice and shake for 10 seconds. Fine-strain into chilled cocktail glass. Garnish with lemon peel.

This recipe was created for a Valentine's Day dinner to fulfill a guest's request for something that everyone would enjoy but that would still have the Waldorf Astoria stamp. This was accomplished by including the decidedly polarizing framboise eau-de-vie. Though this cocktail is easily prepared, its rustic aroma and profile make for quite the unique finish and let you know that you are drinking something special.

Crème de fruits rouges is a four-berry liqueur that has a unique profile. If it's unavailable, any good raspberry (framboise) liqueur or Cassis Liqueur can fill in admirably.

FULL HOUSE/WIDOW'S KISS

1½ oz. Boulard Grand Solage VSOP calvados
¾ oz. yellow Chartreuse
¾ oz. Bénédictine
2 dashes Angostura bitters

Add all ingredients to mixing glass. Add ice and stir for 30 seconds. Strain into chilled cocktail glass. Garnish with lemon peel.

Full House (Savoy Version)

1½ oz. Plantation 3 Stars white rum
¾ oz. Kronan Swedish punsch
¾ oz. Noilly Prat extra dry vermouth

Add all ingredients to mixing glass. Add ice and stir for 30 seconds. Strain into chilled cocktail glass. Garnish with lemon peel.

The *Full House* cocktail found in the Old Books cites equal portions of the three ingredients and calls for apple whiskey in the top slot. The first printed recipe, found in George Kappeler's *Modern American Drinks (1895),* called for the same ingredients but was named the *Widow's Kiss*. To slightly confuse things further, the *Widow's Kiss* found in the Old Books was a Pousse-Café with a beaten egg white and strawberry slice on top.

To sort this all out, I landed on the original *Widow's Kiss* build, but using equal portions resulted in a cocktail that was far too cloying. I gave the lead role over to a refined calvados. (I have served it in equal 1 oz. portions, but I presented it on the rocks and topped it with a couple of ounces of chilled club soda, garnished with a brandied cherry. I named it the **Winter Lowball** and it works surprisingly well.)

As for the Savoy variation, I included it here to avoid any confusion and because it is a far cry from the Waldorf version, though still delicious. Harry Craddock's complex cocktail is worth trying if only to decide which *Full House* you might prefer. As for the title of the cocktail, around the time of the publication of the Old Books, "full house" was the term used in the game of bridge for what we'd call a "grand slam."

FUTURITY

1½ oz. Plymouth sloe gin or Greenhook Ginsmiths beach plum liqueur
1½ oz. Martini & Rossi sweet vermouth
2 dashes Angostura bitters

Add all ingredients to mixing glass. Add ice and stir for 30 seconds. Strain into chilled cocktail glass. Garnish with lemon peel.

Blackthorn (Improved)

1½ oz. Plymouth gin
¾ oz. Plymouth sloe gin or Greenhook Ginsmiths beach plum liqueur
¾ oz. Martini & Rossi sweet vermouth
2 dashes Regans' Orange Bitters No. 6

Add all ingredients to mixing glass. Add ice and stir for 30 seconds. Strain into chilled cocktail glass. Garnish with orange peel.

Van Wyck

2 oz. Hayman's Old Tom gin
1 oz. Plymouth sloe gin or Greenhook Ginsmiths beach plum liqueur
1 dash Regans' Orange Bitters No. 6

Add all ingredients to mixing glass. Add ice and stir for 30 seconds. Strain into chilled cocktail glass. Garnish with lemon peel.

Like the **Floater** and **Suburban**, this cocktail of the Old Books was named for finance maven and stable owner James R. Keene. This is one not to overthink; just picture yourself at the racetrack clubhouse enjoying one of these and you'll be fine.

The shillelagh is cut from the blackthorn bush, whose fruit is the sloeberry, hence the Irish connection. At the Old Bar, the *Blackthorn* earned its name, as it was two-thirds sloe gin and one-third sweet vermouth. Although it's quite digestible at that ratio (you should try it), I always feel that a bit of backbone only helps, hence the Plymouth gin. Other recipes of the day included such varied ingredients as dry vermouth, Dubonnet, and kirschwasser. More robust varieties of vermouth only masked the delicate notes of the sloe gin, but as always, it's up to you. The similarly named **Black Thorn** dates back to the era of the Old Bar but is not included in either book. It's essentially an Irish whiskey–based dry *Robert Burns* with an absinthe rinse, a nice autumnal alternative.

The vermouth-less *Van Wyck* appears nearly as it did in the Old Books except for the orange bitters (which you can omit if you like). An alternate for Plymouth sloe gin is the unique beach plum liqueur from Greenhook Ginsmiths, in Brooklyn, New York, sourced from Long Island plums. If you sub in equal parts Plymouth gin and sloe or plum liqueur, you will have the **Sloe Gin Cocktail** (the original went with equal parts, but you won't want to). This was also known as a **Tyrone**. See **Arctic/Ardsley**, **Ping Pong**, and **Ruby** for variations.

GENERAL HENDRICKS

1 orange wedge (halved)
2 demerara sugar cubes (or 1 tsp. demerara sugar)
3 dashes Angostura bitters
2 oz. Baker's 107 proof bourbon
3 oz. chilled club soda

Add orange, sugar cubes, and bitters to Old Fashioned glass and muddle. Add whiskey and club soda. Fill with large ice cubes and stir briefly to integrate.

A precursor to the mid-twentieth-century version of the **Old Fashioned** (if you limit the soda), this enhanced *Rickey* earns its own entry because of the muddling of the fruit. Though it's quite the refresher in this form, I prefer an orange wedge to the original lemon called for in the Old Books, as orange pairs much more naturally with bourbon. Please do not use a syrup for the sugar component; the abrasiveness of the raw sugar when muddling gets the most out of the rind. I used overproof bourbon at the base because it more than held up to the soda and ice, which is imperative, as you know by now.

GIMLET *(Cordial)* ∎ Classic

2 oz. Greenhook Ginsmiths American dry gin
1 oz. Rose's lime juice cordial

Place both ingredients into mixing glass. Strain into chilled cocktail glass. Garnish with thinly sliced lime wheel.

GIMLET (Sour) ∎ Classic

2 oz. Greenhook Ginsmiths American dry gin
¾ oz. Simple Syrup
¾ oz. fresh lime juice

Place all ingredients into mixing glass. Add ice and shake well. Strain into chilled cocktail glass. Garnish with thinly sliced lime wheel.

This classic cocktail, invented in the mid-1800s as a way to combat scurvy (and a convenient way to get troops to drink lime juice), does not appear in either Old Book by the title of "Gimlet." It was listed as the **St. Peter** and remains extremely popular today. The real point of controversy is in which form one will take his or her lime: fresh or in cordial form. Peacock Alley bartenders will ask a guest's preference prior to serving. It's also notable that the *Cordial* variation is one of only a few cocktails in which the direction is to shake and not stir, though it lacks any real citrus or dairy. Shaking the cocktail aerates the sweetened cordial, making it a bit more potable. I personally prefer the *Sour* version; it's refreshing, classic, and pliable. As you may have noticed, you can sub in rum for the gin and you've got yourself the classic **Daiquiri**.

GINGER COLLINS ∎ Peacock Alley

2 oz. of Ginger and Lemongrass-Infused G'Vine Floraison Gin
(recipe follows)
¾ oz. fresh lemon juice
½ oz. Simple Syrup
½ egg white
1 oz. chilled club soda

Add all ingredients except club soda to mixing glass. Dry-shake for 5 seconds. Add ice and shake for 10 seconds. Strain into ice-filled Collins glass. Top with club soda. Garnish with brandied cherry.

½ c. peeled and chopped fresh ginger
12 lemongrass leaves, cleaned and chopped into thirds
1 750 ml. bottle G'Vine Floraison gin

Add all ingredients to large, airtight glass container. Seal and stir occasionally for 10 days. Double-strain and funnel back into bottle. Lasts up to 2 months.

The *Ginger Collins* is one of our most popular concoctions from the early days at Peacock Alley. This simple Sour caught on with such fervor, guests were requesting it in February. If you plan on featuring this for an event, I suggest preparing a large batch of fresh sour mix ahead of time (see "House-Made Recipes" chapter) for a 1:1 ratio of spirit and sour. It will make service much easier. As usual, you may adjust the amount of soda for your personal taste.

We now cultivate our own fresh lemongrass in our rooftop garden, which makes it very easy to highlight this as a late summer refresher. This is another recipe that Gaz Regan was kind enough to include in his classic *Bartender's Gin Compendium.*

GINGERBREAD MAN ▮ *Peacock Alley*

1½ oz. Vanilla Bean–Infused Plantation Original Dark Rum (recipe follows)
¾ oz. house-made Cinnamon Vodka
¾ oz. heavy cream
½ oz. Monin gingerbread syrup

Place all ingredients into mixing glass. Add ice and shake well. Fine-strain into chilled cocktail glass. Garnish with freshly grated nutmeg.

Split one whole vanilla bean lengthwise, scrape out seeds, and place bean and seeds in bottle. Agitate every other day for a week and begin to use.

This has been a holiday favorite at Peacock Alley for many years and is a fine Eggnog alternate. Guests order it even if I decide not to include it on our list around the holidays. Luckily, we prepare a stash of cinnamon-infused vodka every October, just for these seasonal touches.

GLOBETROTTER ▪ *Peacock Alley*

1½ oz. Banks 7 Golden Age dark rum
1 oz. Meletti amaro
1 oz. Lustau Don Nuño oloroso sherry

Add all ingredients to mixing glass. Add ice and stir briefly to integrate. Strain into Old Fashioned glass filled with large ice cubes or sphere. Garnish with orange peel.

This is one of my favorite sippers, and after developing it I realized that it could also be viewed as a Negroni variation. Either way, it's delicious and possesses a long and complex finish, and for those who partake in such things, it pairs extremely well with a cigar.

GOAT'S DELIGHT

1 oz. Hine VSOP cognac
1 oz. Etter Zuger kirsch brandy
½ oz. Torani or Giffard orgeat syrup
¼ oz. Pernod Original Recipe absinthe
½ oz. heavy cream

Place all ingredients into mixing glass. Add ice and shake well. Fine-strain into chilled cocktail glass. Garnish with brandied cherry.

Here is another Old Bar recipe that needed a modern interpretation. I ramped up the orgeat to help represent the sugar component. When I used the mere dash called for in the original recipe, the cocktail was bitter; when I added simple syrup to make up the difference, the almond component was lost. I also increased the cream component to a half ounce, as the original "spoon" got lost. This planted the cocktail firmly in the dessert drink camp, where I feel it belongs anyway (brandies of any kind sing out for postprandial consumption to me). It is now intriguingly worth a try.

GOODWIN PUNCH

2 oz. Wild Turkey 101 rye
¾ oz. fresh lime juice
½ oz. house-made Demerara Syrup
¼ oz. Lustau Don Nuño oloroso sherry

Place all ingredients into mixing glass. Add ice and shake well. Strain into Old Fashioned glass or Hoffman House goblet filled with ice cubes or sphere. Garnish with fresh seasonal fruit and freshly grated nutmeg.

I only meandered slightly from the original recipe here, subbing in demerara syrup for standard sugar, as it lends a toasted note that pairs so well with the rest of the ingredients.

According to Mr. Crockett, this was named for the supposedly philandering actor Nat C. Goodwin. Old Albert said the drink described the result of his many scrapes, and "of what Nat took, [rather] than what he gave." Whether Mr. Goodwin took more punches than he gave may never be known, but his namesake cocktail sure does pack one. See **Herald Punch** for variation.

GRASSHOPPER ∎ Classic

1 oz. Tempus Fugit crème de cacao
1 oz. Marie Brizard green crème de menthe
1½ oz. half and half

Add all ingredients to mixing glass. Add ice and shake well. Fine-strain into chilled cocktail glass. Garnish with mint leaf.

JADED GRASSHOPPER ❚ *Peacock Alley*

1 oz. house-made Vanilla Vodka or Stolichnaya vanilla vodka
1 oz. Drambuie liqueur
½ oz. Tempus Fugit crème de cacao
½ oz. Marie Brizard green crème de menthe
1 oz. heavy cream

Add all ingredients to mixing glass. Add ice and shake well. Strain into chilled cocktail glass. Garnish with chocolate curls or shavings.

Vanilla Vodka

Split one whole vanilla bean lengthwise, scrape out seeds, and place bean and seeds in bottle. Agitate every other day for a week and begin to use.

The *Grasshopper* is a post-theater classic that gets called for nightly once autumn arrives. For the record green and white crème de menthe are interchangeable, as are white and dark crème de cacao; the color is the only difference. You may also choose to shake with a few sprigs of mint leaves during preparation for an added level of complexity. If doing so, be sure to fine-strain. It's not necessary to fine strain the *Jaded Grasshopper* as the use and texture of chocolate shavings makes double straining redundant. In general, fine-straining cream-based cocktails ensures a luxuriously smooth trip across the palate.

The *Jaded Grasshopper* was created for the restoration of Peacock Alley in 2005. At the time, I had an idea for an expanded cocktail menu in which we would offer classic or forgotten cocktails alongside improved or ramped-up versions. This concept never made it to service because I wanted to feature the new cocktails that we were creating. I felt that if someone wanted a traditional *Grasshopper,* for instance, we could just make one. I must admit that no one ever orders a standard *Grasshopper* after trying the *Jaded* one. Happily, cocktail writer Stew Ellington was kind enough to include the *Jaded Grasshopper* in his very comprehensive 2012 book, *901 Very Good Cocktails.* See **Bradley-Martin** for variation.

GRENADINE FIZZ

1½ oz. chilled club soda
2 oz. Tanqueray Old Tom or London dry gin
¾ oz. fresh lemon juice
¾ oz. house-made Grenadine
¾ oz. half and half (or milk)

Add chilled club soda to small Collins or Fizz glass. Add remaining ingredients to mixing glass. Add ice and shake well. Fine-strain into prepared glass. Stir to integrate. No garnish.

I prepared and tested more than a few variations of this enhanced Fizz and settled on this version. London dry–style gin makes for a slightly drier rendition. The original recipe called for milk, but I opted for the heavier half and half, as it survives the Fizz treatment with ease. See *Fizz* for variations.

GROUNDHOG ▮ *Peacock Alley*

2 oz. Tapatio añejo tequila
½ oz. Marie Brizard white crème de cacao
½ oz. fresh lemon juice
2 dashes house-made Cocoa Bitters

Prepare rim on one side of cocktail glass with unsweetened cocoa powder (optional). Add all ingredients to mixing glass. Add ice and shake well. Strain into chilled cocktail glass. Garnish with orange peel.

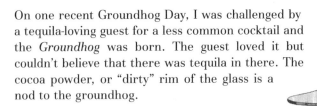

On one recent Groundhog Day, I was challenged by a tequila-loving guest for a less common cocktail and the *Groundhog* was born. The guest loved it but couldn't believe that there was tequila in there. The cocoa powder, or "dirty" rim of the glass is a nod to the groundhog.

GUION

1½ oz. Plymouth gin
1½ oz. Martini & Rossi sweet vermouth
1 dash Regans' Orange Bitters No. 6
⅓ oz. Bénédictine liqueur (for float)

Add all ingredients except Bénédictine to mixing glass. Add ice and stir for 30 seconds. Strain into chilled cocktail glass. Slowly pour Bénédictine over back of bar spoon onto surface of cocktail. Snap a lemon peel to release oils, then discard.

This **Martinez** variation with a final service flourish is a rediscovered cocktail if there ever was one. It was named for a family member of the Guion Line, a steamship company that dominated transatlantic transportation just prior to the time of the Old Bar; I'd say it's safe to assume they were revered guests of the Hotel.

As for the Bénédictine, this is not your typical float, as the heavy liqueur will sink to the bottom of the glass, but your confident use of a bar spoon to complete the presentation will surely wow your guests. See **Merry Widow** for variation.

HANCOCK SOUR/FIZZ

2 oz. chilled club soda
1½ oz. Old Grand-Dad bourbon
½ oz. Appleton Estate Reserve rum
¾ oz. fresh lime juice
½ oz. Simple Syrup
½ egg white

Add chilled club soda to small Collins glass. Add remaining ingredients to mixing glass. Dry-shake for 5 seconds. Add ice and shake well for 10 seconds. Strain into Collins glass. Stir briefly with bar spoon to integrate. Snap an orange peel to release oils, then discard.

This is called a "Hancock Sour" in the Old Books but is, by definition, a Fizz. Anyhow, this unique mash-up turns out to be quite versatile. Mr. Crockett wrote, "according to Bartender Johnnie Solan, this was named in memory of General Winfield Scott Hancock, famous Confederate veteran, who was the Democratic candidate for the Presidency of the United States away back in 1880."

I adapted this by pulling back on both the lime juice and sugar component, which offered more balance and harmony, and enabled both the bourbon and rum to come through. This also allows it to be served up as a *Sour* (without soda). Either way, it's a refreshing summer night's sipper.

HARVARD

1½ oz. Pierre Ferrand 1840 cognac
1 oz. Noilly Prat sweet vermouth
2 dashes Simple Syrup
2 dashes Angostura bitters
1 dash Regans' Orange Bitters No. 6
1 oz. chilled club soda (or Champagne, preferred)

Add all ingredients except club soda to mixing glass. Add ice and stir for 30 seconds. Strain into chilled cocktail glass. Top with club soda or Champagne. Garnish with lemon peel.

Kicking around since even before the opening of the Old Bar, this unique presentation was obviously a favorite of alumni and frequenters. Originally printed in George J. Kappeler's *Modern American Drinks* (1895), it had gone through a transformation since its peak in popularity. It evolved into an enhanced Highball by the 1950s when ex-Waldorf-Astoria publicist Ted Saucier included it in his cocktail collection, *Bottoms Up* (it works just fine that way—just add a touch more soda over ice).

The recipe listed here represents a slightly tweaked hybrid of all of them. The overproof cognac helps with the balance. I wouldn't use a more flavor-forward vermouth, as you will want the other ingredients and bitters to keep their identity. It's a great conversation piece; your guests will be sure to gasp as you pour soda water into their cocktail, but you'll know better and will use Champagne.

HARVEY WALLBANGER ▮ *Classic*

1½ oz. Tito's Handmade vodka
4 oz. fresh orange juice
¾ oz. Galliano

Add vodka and orange juice to ice-filled highball glass. Stir briefly to integrate. Float Galliano on top. Garnish with orange peel or wheel.

The Harvey Wallbanger became extremely popular in the late 1960s. Simple to make and easy to drink, this enhanced Screwdriver (vodka and OJ) was, for good or bad, one of the first wave of cocktails that leaned on its sugar components, and it led the way for the Blue Whales and Melon Balls to follow. It's rumored to have been invented by career barman Donato "Duke" Antone, who supposedly named the drink after a Manhattan Beach surfer who was a regular at Duke's Blackwatch Bar, in Hollywood. The story is most likely fictitious and the true origin lies in a marketing campaign, but I won't quibble, especially with a concoction that has lasted this long. The use of fresh orange juice makes it worth trying, anyway.

A couple of variations of my own have made it to a few Waldorf Astoria menus and events. If you include the strawberry and pink peppercorn–infused Galliano used in our *Peacock Alley Champagne Cocktail* (see *Champagne Cocktail*), you will have the **Shirley Wallbanger**. And once, for a German-themed event, the host requested German twists on classic cocktails and specifically included the Harvey Wallbanger as one to be "Germanized." So I topped a standard HW with the same amount of kümmel, a popular, caraway-flavored liqueur, in lieu of Galliano and the **Hanz Wallbanger** was born.

HERALD PUNCH

1½ oz. Bulleit rye whiskey
1¾ oz. fresh orange juice
¼ oz. house-made Demerara Syrup
2 dashes Regan's Orange Bitters No. 6
½ oz. Myers's rum (for float)

Add all ingredients except rum to mixing glass. Add ice and shake well. Strain into Old Fashioned glass or Hoffman House goblet filled with ice cubes or sphere. Top with rum. Garnish with seasonal fruit.

Mr. Crockett reported that this was a favorite of the old *New York Herald* newspaper staff who frequented the Old Bar. I can see why. I took the liberty of adding orange bitters for a bit of spine and added complexity; other than that, it survives the ages as is. See **Goodwin Punch** and **Jamaica Orange Cocktail** for variation.

1¼ Sailor Jerry spiced rum or homemade **Spiced Rum Infusion**
(recipe follows)

¾ oz Royer Force 53 VSOP
cognac

½ oz. Varnelli Punch alla
Fiamma liqueur

¾ oz. fresh lemon juice

½ oz. Simple Syrup

½ egg white

Add all ingredients to mixing
glass. Dry-shake for 5
seconds. Add ice and shake
for 10 seconds. Strain into
chilled cocktail glass. Garnish
with orange peel.

Spiced Rum Infusion

1 750 ml. bottle amber rum such as Ron del Barrilito 2 Star or
Cruzan dark.

1 vanilla bean, split

1 orange rind (preferably dried)

1 cinnamon stick

6 allspice berries

3 cloves

12 black peppercorns

1 whole nutmeg seed

¼ cup fresh ginger, julienned and crushed

Add all ingredients to an airtight glass container. Let stand for 7
days and taste. If you want a bit more flavor, remove cinnamon
stick and let rest for 3 more days. Fine-strain, then funnel back into
bottle. Best used within 6 months.

What started out as a riff on the classic **Between the Sheets** cocktail (one ounce each of white rum, cognac, and Cointreau with a
quarter ounce of lemon juice, stirred) quickly developed into something completely different. The Varnelli is a sweet herbal liqueur
that kind of tastes like Eggnog without the cream or maybe liquid

fruitcake. It's great around the holidays and blends seamlessly when combined with the spiced rum and cognac.

We use a house-made spiced rum but a commercial brand is fine here or even a dark unspiced version. Be adventurous. The same goes for the cognac. I used a full-flavored one but a lighter variety will allow the rum to shine. A wintertime treat that will be sure find its way into your regular rotation.

HONEY DEW

2 oz. Plantation Original Dark rum
½ oz. New York Distilling Company Perry's Tot navy-strength gin
½ oz. Cocchi Americano aperitif
½ oz. fresh lemon juice
½ oz. Simple Syrup

Add all ingredients to mixing glass. Add ice and shake well. Strain into chilled Old Fashioned glass or Hoffman House goblet filled with crushed or pellet ice. Garnish with orange wheel.

Why this was named the *Honey Dew* is beyond me and any subsequent research. What I can tell you is that it is surprisingly delicious and complex as far as drinks served on crushed ice go. The Old Bar's recipe simply directed the use of vermouth. I've tried it with both dry and sweet, but the Cocchi Americano brings much more to the table. It's a pretty pliable template. If you're using standard ice cubes, reduce the syrup or try it with dry vermouth.

HONOLULU

2 oz. Hayman's Old Tom gin
¼ oz. fresh lime juice
¼ oz. fresh orange juice
¼ oz. fresh pineapple juice
¼ oz. Simple Syrup
2 dashes Angostura bitters

Add all ingredients to mixing glass. Add ice and shake well. Strain into chilled cocktail glass. Garnish with lemon peel.

Honolulu No. 2 *(see Manhattan and Thompson for variations)*

Honolulu No. 3 *(à la Mr. Smith)*

2 oz. Bombay London dry gin
¾ oz. Pierre Ferrand dry curaçao
¼ oz. fresh lime juice
1 dash Angostura bitters
1 dash Regans' Orange Bitters No. 6

Add all ingredients to mixing glass. Add ice and stir for 30 seconds. Strain into chilled cocktail glass. Garnish with lemon peel.

Honolulu (Ensslin Variation)

1½ oz. Portobello Road No. 171 London dry gin
¾ oz. Bénédictine
½ oz. Luxardo maraschino liqueur

Add all ingredients to mixing glass. Add ice and stir for 30 seconds. Strain into chilled cocktail glass. Garnish with lemon peel.

I will begin by saying that the name Honolulu (and Hawaii, in some form or another) seems to have had a hold on pre-Prohibition bartenders. A whole hodgepodge of ingredients represent the *Honolulu* in various forms.

I took the liberty of including pineapple juice in the first version, as it appears in the recipe of *The Savoy Cocktail Book* (1930) and, more important, represents the defining indigenous ingredient. If you want to make the Old Bar variation (and if we are to believe that the transcription was not at fault), just omit the pineapple and add another quarter ounce of simple syrup. Either way, pre-batch the juice/syrup portion for larger gatherings and you have an easy three-ingredient summertime crowd-pleaser.

The *Honolulu No. 2* is an innocuous Manhattan variation. We can only wonder how or why it became attached to an island in the South Pacific, though one possibility is that either Mr. Crockett's interpretation or the actual Old Bar book got the association wrong; or that there was a pineapple wedge involved and it was a missing ingredient as in the *Thompson*, and this was actually meant to be listed as the *Honolulu No. 2,* or you can try them and hope to find out. Jacques Straub's 1914 version happens to be whiskey based, so there may be something to that. There are also post-Prohibition renditions that cite slightly modified (and unnecessary) gin-based versions that closely mirror the original. So there's that too.

As for the Honolulu No. 3 (à la Mr. Smith), the islands are still a stretch ingredient-wise, but at least it's warm-weather appropriate. In *Old Waldorf Bar Days,* this rendition is credited to a Mr. Smith. It's satisfyingly dry with a long finish. If you prefer yours a bit sweeter, sub in Cointreau or Grand Marnier for the dry curaçao. The original recipe did not include bitters of any kind, but I think they are essential. I'll leave it to your imagination to experiment, but I liked the aromatic and orange bitters combination. Peychaud's bitters were also interesting.

Finally, the *Honolulu (Ensslin Variation).* Although not included in any of the Old Bar books, this was the first version found in print, in *Recipes for Mixed Drinks* (1917), by German-born and New York–based barman Hugo Ensslin. It was originally equal parts of all ingredients (shaken with no garnish, and still way too syrupy), but I've revised it to appeal to the modern palate. Now it's a pleasing and balanced "sweet side" after-dinner drink.

HOP TOAD

1½ oz. Appleton white Jamaican rum
1 oz. Rothman & Winter orchard apricot liqueur
½ oz. fresh lime juice

Add all ingredients to mixing glass. Add ice and shake well. Strain into chilled cocktail glass. Garnish with brandied cherry.

WALDORF SPECIAL

1½ oz. Blume Marillen apricot eau-de-vie or Zwack Pecsetes Barack Palinka apricot brandy
1 oz. Combier Abricot liqueur
½ oz. fresh lime juice
2 dashes house-made Peach Bitters or The Bitter Truth Peach Bitters

Add all ingredients to mixing glass. Add ice and shake well. Strain into chilled cocktail glass. Garnish with orange peel (optional).

The Jamaican rum called for in the original recipe would probably have been aged in wood and brought that compromising component to the mix. You can try it if you like, but I think the full-flavored white rum does the job and pairs more suitably with the sweet liqueur. This also works with white rhum agricole. The key is that the rum has some funk but not the stamp of wood, which really does not blend with the lime (that's the culprit!). As for the liqueur, unlike peach brandy, which is a barrel-aged eau-de-vie, when apricot brandy is called for in recipes, it refers to the sweet, cordial variety. I used two different brands here, as each has a unique quality and varying amounts of sweetness, but any one you have around will do.

This cocktail is related to at least two others, the **Hop Frog**, which precedes this recipe in the Old Books (probably named for the Edgar Allan Poe short story) and is the bone-dry variant, with no sweet element at all. The *Hop Frog* is 2:1 lime juice to brandy. Save your juice (and brandy). The other version of note is the **Leaping Frog**, from Tom Bullock's *The Ideal Bartender*. Similar to the Hop Frog in dryness, this has a traditional (Hungarian) apricot brandy (an unsweetened apricot eau-de-vie) in a 2:1 ratio with lime juice, shaken and strained. This variation is only truly palatable if you add a sugar component.

Lastly, the Old Bar books listed a **Waldorf Frappé** but Jacques Straub's *Drinks* cited it as the **Waldorf Special**. I'm going with that, as any drink prepared and chilled with ice could be described as "frappéd," and because it is not served over crushed ice, which would also make it a Frappé. It also included Abricotine, a liqueur that is no longer imported. Using this as a springboard to create something unique, I used apricot eau-de-vie, an apricot-based distillate that, when paired with the apricot liqueur, adds some heft and a spine to this cocktail; I think it approximates the original intention. Although we could make some sort of apricot bitters easily enough, using another stone fruit–based bitters here suffices just fine. See **Charlie Chaplin** and **Yacht Club** for variations.

IDEAL

2 oz. Plymouth gin
1 oz. Cinzano Rosso sweet vermouth
¼ oz. fresh grapefruit juice

Add all ingredients to mixing glass. Add ice and stir for 30 seconds. Strain into chilled cocktail glass. Garnish with grapefruit peel.

ƎLOPPY JOE'ƒ CUBAN ADAPTATION

1.5 oz. Tanqueray London dry gin
1 oz. Noilly Prat extra dry vermouth
¾ oz. fresh grapefruit juice
½ oz. Simple Syrup
½ egg white (optional)

Add all ingredients to mixing glass. Add ice and shake well. Strain into chilled cocktail glass. Garnish with grapefruit peel.

To be honest, I did not hold out much hope for this recipe. I mean, grapefruit *and* sweet vermouth? But once I tried it, I could see why it could have been a specialty of the Old Bar. I would liken it to a brighter, sweet **Martini** with the juice taking on the role that bitters would (that's the reason for the stir). A deviation included in the Old Books substituted the juice for two dashes of grapefruit bitters, which resulted in a **Milo**.

Jack's Manual (1916), practiced a "perfect" rendition of the Old Bar's version, splitting the vermouth between sweet and dry. It didn't wow me.

There's another take in Hugo Ensslin's *Recipes for Mixed Drinks* (1917). It added a quarter ounce of maraschino liqueur, which would of course nudge this into the enhanced **Martinez** category. A nice addition for sure, but have a go at the unadorned version first.

In my opinion, the best step away from the Hotel's take is from Cuba's famous *Sloppy Joe's Bar Book* (1932). It's summertime turn is a real winner. One of the many drinks with a foot in both past and future. You will think that you can pour these all day (you can't!). My only twist on it would be the addition of a half ounce of egg white to lighten it to cloudlike heights.

ISLANDS IN THE STREAM ▮ *Peacock Alley*

2 oz. Banks 5 Island white rum or Plantation 3 Stars white rum
1 oz. St. Germain elderflower liqueur
¾ oz. fresh lime juice
2 dashes Regans' Orange Bitters No. 6

Add all ingredients to mixing glass. Add ice and shake well. Strain into chilled cocktail glass. Garnish with orange peel.

I adapted this Daiquiri variation on the fly for a television shoot that was taking place in the Hotel's Bull and Bear Prime Steakhouse about the time that St. Germain elderflower liqueur was being introduced in 2007. We had submitted cocktails for the show weeks earlier, but they unexpectedly required one more.

It's simply prepared yet complex on the palate; the secret (as always) is not letting the prominent floral/lychee flavor profile of the St. Germain take over the show. The orange bitters and twist add another layer of complexity. Feel free to experiment in the rum slot—this recipe can take it—though I tend to lean on these multi-island blends (hence the title). For an autumnal twist, I also like to infuse the rum with cubed Bosc and/or Bartlett pears for a week or so (use lemon juice, if going that way).

JACK ROSE

2 oz. Boulard Grand Solage VSOP calvados
½ oz. fresh lime juice
½ oz. house-made Grenadine

Add all ingredients to mixing glass. Add ice and shake well. Strain into chilled cocktail glass. No garnish.

ROYAL SMILE *(Peacock Alley Adapted Version)*

1¼ oz. Boulard Grand Solage VSOP calvados
¾ oz. Hayman's Old Tom gin
¾ oz. fresh lemon juice
½ oz. house-made Grenadine
1 dash Regans' Orange Bitters No. 6 (optional)

Add all ingredients to mixing glass. Add ice and shake well. Strain into chilled cocktail glass. Garnish with thin house-made **Dried Apple Chip**.

ROYAL SMILE *(Jacques Straub version)*

¾ oz. Boulard Grand Solage VSOP calvados
¾ oz. Noilly Prat extra dry vermouth
¾ oz. fresh lime juice
¾ oz. house-made Grenadine
½ egg white
1 dash Regans' Orange Bitters No. 6

Add all ingredients to mixing glass and dry-shake for 5 seconds. Add ice and shake well. Fine-strain into chilled cocktail glass. Garnish with orange peel.

Stories abound regarding the origin of this cocktail but even Mr. Crockett, bartender Joseph Taylor, and the other bartenders were pretty convinced they knew the simple truth. Despite a link to a racketeer of the same name whose court case made the headlines of the day, Crockett maintained that it was named for the Jacquemot Rose, whose pink color this cocktail's shade closely resembles. Once I sided with its French origin, replacing the American-made applejack was an easy call. Going with the more refined calvados gave me no choice but to have the good stuff shine. This recipe has published variants in terms of the juice as well. The Old Books required lime, so I went that way, though lemon works just as well. The lime also separates it from the closely related *Royal Smile*.

According to a 1910 *The Chef Magazine* banquet review, "The *Royal Smile* cocktail, lately introduced at the Astor, was part of the decoration, which also included pink roses." The original version included equal parts of each ingredient. In our Peacock Alley adaptation we have ramped up the calvados and switched out London dry gin for Old Tom gin. Substituting the Old Tom allows the calvados to do the heavy lifting, which I feel is the cocktail's intention. There is another interesting variation, from the mid-twentieth century, in which the gin is the star and the calvados takes the backseat. It became extremely popular and was known as the **Pink Lady**. A nice warm-weather variation.

In *Drinks*, Jacques Straub included dry vermouth in his Royal Smile and it plays much better with the directed equal portions than the original spirit-forward Waldorf version. I've added a dash of bitters, but this old-timer is still certainly the crowd-pleaser, one hundred years on.

JAMAICA ORANGE

1½ oz. Appleton Estate V/X rum
1 oz. Carpano Antica sweet vermouth
1½ oz. fresh orange juice
1 dash Regans' Orange Bitters No. 6
1 small pinch powdered cinnamon

Add all ingredients to mixing glass. Add ice and shake well. Strain into chilled cocktail glass. No garnish.

This sipper, made today with quality and fresh products, is quite the seasonal surprise. Although it's already complex, the inclusion of Carpano Antica, orange bitters, and the smallest pinch of ground cinnamon (which was included in the original recipe) adds another level. A delightful holiday-time alternative.

JAMAICA RUM

1½ oz. Appleton Estate Special white rum
½ oz. Tanqueray Rangpur gin (Tanqueray No. Ten, if unavailable)
⅓ oz. house-made Grenadine
⅓ oz. fresh orange juice
⅓ oz. fresh lemon juice
⅓ oz. fresh lime juice
2 dashes Regans' Orange Bitters No. 6

Add all ingredients to mixing glass. Add ice and shake well. Strain into chilled cocktail glass. Garnish with orange peel.

LANDER'S PUNCH

1 oz. Appleton V/X Jamaican rum
1 oz. Tanqueray Malacca gin or Tanqueray No. Ten gin
1 oz. Noilly Prat extra dry vermouth
½ oz. fresh lemon juice
½ oz. Demerara Syrup

Add all ingredients to mixing glass. Add ice and shake well. Strain into chilled Old Fashioned glass filled with large cubes or sphere. Garnish with freshly grated nutmeg and orange peel.

These adapted recipes will certainly become summertime staples. Tanqueray Rangpur, with its lime-forward profile, provides the perfect accompaniment to the other ingredients in the *Jamaica Rum Punch*. Lime or lemon juice was the called-for citrus component but using both along with orange juice adds complexity. Just combine the juices beforehand (the juice of one orange and two each of lemon and lime should do the trick). The grenadine can be adjusted for personal taste but the orange peel produces the first glorious jolt. I present this one served up as it was listed in the "Jamaican Jolifiers" chapter of the Old Bar book, though adding ice would solidify this as the Punch that it is. It works either way.

This is one of Mr. Crockett's Prohibition-era recipes, and with no sugar component, it made for quite the face-twister. I attempted many variations, including Bianco vermouth (aiming to avoid added sugar), white, darker and sweeter rums, gins of all kinds, etc., before finally landing on the listing above. You could use the three-juice mix here as well, but the nutmeg and orange peel make it happen.

JAPALAC

1½ oz. High West Rendezvous rye
1 oz. Noilly Prat extra dry vermouth
¾ oz. fresh orange juice
¼ oz. house-made Raspberry Syrup
1 dash Regans' Orange Bitters No. 6

Add all ingredients to mixing glass. Add ice and shake well. Strain into chilled cocktail glass. Garnish with orange peel.

This cocktail originated at the Old Bar, and as politically incorrect as it sounds, it was named for a commercially available additive that contained a Japanese-based chemical for improving the drying time of paint and varnish. It also helped launch "varnished" as a synonym for overindulgence.

The original recipe calls for equal parts whiskey and vermouth but a nudge to the rye side is a huge improvement, especially when using good, flavorful whiskey.

JAPANESE

2 oz. Royer VSOP cognac
¼ oz. Torani or Giffard orgeat syrup
4 dashes Dr. Adam Elmegirab's Boker's bitters or The Bitter Truth Jerry Thomas bitters

Add all ingredients to mixing glass. Add ice and stir for 30 seconds. Strain into chilled cocktail glass. Garnish with lemon peel.

Created by famed barman Jerry Thomas and first found in print in his *Bartenders Guide* (1862), this "big bang" sipper (and its variants) appeared in more than a few pre-Prohibition cocktail books. It's most likely named for the high-profile New York visits of Japanese statesman in the mid-1800s.

I prepared many different recipe mixes and variants, and though the Old Books' take on this formula made for a nicely enhanced cognac cocktail (using mere dashes of orgeat and bitters), it was Mr. Thomas's original, with its extra helping of each, that won out.

JITNEY

2 oz. Nolet's Silver gin
½ oz. fresh lemon juice
½ oz. fresh orange juice
¼ oz. Simple Syrup
½ egg white
2 dashes Regan's Orange Bitters

Add all ingredients to mixing glass. Dry-shake for 5 seconds. Add ice and shake well for 10 seconds. Strain into chilled cocktail glass. Garnish with orange peel.

According to Mr. Crockett, this one was named for the bus that was contracted "to take the place of Trolley Cars when drivers and conductors went on strike." I'm sure it cooled more than a few regulars off as they waited for the next bus.

I reached for Nolet's Silver gin, with its unique and floral flavor profile, to make this worthy of its own entry. The great thing about this basic Sour is that it's very adaptable and can handle almost any of your favorite spirits in the lead spot. For presentation, I personally prefer this one strained over fresh ice, on the rocks, in an Old Fashioned glass as a summertime crowd-pleaser.

JULEP/SMASH (Basic Recipe)

MINT JULEP

12 mint leaves and one large sprig saved for garnish
½ oz. Simple Syrup
2½ oz. Baker's 107 proof bourbon or other bonded bourbon

Add mint leaves (except mint for garnish) and simple syrup to
pewter Julep cup. Muddle briefly to release oils and aroma from
mint, being careful not to bruise. Pour in bourbon and stir to
integrate. Fill with pebble ice and churn to chill. Fill with more ice.
Smack mint sprig against palm of your hand to release essence,
and add as garnish. Garnish with powdered sugar (optional). Serve
with short silver straw. If you do not have a pewter or silver Julep
cup available, a Collins glass will do.

BRANDY SMASH

2 oz. Royer Force 53 VSOP cognac
½ oz. Simple Syrup
12 mint leaves and one sprig saved for garnish

Add all ingredients to mixing glass (except mint reserved for
garnish). Add ice and shake well. Fine-strain into wineglass or
Hoffman House goblet filled with crushed or pebble ice. Garnish
with mint sprig, orange wheel, brandied cherry, and/or seasonal
fruit.

Okay, here goes: *Juleps* originated primarily as medicinal elixirs in
the late 1700s, evolving into a cocktail from the American South
during the early 1800s. *Smashes* emerged soon after as a less complicated offshoot. It's named for the smashed mint that results from
the shaking and preparation of the cocktail. Though they both contain fresh herbal aromatics (most popularly mint), sugar, and spirit,
the *Smash* became its own category of drink primarily because of
two small but related differences: the method of construction and
the size. In terms of preparation, the *Smash* was usually shaken,
strained, and poured over fresh ice, while the *Julep* was built and
served in the same glass it was prepared in. In regard to size, the
Smash was generally made in a smaller portion than the Julep, de-

signed to be enjoyed quickly (considering its dilution upon preparation), whereas the *Julep* was meant to be savored a bit more slowly.

I think these differences matter less today; I'll take this opportunity to simplify this with a modern definition. Today's cocktail creators have many more paints on their palette than the barmen of the nineteenth century. Any embellishment on the *Julep* at all resulted in the *Smash*. With today's wide variety of available syrups, liqueurs, and craft ingredients, any *Julep* that contains anything other than some form of the ingredients mentioned in the basic recipe here, and that is shaken and not served in the glass that it was prepared in, relinquishes the title of *Julep* and falls under the general descriptor of a *Smash*. This simplifies things if one needs these things simplified. For clarity's sake, it's how I've listed such a cocktail on our menu and it makes for a consistent distinction between the two camps. See **Pineapple Smash** recipe on the next page.

As for the **Mint Julep** itself, cognac, rye whiskey, genever, and even rum were the early base spirits used to prepare it. If you're starting chronologically, the original recipe included cognac in the starring role, though its availability (and subsequent popularity) waned in no small part because of Europe's phylloxera epidemic, which destroyed more than two-thirds of its vineyards. This gave rise to the use of American whiskey as its substitute in general, most notably in the *Julep*. It wasn't until around the Civil War that bourbon came into the fold.

You can prepare it as they would have back then by placing the mint, along with a teaspoon of superfine sugar and one-third ounce of water, in the Julep cup and continue the recipe as listed here. It's nice to try, but the simple syrup makes for a much more consistent result. Adjust sugar as per personal taste.

Though a simple, whiskey-less **Champagne Julep** is listed in the Old Bar book, you can prepare it as in this recipe, with Champagne filling in for the bourbon for a low-alcohol, sweet, and minty Champagne cocktail. What I prefer is making a **Brandy Mint Julep** (the soft yet strong Pierre Ferrand 1840 cognac works well) and for a treat, top it with genuine Champagne. Not to worry, if you're preparing for a crowd, a dry cava or prosecco will most certainly do. There is a **Whiskey Mint Julep** cited in the Old Bar book, which stars rye whiskey (if you split it with cognac it becomes an early version of a *Mint Julep*). I would recommend a strong rye here (Wild Turkey 101 rye more than does the job). A **Presbrey** is a standard rye-based *Julep* topped with a half ounce of rum. A dark

Jamaican variant, such as Smith & Cross's, would have been the choice of the day.

A **Jamaican Mint Julep** is one with, you guessed it, Jamaican rum at its base (the full-bodied Appleton Estate 12 Year Old works great here or even the Smith & Cross navy-strength). The barmen at the Old Hotel added a ton of seasonal fruit to the top of this one along with the mint. Go for broke and sprinkle the whole thing with powdered sugar.

A **Georgia Mint Julep** is made with equal parts cognac and peach brandy (not to be confused with peach liqueur). This is a peach-based eau-de-vie that sees barrel aging. Some smaller craft distillers are now producing varieties of it, but I have included a handmade recipe to substitute if you are unable to procure one of them (see "House-Made Recipes" chapter). As for the recipe itself, I prefer my adaptation of 2:1 cognac to peach brandy ratio. If it's unavailable, a peach liqueur will work; just add a touch more brandy for balance and cut back on the syrup.

The Old Books list only two *Smashes* by name: the *Brandy Smash* described here, along with the **Whiskey Smash**, which would be prepared identically but with rye whiskey taking the lead. You could use bourbon for a sweeter version. Applejack, genever, and rum all make fine alternates, as does this following recipe. See **Cobbler** for variations.

Pineapple Smash ∎ *Classic*

2 oz. Bols genever or New York Distilling Company Chief Gowanus New Netherland gin

½ oz. house-made Raspberry Syrup

¾ oz. pineapple juice

½ oz. Noilly Prat extra dry vermouth or dry Riesling (optional)

12 mint leaves plus a mint sprig for garnish

Add all ingredients to mixing glass (except the mint for garnish and wine, if using). Shake well and fine-strain into a Hoffman House goblet (or wineglass) filled with shaved or pebble ice. Stir briefly with a bar spoon to integrate. Refill with more ice, then top with wine, if using. Garnish with mint sprig and pineapple wedge.

Inspired by Jerry Thomas's large-format *Pineapple Julep*, this is a tremendously refreshing summertime sipper. The vermouth (my preference) or a bone-dry Riesling does wonders for "drying it out," making resisting another slug nearly impossible. The Chief Gowanus is based on an early American recipe for Holland gin (genever). It's rye-based and sees a bit of time in the barrel, retaining its appropriate rustic qualities, making it perfect for a time-machine recipe such as this.

KING CHARLEƧ

1½ oz. Greenhook Ginsmiths Old Tom gin
½ oz. Luxardo maraschino liqueur
1 dash Regans' Orange Bitters No. 6
4 oz. chilled club soda

Add spirits and bitters to Collins glass. Fill with large ice cubes. Add chilled club soda and stir to integrate. Garnish with orange peel, lemon peel, and brandied cherry.

This home-grown favorite was most certainly popular in the Old Bar, if not the survivor it could have been. This is a fine summertime Cooler that is flexible enough to take some personal tinkering. The original recipe called for a standard unaged Old Tom gin but the aged variety added a noticeable complexity to the final result. It also called for more maraschino, which proved too much for me. The half ounce here does the job. The Old Bar book did not include bitters of any kind, but I like a dash of orange, or you could sub in or add a couple of dashes of rhubarb bitters for another unique and refreshing twist. See **Cooler/Highball** for variations.

KINGSTON

2 oz. Appleton Estate Reserve rum
½ oz. Combier kümmel liqueur
¼ oz. St. Elizabeth allspice dram (or The Bitter Truth pimento dram)
1 oz. fresh orange juice
¼ oz. fresh lemon juice

Add all ingredients to mixing glass. Add ice and shake well. Fine-strain into chilled cocktail glass. Garnish with brandied cherry.

Although not exactly the best-known classic of its era, the *Kingston* is a great example of how adventurous some of the old bartenders could be, especially considering their much smaller selection of products compared to what we have available today. It does appear by name in *The Savoy Cocktail Book*, so it had some sort of global audience.

It has a unique flavor profile thanks to the combination of the caraway-flavored kümmel and cherry-based maraschino liqueur. I've added the touch of lemon juice for a bit of grip, but you could use a couple of dashes of acid phosphate or try it without, as they did at the Old Bar. See **Rum Punch** for variation.

KNICKERBOCKER PUNCH

2 oz. Cruzan dark rum
½ oz. Pierre Ferrand dry curaçao
½ oz. Simple Syrup (house-made Raspberry Syrup, optional)
¾ oz. fresh lemon juice
½ oz. Bordeaux Supérieur dry red wine (for float)

TRADITIONAL SERVING:

Squeeze juice from half of a lemon (omit additional juice) and drop rind in mixing glass. Add remaining ingredients and fill with ice cubes. Roll contents 4 to 6 times between mixing glass and shaker, then pour entire contents into Old Fashioned glass or Hoffman House goblet. Float the red wine. Garnish with seasonal fruit.

MODERN SERVING:

Add all ingredients to mixing glass. Add ice and shake well. Strain into Old Fashioned glass or Hoffman House goblet filled with ice cubes or sphere. Float the red wine. Garnish with seasonal fruit.

WALDORF-ASTORIA "JAMAICAN" VARIATION

2 oz. Appleton Estate Reserve rum
¼ oz. house-made Grenadine
½ oz. fresh lime juice
½ oz. fresh orange juice
1 dash Dale DeGroff's pimento bitters or St. Elizabeth allspice dram

Add all ingredients to mixing glass. Add ice and shake well. Strain into Old Fashioned glass or Hoffman House goblet filled with crushed or pellet ice. Garnish with seasonal fruit.

WALDORF-ASTORIA COLLINS VARIATION

2 oz. Rémy Martin 1738 Accord Royal cognac
½ oz. house-made Demerara Syrup
¾ oz. fresh lemon juice
2 dashes Angostura bitters
2 oz. chilled club soda

Add all ingredients except club soda to mixing glass. Add ice and shake well. Strain into Collins glass filled with large ice cubes and top with club soda. Garnish with lemon peel.

The *Knickerbocker Punch* is one of the earliest drink recipes on record, first seen in print in the mid-1800s. The Old Bar had two other separate variations and I've listed them here. Named for the famed club, the traditional *Knickerbocker Punch* called for St. Croix rum but any amber rum of your choice will do here. As for the execution, I've listed two ways; for a third variation, pour the shaken contents directly into the glass. Though it may have been done that way historically, soon enough it makes for a watery drink, especially if you're enjoying it outdoors in the summer. "Rolling" it makes for a distinctly thinner profile but is certainly in line with the recipes of the day and definitely worth a try. The classic shake-and-strain served over large ice cubes will be the winner and crowd-pleaser. The Hotel's twist added a float of dry red wine, **Brunswick**- or **New York Sour**–style. It helps dry it out and adds complexity.

The Jamaican rendition uses two juices and I thought a bit of allspice would center it geographically. They served it over crushed ice at the Old Bar, though cubes work as well.

Both of these drinks were garnished seasonally with berries, pineapple, orange slices, cherries, etc. Feel free to do the same, as this will add to the wow factor for your guests.

The Old Books also list a **White Lion** recipe (which first appears in *Jerry Thomas' Bartenders Guide*), which is essentially the classic Punch version listed here using Jamaican rum as the base, though other variations of the time replace the raspberry syrup with standard simple syrup. I suggest sticking with the raspberry. They served theirs over crushed ice and you can as well. All omit the wine float, which was a Waldorf-Astoria specialty maneuver.

LALLA ROOKH

> **1 oz. Giffard Vanille de Madagascar liqueur**
> **¾ oz. Appleton Estate Reserve rum**
> **¾ oz. Pierre Ferrand Ambre cognac**
> **1 oz. heavy cream**

Add all ingredients to mixing glass. Add ice and shake well. Fine-strain into chilled cocktail glass. Garnish with grated nutmeg.

FIZZ VARIATION (JACQUES STRAUB)

> **2 oz. chilled club soda**
> **1 oz. Giffard Vanille de Madagascar liqueur**
> **½ oz. Appleton Estate Reserve rum**
> **½ oz. Pierre Ferrand Ambre cognac**
> **1 oz. heavy cream**
> **¼ oz. fresh lemon juice**
> **¼ oz. fresh lime juice**

Add chilled club soda to small Collins glass. Add remaining ingredients to mixing glass. Add ice and shake well. Strain into Collins glass. Stir briefly to integrate. Snap orange peel to release oils, then discard.

Named for Sir Thomas Moore's 1817 narrative poem of the same name and first making its appearance in this form in George Kappeler's

Modern American Drinks (1895), this is quite the knockout. Easy drinking but it packs a wallop!

Jacques Straub's 1914 version is a Fizz rendition and very much worth trying. The original called for lime juice. I tried both and couldn't decide, so I went the way of the *Ramos Gin Fizz* and used both.

THE LAST DROP ▪ *Peacock Alley*

2 oz. Citadelle Réserve barrel-aged gin
¾ oz. fresh lemon juice
½ oz. Simple Syrup
¼ oz. Mathilde cassis (black currant) liqueur

Add all ingredients to mixing glass. Add ice and shake well. Strain into chilled cocktail glass. Drip cassis into center of drink, causing it to pool at bottom of glass. No garnish.

The Citadelle Reserve gin is a unique barrel-aged item. If it's unavailable, I would use 1½ ounces of standard dry gin and add a half ounce of Ransom Old Tom gin. The memorable aspect of this cocktail is the cassis, which makes for a last sip that's completely different from the first. A huge summertime hit at Peacock Alley, this recipe was included in Gaz Regan's *Bartender's Gin Compendium*. See **Princeton** for variation.

LAWYER'S REVENGE

2 large swaths orange peel
½ oz. Sacred extra dry vermouth
3 oz. Quinta do Noval 10 Year Old tawny port
2 oz. San Pellegrino mineral water

Twist orange peels into Old Fashioned glass and add vermouth. Muddle briefly to extract oils from peels, then add large ice cubes or sphere. Pour in port wine and top with mineral water. Stir to integrate.

This time traveler makes for quite the afternoon sipper. The original version called for the peels to be muddled in a bit of sugar and water, but it was too sweet for me. The dry vermouth is successful in remedying that issue, especially if you're using a bone-dry and multifaceted one such as Sacred. It adds to the complexity of the cocktail and makes it memorable. Try it both ways. If Sacred dry vermouth is unavailable, you may want to add a dash of orange bitters to get closer to its flavor profile. As for the style of port wine, the standard would have been of the ruby variety, but whenever I have the chance, especially when the wine is the star, I prefer tawny. Again, have some fun and try both. As for the title, this lunchtime treat was probably consumed during long meetings in the Old Bar. Whether the revenge came in the form of the bar tab or invoice is unknown.

LE COOKED GOOSE ∎ *Peacock Alley*

2 oz. Grey Goose vodka
1 oz. fresh lime juice
¾ oz. Smoked Paprika Syrup (recipe follows)
1 dash Dale DeGroff's pimento bitters

Add all ingredients to mixing glass. Add ice and shake well. Strain into chilled cocktail glass. No garnish.

SMOKED PAPRIKA SYRUP

1 c. white sugar
8 oz. water
1 tbsp. smoked paprika

Add all ingredients to saucepan. Simmer for 3 to 5 minutes or until integrated. Let cool and refrigerate. Lasts up to one month.

This one was created with the bar staff for a special partnership with Grey Goose vodka as a "Martini Week" specialty for charity. It's pretty complex as far as these things go, but it really took on its own identity with the addition of the pimento bitters.

A unique alternative to vodka is white rhum agricole (Rhum Clément 80 proof works nicely), but if you'd really like to test the boundaries of your smoked paprika syrup, prepare this with a "wheated" bourbon such as Larceny or Maker's Mark for another level entirely. Serve on the rocks for a nice pairing with barbecue.

LEMON MERINGUE PIE | *Peacock Alley*

1 oz. Crop organic lemon vodka
1 oz. Stolichnaya vanilla vodka
¾ oz. Toschi limoncello
¼ oz. fresh lemon juice
½ oz. Simple Syrup
½ oz. heavy cream
½ egg white
1 dash The Bitter Truth Lemon Bitters or Regans' Orange Bitters No. 6

Add all ingredients to mixing glass. Dry-shake for 5 seconds. Add ice and shake well for 10 seconds. Strain into chilled cocktail glass. Garnish with lemon zest and crushed graham cracker.

Sometimes the requests for cocktails come from left field. This one was requested for a charity event in which the guest's idea was to have NYC pastry chefs submit desserts and have NYC bartenders pair each one with a liquid version. I drew the lemon meringue pie. Though the recipe isn't out of the ordinary, the combination of ingredients and the garnish is what brings this home. The tart lemon zest and crushed graham cracker paired with the creaminess of the egg white and dairy make for a unique texture and long finish. To prepare the graham cracker, just place a couple of crackers in a resealable plastic bag and smash with the palm of your hand or a wooden spoon until pulverized. You can use this method to garnish most any cream-based drink with crushed cookies for a unique presentation.

LIBERAL

1½ oz. Jim Beam Pre-Prohibition Style rye whiskey
1½ oz. La Quintinye Vermouth Royal Rouge
¼ oz. Bigallet China-China Amer

Add all ingredients to mixing glass. Add ice and stir for 30 seconds. Strain into chilled cocktail glass. Garnish with lemon peel and brandied cherry.

Ted Saucier's Bottoms Up Version

2½ oz. Johnny Drum Private Stock 100 proof bourbon
¼ oz. Bigallet China-China Amer
¼ oz. maple syrup
1 dash Regans' Orange Bitters No. 6

Add all ingredients to mixing glass. Add ice and stir for 15 seconds to integrate. Strain into chilled Old Fashioned glass filled with large ice cubes or sphere. Garnish with lemon peel.

An enhanced Manhattan, the original *Liberal* cocktail actually pre-dates the Old Waldorf-Astoria Bar, as it is first found in print in 1895 (the Old Bar didn't open until 1897). It omits vermouth entirely, sharing the portions equally between the rye whiskey and Amer. It works better with a 2:1 ratio, on the rocks. Another recipe from the turn of the nineteenth century uses equal parts of all ingredients with the addition of a quarter ounce of absinthe. Though it's worth a try, I would just add a couple of dashes to the recipe listed here. The dry vermouth version, enhanced with additional maraschino liqueur, is the classic **Brooklyn** cocktail.

A related cocktail found in the Old Books is the **Monahan Special**. It was named after Mike Monahan, its adapter and an Old Bar barkeep. Just use a 2:1 ratio of whiskey to vermouth, the same amount of Amer, and omit the bitters. It's worth a try, but keep the bitters and it may be the best of them all, though it inches ever closer to the modern Manhattan.

The newly released La Quintinye Vermouth Royal Rouge is a singular item with a huge cocoa finish, kind of like the anti–Carpano Antica (with its vanilla-leaning profile). It stands out here and helps give this recipe its own identity.

There is a **Cuban Liberal** in the Old Books, which is also worth sampling. Just use a good, dark, full-bodied rum in place of the rye for best results (and although it's not Cuban in origin, I personally like an aged rhum agricole. Its dry flavor profile makes for the most balanced result).

In *Bottoms Up,* Waldorf-Astoria press manager Ted Saucier had a sweeter bourbon version. Removing the vermouth and somehow finding room for maple syrup in the recipe and after much trial and error, I settled on the method described.

LLAMA ∎ *Peacock Alley*

1½ oz. Pisco 100 Acholado pisco (Peru)
1 oz. Giffard Pamplemousse Rose liqueur
1 oz. Wölffer rosé wine or any Provence-style rosé
½ oz. fresh lemon juice
2 dashes The Bitter Truth grapefruit bitters

Add all ingredients to mixing glass. Add ice and shake well. Strain into chilled cocktail glass. Garnish with grapefruit peel.

This unique and refreshing summer cocktail can also be prepared as a bowled Punch for a surefire crowd-pleaser (you can double the wine portion). The dry, light-bodied rosé makes this an airy sipper, while the grapefruit liqueur adds contrast to the floral notes of the wine. A new go-to summer tradition in the making.

LOENSKY COCKTAIL ∎ *Peacock Alley*

2 oz. Chivas Regal 12 Year Old blended Scotch whisky
¾ oz. Noilly Prat extra dry vermouth
¼ oz. Combier kümmel liqueur
1 dash Regans' Orange Bitters No. 6

Add all ingredients to mixing glass. Add ice and stir for 30 seconds. Strain into chilled cocktail glass. Garnish with lemon peel.

This recipe is based on the Loensky Pousse-Café-style post-dinner tipple. The ingredients worked so well in that form that I thought that with a bit of tinkering, something of wide appeal with a modern twist could be created.

The original sees three-quarters of an ounce of kümmel poured into a one-ounce pony glass, then topped with a touch of blended Scotch. The new adaptation reverses the roles, which results in a tangy and unique medium-dry Rob Roy variation. I use only a quarter ounce of kümmel when enjoying one myself, but you could easily change the liqueur and vermouth to a half ounce each for a richer result. Either way, this type of cocktail sits firmly in my personal wheelhouse, so I'd place this at the top of my newfound-favorites list. I hope you will as well.

LOVE

1½ oz. Berry Bros. & Rudd No. 3 London dry gin
1½ oz. Carpano Antica sweet vermouth
½ egg white

Add all ingredients to mixing glass. Dry-shake for 5 seconds. Add ice and shake well for 10 seconds. Fine-strain into chilled cocktail glass. Snap orange peel to release oils, then discard.

SOUL KISS (WALDORF-ASTORIA VERSION)

2 oz. Hayman's Old Tom gin
1 oz. Noilly Prat extra dry vermouth
½ egg white

Add all ingredients to mixing glass. Dry-shake for 5 seconds. Add ice and shake well for 10 seconds. Fine-strain into chilled cocktail glass. Snap orange peel to release oils, then discard.

SOUL KISS (JACK GROHUSKO VERSION ▌ 1916)

1½ oz. Byrrh Grand quinquina aperitif
¾ oz. Rittenhouse bonded rye whiskey
¾ oz. Noilly Prat extra dry vermouth
½ oz. fresh orange juice
1 dash Horsford's acid phosphate

Add all ingredients to mixing glass. Add ice and shake well. Strain into chilled cocktail glass. Garnish with orange peel.

Oh, what a little egg white can do. At the end of the day, this frothy Martini variation takes the cake when it comes to being more than the sum of its parts. On paper, it may not look like much, but each ingredient plays its role. The original recipe of the *Love* called for Old Tom gin but resulted in a cocktail that veered a little too close to the sweet side. The London dry keeps things in order. This is one of the Waldorf-Astoria's original cocktails that we may have to fall in love with all over again. A similar cocktail, later listed as the **White Elephant**, uses a 2:1 ratio of gin to vermouth. If you go that way, utilize an Old Tom gin. It will make for a softer cocktail. I can recommend trying both.

Another listed variation is the *Soul Kiss*, named for a saucy musical comedy of the time. This adaptation flips the base gin again, using Old Tom where London dry was called for because of the inclusion of dry vermouth. If you use equal parts, you'll have what the Old Books called a **Tango**. Feel free to add a dash of simple syrup for a bit of balance if you like, though it's more than fine without. The lack of bitters helps retain their identity, though you may add a drop if you like.

Another more referenced rendition from the days of the Old Bar is from *Jack's Manual* (1916); it takes its adoration in another direction entirely. Whereas our *Love* and *Soul Kiss* seem to be squarely related, this aromatized wine–based cocktail has its heart in another place. I took the liberty of adding a dash of acid phosphate for a bit of backbone, as orange juice is in perpetual need of one. If you have run out of acid phosphate, a dash of lemon juice will do the trick.

LUCKY NUMBER ∎ *Peacock Alley*

1½ oz. Maker's 46 whiskey or Stranahan's Colorado whiskey
¾ oz. Lustau Don Nuño oloroso sherry
½ oz. Château Petit Guiraud Sauternes
¼ oz. fresh lemon juice
1 bar spoon Bonne Maman orange marmalade

Add ingredients to mixing glass. Add ice and shake well. Fine-strain into chilled cocktail glass. Garnish with orange peel.

This cocktail was originally created for the release of the first line extension of Maker's Mark (Maker's 46—though Stranahan's Colorado whiskey makes for a unique finish as well). The toasted notes of the sherry and marmalade harmonize perfectly and the end result brings to mind cool autumn days. As for the Sauternes, any table or entry label will do. You do not need your best, just something that you can drink on its own.

We serve this with a candied orange peel prepared by our executive pastry chef Charlie Romano and his staff, but a fresh twist of orange peel will more than do the job. You can enjoy this presented up or with a large ice cube or two.

MACAROON ∎ *Peacock Alley*

1½ oz. Żubrówka bison grass vodka
1 oz. Pierre Ferrand Pineau des Charentes
½ oz. Luxardo amaretto
½ oz. fresh pineapple juice
2 dashes (or ⅛ oz.) Combier kümmel liqueur
2 oz. chilled club soda

Add all ingredients except club soda to mixing glass. Add ice and shake well. Strain into Collins glass filled with ice cubes. Top with club soda. Stir briefly to integrate. Garnish with toasted shredded coconut. (Toast shredded coconut in pan over medium heat, stirring frequently for three to five minutes until toasted. Allow to cool and store in airtight container.)

In an effort to fill a request for a macaroon-themed summer wedding, I opted to forgo the easy but seasonably unsuitable cream-based, pastel-colored dessert drink for this unique refresher instead. The bison grass–infused vodka has a natural coconut note to it that lent a subtle flavor without screaming it. Pineau des Charentes is a classic French fortified wine that brings complexity and some sweetness to the mix. Though not traditional, the pineapple element makes it familiar, the kümmel makes it unique, and the toasted coconut brings it all home. The bride blushed.

2 oz. Pierre Ferrand Ambre cognac
½ oz. fresh lime juice
½ oz. house-made Grenadine

Add all ingredients to mixing glass. Add ice and shake well. Strain into chilled cocktail glass. Garnish with orange peel.

This cocktail, named for the frisky, early twentieth-century actress and sex symbol, is found in Oscar Tschirky's *100 Famous Cocktails* (1934). There are other cocktails that bear her name but this one most closely resembles the formula for namesake cocktails of the day (see **Charlie Chaplin**). They all include a strong base ingredient, citrus, and a sugar component, usually in the form of a liqueur. As far as these things go, the *Mae West* delivers. I usually prefer lighter and more floral cognacs for cocktail use and would steer clear of full-bodied brandies, as they would dominate here.

A similar recipe that was also a favorite of Tschirky's was his **Martell Cocktail**, which substituted honey syrup for the grenadine. Again, try it with a lighter-bodied cognac so the honey can shine through. Finally, you can substitute lemon juice for the lime; just reduce the sweetener by half for a more balanced result and **Sidecar** alternate.

MAI TAI ∎ *Classic*

1 oz. Appleton Estate Reserve Jamaican rum
1 oz. Rhum J.M VSOP agricole
1 oz. fresh lime juice
½ oz. Pierre Ferrand dry curaçao or Marie Brizard orange curaçao
½ oz. Torani or Giffard orgeat syrup
1 dash Angostura bitters

Add all ingredients to mixing glass. Add ice and shake well. Strain into Old Fashioned glass filled with crushed or pellet ice. Garnish with mint sprig.

Most commonly credited to Bay Area tiki restaurateur "Trader" Vic Bergeron (or another local restaurant legend, Don the Beachcomber; sometimes neither), this summertime staple is often requested by our guests. Early recipes included a Jamaican rum that is no longer produced, but just as Trader Vic did, we add the funky rhum agricole at Peacock Alley. I like the complexity that it and the dry curaçao bring to the table. Standard curaçao is a touch sugary but might appeal to those with a bit of a sweet tooth. This one goes easy on the garnish, as the fresh mint's aroma adds more than enough to this complex offering, though you can add a twist of an orange peel if you'd like. See *Fog Cutter* for variation.

MANHATTAN

2 oz. Rittenhouse bonded rye whiskey
1 oz. Cinzano Rosso sweet vermouth
2 dashes Angostura bitters

Add all ingredients to mixing glass. Add ice and stir for 30 seconds. Strain into chilled cocktail glass. Garnish with brandied cherry (or lemon peel).

By most accounts, the *Manhattan* cocktail predates the Waldorf-Astoria Hotel by at least twenty years, but vermouth as a cocktail ingredient was reaching its peak by the time of the Old Bar. In my opinion, all New Yorkers should be proud of this New York City creation. It is one of the first to soften the original *Cocktail* by tempering it with vermouth and, by doing so, ensuring its longevity as a nightly tipple. As with most of the first editions of these types of cocktails, the vermouth was added in equal portion with the base spirit or even in reverse proportion to today's *Manhattan*. I have adapted it here with the modern presentation and palate in mind.

The best renditions are those made with rye whiskey as the base. The higher the proof, the better. Bourbon works fine; just be sure to use a strong one, as it will help the naturally sweeter style of the whiskey stand up to the vermouth and bitters. I prefer 2:1 ratio of whiskey to vermouth, but it is product dependent. Raising the spirit portion up a quarter to half an ounce is recommended when using a whiskey with less alcohol or utilizing a fuller-flavored vermouth such as Punt e Mes.

As for the bitters, I like some variety here. In the winter, aromatic bitters are my choice, whereas I'll choose the orange variety for a predinner drink on a warm evening. Yes, you will notice a difference. Our culinary director, David Garcelon, insists on aromatic bitters all year round, and I wouldn't argue, but the choice remains yours. You can even use both. I won't tell. As with the *Old Fashioned*, just by altering the bitters, you can enjoy a slightly different cocktail every day. (See bitters recommendations in "Bitters" section.)

Much has been made over the final garnish of a proper *Manhattan,* so I will just say this: life is short—go for broke and twist a lemon peel over the drink and drop a brandied cherry in it. Now you have it.

In the Old Books, variations are as plentiful as you want. Direct descendants include the **Manhattan No. 2**, which uses Irish whiskey as its base and a pinch of sugar (see *Rob Roy* for variation) and another favorite of mine, the **Cuban Manhattan**, in which we use Bacardi 8 Year Old dark rum with orange bitters and a twist for remarkable results (also listed as the **Palmetto** in the Old Books, which used a St. Croix rum; Cruzan Estate Diamond dark rum will work great here but any full-bodied rum will do). The apple brandy–based version is called a **Marconi Wireless** and it's a favored variation once autumn rolls around. It was named for Nobel Prize–winning Italian engineer Guglielmo Marconi and his famous radio transmitter (which was the first to send signals across the Atlantic Ocean). Though the device did not survive, recent surveys of cocktail lists prove that this recipe has. I really like the 7$^{1}/_{2}$ Year Old expression of Laird's apple brandy (it is, more or less, American calvados). If it's unavailable, go with a calvados proper.

The Old Books include **Star** and **Normandie** cocktails (names for an old Broadway hotel), both of which are composed of equal amounts of apple brandy and vermouth. The defining characteristic of the fruit gets lost in these; I recommend sticking with this version. Thanksgivings will never be the same.

Lastly, by far the most famous rendition of all is the Manhattan's Scotch whisky brother, the **Rob Roy**.

Dry Manhattan

2 oz. WhistlePig 10 Year rye whiskey
1 oz. Dolin de Chambery dry vermouth
2 dashes Regans' Orange Bitters No. 6

Add all ingredients to mixing glass. Add ice and stir for 30 seconds. Strain into chilled cocktail glass. Garnish with lemon peel.

There are two Beadleston cocktails, both named for a local brewer who supplied the Old Bar with much of its beer. Research for these cocktails unearthed the existence of a Dougherty's Private Stock whiskey, which could be the "Private Stock Whiskey" called for in the *Old Waldorf Bar Days* recipe. This is an extinct Pennsylvania bonded rye, aged thirteen years, and is probably best simulated by the currently available ten-year-old WhistlePig rye. The **Beadleston No. 1** called for equal parts whiskey and dry vermouth and is worth a try (see **Manhattan Junior**). The lemon peel is my idea—it seems to tie the room together. See **Rob Roy** for **Beadleston No. 2**.

The basic *Dry Manhattan* recipe here was used for the **Brown University** and the **Rosemary** cocktails (named for the Broadway production, it was invented for the cast party to celebrate the 1897 opening of the play held at the Old Hotel), save for the inclusion of bourbon instead of rye as the base spirit, and the omission of bitters. I recommend using an orange peel as the garnish when using bourbon, and include orange bitters anyway. If nothing else, you now know that the *Dry Manhattan* has an original name (or two).

Perfect Manhattan

2 oz. Knob Creek straight rye whiskey
¾ oz. Noilly Prat extra dry vermouth
¾ oz. Cinzano Rosso sweet vermouth
2 dashes Regans' Orange Bitters No. 6

Add all ingredients to mixing glass. Add ice and stir for 30 seconds. Strain into chilled cocktail glass. Garnish with lemon peel.

The **Perfect Manhattan** is also listed as **Honolulu No. 2** in the Old Books. How or why that connection was made remains a mystery, but I will chalk it up to a poor recipe transcription by a bartender or a misinterpretation on the part of Mr. Crockett. More obvious is that this is the seasoned veteran's *Manhattan* of choice, and for good reason. Complex yet very sippable, it makes for a fine cocktail on any occasion. Again, higher-proof whiskey is the key, and bourbon works well here too. You could also ratchet up the lead spirit by a half ounce if using a less robust whiskey. See **Thompson** for variation.

Manhattan Junior

1½ oz. Rittenhouse bonded rye whiskey
1½ oz. Carpano Antica sweet vermouth

Add ingredients to mixing glass. Add large ice cubes and stir for 30 seconds. Strain into a chilled cocktail glass. Garnish with orange peel.

The ratios for this *Manhattan Junior* are the same as those in the first printed version of the cocktail (though it also included a couple of dashes each of gum syrup and aromatic bitters). Mr. Crockett's instructions clearly state, "No Bitters," but I prefer to follow this recipe to the letter and exclude them only if using Carpano Antica, Punt e Mes, or another full-flavored sweet vermouth. If you find yourself with a more restrained vermouth, adding a couple of dashes of bitters will make for a much more interesting and balanced result.

1860 Manhattan ∎ *Peacock Alley Variation*

2 oz. Elijah Craig 12 Year Old single-barrel bourbon
1 oz. Noilly Prat sweet vermouth
¼ oz. Pierre Ferrand dry curaçao (or Luxardo maraschino liqueur)
2 dashes Angostura bitters

Add all ingredients to mixing glass. Add ice and stir for 30 seconds. Strain into chilled cocktail glass. Garnish with brandied cherry.

One of our most popular cocktails, the *1860 Manhattan* has the distinction of being on the menu since Peacock Alley's restoration in 2005. Our take on the Manhattan is based on early recipes of the era that added accoutrements to their cocktails. Some had the ingredient ratio reversed, with vermouth taking the lead role. Some added gum syrup (see "Syrups"), curaçao, or maraschino as flavor enhancers. To adapt for a modern palate, we leaned toward the orange, since, believe it or not, maraschino liqueur was not as widely available in 2005 as it is today, though both lend the "What is *that?*" character that most of the best cocktails possess. As for the bitter component, we strictly use our house-made aromatic bitters, but you will not go wrong with experimentation here.

One of the more enjoyable parts of my job involves choosing barrels of whiskey that will one day be included in this special cocktail. Typically, we work with a distillery to purchase a commercially unavailable single barrel of bourbon (rye whiskey is more difficult to procure in this manner). The distillery will send barrel samples, and after we've tasted several—usually at barrel strength, but sometimes properly diluted—we choose what we feel will work best in the cocktail. That usually means the whiskey has characteristics that will shine when integrated with other ingredients—spice notes, tannins, and viscosity all play a role—and after about six weeks the entire barrel arrives, bottled and usually with special labeling indicating the pedigree of this unique spirit. Our guests have expressed overwhelming satisfaction knowing that they are taking part in a unique experience that they can enjoy only at the Waldorf Astoria. See **Brooklyn**, **Liberal**, **Rob Roy**, and **Waldorf** for variations.

MARBLE HILL

2 oz. New York Distilling Company Dorothy Parker gin
1 oz. Byrrh Grand quinquina aperitif (or Dubonnet)
1 oz. fresh orange juice
2 dashes Abbott's bitters

Add all ingredients to mixing glass. Add ice and shake well. Strain into chilled cocktail glass. Garnish with orange peel.

Although geographically connected to the Bronx, Marble Hill is, by law, the most northern part of the borough of Manhattan. It was separated from the island during the construction of the Harlem River Ship Canal in 1895. It remained an island until 1914, when the Harlem River was filled in on the north side, connecting it to the Bronx and cementing its association with the wrong borough. The only place that this makes any kind of sense is in the world of cocktails, as its pedigree makes it a fine alternative to the *Bronx* cocktail.

I used an NYC-made gin to keep with the theme, and while the original called for Dubonnet, I prefer Byrrh aperitif (pronounced "beer"); its flavor profile is a better match with the other ingredients (and it was around back then). In an effort to add a bit of spine to this easy sipper, I added the unique Abbott's bitters, but most any will do in this slot. Be adventurous and make it your own. It's great over ice in the warmer weather as well.

MARGARITA ∎ *Classic*

2 oz. Siete Leguas blanco tequila
1 oz. Combier liqueur d'orange
1 oz. fresh lime juice

Add all ingredients to mixing glass. Add ice and shake well. Strain into Old Fashioned glass filled with fresh ice. Garnish with lime wheel. Salted half rim, optional.

(ALL-IN) MARGARITA ∎ *Peacock Alley*

1½ oz. Siembra Azul blanco tequila
½ oz. Del Maguey Vida mezcal
½ oz. Cointreau
½ oz. Agavero liqueur
¾ oz. fresh lime juice

Add all ingredients to mixing glass. Add ice and shake well. Strain into Old Fashioned glass filled with fresh ice. Garnish with lime wheel. Salted half rim, optional.

A twentieth-century classic, the *Margarita* has gone through enough permutations to produce many unique variations. Its first appearance in print is in London's *Café Royal Cocktail Book* (1937) as the **Picador**, though this *Daisy* has been served in some form since spirits, juice, and sugar were first combined. I'll just say that like most things in life, it's best to keep it simple. You can alter the ingredients incrementally to suit your own taste, but at the end of the day the three-ingredient version is best. Some find a touch of agave syrup adds a pleasant viscosity, in which case you'd adjust the orange liqueur accordingly to balance out the sweetness. We use a good 100 percent blanco as a standard, but a reposado tequila adds a depth of flavor and is a nice treat.

You can try a *Margarita* served up as a predinner cocktail, but if you're planning to enjoy more than one, nothing makes summer afternoons more agreeable than a *Margarita* on the rocks. As for salt, I prefer not to salt the rim, but when in the mood, I drop a pinch of kosher salt into the mixing glass prior to shaking. It won't taste salty but will be slightly more balanced, like in a **Paloma**. Resistance to taking another sip will be futile.

The *(All-In) Margarita* was a result of a happy accident. We were prebatching Mezcal-enhanced *Margaritas* for a large event when one of the catering managers who was lending a hand mistakenly assumed Agavero was a form of curaçao or triple sec and added it to the batch. In actuality, it is a tequila-based liqueur flavored with the Mexican-grown damiana flower. When taste-tested, the drinks made with the Agavero had their own unique flavor profile. When we realized what had happened and identified the oddball ingredient, this refined rendition was born. It is quite the powerhouse, so utilizing crushed or pellet ice is a nice alternative serving. You can also omit the Agavero liqueur and prepare a standard *Margarita* and float the Mezcal on top for a smoky version. It makes a great pairing with barbecue.

For our **Border Flower**, we use Gran Centenario Rosangel as the base of a standard *Margarita*. It is a reposado tequila that is finished in port barrels for two months, then infused with hibiscus flowers. We then top it with three drops of rose water and three baby rose petals as garnish. Aside from being a highly enjoyable variation on the theme, the buds are so visually striking they almost always command orders from nearby tables. If Rosangel is unavailable, any favorite reposado will do. A charming *Margarita* if there ever was one.

MARMALADE

1½ oz. Plymouth London dry gin
¾ oz. Cinzano Rosso sweet vermouth
¾ oz. Noilly Prat extra dry vermouth
1 bar spoon Bonne Maman orange marmalade

Add all ingredients to mixing glass. Add ice and shake well. Fine-strain into chilled cocktail glass. Garnish with orange peel.

At first glance this could be easily dismissed as yet another *Bronx* cocktail alternate. The difference here is the actual marmalade, which, strangely enough, was not included in the transcribed recipe of the Old Books. Then it was just shaken with a couple of orange slices, but as with the *Amsterdam* cocktail, I couldn't resist giving it a proper nod and worthy connection to the title.

I've been making cocktails a long time and every once in a while I come across one in which the addition of bitters somehow brings out a sweet note in a recipe, and this is one, so I omitted them. The dual vermouths add enough complexity, as does the toasty marmalade. Look for this one to surprise you.

MARTINEZ

1½ oz. Tanqueray Old Tom gin
1½ oz. Martini & Rossi sweet vermouth
¼ oz. Luxardo maraschino liqueur
2 dashes Angostura bitters *or* Dr. Adam Elmegirab's Boker's bitters

Add all ingredients to mixing glass. Add ice and stir for 30 seconds.
Strain into chilled cocktail glass. Garnish with orange peel.

BRIDAL

2 oz. Plymouth gin
1 oz. Martini & Rossi sweet vermouth
¼ oz. Luxardo maraschino liqueur
2 dashes Regans' Orange Bitters No. 6

Add all ingredients to mixing glass. Add ice and stir for 30 seconds.
Strain into chilled cocktail glass. Garnish with orange peel.

SILVER

1½ oz. Portobello Road No. 171 London dry gin
1½ oz. Noilly Prat extra dry vermouth
¼ oz. Luxardo maraschino liqueur
2 dashes Regans' Orange Bitters No. 6
⅛ oz. Gum Syrup (optional)

Add all ingredients to mixing glass. Add ice and stir for 30 seconds.
Strain into chilled cocktail glass. Garnish with lemon peel.

PEACOCK ALLEY MARTINEZ

2 oz. Ransom Old Tom gin or Greenhook Ginsmiths Old Tom gin
1 oz. Martini & Rossi sweet vermouth
¾ oz. Noilly Prat extra dry vermouth
¼ oz. Luxardo maraschino liqueur
1 dash Angostura bitters
1 dash Regans' Orange Bitters No. 6

Add all ingredients to mixing glass. Add ice and stir for 30 seconds.
Strain into chilled cocktail glass. Garnish with lemon peel.

SOUTH OF THE BORDER MARTINEZ ∎ *Peacock Alley*

2 oz. Cazadores reposado tequila
1 oz. Carpano Antica sweet vermouth
¼ oz. Luxardo maraschino liqueur
2 dashes house-made Cocoa Bitters (or Fee Brothers Aztec
chocolate bitters)

Add all ingredients to mixing glass. Add ice and stir for 30 seconds. Strain into chilled cocktail glass. Garnish with orange peel.

First found in print in1884 (yes—1884!) in O. H. Byron's *The Modern Bartenders' Guide*, the *Martinez* was described as an enhanced gin-based Manhattan, and I wholeheartedly agree, especially if you take into account that some of the first Manhattan recipes included touches of gum syrup, absinthe, curaçao, or maraschino. Ultimately, it became one of the first wave of cocktails to capitalize on vermouth's newfound popularity, in the late nineteenth century. From that point forward, a significant percentage of memorable cocktails contained an aromatized wine of some sort (as you can tell from the number of recipes in this book alone).

Incidentally, the *Martinez* (traditionally prepared with genever or Old Tom gin) is not listed by name in either of the Old Books; besides Martini cocktails that omit the defining maraschino element, the recipe for the *Bridal* comes closest. You can view this as a modern take on the classic proportions, as it leans on the gin and better represents the modern palate.

The *Silver*, at its heart, is simply a dry, modern *Martinez*. It first appeared in print in Harry Johnson's *Bartenders' Manual* (1900) with London dry gin in the starring role, and later with genever taking the lead. The Old Books simply state "gin," which I have interpreted as meaning London dry, since other variants are listed as such (Old Tom, genever/Holland, Plymouth). You don't have to sweeten this cocktail at all, so just omit the syrup entirely or use an Old Tom gin if that's your preference. You can also just bump the maraschino up to a third of an ounce if leaning on the sweet side of things. With all of these recipes you can use a 2:1 spirit-to-vermouth ratio for an alternate presentation. It's certainly appropriate on Friday nights.

As for the alternate versions, our Peacock Alley rendition of the classic *Martinez* includes barrel-aged Old Tom gin. This results in a unique flavor profile, as the herbal and toasted notes of the gin are both displayed. The addition of dry vermouth and two types of bitters lends an adult complexity to the finish. We purchased large used bourbon barrels from Tuthilltown Sprits distillery, in upstate New York, and filled them with New York Distilling Company Perry's Tot navy-strength gin. After aging for two months, the gin absorbs the sweet notes of the whiskey while the heat of this high-proof spirit is tempered, making for one heck of a singular sensation (and a great gin and tonic as well!). This is another cocktail that I have trouble taking off the menu. The two commercially available barrel-aged gins, Ransom and Greenhook Ginsmiths, are excellent products and shine in this recipe.

Finally, our own *South of the Border Martinez* uses tequila as the base spirit and takes advantage of the Carpano Antica sweet vermouth and tequila's natural, happy coexistence with cocoa. A unique offering for sure. See **Guion** and **Turf** for variations.

MARTINI

The following recipes are reprinted in the form that they appear in the Old Books.

Though other, more practiced renditions may be currently used, I've opted to feature the Old Bar's adaptations, as they are excellent drinks in their own right. Included here are only recipes of cocktails with some sort of gin taking the lead with added vermouth and bitters, served up with no adornment other than an olive, citrus peel, or onion as garnish. In an effort to compartmentalize them, if for no other reason than to have all of the variations on the theme in one section for easier replication, I tried to "umbrella" as many as made sense.

The first recipe is the workaday version, a starting point, if you will. It is followed by the six variants with the grand title of "Martini." What follows from **Amsterdam** to **Newport** are the remaining titled siblings. All told, this section holds about sixty versions, each one unique and each worth trying.

This first recipe represents a modern take in the manner in which we serve a classic dry *Martini* in the Hotel today. You may adjust for personal taste accordingly.

MARTINI ▪ *Modern*

3 oz. Beefeater London dry gin
½ oz. Noilly Prat extra dry vermouth

Add ingredients to mixing glass. Add ice and stir for 30 seconds. Strain into chilled cocktail glass. Garnish with lemon peel and/or Queen Anne olive (optional).

Add a pickled cocktail onion as garnish for a modern-day **Gibson.***

MARTINI ▪ *Fifty Fifty/Dry*

1½ oz. Tanqueray London dry gin
1½ oz. Noilly Prat extra dry vermouth

Add ingredients to mixing glass. Add ice and stir for 30 seconds. Strain into chilled cocktail glass. Garnish with lemon peel and/or Queen Anne olive (optional).

Originally listed as a "Martini (Dry No. 2)."
　　Also listed as **Cornell**, **Gibson**, **Lynne**.
　　Add orange bitters for a **St. Francis**.
　　Use Plymouth gin for **Shake-Up Silo**, **Lewis**, **My Own**.
　　Use Plymouth gin and orange bitters for **Dewey**, **Marguerite**.
　　Use Plymouth gin, orange bitters, and orange peel for **Delmonico**,
Racquet Club.
　　Use Hayman's Old Tom gin and Angostura bitters for **West India**.

MARTINI ▪ *Dry*

2 oz. Beefeater London dry gin
1 oz. Noilly Prat extra dry vermouth†

---

* *Prior to its modern interpretation as a dry Martini with a pickled onion garnish, the Gibson was a singular cocktail at the turn of the nineteenth century. It was different from the Martini inasmuch as it was dry (both in amount and style of vermouth) and it contained no bitters, which were a mandatory if not a defining ingredient of a standard Martini. This made the Gibson the Martini that we all enjoy today. The addition of the onion came later.*

† *The original recipe listed bianco vermouth as an alternate.*

Add ingredients to mixing glass. Add ice and stir for 30 seconds. Strain into chilled cocktail glass. Garnish with lemon peel and/or Queen Anne olive.

Also listed as **Mrs. Thompson.**
Add orange bitters for **Good Times.**
Use Plymouth gin and orange peel for **Gibson No. 2.**
Use Plymouth gin and orange bitters for **Hoffman House.**

MARTINI ∎ *Fifty Fifty/Sweet*

1½ oz. Hayman's Old Tom gin
1½ oz. Cinzano Rosso sweet vermouth
Regans' Orange Bitters No. 6

Add all ingredients to mixing glass. Add ice and stir for 30 seconds. Strain into chilled cocktail glass. Garnish with lemon peel.

Also listed as **Bradford, Gold, Olivet.**
Omit bitters for **Thanksgiving.**
Use Beefeater London dry gin for **Pell, Shafter, Walter Monteith.**
Use Beefeater London dry gin and omit bitters for **Dowd.**
Use Plymouth gin for **Lone Tree.**
Use Plymouth gin and orange peel for **Christ (No. 1).**
Use Plymouth gin, orange bitters, and Angostura bitters for **Hearst.**

MARTINI ∎ *Sweet*

2 oz. Bombay London dry gin
1 oz. Martini & Rossi sweet vermouth
Regans' Orange Bitters No. 6

Add all ingredients to mixing glass. Add ice and stir for 30 seconds. Strain into chilled cocktail glass. Garnish with lemon peel.

Also listed as **Down.**
Use orange twist for **Delatour.**

Omit orange bitters and use three dashes Peychaud's bitters for *Hilliard.*

Omit bitters for *Hamlin.*

Omit bitters and add orange twist for *Rossington.*

Use Plymouth gin, omit orange bitters, and use Angostura bitters for *Club Cocktail No. 2.*

MARTINI ▮ Perfect

1½ oz. Bombay London dry gin
¾ oz. Martini & Rossi sweet vermouth
¾ oz. Noilly Prat extra dry vermouth
Regans' Orange Bitters No. 6

Add all ingredients to mixing glass. Add ice and stir for 30 seconds. Strain into chilled cocktail glass. Garnish with lemon peel.*

Omit bitters for *MacLean, Mr. Vandervere.*

Use Hayman's Old Tom gin and omit bitters for *Somerset.*

Use Plymouth gin and omit bitters for *Grand Vin.*

Use Plymouth gin, omit bitters, and add orange peel garnish for *H. P. Whitney.*

MARTINI ▮ Equal Parts

1 oz. Tanqueray London dry gin
1 oz. Martini & Rossi sweet vermouth
1 oz. Noilly Prat extra dry vermouth
Regans' Orange Bitters No. 6

Add all ingredients to mixing glass. Add ice and stir for 30 seconds. Strain into chilled cocktail glass. Garnish with lemon peel.

Also listed as *Hall.*

Omit bitters for *Perfect No. 2.*

Omit bitters and use orange peel as garnish for *Pomeroy, Rossington No. 2.*

Use Hayman's Old Tom gin for *Somerset.*

---

* The original recipe omitted bitters and included a green (Queen Anne) olive. Please don't.

Use Plymouth gin with orange peel twist for **Johnson.**

Use Plymouth gin, omit bitters, and use orange peel garnish for **Perfect.**

Use Plymouth gin, omit orange bitters, use two dashes of Peychaud's bitters, and add orange peel garnish for **Jimmie Lee.**

AM∫TERDAM ▪ *Genever*

2 oz. Bols genever
½ oz. Cinzano Rosso sweet vermouth
½ oz. Noilly Prat extra dry vermouth
Regans' Orange Bitters No. 6

Add all ingredients to mixing glass. Add ice and stir for 30 seconds. Strain into chilled cocktail glass. Garnish with orange peel.

Of the many edits that I made to the original recipe, this was one of the most obvious. The London dry gin called for in the Old Books does not exactly link itself to Amsterdam, hence the inclusion of a Holland genever spirit here. The recipe was also vague as to which vermouth to use. After trying both separately, I've opted to use both together, making this a "perfect" genever Martini as well as giving it its own identity. It is also one of the relatively few cocktails in the Old Books that specify a garnish, calling for a lemon peel. I think in this version, the orange peel complements the natural complexity of the combination of ingredients and coexists with the bitters as well. See **Turf** for variation.

EA∫Y ▪ *Enhanced*

2¾ oz. Bombay London dry gin
¼ oz. Carpano Antica sweet vermouth

Add ingredients to mixing glass. Add ice and stir for 30 seconds. Strain into chilled cocktail glass. Garnish with lemon peel.

If using a less robust vermouth, add another quarter ounce, along with a dash of orange bitters. This one is a surprising new favorite. It does so much with very little. See **All Right** for variation.

2½ oz. Hayman's Old Tom gin*
¼ oz. Noilly Prat extra dry vermouth
¼ oz. Martini Gran Lusso sweet vermouth
1 dash Regans' Orange Bitters No. 6

Add all ingredients to mixing glass. Add ice and stir for 30 seconds. Strain into chilled cocktail glass. Garnish with lemon peel.

Also listed as "Sunshine."

Use Bombay London dry gin and omit bitters (keep them in anyway) for **Gladwin.**

Newport ▮ *Unique Blend*

1¼ oz. Tanqueray London dry gin
1¼ oz. Noilly Prat extra dry vermouth
¾ oz. Carpano Antica sweet vermouth

Add all ingredients to mixing glass. Add ice and stir for 30 seconds. Strain into chilled cocktail glass. Garnish with orange peel.

▪ ▪ ▪

I am of the generation that when someone brings up the subject of the *Martini*, this is the cocktail that comes to mind: Primarily London dry gin with a touch of dry vermouth, garnished with an unstuffed Queen Anne olive and, if I'm really in the mood, a lemon twist. It is, after all, how my parents and their cohorts enjoyed theirs. One (or if at home, two) before dinner, stirred, cold, and bracing. The gin—very juniper-forward, in a way that few distilleries produce the spirit today—is part of the reason that pro–vodka Martini people grimace at the thought of a gin-based cocktail. This is the spice-leaning spirit they are thinking of. In terms of flavor, gin has moved toward the center, but in a manner that lifts and broadens the entire spirit. Ramping up the citrus, floral, and botanical notes, keeping the juniper and licorice on the edges, and even incorporating cucumber and some other unique ingredients into the

---

* *If using a stronger Old Tom gin (over 80 proof), pull back on the gin by half an ounce and add a quarter ounce each of dry and sweet vermouth for a more balanced result.*

distillation process is transforming this once-intimidating spirit and elevating it to such crowd-pleasing heights. There are a fair share of classic-styled London dry gins being produced (and it better stay that way), and I strongly suggest trying them. Anything that can have your guests expand their horizons and move away from the completely bland is a good thing. Don't get me wrong, I think vodka is a fine spirit, and it too has improved over the years. I will say that nothing comes close to it as a pairing for smoked fish or caviar, but personally, I feel it lacks the character and charm that gin has in spades.

As for the category itself, the *Martini*, in any incarnation, predates the Old Bar by several years, with the first Old Tom/sweet vermouth version first found in print in 1884. The first dry (1:1 ratio) version seems to have come into being around the early 1890s. Then, somewhere around the time of the Old Hotel, there are several named cocktails that are listed in the Old Books made with a 2:1 ratio of dry gin to dry vermouth. Others follow, save for a ratio difference here and a dash of bitters there. In the end it really doesn't matter. These drinks and their kind were popular in their day, were simple and satisfying enough to be served in houses both public and private, and have thankfully survived to be enjoyed today.

Having so many variations of the cocktail to grapple with forced me to incorporate strict parameters as to what would define a *Martini*. As I have mentioned in the introduction to this section, only recipes with gin, vermouth, and/or bitters were included. Any cocktail recipe with enhancements such as absinthe rinses, drops of grenadine, and the like were separated out and received their own entries. Although I've opted not to list it, the modern-day **Dirty Martini** variation, with its ample amount of added olive brine, would certainly fall into this category.

Now, let's get down to the nitty-gritty. A *Martini* is never, ever shaken, and no, shaking does not make it any colder. Professors have been hired, equipment rented, and tests performed. If you stir your cocktail for the proper amount of time, relative to the size of your ice, your *Martini* will reach its desired state of arctic chill while maintaining its leaden imprint on your palate—and all without shards of ice continuing to dilute it for minutes after serving. That goes for 95 percent of all recipes not containing dairy or fruit juice. My closing thought on the subject is this: so important is the stirring of the cocktail that when someone is preparing one for me and he does nothing else right but stir it, he is already home.

Like the *Old Fashioned*, the *Martini* has evolved through the years. Its relationship with vermouth went from a full-on partnership (first with the sweet/Italian and then the dry/French style) to that of a longtime colleague who has moved to the sister office across town and whom you only see at the company picnic. The first variants were pretty sweet, as they were 1:1 ratios of Old Tom gin and sweet vermouth (some early recipes even included dashes of gum syrup!). Even when adventurous barmen of the late 1800s ramped up the Old Tom and cut back the sweet vermouth, it wasn't enough to add real longevity to these versions. They live on more famously and with tangible enhancements as a *Martinez*, for one.

For recipes that include sweet vermouth but do not call for bitters and you want to stay within the intended results, this would be a good time to use a more full-flavored vermouth such as Carpano Antica, Punt e Mes, or Martini Gran Lusso. You could include barrel-aged Old Tom gins such as Greenhook Ginsmiths and Ransom along with these full-bodied vermouths for more robust results, but you are certainly getting into Manhattan territory if you do. As you can probably already tell, a very thin line separated most of these concoctions. I think their strengths lay in their ability to retain their own identity despite their similarities.

The dry version of this cocktail was due another fate entirely. Originally, a Dry Martini meant the use of London dry gin (as opposed to the sweeter Old Tom gin) and dry or French vermouth. It wasn't necessarily related to the amount of vermouth used. As you can see by the early recipes listed here, vermouth mostly split equal billing with the preferred gin of choice. As time went on, and especially post-Prohibition, vermouth was used less and probably grew increasingly rancid because it became less desirable as an ingredient in general. By the 1960s, the gin was served well chilled, diluted with ice, and with barely any added vermouth. To this day, there are holdovers who shudder at the thought of vermouth in their *Martini*.

The interesting thing is, if you omit the vermouth, you are not having a *Martini* at all. The Old Books listed this cocktail as a **Bunyan** (please see this entry for some appealing variations). I maintain that vermouth is an essential part of the cocktail and is its defining ingredient.

When you're purchasing vermouth for home use, I suggest buying half bottles (375 ml.) and keeping them in the refrigerator. They will be depleted more quickly and remain fresh for at least one month or more. You can also cook with it if rotation is an issue. As for bitters, I personally think that they are optional in the modern-day dry version, where gin is the star and does the heavy lifting. If making a *Fifty Fifty* or even a "wet" rendition (one with a 2:1 ratio of gin to vermouth), a dash or two of orange bitters are indispensable and really perks things up.

Most pre-Prohibition cocktail recipes were quite stingy when it came to garnishes and instructions. I think it may be because the use of something as common as citrus peels was just assumed, as most of these books were written for bartenders. Either way, lemon peel works in all of these recipes, though some specifically called for an orange twist or an olive. In the listings here, I tried to be as specific as possible and link a particular garnish to its corresponding recipe in the Old Books. Though, as I've mentioned, the garnish is entirely up to you, especially if none is listed. But I would avoid the use of olives as a garnish in any recipe containing sweet vermouth. As a side note, I personally enjoy what I call a "Dickens" garnish in my dry Martini as it incorporates both an "Olive & Twist" (wink and nudge inserted here!).

Lastly, at Peacock Alley we hand-stuff our own Queen Anne olives with Gorgonzola cheese for one of the most decadent garnishes (and bites) you can possibly have. I strongly suggest doing so yourself. Simply place some room-temperature cheese (of your choice, just make it as savory as you can take it) in a small plastic bag and mash until smooth. Then cut a small end from the corner of the bag to "pipe" or squeeze it into the olives. It's a bit laborious but your guests will love you for it. By the way, in this case there is no commercial product that comes close to the home-made item.

MCKINLEY'S DELIGHT/
REMEMBER THE MAINE

2 oz. Michter's rye whiskey
¾ oz. Martini & Rossi sweet vermouth
½ oz. Rothman & Winter orchard cherry liqueur or Heering cherry liqueur
¼ oz. Pernod liqueur

Add all ingredients to mixing glass. Add ice and stir for 30 seconds. Strain into chilled cocktail glass. Garnish with brandied cherry.

This one, named for assassinated president William McKinley and then appropriated as a commemorative cocktail for the USS *Maine* battleship (which sank in Havana Harbor in 1898 and became a catalyst for the Spanish-American War). As far as cocktails go, this one pops up on menus every now and then. It works fine as the enhanced **Manhattan** that it is. A somewhat adventurous alternative.

MERRY WIDOW (Or Mary Garden) ▌
(Waldorf-Astoria Version)

1½ oz. Byrrh Grand quinquina aperitif (Maurin quina or Dubonnet, if unavailable)
1½ oz. Noilly Prat extra dry vermouth
¼ oz. Luxardo maraschino liqueur or Grand Marnier (optional)
1 dash Regans' Orange Bitters No. 6

Add all ingredients to mixing glass. Add ice and stir for 15 seconds to integrate. Strain into chilled cocktail glass. Garnish with brandied cherry.

POET'S DREAM (ADAPTED)

2 oz. Tanqueray London dry gin
1 oz. Noilly Prat extra dry vermouth
½ oz. Bénédictine liqueur
2 drops Émile Pernot Vieux Pontarlier absinthe

Add all ingredients to mixing glass. Add ice and stir for 30 seconds. Strain into chilled cocktail glass. Garnish with lemon peel.

What became recognized as the Waldorf-Astoria version of the *Merry Widow* cocktail was more than likely a little-seen tipple (named for an opera singer of the day) known as the *Mary Garden*. Some earlier printed recipes of the *Merry Widow* (probably named for the nineteenth-century operetta) also cite it as the *Mary Garden*. In *Recipes for Mixed Drinks* (1917), New York bartender Hugo Ensslin includes gin along with several enhancements. The kicker is, his is the first book to include both the *Mary Garden* and the *Merry Widow* in the forms listed here. Even Oscar Tschirky's pal Jacques Straub, in *Drinks* (1914), listed the *Mary Garden* as the *Merry Widow*. By the time Mr. Crockett recorded the Waldorf's version in 1931, the two drinks were one, though both versions have survived the ages, and for good reason.

The Waldorf's *Widow* is a lighter recipe, perfect for warmer weather. If opting for one of the enhancements, try both, as they each have something unique to offer. Be adventurous here: almost anything can work—Chartreuse, kümmel, etc. You will realize how much a mere quarter ounce brings to the table. The Hugo Ensslin, gin-based version, is perfect for whenever you're in the mood for a **Martini** but have a hankering for something a little bit different.

Finally, the *Poet's Dream* is listed as such in the books but is obviously influenced by the *Merry Widow*, if not incorrectly listed with equal parts of gin, vermouth, and Bénédictine. It was not the best cocktail in the world, so I've adapted it based on the earlier published recipe (1916). Mr. Straub's version omits the absinthe. *The Savoy*'s (1931) does not. See **Guion** and **Salomé** for variations.

METROPOLE

2 oz. Hine VSOP cognac
1 oz. Sacred extra dry vermouth
¼ oz. Gum Syrup or Simple Syrup
2 dashes Peychaud's bitters
1 dash Regans' Orange Bitters No. 6

Add all ingredients to mixing glass. Add ice and stir for 30 seconds. Strain into chilled cocktail glass. Garnish with brandied cherry and lemon peel.

Named for the old Times Square area, Hotel Metropole (which closed in 1912) was, Mr. Crockett implied, quite the after-hours joint. This nineteenth-century cocktail's original recipe called for equal parts brandy and vermouth, and you can make it as such, but I think that this adapted version makes for the better nightcap.

For a similar cocktail of the era, the **Metropolitan**, just switch out these bitters for three dashes of Angostura bitters. The Old Books recipe for this cocktail leaned quite heavily on a defunct brand of bitters (Manhattan Bitters) in ounce form. If you are feeling adventurous, add a few more dashes of Angostura (incrementally) until you reach your desired level of spiciness. These recipes date back to their first appearance in print in 1884 and joined a whole new genre of drinks that included a newly popular import, vermouth.

Another adventurous way to approach either of these cocktails would be to omit the syrup and dry vermouth and add one ounce of bianco-style vermouth (the sweetened, clear version—I like Contratto bianco here) or even Cocchi Americano, for a slightly different take. These are interesting tweaks that don't veer too far from the original intention but add a bit of variety and complexity to the final result.

MILK PUNCH

2 oz. Pierre Ferrand 1840 cognac or Royer Force 53 VSOP cognac
½ oz. Simple Syrup
1½ oz. whole milk

Add all ingredients to mixing glass. Add ice and shake to integrate. Fine-strain into Old Fashioned glass filled with large ice cubes. Garnish with freshly grated nutmeg.

Dating back to 1600s England, milk Punches peaked in popularity in the late 1800s, but were called for often enough at the Old Bar that several variations were included in the Old Books. The **Jamaica Milk Punch** split the spirit portion with Jamaican rum (Appleton Estate Reserve is recommended). A classic.

The **Whiskey Milk Punch** is just that: rye whiskey used in the recipe here. It also does the job nicely. The **New Orleans Milk Punch** adds a couple of drops of pure organic vanilla extract (and the cognac can be subbed out for high-proof bourbon as an alternate) and in my opinion is probably the best variation of them all. I took that recipe one step further and steeped bourbon with a couple of whole vanilla beans for about two weeks with tremendous results.*

---

* Split one whole vanilla bean lengthwise, scrape out seeds, and place bean and seeds in bottle. Agitate every other day for a week and begin to use.

Boston Milk Punch

1 oz. Cruzan Estate Diamond dark rum
1 oz. Crown Royal Canadian whiskey
¾ oz. Simple Syrup
2 oz. whole milk
Freshly grated nutmeg

Add all ingredients to mixing glass. Add ice and shake well. Fine-strain into wineglass or goblet. Garnish with a pinch of freshly grated nutmeg.

This old variation of the classic *Milk Punch* has two base spirits and is not served on ice, which earns this its own entry. I particularly like the inclusion of the nutmeg grated directly into the mixing glass prior to shaking. The original recipe specifies St. Croix rum, hence the inclusion of Cruzan rum, but any rich, dark rum will do. I've chosen the flavorful but unobtrusive Crown Royal for the whiskey portion, which adds to the pleasing viscosity and has little burn. All in all, it's a nice alternative to an **Alexander,** especially around the holidays.

Cream Punch

1½ oz. Rémy Martin 1738 Accord Royal cognac
1 oz. Combier Liqueur d'Orange
1½ oz. whole milk

Add all ingredients to mixing glass. Add ice and shake well. Fine-strain into chilled cocktail glass. Garnish with freshly grated nutmeg.

These simple ingredients make for a classic *Milk Punch* variation. The secret here, as in all milk Punches, is the use of whole milk rather than cream. You don't want a heavy after-dinner drink as the idea is to be able to enjoy more than one. You may present this on ice as you would a standard *Milk Punch*. See **Alexander** for variations.

MILLIONAIRE

2 oz. Berry Bros. & Rudd No. 3 London dry gin
1 oz. Noilly Prat extra dry vermouth
¼ oz. house-made Grenadine
1 dash Regans' Orange Bitters No. 6

Add all ingredients to mixing glass. Add ice and stir for 30 seconds. Strain into chilled cocktail glass. Garnish with orange peel.

Mr. Crockett's original transcription was simply "Dry Martini with Grenadine on top." Well, right off the bat I knew that was not going to work. The heavy-bodied grenadine would just sink to the bottom of the cocktail glass, leaving an incongruous last sip. What *did* work was mixing it with the gin and vermouth and adding a dash of orange bitters to temper and balance the whole thing. Another of the Old Books' pleasant surprises. You can omit the bitters for a slightly sweeter result, but if you do, I recommend a lemon twist.

MISSISSIPPI PUNCH

1½ oz. Courvoisier VSOP cognac
¾ oz. Appleton Estate 12 Year Old rum
¾ oz. Jim Beam bourbon
½ oz. Simple Syrup
½ oz. fresh lemon juice

Add all ingredients to mixing glass. Add ice and shake well. Strain into Old Fashioned glass or Hoffman House goblet filled with ice cubes. Garnish with orange wheel and seasonal fruit.

This old Punch dates back to the mid-1800s and actually called for larger portions of each ingredient. I kept it in line with a modern serving and reduced it accordingly. Although this is a strong, slow sipper, you can be adventurous and move the rum into the lead spot or, if you like, use equal portions of each. Don't worry, this sturdy recipe can take it. You could also roll this one for a traditional presentation. The original recipe specifies crushed ice, but as with any Punch, ice cubes would be the usual call.

MOJITO

12 fresh mint leaves (plus one sprig reserved for garnish)
¾ oz. Simple Syrup
2½ oz. Bacardi y Cia Heritage white rum
1 oz. fresh lime juice
2 oz. chilled club soda

Add mint and simple syrup to mixing glass and muddle. Add rum and lime juice and fill with ice. Shake well and double-strain into Collins glass filled with fresh ice. Top with club soda. Garnish with reserved mint sprig.

New Mexico Mojito ❘ *Peacock Alley*

Fresh cilantro leaves (enough to fill the center of your cupped palm)
4 fresh mint leaves
¾ oz. organic light agave syrup (1:1 ratio of agave and water)
2½ oz. 86 Co. Cabeza blanco tequila
1 oz. fresh lime juice
2 oz. chilled club soda

Add cilantro, mint, and agave syrup to mixing glass and muddle. Add tequila and lime juice and fill with ice. Shake well and double-strain into Collins glass filled with fresh ice. Top with club soda. Garnish with lime wheel.

Peach

(Build for presentation in order listed)

BUILD IN A PINT GLASS:
¾ oz. Simple Syrup
12 fresh mint leaves (plus one sprig reserved for garnish)

MUDDLE GENTLY:
½ oz. fresh lemon juice
½ oz. fresh lime juice
2½ oz. Bacardi y Cia Heritage white rum

Fill with alternating layers of shaved or pellet ice and peach slices.

Top with shaved or pellet ice. Garnish with mint sprig. Serve with straw.

This classic has become synonymous with summertime parties, though what most people don't realize is that versions of it have been served for centuries. In fact, a simple rendition of this recipe is listed in the Old Books, and I like to picture plenty of these things going over the Old Bar, in that high-ceilinged and non-air-conditioned room. I know one thing for certain: the moment the heat rises past 80 degrees on the island of Manhattan, requests for *Mojitos* go up with every degree at Peacock Alley (and every other bar in town).

Demerara syrup can be substituted for the white simple syrup for a slightly earthier result. You would be missing out if you didn't try it at least once.

A good bartender's tip is to "clean" the shaker by pouring some club soda into the shaker tin and swirling it around to combine with anything left over from the shaking of the drink and then pour that on top of the drink as a bit of a flavorful bonus.

The *New Mexico Mojito* is a cilantro-tinged variation which leans on the herbal notes and agave nectar for the sugar component. I created it for those who occasionally want to deviate from the classic version.

As for the *Peach*, it's listed strictly for its presentation purposes as it was in the Old Books. If you'd like a **Peach Mojito**, simply prepare a basic *Mojito* and add a cubed third of a ripe peach, muddled along with the mint and sugar.

MONKEY GLAND ∎ *Classic*

2 oz. Bombay London dry gin
1 oz. fresh orange juice
¼ oz. house-made Grenadine (or Raspberry Syrup)
¼ oz. Émile Pernot Vieux Pontarlier absinthe
¼ oz. fresh lemon juice or 3 dashes Horsford's acid phosphate

Add all ingredients to mixing glass. Add ice and shake well. Strain into chilled cocktail glass. No garnish.

MONKEY MARGARITA ▪ *Peacock Alley*

2 oz. Fidencio Classico Mezcal Vida mezcal
1 oz. fresh orange juice
¼ oz. Émile Pernot Vieux Pontarlier absinthe
¼ oz. Cointreau
¼ oz. fresh lime juice
¼ oz. house-made Grenadine

Add all ingredients to mixing glass. Add ice and shake well. Fine-strain into chilled cocktail glass. Garnish with orange peel.

RUSSIAN GRAND DUKE ▪ *Oscar Tschirky's 100 Famous Cocktails*

2 oz. Russian Standard vodka or Martell VSOP cognac
1 oz. fresh orange juice
½ oz. Simple Syrup
¼ oz. Pernod Original Recipe absinthe
1 dash Regan's Orange Bitters No. 6

Add all ingredients to mixing glass. Add ice and shake well. Strain into chilled cocktail glass. Garnish with orange peel.

This is yet another Prohibition-era cocktail and you can see why it was popular. Although created in Europe, where proper spirits were available, it was still potable if you used less than top-quality gin, as the other ingredients propped it up. Whether true or not, it is supposedly titled for a technique that included the grafting of actual monkey glands to human glands to help aid in the raising of the male libido. No further comment here.

Other variations of the day included the substitution of Bénédictine for the absinthe. The result is a different animal altogether, but is worth a try. Most recipes called for the inclusion of grenadine as the sweetener, but raspberry syrup was also listed in some early recipes and I prefer it. Not only is it sweet, but it adds a bit of tang to the mix, which the orange juice can use. Somewhere along the line, I began adding a couple of dashes of lemon juice to this cocktail and now I cannot enjoy it without. If you want to avoid the addition of another citrus fruit, I have also topped a standard *Monkey Gland* with a few drops of our house-made cranberry bitters, though orange bitters would work in a pinch. You can argue that with all of these adaptations it kind of becomes another cocktail, but so be it. At the end of the day, that's how cocktails are born.

The *Monkey Margarita* was a Repeal Day celebration cocktail in which a twist on a Prohibition-era classic was requested and I came up with this. I really like the savory note of the entire recipe. You could easily switch in a good reposado tequila for the mezcal, if you so wish.

Oscar Tschirky's *100 Famous Cocktails* includes a *Russian Grand Duke*. Why he used cognac as the base spirit for this close cousin of Harry MacElhone's *Monkey Gland* may never be known, though their similarity cannot be denied. This complex sipper is listed as the "Russian" in the Old Books. Mr. Crockett alludes that there was another cocktail in which vodka took the lead "but was seldom called for." With no other mention of another "Russian" cocktail, I made the assumption that the vodka-based *Russian* was just that, the same cocktail with vodka in the lead. I tried it and liked it, so we're keeping it.

MONTANA

1 oz. Royer VSOP cognac
1 oz. Noilly Prat extra dry vermouth
1 oz. Graham's ruby port wine
1 dash Regans' Orange Bitters No. 6 (optional)

Add all ingredients to mixing glass. Add ice and stir for 30 seconds. Strain into chilled cocktail glass. Garnish with orange peel.

According to Mr. Crockett, many of the patrons of the Old Bar hailed from this fine state; I guess this cocktail was their idea. Either way, it's a unique item. I used ruby port, which is most likely what would've been on hand in the time of the Old Bar, though a tawny makes for an interesting result. Try both.

I found an earlier version in Jacques Straub's *Drinks* (1914) that included Angostura bitters and anisette. Try as I might to fix it, it remained a mishmash. If I were to modify this recipe at all, I would pull back on the dry vermouth and port by a quarter of an ounce each and add half an ounce to the cognac slot for a more robust cocktail with a long and interesting finish.

MONT BLANC FIZZ

2 oz. chilled club soda
2 oz. St. George Absinthe Verte
1 oz. orgeat syrup
½ egg white

Add chilled club soda to small Collins or Fizz glass. Add remaining ingredients to mixing glass. Dry-shake for 5 seconds. Add ice and shake for 10 seconds. Strain into small Collins or Fizz glass. Stir quickly with bar spoon to integrate. No garnish.

This looked like yet another recipe that was going to take major tinkering to make it palatable, but I couldn't have been more wrong. The note from *Old Waldorf Bar Days* read, "It took an imaginative bartender to see a resemblance to a white-topped mountain in a foaming glass." Believe me, after one of these strong Fizzes, you might be seeing other sights as well. The full two ounces of absinthe means this packs quite the punch. If you wanted to tone it down a bit (or have more than one), Pernod or Ricard pastis could fit the bill in that slot.

MORNING GLORY FIZZ

2 oz. chilled club soda
2 oz. Compass Box Great King St. blended Scotch whisky
¾ oz. lemon juice
½ oz. Simple Syrup
2 dashes Émile Pernot Vieux Pontarlier absinthe
½ egg white

Add club soda to small Collins or Fizz glass. Add remaining ingredients to mixing glass. Dry-shake for 5 seconds. Add ice and shake for 10 seconds. Strain into small Collins or Fizz glass. Stir briefly with bar spoon to integrate. Twist lemon peel to release oils, then discard.

BRANDY MORNING GLORY FIZZ

1½ oz. chilled club soda
1 oz. Hardy VSOP cognac
1 oz. Michter's US 1 single-barrel straight rye whiskey

¼ oz. Combier Liqueur d'Orange

2 dashes Émile Pernot Vieux Pontarlier absinthe

2 dashes Dr. Adam Elmegirab's Boker's bitters or Angostura bitters

Add club soda to small Collins or Fizz glass. Add remaining ingredients to mixing glass. Add ice and stir for 60 revolutions. Strain into small Collins glass. Stir to incorporate club soda. Twist lemon peel to release oils, then discard.

This classic Fizz predates the Old Bar by at least ten years and deserves to see a comeback. It's airy, and with a lighter Scotch whisky at the base, it can make quite the Bracer. It's also nice during late afternoons in the summertime . . . possibly enhanced by pairing it with a fresh oyster or three!

As for the brandy variation, it is one of the first multispirit cocktails with both whiskey and brandy sharing top billing. This must've been quite the best seller at the Old Bar, as it covered a lot of ground. The ingredients here all matter; the club soda does not hide much. Traditionally, one would add in a touch of superfine sugar when incorporating the soda water, but I think it can do without it. Substitute Champagne for the club soda when something really special is in order.

NATALE DOLCE *(Holiday)* ∎
Peacock Alley

1 oz. Sailor Jerry Spiced rum
1 oz. Varnelli Punch alla Fiamma liqueur
1½ oz. Moccia Zabov zabaglione liqueur

Add all ingredients to mixing glass. Add ice and shake well. Double-strain into Old Fashioned glass filled with large ice cubes or sphere.
Garnish with small amount of freshly grated nutmeg.
Additional optional garnish: French vanilla tuile wafer served on side plate.

Made since 1946, Zabov cream liqueur is based on the classic Italian cream zabaglione. For those who aren't familiar, it's a vanilla custard with a touch of Marsala wine. This liqueur pulls back on that profile, leaning it a bit toward a liquid crème brûlée. What I like about it is its versatility and ease of use, as it negates the need for double-boiling eggs and sugar.

Varnelli Punch alla Fiamma is a rum-based liqueur that is quite heavily spiced and also traditionally served around the holidays. You can substitute a brandy of your choice in the spiced rum slot for another interesting serving. Either way, this is just made for the holiday season as a simple, quickly prepared Eggnog alternative.

NATASHA ▮ *Peacock Alley*

1½ oz. Rittenhouse bonded rye whiskey
1 oz. Amaretto Disaronno liqueur
¾ oz. fresh lemon juice
¼ oz. Simple Syrup
½ egg white

Add all ingredients to mixing glass. Dry-shake for 5 seconds. Add ice and shake well. Fine-strain into chilled cocktail glass. Snap grapefruit peel to release oils, then discard.

Created for a Valentine's Day event in 2001, this is a simple yet beguiling hybrid of a Whiskey and Amaretto Sour. We've occasionally added a cinnamon-sugar rim to half of the glass, but I'll leave that up to you. The grapefruit twist dries the top off nicely and lifts it to another dimension. Appealing to nearly everyone, this would make a great cocktail for a large gathering or event. For a twist, try with Smith & Cross navy-strength rum in the whiskey slot.

NEGRONI ▮ *Classic*

1½ oz. Beefeater London dry gin
1 oz. Cinzano Rosso sweet vermouth
1 oz. Campari

Add all ingredients to mixing glass. Add ice and stir for 15 seconds. Strain into Old Fashioned glass filled with large ice cubes or sphere. Garnish with orange peel.

ALLEY NEGRONI ▮ *Peacock Alley*

1½ oz. Bols genever
1 oz. Dimmi Liquore di Milano
1 oz. Campari

Add all ingredients to mixing glass. Add ice and stir for 15 seconds. Strain into Old Fashioned glass filled with large ice cubes or sphere. Garnish with orange peel.

The extra half ounce of genever is the secret touch here, as it thins out the viscosity of the Dimmi and Campari. Its malty flavor profile pairs extremely well with these liqueurs. This is a true alternative to the classic, as it strays far enough from shore but still manages to keep a few toes on land.

Winter's Nap/Spring Awakening ▮ *Peacock Alley*

1½ oz. Belvedere vodka
1 oz. Cocchi Americano
1 oz. Aperol

Add all ingredients to mixing glass. Add ice and stir for 15 seconds. Strain into Old Fashioned glass filled with large ice cubes or sphere.

Garnish *Winter's Nap* with a rosemary sprig (slapped in hand prior to adding to glass to release essence).

Orange or lemon peel for garnish makes this a *Spring Awakening*.

This cocktail was created for a vodka-themed event; the lighter Aperol, standing in for Campari, makes for a nice accompaniment. The finish is surprisingly multidimensional. Lighter and more floral forward, it can be thought of as the *Negroni*'s sister. Obviously, lighter and more floral gins work as well.

Negroni Bianco ▮ *Peacock Alley*

1½ oz. 86 Co. Ford's London dry gin
1 oz. Dimmi Liquore di Milano
1 oz. Salers Gentiane aperitif

Add all ingredients to mixing glass. Add ice and stir for 15 seconds. Strain into Old Fashioned glass filled with large ice cubes or sphere. Garnish with orange and lemon peel.

You could replace the Salers with Cocchi Americano for a slightly less bitter result, but you would be kind of missing the point. I think this is a perfectly balanced combination; it has been a summertime staple of the Peacock Alley Bar menu for years. I like the dual citrus notes of the peels here. Gaz Regan was kind enough to include an adapted version of this recipe in his now-classic book, *The Negroni* (2012).

RED SHIPS OF SPAIN ▮ *Peacock Alley*

1½ oz. Plymouth gin
1 oz. Calisaya liqueur
1 oz. Lustau Don Nuño oloroso sherry

Add all ingredients except Calisaya to mixing glass. Add ice and stir for 15 seconds. Strain into Old Fashioned glass filled with large ice cubes or sphere. Garnish with grapefruit peel.

The *Red Ships of Spain* was created for a dinner in Bull and Bear Prime Steakhouse featuring Spanish wines. The American-made Calisaya liqueur is based on the no longer exported Spanish version. It fills the role that Campari usually does, adding viscosity. The sherry dries it out, making this rendition best enjoyed after dinner, as it was that evening. The grapefruit twist complements the finish.

The *Negroni*, though not mentioned in either of the Old Books, is a product of the Prohibition era and earns its entry here for two main reasons. The first is that if the Old Bar had been able to exist into the era of this drink's popularity, it surely would have been a huge hit; its brawny flavor profile would have fit right in with some of the Old Bar's other offerings. The second is that after languishing at the periphery of cocktail culture for many years, this complex combination of ingredients has become one of the most requested items in the past decade. So popular is this now-classic that it seems every establishment in the world knows how to prepare it, and they also have a variation or two of their own. It's only fitting, as the original *Negroni* is actually based on a variation itself, which omitted the gin and added club soda to become the **Americano**. And that is based on another variation, the **Milano-Torino** (Campari, sweet vermouth, rocks, orange peel), which dates back to the nineteenth century. Anyway, it seems that this recipe was made to be modified and boy, does it take to it.

At Peacock Alley, we've created at least four over the years, which I have included here. They are all unique and (most) don't mind being adjusted for your personal taste. As for the original, standard recipes call for equal parts of gin, Campari, and vermouth, but I feel a touch more gin props the whole thing up nicely and enables it to last a bit longer over ice. I also prefer to integrate the ingredients briefly prior to serving over fresh ice. One exception would be if serving outdoors in the warmer weather. Feel free to use equal portions and build the drink directly in the glass on a humid day to avoid over-diluting. I still don't know how, at the very beginning of their reemergence in popularity, *Negroni*s were being served up, but they were. Although I think the dilution from the ice cubes are an integral part of the experience, I also think it essential that the concoction remain as cold as possible to the last sip. This is only possible if served on ice. Incidentally, if you substitute bourbon for the gin, and serve it up, you will have the even older but newly popular **Boulevardier** cocktail. I wouldn't be afraid to present this on the rocks as well.

As for the vermouths, feel free to experiment, as they will all bring variations to the theme. I prefer fuller-bodied styles such as Punt e Mes in the cooler months, but the choice remains yours.

NETHERLAND (or Sherry-Netherland)

2 oz. Martell VSOP cognac
¾ oz. Cointreau
2 dashes Regans' Orange Bitters No. 6

Add all ingredients to mixing glass. Add ice and stir for 30 seconds. Strain into chilled cocktail glass. Garnish with lemon peel (optional).

This was the signature cocktail of NYC's old Hotel New Netherland (though its replacement resides on the same footprint as the original, Prohibition-era construction probably could not see an end to the dry years and excluded a proper barroom). This orangey-boozy thing is just one ingredient away from greatness; add lemon juice and you'll have the immortal **Sidecar**. You can also utilize the intended Grand Marnier in the supporting role for a slightly heavier variant, especially as an after-dinner item, maybe served over ice cubes or a sphere.

NEW ORLEANS COCKTAIL

2.5 oz. Carpano Antica sweet vermouth (chilled)
1 dash Regans' Orange Bitters No. 6
1 dash Angostura bitters
2 oz. chilled club soda

Add all ingredients to mixing glass. Add ice and stir for 10 seconds to integrate. Strain into Champagne coupe. Top with chilled club soda. Garnish with orange or lemon peel.

This refreshing quaff has been enjoyed in some form for 150 years or so. The barmen of the Old Bar served theirs in a Fizz glass, but the version that first appeared in print, in *The Cocktail Book: A Sideboard Manual for Gentlemen* (1900), places it in the more elegant champagne coupe. You may want to use an extra dash or two of bitters if using a more restrained style of vermouth. In fact, to keep it more geographically correct, forego Angostura and opt for Peychaud's bitters instead. A real summertime winner, when a stronger cocktail would be overdoing it. The **Creole** cocktail adds a half ounce of absinthe and omits the aromatic bitters and soda. Simply served up, I would incorporate a more traditional vermouth such as Martini & Rossi when pairing with absinthe. The **Crook** cocktail was an identical entry to the *Creole* in both Old Books.

NIGHTCAP

2 oz. Bacardi 8 Year Old rum (or Rhum Clément VSOP agricole rum)
1 oz. Grand Marnier
1 egg yolk
⅓ oz. heavy cream (optional)

Add all ingredients to mixing glass. Add ice and shake well. Fine-strain into chilled cocktail glass. No garnish.

Found in the "Cuban Concoctions" chapter of *The Old Waldorf-Astoria Bar Book* and calling for Bacardi in the rum slot, I had to make the assumption that dark rum would've been in the lead role. I prefer a drier, aged agricole, but the Bacardi 8 Year Old works great as well. Other curaçaos resulted in thin finishes, while Grand Marnier helped give this cocktail its identity. For even more luxury not included in the original recipe, a touch of heavy cream really brings this one home. It fills in the holes that the egg yolk doesn't quite get to.

NORTHERN LIGHTS ❚ *Peacock Alley*

1¼ oz. Pierre Ferrand Ambre cognac
¾ oz. Aalborg akvavit
½ oz. Tempus Fugit crème de cacao
½ oz. Cocchi Americano Bianco

Add all ingredients to mixing glass. Add ice and stir for 30 seconds.
Strain into chilled cocktail glass. Garnish with lemon peel.

Created as a unique and complex after-dinner cocktail, this exhibit
has plenty going on, including an unexpectedly long, honeyed finish.
In an effort to ensure that we aren't missing anything in the build,
dry vermouth in the Cocchi slot makes for a slightly more austere
variation. The caraway notes of the akvavit really sets this one
apart. A good cognac will shine through in the final result, though
you may want to lean on more feminine styles as we do here.

NUMBER THREE

2 oz. Berry Bros. & Rudd No. 3 gin
¾ oz. Noilly Prat extra dry vermouth
¼ oz. Varnelli l'Anice Secco Speciale anisette
1 dash Regans' Orange Bitters No. 6

Add all ingredients to mixing glass. Add ice and stir for 30 seconds.
Strain into chilled cocktail glass. Garnish with lemon peel.

This cocktail is actually not named for the recently produced gin of
the same name, but it made sense to try it. As for the anisette,
Varnelli's is, without a doubt, my favorite on the planet. It's drier,
and higher in alcohol than most, so it would be difficult to duplicate
the best version of this cocktail without it. As for alternatives, an
additional quarter ounce of dry vermouth with a standard sweet
anisette might get you a bit closer. Also found as a ***Marguerite*** in
Harry Johnson's 1934 *Bartenders Manual*. Other renditions of that
place curaçao in the anisette slot, which is worth a try.

OJEN (HERBSAINT) FRAPPÉ

1¼ oz. Pernod Original Recipe absinthe
1 oz. Herbsaint
¼ oz. Simple Syrup

Add all ingredients to mixing glass. Add ice and stir for 30 seconds. Strain into chilled Old Fashioned glass filled with crushed or pellet ice. Garnish with three dashes of Peychaud's bitters.

Ojen ("oh-hen") is a Spanish aguardiente (similar to cachaça or rum in terms of distillation but flavor and styles vary based on origin) that was especially popular in New Orleans in its day. Though it's no longer exported, Chris Hannah, bartender of the famous Arnaud's French 75 bar, in New Orleans, offered this fine alternate recipe. According to Mr. Crockett, the bartenders at the Old Bar served this concoction with seltzer. Whether they used it to top off the cocktail or served on the side isn't clear, so I'll just recommend a nice cold glass of club soda presented as a chaser. A durable and colorful summer refresher. See *Absinthe Frappé* (*California* and *New York* versions) for variations.

OLD FASHIONED ▮ *Pre-Prohibition Version*

1 demerara sugar cube
2 dashes Angostura bitters
2 oz. Rittenhouse bonded rye whiskey

Add sugar cube and bitters to mixing glass. Muddle to dissolve sugar. Add whiskey and ice and stir for 15 seconds to integrate. Strain into Old Fashioned glass filled with large ice cubes or sphere. Garnish with lemon peel.

OLD FASHIONED ▮ *Mid-Twentieth-Century Variation*

1 orange slice (thin half wheel)
1 brandied cherry
1 demerara sugar cube
2 dashes Angostura bitters
1 dash Regans' Orange Bitters No. 6
2½ oz. Elijah Craig 12-Year-Old single-barrel bourbon

Add orange slice and brandied cherry to Old Fashioned glass. Add sugar cube and bitters, then muddle to dissolve sugar. Add whiskey and stir, making sure sugar is dissolved. Add large ice cubes and stir briefly to integrate. Garnish with orange wheel and brandied cherry "flag."

There is probably no drink in the world that garners more personal variation than the *Old Fashioned.* We'll have to start with its predecessor because, as we all know, for something to be old-fashioned, it once had to be new.

Despite claims from historical characters and organizations, there is no doubt that the *Old Fashioned* evolved from the *(Whiskey) Cocktail* (see **Cocktail**) and can claim no one creator. Spirit, sugar, water, and bitters are the four ingredients that succinctly define a cocktail in the first recipe for the concoction, appearing in print in 1806. As the nineteenth century wore on, tastes changed (as they are apt to do) and other enhancements were added to this simple recipe. Absinthe, curaçao, orgeat syrup, and the like were added over time and so this became the recipe that imbibers of the day hearkened back to when they wanted something "old-fashioned." One difference was that the *Cocktail* was served up while the *Old Fashioned* was served on ice, a newfound amenity that was becoming more and more common.

In the *Old Fashioned* entry in the Old Books, Mr. Crockett mentions that the drink "was introduced by, or in honor of, Col. James E. Pepper, of Kentucky, proprietor of a celebrated whiskey of the period. It was said to have been the invention of a bartender at the famous Pendennis Club in Louisville, of which Col. Pepper was member." This has proven to be nothing more than poetic license on the part of either Col. Pepper or whoever passed along the information to Mr. Crockett. The boys at the Old Bar would've been well aware of the cocktail's existence long before the arrival of Col. Pepper; the Old Bar opened in 1897.

As for the variations, time has molded expectations for what this cocktail should be. I think the blame for its regression from classic sipper to fruit-forward minipunch can be squarely placed on the shoulders of Prohibition. What were once enhancements on pretty decent spirits or whiskey were forced to become cover-ups for subpar hooch. That's how the citrus component got thrown in and muddled along with the sugar, instead of simply being the finishing touch.

That said, my first Old Fashioned was this muddled-fruit incarnation, as was probably the case for anyone else who tasted one in the twentieth century.

I have made plenty of them in my day, but by the time we reopened Peacock Alley in 2005, this was exactly the type of bastardized recipe we set out to right or, at the very least, bring attention to the original version. Still, I do think that there is room for both in this world.

Somewhere in between, the original version of the cocktail swung back into the public consciousness, which led to another issue. Our bartenders at Peacock Alley used to have quite the postshift bull sessions as they tried to guess which variation any one particular guest would prefer. The well-heeled businessman must want the muddled-fruit variety; the flannel-wearing rock star must want the pre-Prohibition version. . . . Exactly wrong. We caved and it became the guests' request, and we now simply ask for preference upon ordering.

As for the soul of the cocktail, almost anything works here, and like the original Whiskey Cocktail, it would've been called for by its lead spirit. I prefer rye (which would be the historically correct choice), but any whiskey will do. Bourbon pairs well with the fruited version and orange peel. Of course, there was a **Bacardi Old Fashioned** in the Old Books. Go with a dark variety of rum and you will be fine; I like an aged agricole. Its dry profile meets the sugar component halfway for a very balanced result.

In general, higher-proof labels shine, since the *Old Fashioned* is a cocktail meant to be sipped and savored. You could build these in the serving glass; however, although the dilution rate will eventually meet anyone's satisfaction, it's the bitters that benefit most from the mixing glass preparation. This way they get the chance to fully intermingle with the whiskey and make it the cocktail that it was meant to be. At the very least, your first one should be prepared in the mixing glass.

Another key is matching the bitters to the base ingredient. One variation from the Old Books was called the **Southgate**. Its lone deviation was the use of Boonekamp bitters; these are again being produced, but the much-easier-to-find Underberg bitters make a fine substitution. And although it may be historically dubious, the use of unique bitters (or even standard Angostura) helps make the unheard-of **Vodka Old Fashioned** something to be had. (Who said vodka doesn't work in classic cocktails? We tried it and liked it, so here it is.) It makes a great platform for some of your homemade, artisanal, and off-the-beaten-path bitters varieties. A genever-based *Old Fashioned* is a personal summertime favorite (The Bitter Truth's Jerry Thomas bitters are a natural pair).

For the sugar note, I tend to lean on the demerara cube, as it delivers more than just sweetness to the mix. An agave or maple syrup would also bring a nice twist to tried-and-true classic presentations. I recommend using standard simple syrup for large parties, for quickly preparing more than a few; just use less syrup than you would sugar. About a third of an ounce is where the magic happens.

The importance of ice in this cocktail cannot be overstated. Investing in rubber ice molds for a large two inch sphere or cube will make a huge difference, as it will slow dilution while keeping the cocktail at its proper temperature. For a different take on the citrus element, try twisting a lemon peel (or orange if using bourbon) into the chilled Old Fashioned glass to release oils, then discard. Prepare the rest of the drink as usual.

For the *Mid-Twentieth-Century Variation*, the orange slice (yes, pulp included) must be thin. Although this is traditionally muddled with a neon red maraschino cherry, I opt to use a brandied cherry for an adult twist. A few quick taps with the muddler to release the fruits' juices will do the trick; no need to muddle into a mush. I do stop short of topping it with soda of any kind. There is no benefit in that at all, and anyway, it received its own entry at the Old Bar. See **General Hendricks** for variation.

I think the simple preparation of this cocktail is part of its allure, and it is a good stepping-stone to more complicated recipes that will follow as your palate becomes increasingly adventurous over time. After all, you will earn a bit of experience with the tools that are required to make any number of cocktails—the muddler, jigger, peeler . . . You will look like a pro in no time.

I've included two of our own variations below.

COCOA OLD FASHIONED *Peacock Alley*

1 orange peel (about 3 inches long)
2 dashes house-made Aromatic Bitters
1 demerara sugar cube
2 oz. Cocoa-Infused Whiskey (Stranahan's Colorado; recipe follows)

Add orange peel, bitters, and sugar cube to Old Fashioned glass. Muddle to incorporate and dissolve sugar. Add whiskey and stir, making sure sugar is dissolved. Add ice and stir briefly to chill. Garnish with orange peel.

Cocoa-Infused Whiskey

½ cup Noel cocoa nibs (France)
1 750 ml. bottle Stranahan's Colorado whiskey

Place ingredients in airtight glass jar for 3 to 5 days, stirring occasionally. Fine-strain and funnel back into bottle. (Do not let macerate any longer, as the result becomes overly bitter.) Best if used within 6 months.

This unique hybrid *Old Fashioned* incorporates Colorado's multi-grain whiskey. Its complex and creamy taste profile pairs so well with the cocoa and the orange that the result is somehow savory and sweet at the same time. Created for the 2014 Super Bowl events hosted by the Hotel, this turned out to be just the thing to ease the disappointment of the Denver Broncos fans.

YULETIDE OLDE-FA/HIONED ∎ *Peacock Alley*

1 demerara sugar cube
3 dashes Dale DeGroff's pimento bitters (or St. Elizabeth allspice dram)
2½ oz. Apple, Pear, and Orange Peel–Infused Bourbon (Henry McKenna; recipe follows)
1 large swath lemon peel

Add sugar cube and bitters to Old Fashioned glass. Muddle to incorporate and dissolve sugar. Add whiskey and stir, making sure sugar is dissolved. Add ice and stir briefly to chill. Garnish with lemon peel.

Apple, Pear, and Orange Peel–Infused Bourbon

2 Fuji apples
1 Bosc pear
1 whole orange rind (peeled, with as little pith as possible)
1 750 ml. bottle Henry McKenna bonded bourbon

Wash fruit. Core and cube apples and pear. Place in airtight glass container along with orange peel. Add bourbon and macerate for at least 10 days, stirring occasionally. Fine-strain and funnel back into bottle.

In an effort to create a holiday-themed *Old Fashioned,* I used the fruits of the season to impart their essence into a full-bodied bourbon. The pimento bitters, with notes of allspice, nutmeg, and clove, seal the seasonal deal. A real treat.

You can also add a favorite spice to the bottle of fruit-infused whiskey as it infuses, for yet another layer of flavor. Think two or three cloves (a little goes a long way) or one cinnamon stick added a day or two before straining. These will most definitely help impart festive flavors to your newly decorated classic holiday cocktail.

ORANGE BLOSSOM

1 oz. Hayman's Old Tom gin (or Tanqueray No. Ten gin)
1 oz. Cinzano Rosso sweet vermouth
1 oz. fresh orange juice

Add ingredients to mixing glass. Add ice and shake well. Strain into chilled cocktail glass. Garnish with orange peel.

ORANGE BLOSSOM No. 2

1½ oz. Beefeater 24 gin
1½ oz. fresh orange juice
2 dashes Regan's Orange Bitters (optional)

Add all ingredients to mixing glass. Add ice and shake well. Strain into chilled cocktail glass. Garnish with orange peel.

In an effort to mask the rough-hewn flavor profile of illegal, "bath-tub" gin, this drink reached the apex of its popularity during Prohibition. Following the Old Books recipe with unaged Old Tom gin, the drink was quite satisfying. Looking to lift it up, I originally attempted tweaking the vermouth aspect, forgoing the classic re-served style for the heavyweight Punt e Mes or Carpano Antica. Those styles dominated the production. With no help there, I adapted the recipe with a citrus-forward, aromatic gin in Tanqueray No. Ten. It lent some backbone without screaming its presence and its citrus notes made for quite the addition. Genever is also a nice alternative. The dry version of this cocktail, subbing in dry ver-mouth for sweet, is an **Eddy** (named for a diplomat). A couple of drops of organic orange flower water is also an optional addition and obviously, the "perfect" version (equal parts sweet and dry ver-mouth) is a **Bronx**.

The **Orange Blossom No. 2** alternative omits vermouth entirely. An identical version of this recipe appears as the **Adirondack** and specifies Gordon's gin. If you sub in Jamaican rum here, you have what the Old Books called a **Lifesaver**.

The original recipes did not include bitters of any kind, but once you try these drinks with a dash or two of orange bitters, there is no going back. Also, the addition of a tiny amount of orange liqueur, such as Combier's Liqueur d'Orange or Cointreau, ramps up the orange aspect and adds a touch of sweetness. It's a great supple-ment. For a **Cuban Blossom**, sub in an aged white rum for the gin and add a quarter ounce of Luxardo maraschino liqueur. A bit more of an interesting and satisfying alternative.

The last namesake recipe is the **Waldorf Bronx**, which appears, strangely enough, within the Manhattan-like "Waldorf" cocktail entry in *Old Waldorf Bar Days*. In it, Mr. Crockett notes that it was never entered into the actual Bar Book but that it was a popular verbal order by those who "sometimes tired of the ordinary Bronx." He cites Johnnie Solan again, offering that "it was composed of two-thirds gin, one-third orange juice, and two slices of fresh pineapple." It is at its heart a pineapple-enhanced *Orange Blossom No. 2*. See **Bronx/Queens** for variation.

PALL MALL (HIGHBALL)

1 oz. New York Distilling Company Dorothy Parker gin
1 oz. Pierre Ferrand Ambre cognac
1 oz. La Quintinye Vermouth Royal Rouge
2 oz. chilled club soda

Add all ingredients to Collins glass. Add large ice cubes and stir briefly to integrate. Garnish with orange peel.

This deservingly popular Highball of its day appears in a couple of recipe books that predate the Hotel. One version pushes the cognac portion up a touch, but I wouldn't. The only measure of volume that I would be concerned with is the soda, if you're planning on enjoying more than one. This survivor is quite surprising, especially when using adventurous and modern gins and vermouths. A real find.

PALOMA ▮ *Classic*

2 oz. Espolòn blanco tequila
½ oz. fresh lime juice
⅓ oz. Simple Syrup
1 pinch kosher salt
1 oz. fresh grapefruit juice
2 oz. chilled club soda

Add first four ingredients to chilled Collins glass. Add ice and stir to integrate. Add chilled club soda and grapefruit juice. Stir briefly to integrate. Garnish with grapefruit peel or lime wheel.

PALOMA FLORA ∎ *Peacock Alley*

2 oz. Gran Centenario Rosangel hibiscus-infused tequila
½ oz. fresh lime juice
1 pinch kosher salt
3 oz. San Pellegrino Pompelmo grapefruit soda

Add all ingredients except grapefruit soda to Collins glass. Add ice. Fill with soda and stir briefly to integrate. Garnish with grapefruit peel or lime wheel.

Very few midsummer Coolers succeed in doing the job quite like a *Paloma*.

There are other grapefruit sodas out there (Ting, Jarritos, etc.), or you could even make one from scratch using fresh grapefruit juice, simple syrup, and club soda, as in the classic version, but why bother? This is meant to be made quickly, with little fuss. I've included both here for completion's sake. Try both. This Peacock Alley variation differs from the classic only by using a hibiscus-infused tequila, which adds a slight fruitiness and a bit of a cocoa note.

The classic presentation includes preparing the rim of the Collins glass with kosher salt, but I prefer including it in the build for a more balanced and savory result. If using grapefruit soda, use a standard 100 percent agave blanco tequila and prepare as you would the *Paloma Flora*.

PAN-AMERICAN

½ fresh lemon, quartered
1 bar spoon demerara sugar
2 oz. George Dickel rye whisky

Add lemon and sugar to mixing glass. Muddle to release oils and juice. Add whiskey and fill with ice. Shake well and pour entire contents into chilled Old Fashioned glass. Serve with straw.

This sipper was created at the Old Bar to commemorate the efforts of diplomat John Barrett and Andrew Carnegie in the development of the Pan-American Union and the construction of its building in Washington, D.C. (now the Organization of American States). President William Taft planted a "peace tree" during the building's dedication ceremony in 1910. In 2010, President Barack Obama planted one in a renewed dedication of solidarity for the next hundred years.

Though the instructions varied between the two books (first served up, then on ice), I believe that because of the muddling of the lemon and sugar, it became easy for me to view this as a whiskey/lemon *Caipirinha* and I chose that version to represent this entry, which isn't a bad thing at all. If you're presenting it in a cocktail glass, as later recipes do, I would simply use a third of an ounce each of lemon juice and demerara syrup to the rye whiskey, add ice, stir, and strain to err on the side of tradition.

PEACH BLOW FIZZ

3 oz. chilled club soda
½ small, ripe yellow peach (cubed)
½ oz. fresh lemon juice
1 oz. Combier Pêche de Vigne liqueur
2 oz. Hayman's Old Tom gin
1 drop pure vanilla extract
1 oz. heavy cream

Add chilled club soda to small Collins or Fizz glass. Add peaches and lemon juice to mixing glass and muddle. Add remaining ingredients and shake for at least 20 seconds. Fine-strain into prepared glass. Stir briefly to integrate.

First found in print in 1895 in George Kappeler's *Modern American Drinks,* this concoction actually used strawberries as the base fruit and the name came from the peachy hue of the finished product. Other sources stick to the fruit in the title, as does Old Waldorf Bar Days. The Waldorf recipe was the only one that omitted cream of any kind. I viewed that as an oversight and added it for consistency's sake, as the creamless version was less than inspiring. I also added peach liqueur to ramp up the peach flavor while providing a bit of a sugar component. Finally, I added a drop of pure vanilla extract simply because it pairs so well with both the peach and cream. Best made in mid- to late summer, when peaches are at their sweetest, this is one that is worth the effort.

PEACHY PEACOCK COBBLER ∎ *Peacock Alley*

2 oz. Peach-Infused Larceny bourbon
1½ oz. dry red wine (a medium- to full-bodied cabernet sauvignon works best here)
½ oz. Simple Syrup
2 dashes house-made Peach Bitters or The Bitter Truth Peach Bitters
1 peach (half cubed, half sliced)

Add cubed peach and bitters and muddle briefly. Add remaining ingredients except sliced peach to mixing glass. Add ice and shake well. Strain into steel or pewter Julep cup filled with pellet or crushed ice (a Hoffman House goblet or wineglass can work as well). Garnish with reserved sliced peach, fresh mint, and powdered sugar. Serve with straw.

PEACH-INFUSED BOURBON

Add 3 to 4 peaches to airtight glass jar. Add 1 liter bourbon and infuse for 7 to 10 days. Fine-strain and funnel back into bottle. Best used within three months.

This should become a summertime staple. The softer, "wheated" bourbon is very agreeable with the wine and fruit. You may want to pull back on the simple syrup if you prefer a drier profile or if your peaches are very ripe. The homemade peach bitters is simple enough to make and you can use it all summer long, even in your bourbon-based *Manhattans*. See **Cobbler** for variation.

PEACOCK *(Old Books Version)*

2 oz. Rémy Martin 1738 Accord Royal cognac
¼ oz. Bigallet China-China Amer
1 dash Émile Pernot Vieux Pontarlier absinthe

Add all ingredients to mixing glass. Add ice and stir for 30 seconds. Strain into chilled cocktail glass. Garnish with lemon peel.

This short, complex, and flavorful tipple stands as one of the finest surprises in the entirety of the Old Books. The creaminess of the cognac, the orange notes of the Amer, and the lingering flourishes of the absinthe all compete yet reside so harmoniously together. It's a must-try.

According to Ted Saucier in *Bottoms Up* (1951), there was a **Peacock Gallery** cocktail that was served in the early days of the new Hotel. It replaced the Amer with a few dashes of Abbott's bitters. Now that versions of these particular bitters are back on the market, you can try it if you like. It's an adequate enough cocktail, though a touch of gum syrup or simple syrup is needed to really make it happen. For the record, it also appeared in Oscar Tschirky's book as "Peacock Alley." Tschirky himself used the über-premium Martell's Cordon Bleu cognac, but I would save it to be enjoyed neat. Try this version around the holidays.

THE PEACOCK *(2005 Version)*

1½ oz. Ketel One vodka
1½ oz. Pama liqueur
¼ oz. Combier Liqueur d'Orange
¼ oz. fresh lemon juice
1 dash Regans' Orange Bitters No. 6

Add all ingredients to mixing glass. Add ice and stir for 30 seconds. Strain into chilled cocktail glass. Garnish with lemon twist.

This was the first signature cocktail of the newly restored Peacock Alley in 2005, created with our opening assistant general manager, Evelyn Hsu Ciszak. The first rendition included an upscale cognac barrel–finished vodka but any premium variety works just fine here. The bitters add balance and when the drink is stirred (despite the inclusion of lemon juice, which plays a supporting role), it becomes the throwback cocktail it was meant to be.

2 oz. Cranberry-Infused Vodka (recipe follows)
½ oz. Marie Brizard Apry apricot liqueur
1 oz. fresh lemon juice
½ oz. Simple Syrup
½ egg white

Add all ingredients to mixing glass and dry-shake for 5 seconds. Add ice and shake well. Fine-strain into chilled cocktail glass. Twist lemon peel to release oils, then discard. Garnish with dried apricot (optional).

Cranberry-Infused Vodka

Place 2 c. fresh (or frozen) cranberries in airtight glass container. Add 32 oz. vodka. Seal and let rest for at least 1 week. Fine-strain and funnel back into bottle.

Conceived as a **Cosmopolitan** alternative, it succeeds in spades. It soon displaced the spirit-forward first rendition of *The Peacock* as our signature cocktail. For daily service, we do not prepare it with lemon juice, syrup, and egg white à la minute. Instead, we make a sour mix, which incorporates all of these ingredients and more (see "House-Made Recipes" chapter). Since this is our bestselling cocktail, we had to find a way to shorten service time as much as possible. Homemade sour mix is a good idea to have around for house parties as well. As for garniture, we went through various phases that included garnishes such as rainbow-colored glasslike candy peacocks to simple lemon twists before settling on the distinctive, if less visually striking dried apricot. It serves its purpose of identifying itself at the service end of our extremely busy bar.

PEACOCK ALLEY ∎ *(Ted Saucier Bottoms Up)*

2 oz. Rhum J.M agricole white rhum (100 proof)
¾ oz. fresh lime juice
½ oz. maple syrup

Add all ingredients to mixing glass. Add ice and shake well. Strain into chilled cocktail glass. Garnish with freshly grated nutmeg.

This is another cocktail that, according to Ted Saucier, was served in the early days of the New Waldorf-Astoria.

It was originally composed of Charleston rum, a creation of the American South whose best days were already behind it in the time of the Old Bar. Rum distilleries in the area were already on their last legs in the nineteenth century, never mind the mid-twentieth century. Either way, I would imagine this is not something to be sipped gently at the end of the day. You could settle anywhere, but I landed on a higher-proof rhum agricole. This cane rum will have some link to the style of the original ingredient. But don't overthink it, as it could have simply been something an adventurous bartender came up with on the fly, with no motives of posterity. Either way, it makes for an interesting fall or winter Daiquiri alternative. The nutmeg was my idea.

PEGGY O'NEILL PUNCH

1 orange wedge

½ lime wedge

2 dashes Abbott's bitters (Regans' Orange Bitters No. 6, if unavailable)

2 oz. Bulleit rye whiskey

¼ oz. Marie Brizard Parfait d'Amour liqueur

1 oz. chilled club soda (optional)

Add fruit and bitters to mixing glass. Muddle briefly to release oils and juice from fruit. Add whiskey and liqueur. Add ice and stir for thirty seconds. Strain into Old Fashioned glass filled with large ice cubes or sphere. Top with club soda (optional). Garnish with fresh mint sprig.

This was one of the hardest recipes to grapple with. The original recipe's direction lacked detail, and Mr. Crockett's transcription was the culprit. When I followed it to the letter, I just could not get the lime peel to cooperate with the other ingredients. My friend (and distiller) Allen Katz was also left less than satisfied and we independently arrived at similar solutions. We let orange come to the rescue, not only to temper the lime but also to help blend with the candy notes of the Parfait d'Amour. The Abbott's bitters, with their multilayered complexity, helped add a bit of tannin to the final product. I thought the rye whiskey may have been holding it back, but when I replaced it with bourbon, it landed on the sweet side. The grassy notes of the rye make for a more balanced finish.

The drink's namesake, according to Mr. Crockett, was the beautiful and witty daughter of a Washington, D.C., tavern keeper. She was a thrice-married debutante whose first husband, a navy man, committed suicide. Her second husband was Major J. H. Eaton, who became Andrew Jackson's secretary of war, though it was she who scandalously had the president's ear. Her third husband was a much younger dancing instructor, who spent his way through most of her money before she divorced him. Mr. Crockett thought this a good story. I found it utterly depressing and immediately saluted a *Peggy O'Neill Punch* in her honor.

PEPSIN TODDY

2 oz. Rittenhouse bonded rye whiskey

½ oz. Simple Syrup

3 oz. chilled club soda

3 dashes house-made Pepsin Bitters or ¼ oz. Cinzano Rosso sweet vermouth

Add simple syrup and rye whiskey to chilled Collins glass or tumbler. Stir briefly to integrate. Add large ice cubes or sphere. Add club soda and stir again to integrate. No garnish.

This recipe was listed as a "Toddy" in the Old Books, though with the addition of bitters (and club soda), that isn't technically correct. Either way, the bitters are the interesting part here. Though pepsin bitters are no longer produced, it's rumored that the base of pepsin bitters went on to become the leading flavor profiles in Dr Pepper and Pepsi. I took the liberty of devising a bitters based on Dr Pepper in an effort to use at least one unique ingredient in this simple Highball. It's exactly the summer Cooler you think it is.

PICK ME UP

2 oz. Dolin de Chambery sweet vermouth

1 oz. Kübler absinthe

3 dashes acid phosphate

Add all ingredients to mixing glass. Add ice and stir for 30 seconds. Strain into chilled cocktail glass. Garnish with lemon peel.

Pick Me Up No. 2

1 oz. Pierre Ferrand Ambre cognac
1 oz. Carpano Antica sweet vermouth
1 oz. Kübler absinthe

Add all ingredients to mixing glass. Add ice and stir for 30 seconds. Strain into chilled cocktail glass. Garnish with lemon peel.

Most early recipes (and even more modern takes) with this name include lighter and/or softer ingredients such as gin and Champagne as base ingredients and soda and milk as modifiers. Not these two. The Waldorf-Astoria version of the *Pick Me Up* cocktail is directly related to the **Duchess**, as it omits the dry vermouth and bitters but adds a couple of drops of acid phosphate. I prefer a 2:1 ratio of vermouth to absinthe here, but it's up to you, as are the styles of vermouth and absinthe. I chose less assertive versions of both in an attempt to stay faithful to its name. As for the *Duchess*, prepare as you would the **Pick Me Up** by using equal parts absinthe, sweet and dry vermouth, and a couple of dashes of orange bitters. First found in print in 1917, this pre-Prohibition cocktail is also a fine representation of its era. I tried tinkering with the proportions of ingredients but settled on the original recipe (a quarter ounce of gum syrup adds viscosity and a slightly sweeter profile and is worth a try). Ted Saucier, in *Bottoms Up*, used aromatic bitters in lieu of the orange. To me it actually makes more sense and is definitely worth tasting. Without bitters at all, it becomes a **Loftus**, which was named for the then-popular British comedienne and vaudeville headliner Cissy Loftus.

The *Pick Me Up No. 2* is actually the *Pick Me Up* listed in Jacques Straub's *Drinks*. Mr. Straub probably had access to the Old Bar's book and as a result his variations are valid. His version includes cognac and may have seen action at the Old Bar in this form. I landed on Carpano Antica in the vermouth slot, as it adds a chocolate/cherry note when added to the fruit-forward Ferrand cognac. See **Duke** for variation.

PINEAPPLE FIZZ

2 oz. Plantation 3 Stars white rum
1 oz. fresh pineapple juice
½ oz. fresh lemon juice
½ oz. house-made Demerara Syrup
½ egg white
1 dash Angostura bitters
1½ oz. chilled club soda

Add chilled club soda to small Collins or Fizz glass. Add remaining ingredients to mixing glass. Dry-shake for 5 seconds. Add ice and shake for 10 seconds. Fine-strain into prepared glass. Stir briefly to integrate. No garnish.

Freshly pressed pineapple juice will make all the difference here, but canned will work in a pinch (just not from concentrate); just adjust demerara syrup accordingly. Originally excluding lemon juice, I find it essential for the balance of this refreshingly simple summertime sipper. The added bitters lend complexity and extend its finish on the palate. As with most Fizzes, it makes for a fine Bracer or brunch treat as well.

PING PONG

1½ oz. Plymouth sloe gin or Greenhook Ginsmiths beach plum gin liqueur
1½ oz. Noilly Prat extra dry vermouth
2 dashes Regans' Orange Bitters No. 6

Add all ingredients to mixing glass. Add ice and stir for 30 seconds. Strain into chilled cocktail glass. Garnish with lemon peel.

PING PONG (IMPROVED)

1½ oz. Plymouth gin
¾ oz. Plymouth sloe gin or Greenhook Ginsmiths beach plum gin liqueur
¾ oz. Noilly Prat extra dry vermouth
2 dashes Regans' Orange Bitters No. 6

Add all ingredients to mixing glass. Add ice and stir for 30 seconds. Strain into chilled cocktail glass. Garnish with lemon peel.

TIPPERARY (OLD BAR VERSION)

2 oz. Plymouth sloe gin or Greenhook Ginsmiths beach plum gin liqueur
1 oz. Noilly Prat extra dry vermouth
¼ oz. fresh lemon juice

Add all ingredients to mixing glass. Add ice and stir for 30 seconds. Strain into chilled cocktail glass. Garnish with lemon peel.

PING PONG FIZZ

1½ oz. chilled club soda
2 oz. Doc's hard apple cider (NY) or other dry cider
½ oz. Laird's bonded applejack (optional)
¾ oz. fresh lemon juice
½ oz. Simple Syrup
1 egg yolk
1 dash Angostura bitters

Add chilled club soda to small Collins or Fizz glass. Add remaining ingredients to mixing glass and dry-shake for 5 seconds. Add ice and shake for 10 seconds. Fine-strain into prepared glass. Stir to incorporate. No garnish.

The *Ping Pong* was named for the very popular game at the turn of the nineteenth century and the table set that was purchased for the guests of the Old Bar by the owner George C. Boldt. Mr. Crockett maintained that the guests drank so many of these that they saw "three or four [balls] going over the net, instead of one." This one is much more potable than its sweeter sibling, the **Futurity**. The original was simply equal parts sloe gin and dry vermouth with orange bitters. Though I can see that recipe easily being consumed in copious amounts, it still had room for some improvement, and that came in the form of the added gin. This is one of my favorite finds, and it will most definitely find its way onto the Peacock Alley cocktail list.

As for the *Tipperary*, it has no link to Ireland other than Mr. Crockett's recollection as a favorite of a "fond exile." The added lemon juice separates it from the previous versions. See **Tipperary** for accepted standard.

Finally, there was yet another "Ping Pong," which was listed in the "Punch" chapter but was a bland representative. Using all of its ingredients, I interpreted it as a cider-based Fizz. It included the whole egg, which I've adapted by using only the yolk, making it a **Golden Fizz**. I've also added a touch of applejack for a bit of oomph. A refreshing autumnal Bracer either way.

PISCO SOUR ∎ *Classic*

2 oz. Pisco 100 Acholado pisco (Peru)
¾ oz. fresh lime juice
¾ oz. Simple Syrup
½ egg white
3 drops Angostura bitters (for garnish)

Add all ingredients (except bitters) to mixing glass and dry-shake for 5 seconds. Add ice and shake for 10 seconds. Fine-strain into chilled coupe or footed Sour glass. Garnish with Angostura bitters in center of cocktail.

SUITE MARILYN ∎ *Peacock Alley*

2 oz. Pisco 100 Acholado pisco (Peru)
1 oz. St. Germain liqueur
¾ oz. fresh lime juice
½ egg white
1 dash Regans' Orange Bitters No. 6

Add all ingredients to mixing glass and dry-shake for 5 seconds. Add ice and shake for 10 seconds. Fine-strain into chilled coupe or footed Sour glass. Garnish with orange peel.

Though not included in either of the Old Books, this oft-requested refresher deserves an entry here. It's historically prepared using only lime juice, but I think adjusting it with a quarter ounce of lemon juice tempers the final result quite nicely. Either way, it's a summertime classic for a reason.

Although it's well known that Marilyn Monroe loved Champagne,

I cannot imagine her having much to quibble with over this refreshing Sour. She made the Waldorf Towers her residence for eight months in 1955, subleasing her suite from its owner, the British actress Leonora Corbett. Created for an anniversary event hosted there, *Suite Marilyn* was very popular, as guests assumed that the drink was a favorite of hers. I did not have the heart to disappoint them. I have also served this on the rocks and topped it with a touch of Champagne as an alternative decadent presentation.

PLANTER'S PUNCH

2 oz. Myers's Original dark rum
½ oz. fresh lime juice
½ oz. fresh lemon juice
½ oz. fresh orange juice
¼ oz. house-made Demerara Syrup
⅓ oz. house-made Falernum Syrup

Add all ingredients to mixing glass. Add ice and shake well. Strain into Old Fashioned glass or Hoffman House goblet filled with large ice cubes or sphere. Stir briefly to integrate. Garnish with citrus wheels and/or seasonal fruit.

This traditional serving was transcribed as consisting simply of rum and citrus juices—innocuous enough, but small modifications elevate it tremendously. For one, we add our house-made Falernum. It's a lime-and-spice-infused rum-based syrup that hails from the Caribbean. Once it's prepared, the infused base spirit lasts practically forever and you can just add simple syrup as needed. I promise that if you make one batch in the springtime, by the end of summer it will be gone. Club soda was added in some old recipes, though I wouldn't bother. Although served at the Old Bar and obviously prior, these types of drinks would reach their peak of popularity during the mid-twentieth-century tiki craze. As a testament to their durability, they are currently found on cocktail lists all over the world. They are meant to be adjusted for personal taste, so have some fun with them.

POLO

2 oz. Appleton Estate white rum
½ oz. fresh orange juice
½ oz. fresh lemon juice
¼ oz. house-made Demerara Syrup
2 dashes Regans' Orange Bitters No. 6

Add all ingredients to mixing glass. Add ice and shake well. Strain into chilled cocktail glass. Garnish with brandied cherry.

This simple mix will be sure to take the place of your standard summertime Daiquiri at the first sip. The Appleton white rum lends a long hint of coconut to its finish. The original did not include any added sugar or bitters of any kind, but they will add a welcome complexity. According to Mr. Crockett, it was named for the game of kings, and not the explorer.

There is an earlier version of the *Polo* that appears in Jacques Straub's *Drinks* (1914), which is composed of equal parts Old Tom gin, grapefruit, and orange juices. It's pleasing enough; just sub those ingredients into the template above.

POMPIER *(Cascade/Vermouth Cassis)*

2½ oz. La Quintinye Royal extra dry vermouth
¾ oz. Lejay crème de cassis de Dijon
2 oz. chilled club soda

Add ice to Collins glass. Add vermouth and crème de cassis. Top with club soda and stir quickly to integrate. Garnish with lemon peel.

Traditionally recognized as both a *Pompier* and a *Vermouth Cassis* (and is also listed as a "Cascade"), this fills the bill as a lower-alcohol alternative with plenty of flavor to spare. *Pompier* is a French term for *fireman*; this summertime Cooler is sure to refresh your overheated guests. This is another recipe that would take well to fuller-flavored vermouths, as I used here. The lemon twist was not originally included but is essential now.

PRE/IDENTE

1½ oz. Diplomático Reserve rum
¾ oz. Dolin de Chambery Blanc vermouth
¾ oz. Noilly Prat extra dry vermouth
¼ oz. house-made Grenadine
¼ oz. Pierre Ferrand dry curaçao (optional)
1 dash Regans' Orange Bitters No. 6

Add all ingredients to mixing glass. Add ice and stir for 30 seconds. Strain into chilled cocktail glass. Garnish with orange peel and brandied cherry.

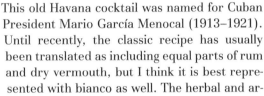

This old Havana cocktail was named for Cuban President Mario García Menocal (1913–1921). Until recently, the classic recipe has usually been translated as including equal parts of rum and dry vermouth, but I think it is best represented with bianco as well. The herbal and aromatic notes of the dry vermouth offset and complement the sweeter profile of the vermouth bianco, and the grenadine and curaçao. Some form of orange curaçao is optional and does lend a sparkle, as do the bitters. You can remove one sugar component if using the other. Perfect for guests who claim an aversion to rum . . . or vermouth!

PRE/IDENT'/ GHO/T *("Banshee" Improved)*

▌ *Peacock Alley*

1 oz. Tuthilltown Hudson New York corn whiskey
1 oz. Tempus Fugit crème de cacao
1 oz. Giffard Banane du Brésil (crème de banana)
1 oz. heavy cream

Add all ingredients to mixing glass. Add ice and shake well. Fine-strain into chilled cocktail glass. Top with small chocolate curls or shavings for garnish.

This is a delicious variation on the forgotten dessert cocktail the *Banshee*. This version adds a backbone of white whiskey, which for me makes all the difference. The high-quality cordials also do their part to make this more than just a sweet tooth's favorite. They are complex and should be tried on their own to fully appreciate their merits. Using a microplane for the shavings makes this crowd-pleaser go down even easier. Inspired by the Presidential Suite (Room 35A), and the ghosts whose presence I (almost) felt.

PRINCE

2 oz. Bulleit rye whiskey
¼ oz. Tempus Fugit crème de menthe
2 dashes Regans' Orange Bitters No. 6

Add all ingredients to Old Fashioned glass. Add large ice cubes or sphere. Stir briefly to integrate. Garnish with lemon peel.

Though served at the Old Bar, this simple, prepared-in-the-serving-glass cocktail seems like it is straight out of the 1960s, when this method was popular. Anyway, the well-made liqueur adds just enough sweetness and viscosity to make it memorable. It's worth a try after dinner. See **Stinger** for variation.

PRINCE HENRY

2 oz. Spencerfield Spirit Edinburgh dry gin
1 oz. Noilly Prat extra dry vermouth
⅓ oz. Tempus Fugit crème de menthe
1 dash Regans' Orange Bitters No. 6

Add all ingredients to mixing glass. Add ice and stir for 30 seconds. Strain into chilled cocktail glass. Garnish with lemon peel.

Named for German Prince Henry's 1902 visit to the United States and his stay at the Old Hotel, this is yet another example in which a bit of enhancement goes a long way. I'm not saying that I would have one of these every day, but I can certainly find room for it in my rotation. Originally prepared with Old Tom gin and sweet vermouth, this dry version is the way to go. The lemon peel is essential. It's also charming on the rocks, with a fresh sprig of mint as garnish.

The Old Books include a **Cuban Prince**, which allows sweet vermouth to be the modifier. Stick with a flavorful white rum such as 86 Co. Caña Brava or Plantation 3 Stars in the gin slot and follow the template here for exemplary results.

PRINCETON

2½ oz. Ransom barrel-aged Old Tom gin or Greenhook Ginsmiths Old Tom gin
2 dashes Regans' Orange Bitters No. 6
½ oz. chilled club soda

Add gin and bitters to mixing glass. Add ice and stir for 30 seconds. Strain into chilled cocktail glass. Add club soda directly into cocktail. Snap lemon peel over surface to release oils, then discard.

George Kappeler Version (1895)

2½ oz. Tanqueray Old Tom gin or Hayman's Old Tom gin
2 dashes Regans' Orange Bitters No. 6
½ oz. Graham's ruby port wine

Add gin and bitters to mixing glass. Add ice and stir for 30 seconds. Strain into chilled cocktail glass. Pour port into jigger and pour down side of rim so it slides down side of glass. Snap lemon and orange peels to release oils, then discard.

The Waldorf Astoria version of this cocktail can take some experimentation regarding gin style, though the barrel-aged versions of Old Tom gin bring something extra to the table.

If you prepare this cocktail using a hearty rye whiskey (WhistlePig or Rittenhouse work well here) and Angostura bitters, you will have the **Amaranth**. An additional trick to this one was adding a touch of confectioners' sugar to it just after the club soda for a little extra foaming action. This maneuver was a staple of pre-Prohibition hotel bars. You can do the same for the *Princeton*.

Mr. Crockett states that the *Princeton* cocktail was named for the alumni who apparently took it as a rite of passage to visit the Old Bar. They must've gotten around, as they apparently spent time at the old Holland House as well, because bartender and author George J. Kappeler also had a rendition. His was another visually striking version, presented as a "two-tone" cocktail in which the port wine pooled at the bottom of the glass and made for a "two drinks for the price of one" enterprise. Do limit the gin to unaged varieties, as barrel-aged versions tend to muddy the pairing with the port. See **The Last Drop** for variation.

QUEEN CHARLOTTE

> **3 oz. Bordeaux Supérieur red wine or dry red wine of choice**
> **¾ oz. house-made Raspberry Syrup**
> **3 oz. Q lemon soda (or other cane syrup–based variety)**

Add wine and raspberry syrup to chilled Collins glass. Add large ice cubes. Add lemon soda and stir to integrate. Garnish with mint sprig.

Named for the capital city of the United States Virgin Islands, Charlotte Amalie, the original recipe called for the wine to simply "flavor" the soda, but a touch more adds the proper body and effervescence. As alcohol is a relatively small part of this midday refresher—and by all means it can stay that way—I wouldn't shrug at adding a nudge of gin if enjoying at sundown.

QUEEN ELIZABETH

> **2½ oz. Appleton Estate 12 Year Old Jamaican rum**
> **¼ oz. fresh lime juice**
> **⅓ oz. house-made Grenadine**
> **2 dashes Regans' Orange Bitters No. 6**

Add all ingredients to mixing glass. Add ice and stir for 30 seconds. Strain into chilled Old Fashioned glass with large ice cubes or sphere. Garnish with orange peel and brandied cherry.

Though there were other renditions, this one seems to be a proprietary recipe of the Old Bar. Calling for five parts of Jamaican rum, there is no doubt about its intention (use the good stuff here). I adapted it by adding bitters for backbone and stirring it (the original recipe directed shaking it). This will make a fine summertime predinner tune-up. I would be careful, though, as it is quite the strong one. Be sure that the air-conditioning is working.

THE QUIET MAN *(St. Patrick's Day)* ❚ *Peacock Alley*

- **1½ oz. Bushmills Irish whiskey**
- **¾ oz. French roast coffee (chilled)**
- **½ oz. Irish Mist liqueur**
- **½ oz. Amaretto Disaronno**
- **¼ oz. fresh orange juice**
- **1 drop pure vanilla extract**

Add all ingredients to mixing glass. Add ice and stir for 30 seconds. Strain into chilled cocktail glass. Garnish with orange twist.

The original intention and inspiration for this cocktail was a dairy-free and drier version of Baileys Irish cream. Although other models came closer in flavor profile to the intended target, this rendition is, for me, the most enjoyable. As always, just chill the morning's leftover coffee and use at night for cocktails.

Or you could do what I do when I want to lift this to another level (making it what I call an ***Irish Goodbye***): Prepare the recipe as listed here and include two ounces of heavy cream, shake then strain into two chilled cocktail glasses for a strong and complex after-dinner treat for a special guest. Crème de cacao can stand in for the Irish Mist for yet another twist. I really enjoy these types of recipes; they are fine, old-school holiday or wintertime offerings that rely on a little extra "mixology" and result in special and worthy returns.

RABBIT'S DILEMMA ❙ *Peacock Alley*

1½ oz. George Dickel No. 12 Tennessee whiskey
¼ oz. house-made Cinnamon Vodka
1½ oz. fresh carrot juice (or Bolthouse Farms, if unavailable)
½ oz. house-made Demerara Syrup
¼ oz. fresh lemon juice
2 dashes house-made Cocoa Bitters (or Fee Brothers Aztec
**   chocolate bitters, if unavailable)**

Add all ingredients except bitters to mixing glass. Add ice and
shake well. Strain into Old Fashioned glass filled with large cubes or
sphere. Top with bitters. Garnish with carrot wheel set vertically on
rim of glass.

This recipe relies very heavily on house-made ingredients, but the
final result makes it worth the effort. An autumnal treat, this went
through more than a few variations, even including a house-made
butternut squash syrup (which kind of got lost in the mix). The
house-made cocoa bitters sets a high bar and the full-bodied
Tennessee whiskey and cinnamon vodka profile brings home the
long and complex finish.

RAMOS GIN FIZZ *(a.k.a. New Orleans Fizz)*

- **2 oz. chilled club soda**
- **2 oz. Beefeater London dry gin (or Hayman's Old Tom gin)**
- **½ oz. lemon juice**
- **½ oz. lime juice**
- **¾ oz. Simple Syrup**
- **1 oz. heavy cream**
- **3 drops orange flower water**
- **2 drops pure vanilla extract (optional)**
- **½ egg white**

Add chilled club soda to small Collins glass. Add remaining ingredients to mixing glass and dry-shake for 5 seconds. Add ice and shake for 10 seconds. Strain into Collins glass. Stir quickly with bar spoon to integrate. No garnish.

Listed in the Old Books as the geographically correct **New Orleans Fizz**, this classic is one of my personal favorites. Legend has it that bartender Henry C. Ramos created it in 1888 at the Imperial Cabinet Saloon. Using up to two dozen "shaker boys" on a busy Mardi Gras Day, the bartenders would pass along these ice cold shakers in a relay to ensure the proper level of frostiness.

Although it's not traditionally added, some of New Orleans' finer establishments include vanilla extract as a "secret ingredient." I like it, so I've incorporated it here. Today the *Ramos Gin Fizz* is properly served with historical authority at the famous Sazerac Bar in the Roosevelt Hotel in New Orleans (a Waldorf Astoria Hotel). See *Fizz* for variations.

RASPBERRY BERET ▮ *Peacock Alley*

- **2 oz. Spiced Rum Infusion (Appleton Estate Reserve or Sailor Jerry; recipe follows)**
- **1½ oz. fresh raspberry puree (or Les vergers Boiron, Perfect Purée, or Ravifruit)**
- **½ oz. Luxardo Triplum orange liqueur**
- **¼ oz. fresh lemon juice**
- **1 dash Angostura bitters**

Add all ingredients to mixing glass. Add ice and shake well. Strain into chilled cocktail glass. Garnish with mint sprig.

Spiced Rum Infusion

1 750 ml. bottle Appleton Reserve rum
2 tablespoons black peppercorns
1 orange rind
4 Calamyrna or Turkish dried figs, halved
1 Fuji apple, cored and cubed
¼ cup fresh ginger, julienned and crushed
¼ cup dried coriander seeds
1 vanilla bean, split

Add all ingredients to an airtight glass container. Let stand for 7 days and taste. If you want a bit more flavor, infuse for 3 more days. Fine-strain, then funnel back into bottle. Best used within 6 months.

ʃOUTHERN GENTLEMAN ▮ *Peacock Alley*

1½ oz. Elijah Craig 12 Year Old bourbon
1½ oz. fresh Raspberry Puree (or Les vergers Boiron or Ravifruit)
⅓ oz. Luxardo Triplum orange liqueur
⅓ oz. Luxardo maraschino liqueur
2 dashes Angostura bitters

Add all ingredients to mixing glass. Add ice and shake well. Strain into chilled cocktail glass. Garnish with mint sprig and lemon peel.

These complex yet extremely drinkable cocktails hearken back to our opening in 2005. We often use commercial frozen purees strictly for the sake of consistency, though instructions for homemade purees can be found in the "House-Made Recipes" chapter.

The house-made spiced rum infusion in the *Raspberry Beret* was created for a food and spirits pairing event. We happened to have some left over and we created this cocktail.

I did not want to simply swap out the base spirits, so with the addition of the maraschino liqueur, the *Southern Gentleman* became its own cocktail entirely. Enjoy with caution—the bourbon is well hidden by the other flavor components and because this combination is so easy drinking, it's sure to sneak up on some.

REES

1½ oz. Hayman's Old Tom gin
¼ oz. Punt e Mes sweet vermouth
1 dash Émile Pernot Vieux Pontarlier absinthe
1 dash Angostura bitters

Add all ingredients to mixing glass. Stir briefly to integrate (no ice). Pour into Sherry cocktail glass. No garnish.

This unique serving was named for a personal friend of George C. Boldt, the first general manager (and part owner) of the Old Waldorf Hotel, in 1893. The original recipe instructed, "to be served warm—no ice." You may balk, but with the first sip, you'll find that they had something here. Now, would I have one every day? Probably not, but as a midwinter's wee nip, unabashedly and without a doubt. As for the vermouth, the more robust, the better. Feel free to explore and use some new American-style gins here, as long as they hover around 80 proof. Anything stronger and you will probably have to add water. On that note, you may want to add a quarter of an ounce or so of chilled mineral water anyway, to help release some of the more complex flavor components. This one is a real winner. See **Creole Lady** for similar presentation.

RIDING CLUB

3 oz. Cocchi Barolo Chinato quinquina or Bonal quinquina aperitif
3 dashes Horsford's acid phosphate
2 dashes Angostura bitters

Add all ingredients to mixing glass. Add ice and stir for 30 seconds. Strain into chilled cocktail glass. Garnish with lemon twist.

(MONTAUK) RIDING CLUB ❙ *Classic*

2 oz. Castarède Sélection Armagnac
1 oz. Cocchi Barolo Chinato quinquina or Bonal quinquina aperitif
3 dashes Horsford's acid phosphate
2 dashes Angostura bitters

Add all ingredients to mixing glass. Add ice and stir for 30 seconds. Strain into chilled cocktail glass. Garnish with lemon twist.

Originally debuting in print in George Kappeler's *Modern American Drinks* (1895), the *Riding Club* and its variants are odes to New York's social clubs of the same name. Whether or not the Old Book included a base spirit may never be known, but the *Montauk Riding Club* incorporates brandy into the mix. I like the result when using Armagnac but most any brandy will do. The original recipe called for equal measures of brandy and Calisaya, but I think it has more character if you allow the brandy to lead the procession. It also did not include bitters of any kind, but I added two dashes of gum syrup instead (see "House-Made Recipes"). The acid phosphate adds acidity without a citrus element. In the end, these are classic digestifs—and you should enjoy them as such. See **Calisaya** for variation.

RIO GRANDE ∎ Classic

1 oz. Espolòn reposado tequila
1 oz. Hayman's Old Tom gin
1 oz. Cinzano Rosso sweet vermouth
3 dashes house-made Cocoa Bitters or Fee Brothers Aztec
    Chocolate Bitters

Add all ingredients to mixing glass. Add ice and stir for 30 seconds. Strain into chilled cocktail glass. Garnish with orange peel.

This recipe made its debut in the *Café Royal Cocktail Book*, published in 1937. I am including it here because it's one of the few examples of a tequila-based recipe of the era and one that I can easily imagine being served at the Old Bar. We have featured it for a few dinner events with great success. The original called for it to be shaken and included London dry gin, but the sweeter Old Tom gin does the trick. The type of tequila was not specified, but it works well with a 100 percent agave reposado. It helps soften the mouthfeel and extend the finish. The cocoa bitters and orange twist were also not originally included but are now essential.

ROB ROY

2 oz. Chivas Regal 12 Year Old blended Scotch whisky
1 oz. Dolin de Chambery sweet vermouth
2 dashes Regans' Orange Bitters No. 6

Add all ingredients to mixing glass. Add ice and stir for 30 seconds. Strain into chilled cocktail glass. Garnish with lemon peel.

ROB ROY ▮ *Dry*

2 oz. Haig Dimple Pinch 15 Year Old Scotch whisky
¾ oz. Noilly Prat extra dry vermouth
2 dashes Regans' Orange Bitters No. 6

Add all ingredients to mixing glass. Add ice and stir for 30 seconds. Strain into chilled cocktail glass. Garnish with lemon peel.

The *Rob Roy* is the most famous cocktail credited to the fellows at the Old Bar. It was named for the Reginald De Koven–composed "romantic comic operetta *Rob Roy.*" This Herald Square Theatre production, near the Old Hotel, is based on the life of one Robert Roy MacGregor (and by association, the Sir Walter Scott novel). This cocktail, like many others, was intimately linked to happenings that were part of the social consciousness of the day. Not much has changed over the past hundred years. The original recipe remains largely intact, with only the ratio of Scotch to vermouth adjusted to about 2:1; the Old Books called for equal amounts of each. If you tried it that way (and you should), you would be having a **Highland** or an **Express**—both were identically listed. I leaned on the 2:1 ratio here for the modern presentation.

As with the *Manhattan*, the cocktail to which this is most closely related, there is no need to ask for a "sweet" variation when requesting one at a bar, as using sweet vermouth is the standard preparation. If ordering a "dry" version, you will have to specify. The Old Books recognized this dry rendition as a **York** or a **Beadleston No. 2**. Both Beadleston cocktails were named for a local brewer who supplied the bar with much of its beer. I think it's safe to assume that he was also quite the customer. By the way, this is one of my mother's favorite cocktails, and although not a stickler for most things, she will ask a waiter to return with a "dry" Rob Roy if he happened not to get her order correct. Ninety percent of all

Rob Roys served are of the sweet variety. (See **Manhattan** for **Beadleston No. 1**.) The ratio of whiskey to vermouth can be adjusted for personal taste, but I would not veer much further than adding another half ounce of whiskey if you're in the mood for something stronger. Anything past that and you may as well be a time traveler from 1977.

Because of the hotel's history and clientele, I often receive unusual requests, and it was from one such request that the *Rob Royce* was born. This one, from an in-flight private jet publication, required an "expensive version" of a classic cocktail. For obvious reasons, we drew the Rob Roy, and to answer the call of our general manager at the time, Eric Long, I created the **Rob Royce**. It's an ultra premium "1860"-styled, enhanced Rob Roy. I used the Macallan 18, Carpano Antica sweet vermouth, and a touch of Grand Marnier's 100th Anniversary edition. An exercise in excess for sure.

Another often requested rendition is the **Perfect Rob Roy**, which splits the vermouth portion of the recipe equally between sweet and dry. Try it with some of the newly released amber vermouths as an alternate.

Back to the Old Books; there were two Irish whiskey renditions, both including equal parts Irish whiskey and sweet vermouth, with the type of bitters used as the defining ingredients. The **Emerald** used Angostura, and the **Rory O'More**—named for the seventeenth-century Irish rebel leader—included orange bitters (other books of the era also reference this as a **Paddy**). I prefer it to the *Emerald*, as the aromatic Angostura bitters blanket the delicate floral and fruit notes of the Irish whiskey (go with a full-bodied, pot still rendition here), but I certainly recommend trying both (with a 2:1 ratio of whiskey to vermouth), if only to come to your own conclusion. See **Robert Burns** for variation.

ROBERT BURNS

2 oz. Spencerfield Spirit Sheep Dip or Johnnie Walker Black blended Scotch whisky

1 oz. Martini & Rossi sweet vermouth

2 dashes Émile Pernot Vieux Pontarlier absinthe

1 dash Regans' Orange Bitters No. 6

Add all ingredients to mixing glass. Add ice and stir for 30 seconds. Strain into chilled cocktail glass. Garnish with lemon twist.

Bobby Burns ▮ *Harry Craddock Variation*

- **2 oz. Spencerfield Spirit Sheep Dip or Johnnie Walker Black blended Scotch whisky**
- **1 oz. Dolin de Chambery sweet vermouth**
- **¼ oz. Bénédictine liqueur**
- **1 dash Regans' Orange Bitters No. 6**

Add all ingredients to mixing glass. Add ice and stir for 30 seconds. Strain into chilled cocktail glass. Garnish with lemon twist.

Tale of Two Roberts ▮ *Peacock Alley*

- **2 oz. Spencerfield Spirit Sheep Dip or Johnnie Walker Black blended Scotch whisky**
- **1 oz. Cinzano Rosso sweet vermouth**
- **¼ oz. Bénédictine liqueur**
- **2 dashes Émile Pernot Vieux Pontarlier absinthe**

Add all ingredients to mixing glass. Add ice and stir for 30 seconds. Strain into chilled cocktail glass. Garnish with lemon twist. Serve three small shortbread cookies on side plate.

This is another creation credited to the Old Waldorf-Astoria, and it's basically a *Rob Roy* with an absinthe enhancement. According to Mr. Crockett, it was named for the gentleman who sold cigars to the Old Bar, probably for the now-defunct Robert Burns Cigar Company, of which, I imagine, they sold many (though there was a "Robbie Burns" Scotch whisky being imported at the time of the Old Bar as well). Naming a favorite cocktail for a regular guest was not uncommon, and there are more than a few in this book. The *Robert Burns* is a simply decorated cocktail for the ages. The one difference here is that unlike with the Manhattan and the Rob Roy, I would not recommend ramping up the Scotch whisky. These are all pretty delicately balanced cocktails that rely on harmony to

succeed. If you are in the mood for something stronger, it may be in your best interest to enjoy a simple dram.

Now, the more popular variation with Benedictine as the enhancing ingredient, from the Savoy's Bobby Burns, was clearly named for the Scottish poet (most famously known for "Auld Lang Syne"), as the recipe note in *The Savoy Cocktail Book* states that the drink was a "very fast mover on St. Andrew's Day." As for the cocktail itself, the original omitted bitters of any kind, but a dash of the orange variety works for a bit of backbone. Although it was traditionally served with equal measures of whisky and vermouth, I've adapted it here for the modern palate.

Also of note is the **Black Thorn**, surprisingly not included in the Waldorf books and first found in print in Harry Johnson's *Bartender's Manual* (1900). It's simply the Irish whiskey rendition of the *Burns*, made using a dry vermouth and absinthe rinse. Just use a full-bodied whiskey here (2:1 Redbreast 12 Year Old to dry vermouth will do). Aromatic bitters was the original call, though bravery will be rewarded.

Finally, there is the *Tale of Two Roberts*, a combination of the previous two that I came up with a few years ago. I think it's the tastiest of the three, as it includes the herbal notes of absinthe and the sweetness of Bénédictine for the most complex finish. On this one, I would avoid bitters of any kind, since they tend to muddy up the mix. David Embury, author of the classic *The Fine Art of Mixing Drinks,* preferred Drambuie to augment his version because it's a Scotch-based liqueur, but I disagree for that same reason. Please try one and decide for yourself.

ROBIN

2½ oz. Famous Grouse Black Grouse blended Scotch whisky or Johnnie Walker Double Black blended Scotch whisky
½ oz. Calisaya liqueur

Add ingredients to mixing glass. Add ice and stir for 30 seconds. Strain into chilled cocktail glass. Garnish with lemon twist and brandied cherry.

Jacques Straub, in his 1914 book, *Drinks,* had the Scotch whisky taking the lead with only dashes of Calisaya. After sampling nearly every variation in between, I landed on the proportion listed here for its balance, though the ratio can be adjusted for taste, mood, or simply the time of day. The Calisaya elevates this to a singular sensation. The slightly peated whisky shines through for a remarkably strong marriage. You could also present this as an alternate to the **Rusty Nail** by simply floating the liqueur over the whisky, in an ice-filled Old Fashioned glass. See **Floater** for variations.

ROCK AND RYE

2 oz. New York Distilling Company Mister Katz's Rock & Rye

Add to chilled Old Fashioned glass and serve. Garnish with lemon twist and brandied cherry on skewer.

Although there were plenty of bottled versions produced, early bartenders would've doctored up their own *Rock and Rye* by adding personal enhancements to some rough-and-tumble rye whiskey of the day. Citrus and cherries, along with rock candy or syrup and a selected spice or two (some stalwarts included cinnamon, star anise, and clove) would all be added to the "hearty" and young spirit. It was also quite commonplace for a stick of rock candy to be served with your neat rye whiskey, but as the liquor improved, the necessity for such enhancements declined. By the time of the Old Bar, I think this ceremony was merely a step of service.

This recipe includes a commercially produced finished product, which is the result of sweetening the rye whiskey, post-aging, and adding bing cherries, orange peels, and cinnamon. The whiskey is then filtered before bottling for the multifaceted sipper you have today.

Traditionally accepted as a tonic for the common cold and other ailments, most likely due to the inclusion of a citrus element (though the promise of reduced taxes during the height of the temperance movement probably played the greatest role regarding the seeding of this tall tale), **Rock and Rye** found a space on most back bars until the 1980s or so.

On a personal note, I like to add the peels of half a lemon, half an orange, and a few brandied cherries to the bottle in an effort to replicate the soul of the Old Bar. One last secret: You can serve it on the rocks and add a dash or two of aromatic bitters for an instant Old Fashioned. I won't tell anyone.

ROMAN PUNCH

1 oz. Appleton Estate Extra Jamaican rum
½ oz. Rémy Martin 1738 Accord Royal cognac
½ oz. Luxardo Triplum triple sec
¾ oz. fresh lemon juice
½ oz. house-made Raspberry Syrup
½ oz. Graham's ruby port wine (for float)

Add all ingredients except port wine to mixing glass. Add ice and shake well. Strain into Old Fashioned glass or Hoffman House goblet filled with large ice cubes or sphere. Float port wine on top. Garnish with one raspberry (optional).

This nineteenth-century creation has survived from the Civil War era straight through until today. The *Roman Punch* first found itself in print in *Jerry Thomas' Bartenders Guide* (1862), and it appears here almost faithfully. I have adapted it so that the sweet components of the recipe carry their weight without the need to add more sugar. I've also included Mr. Thomas's raspberry syrup, as the Old Bar books omitted it. Other even older recipes fold in meringue egg whites, which are probably best reserved for larger-format servings.

Not only is this a "big bang" creation, it also has a timeless flavor profile, meant to be enjoyed by everyone. Using another fortified wine such as Madeira, sherry, or tawny port as a finish is also encouraged. If using a Hoffman House–style goblet or wineglass, feel free to add more seasonal fruit for a ramped-up presentation.

ROMAN HOLIDAY ∎ *Peacock Alley*

2 oz. Bombay Sapphire London dry gin
½ oz. Aperol
½ oz. Cynar
1 oz. fresh orange juice (blood orange juice, if in season)

Add all ingredients to mixing glass. Add ice and shake well. Strain into chilled cocktail glass. Garnish with orange peel and brandied cherry.

Created for a promotional event in 2010, this satisfying hybrid can also be served on the rocks with a splash of soda for the hottest of summer afternoons. If you're leaning toward this presentation and are in the mood for a more bitter result, try pulling back on the gin by half an ounce to allow the bitter and amaro to lead.

ROOFTOP MAGIC ▌ *Peacock Alley*

2 oz. Black Cherry–Infused Bourbon (Henry McKenna; recipe follows)
1 oz. Cinzano Rosso sweet vermouth
¾ oz. Empire Brewing Company Downtown Brown ale or other brown ale (flat)
¼ oz. house-made Honey Syrup
1 dash Angostura bitters

Add all ingredients to mixing glass. Add ice and stir for 30 seconds. Strain into chilled cocktail glass. Garnish with brandied cherry.

Black Cherry-Infused Bourbon

1 c. fresh black cherries, split
1 750 ml. bottle Henry McKenna bonded bourbon

Place all ingredients in airtight glass container for 7 days. Fine-strain and funnel back into bottle. Best if used within two months.

This unique cocktail was created for a media event for our in-house weekly magic show. The magic part of the cocktail is that we made the bubbles in the beer disappear . . . ha! Simply pour the beer into a container and leave it covered in the refrigerator for two days, then use as you would any other ingredient. The original beer was our Waldorf Buzz brown ale, made by Empire Brewing Company, in Syracuse, New York. It incorporated our "Top of the Waldorf" honey in the fermentation process and was a huge success. The honey syrup was also made with our rooftop honey, culled from our rooftop hives, and the bitters were house-made as well. Despite the use of honey in this cocktail, it is not as sweet as you might think. The assertive, dry brown ale does its job (along with the bitters) of drying out the finish while leaving you wanting another sip.

ROOSEVELT PUNCH/SOUR

2 oz. Laird's bonded applejack
¾ oz. fresh lemon juice
½ oz. house-made Demerara Syrup
½ oz. Pierre Ferrand Ambre cognac
1 dash Angostura bitters (optional)

PUNCH PRESENTATION:

Add all ingredients except cognac to mixing glass. Add ice and shake well. Strain into Old Fashioned glass or Hoffman House goblet filled with large ice cubes or sphere. Top with cognac. Garnish with orange peel and brandied cherry.

SOUR PRESENTATION:

Add all ingredients except cognac to mixing glass. Add ice and shake well. Strain into chilled cocktail glass. Garnish with brandied cherry.

Named for President Theodore Roosevelt, this entry as it appears here is adapted for a modern presentation. The *Roosevelt Punch* listed in both of the Old Books called for half of a lemon to be muddled along with a teaspoon of demerara sugar. If going the traditional route, just add the applejack post-muddle, add ice, and shake. Strain over fresh ice and top with cognac. Make no mistake, this is quite the powerhouse tipple and should be treated as such. An additional ounce of water in the build here would be traditional (and probably necessary).

Since there is a *Roosevelt Sour* (a.k.a. Jersey Sour) that was served up, we can use the same recipe. Its quirk is that it omits the cognac, but you don't have to. I recommend preparing as directed here except cut the applejack by half an ounce. This will ensure the most balanced and agreeable mix. The bitters were not mentioned, but I find them essential, especially in the *Sour* presentation.

ROSEMARY'S, MAYBE? ∎ *Peacock Alley*

2 oz. 86 Co. Aylesbury Duck vodka
½ oz. St. Germain liqueur
1 oz. fresh grapefruit juice
2 dashes house-made Peach Bitters or The Bitter Truth peach bitters
One sprig rosemary

Add all ingredients to mixing glass. Add ice and shake well. Fine-strain into chilled cocktail glass. Garnish with freshly grated nutmeg.

Created for a special food pairing menu, this was a guest favorite for a few consecutive summers after it debuted in 2007. Now that I've revisited it, I can see why. It's a refresher that you can also serve on ice. If peach bitters are unavailable, orange will most certainly do and yes, the rosemary sprig gets shaken in the mix.

RUBY

2 oz. Rothman & Winter orchard cherry liqueur
1 oz. Noilly Prat extra dry vermouth
¼ oz. Luxardo maraschino liqueur
5 dashes Horsford's acid phosphate
2 dashes Regans' Orange Bitters No. 6

Add all ingredients to mixing glass. Add ice and stir for 30 seconds. Strain into chilled cocktail glass. Garnish with lemon peel.

RUBY ❙ *William "Cocktail" Boothby Variation*

1½ oz. Plymouth sloe gin or Greenhook Ginsmiths beach plum gin liqueur
1½ oz. Martini and Rossi sweet vermouth
¼ oz. Heering cherry liqueur
1 dash Regans' Orange Bitters No. 6

Add ingredients to mixing glass. Add ice and stir for 30 seconds. Strain into small cocktail glass. Garnish with lemon peel.

RUBY ❙ *Jack Grohusko Variation*

2½ oz. Hayman's Old Tom gin
5 dashes Peychaud's bitters

Add ingredients to mixing glass. Add ice and stir for 30 seconds. Strain into chilled cocktail glass. Garnish with lemon peel.

This creation of the Old Bar is a lower-alcohol sipper with plenty of flavor. Should you make the recommended investment of acid phosphate, you will find ways to use this revelatory item from the past.

What was probably the original version of this cocktail and most likely the one the bartenders of the Old Bar riffed on to create their own *Ruby* was culled from *World Drinks and How to Mix Them* (1908). Later versions added London dry gin and even egg whites. Stick with this recipe and you won't go wrong, especially with the beach plum liqueur, which manages to stand out in this crowd. See **Futurity** for variations.

Another *Ruby* cocktail of the era simply fused London dry gin with Peychaud's bitters to less-than-life-changing results, but it really took off with the sweeter (and lower-alcohol) Old Tom gin taking the lead (I took the liberty of making the commonsense move and added a lemon twist, to predictably outstanding results). From *Jack's Manual* (1916), it has become one of my favorites. See **Bunyan** for variation.

RUM PUNCH

2 oz. Santa Teresa 1796 Ron Antiguo de Solera rum
¾ oz. fresh lemon juice
½ oz. house-made Demerara Syrup
1 dash Regan's Orange Bitters
1 dash Angostura Bitters

Add all ingredients to mixing glass. Add ice and shake well. Strain into Old Fashioned glass or Hoffman House goblet filled with crushed or pellet ice. Garnish with brandied cherry and orange slice (seasonal berries, optional).

RUM AND FRUIT PUNCH

2½ oz. Appleton Estate V/X Jamaican rum
¼ oz. Combier kümmel Liqueur
¼ oz. Benedictine Liqueur
½ oz. fresh orange juice
½ oz. fresh pineapple juice
½ oz. fresh lemon juice

Add all ingredients to mixing glass. Add ice and shake well. Strain into Old Fashioned glass or Hoffman House goblet filled with large ice cubes or sphere. Garnish with brandied cherry and orange slice (seasonal berries, optional).

Though it's traditionally prepared with a bit of water, we can forgo that custom with this Punch, since we're serving over crushed ice (Punches are typically served with large ice cubes). Go with a dark variety of rum here. The demerara syrup also adds a richness that helps give this one its own identity, and a touch of bitters aids in balancing the result and helps keep it alive on the ice.

The *Rum and Fruit Punch* is a complex, crowd-pleasing combination. I like how some of the old recipes reflect the adventurous spirit of the day. Although some barkeep may have just grabbed any bottle on the bar looking to accent a basic recipe, I would like to think that it took more than a bit of trial and error to land on such a lasting and complex combination. See **Kingston** for variation.

∫ALOMÉ

1½ oz. Byrrh Grand quinquina aperitif (Maurin quina or Dubonnet, if unavailable)
1½ oz. Martini & Rossi sweet vermouth
¼ oz. Pernod Original Recipe absinthe
1 dash Regans' Orange Bitters No. 6

Add all ingredients to mixing glass. Add ice and stir for 30 seconds. Strain into chilled cocktail glass. Garnish with lemon peel.

∫ALOMÉ ▮ *Jacques Straub Variation*

1½ oz. Portobello Road No. 171 London dry gin
¾ oz. Noilly Prat extra dry vermouth
¾ oz. Martini & Rossi sweet vermouth
1 dash Regans' Orange Bitters No. 6
12 celery leaves

Add all ingredients to mixing glass. Add ice and stir for 30 seconds. Fine-strain into chilled cocktail glass. No garnish.

∫ALOMÉ ▮ *Harry Craddock Variation*

1 oz. Portobello Road No. 171 London dry gin
1 oz. Noilly Prat extra dry vermouth
1 oz. Byrrh Grand quinquina aperitif or Maurin quina (Dubonnet, if unavailable)
1 dash Regan's Orange Bitters No. 6

Add all ingredients to mixing glass. Add ice and stir for 30 seconds. Strain into chilled cocktail glass. Garnish with lemon peel.

Named for the crazed biblical character with a penchant for severed heads, and subsequently the popular Oscar Wilde play from the turn of the twentieth century, this pleasant cocktail is a product of its era but can most certainly be enjoyed today. The Old Bar's version is an absinthe-laced, aromatized wine–based aperitif. Note that the wines should already be chilled. Be sure not to over-stir and dilute the final product; stir just enough to integrate the absinthe.

The Straub version, from *Drinks*, has celery leaves as an oddball ingredient. Using just enough adds an herbal touch that does not identify itself on the palate but contributes a simultaneously fresh and slightly bitter note. A complete surprise.

Mr. Craddock's version, from *The Savoy Cocktail Book,* is a sort of hybrid of the first two. Lighter and definitely worth sampling.

ſANGAREE ▮ *Old Bar Variation*

1½ oz. Greenhook Ginsmiths beach plum gin liqueur or Plymouth sloe gin
1½ oz. Noilly Prat extra dry vermouth
¼ oz. Simple Syrup
2 dashes Horsford's acid phosphate
2 dashes Angostura bitters

Add all ingredients to mixing glass. Add ice and stir for 15 seconds. Strain into Old Fashioned glass filled with large ice cubes or sphere. Garnish with freshly grated nutmeg.

PORT WINE ſANGAREE (ſTANDARD)

3 oz. Graham's ruby port wine (sherry or Madeira, optional)
¼ oz. Simple Syrup

Add all ingredients to mixing glass. Add ice and stir for 15 seconds. Strain into Old Fashioned glass filled with large ice cubes or sphere. Garnish with freshly grated nutmeg.

Rum Sangaree/Punch

2 oz. Appleton Estate Reserve Jamaican rum
1 oz. chilled water
¼ oz. house-made Demerara Syrup (or Simple Syrup)
¼ oz. Quinta do Noval 10 Year Old tawny port wine (optional, for float)

Add all ingredients except port wine to mixing glass. Add ice and stir for 15 seconds. Strain into Old Fashioned glass filled with large ice cubes or sphere. Float port wine if using. Garnish with freshly grated nutmeg.

The *Sangaree* originated in Spain, and should utilize Spanish wines. It represents one of the oldest families of prepared drinks. Dating back to the 1700s, the port, Madeira, and sherry variations are standards. These are wine-based **Toddies** and what mainly separates the *Sangaree* from the popular Sangria is the omission of citrus of any kind.

Though this drink is traditionally made by dissolving sugar and water, then adding the main ingredient, I find it best to cut to the chase and use syrup. Not only will it integrate easier, it will be much more manageable when it comes to consistently portioning the sugar level. If using a drier sherry such as fino, the half ounce of syrup may be welcome, though I would pull it back or consider not using it at all if you're going with a Pedro Ximénez sherry or ruby port.

Over time, the category expanded to include a bit of spirit. The Old Bar's Sangaree goes even further and incorporates bitters and acid phosphate. Mr. Crockett's transcription omitted sugar, but I've included it here for balance.

The *Rum Sangaree* is not a *Sangaree*, but makes for quite the sipper and, like a **Punch**, is meant to stretch the base spirit, hence the addition of water. Try with genever, añejo tequila, or an entry-level Armagnac for unique offerings. Again, the sugar level and port wine float are a completely personal call and should correlate with the base spirit, though the nutmeg remains essential for all of them. Here's where a tawny port or oloroso sherry float will shine.

SATCHMO AT THE WALDORF ▮ *Peacock Alley*

- **1 oz. Smith & Cross navy-strength rum**
- **1 oz. Lustau Don Nuño oloroso sherry**
- **1 oz. fresh pineapple juice**
- **½ oz. fresh lemon juice**
- **½ oz. Simple Syrup**
- **¼ oz. fresh egg white**
- **2 oz. any Belgian-style witbier (reserved for finish)**
- **5 drops Peychaud's bitters (reserved for garnish)**

Add all ingredients except beer and bitters to mixing glass. Add ice and shake well. Strain into chilled pilsner glass filled with ice cubes. Top with beer. Top with bitters, for garnish.

In keeping with the tradition of the Old Bar, this was created for the 2014 off-Broadway production of the same name. Its producers asked me if I could create something to commemorate Louis Armstrong's last shows, which were held in the Hotel's Empire Room during March 1971. Riffing on Mr. Armstrong's New Orleans roots led to this satisfying refresher. I wish "Satch" were around to try this bittersweet post-performance quaff. I imagine him wiping his brow with his famous handkerchief and slaking his thirst, raising his glass in my direction with approval, and then taking another long sip.

SAVANNAH

- **½ egg white**
- **2 oz. Plymouth gin**
- **1 oz. fresh orange juice**
- **¼ oz. Tempus Fugit crème de cacao**

Add ingredients to mixing glass and dry-shake for 5 seconds. Add ice and shake for 10 seconds. Fine-strain into chilled cocktail glass. Garnish with orange peel.

Though there isn't much historical information on this crowd-pleasing entry, that is just fine; we will let the perfect pairing of orange and chocolate speak for itself. I am very proud of this proprietary concoction, as it is one of my favorites when I'm in the mood for something deceptively strong but equally delicious.

ƒAZERAC

1 sugar cube

3 dashes Peychaud's bitters

2 oz. Wild Turkey 101 rye whiskey or Pikesville 110 proof rye whiskey

¼ oz. Émile Pernot Vieux Pontarlier absinthe (or Herbsaint liqueur)

Add ice and a splash of cold water to Old Fashioned glass to chill. Add sugar cube and bitters to mixing glass and muddle until integrated (about 5 seconds). Add whiskey and stir briefly to combine. Add ice and stir for 20 seconds. Discard ice from prepared Old Fashioned glass. Add absinthe and roll glass to coat, then discard. Strain contents of mixing glass into prepared Old Fashioned glass. Snap lemon peel to release oils, then discard.

Born in late-nineteenth-century New Orleans, this time traveler has hardly wavered in popularity (in New Orleans, at least) and is more in demand today than ever before (everywhere). That it found its way into the Old Books is a testament to how well-traveled it was. At its heart, it's simply a *(Whiskey) Cocktail* with Peychaud's bitters and an absinthe rinse, but its legend and preparation makes it so much more. By the time of the Old Bar, Mr. Crockett noted that they adorned their rye version of the Sazerac with an additional dash of sweet vermouth (please don't—that's more or less a *Waldorf*). If using the originally intended cognac in the lead role, I prefer a more masculine variety here, as it holds up to the other ingredients and the dilution best.

Another favorite variation of mine is a calvados version. I would add two dashes of aromatic bitters along with the Peychaud's; it works wonders. Laird's bonded applejack can work too, for an American twist.

This is certainly one of the top ten cocktails to have in your repertoire when you need to impress guests with your bartending skills. Simply packing crushed ice into an Old Fashioned glass while building the cocktail in a separate mixing glass will lend an air of anticipation to the proceedings, not to mention coating said glass with absinthe. Just be sure to practice the timing once or twice prior to your event to guarantee success.

This is one cocktail in which I will insist on the sugar cube, as it adds the perfect amount of sweetness. It always seems to me that syrup, no matter how little, tends to infiltrate its core, making the final result too sweet. One exception I will make is a touch of gum syrup (only if you already have it on hand), as the slightly sweet profile of the drink is offset and somehow enhanced by the added viscosity and creaminess of the gum syrup. It is certainly worth a try.

One of the premier bars to experience both the *Sazerac* and the *Ramos Gin Fizz* is the Sazerac Bar, in the lobby of the famous Roosevelt Hotel in New Orleans (a Waldorf Astoria hotel), the spiritual home of these classics. Be sure to engage bar manager Russ Bergeron, as he is well versed in the history of both his hotel and his city.

SHANDYGAFF

6 oz. Tröegs HopBack amber ale (Pennsylvania) or Bass ale (England)

6 oz. Q or Boylan ginger ale or other cane-based ginger ale or ginger beer (chilled)

Combine ingredients in chilled pilsner glass or mug. Stir briefly to integrate.

When the NYC summer heats up, we are sure to fill a few requests for these during lunch service and into the afternoon. A classic of English pubs of the nineteenth century, it has lost some of its popularity there but continues to be ordered around the world. The name comes from London slang for "pub water" or "pint of beer" ("shant of gatter"—*shanty* means "public house" and *gatter* means "water"). This was traditionally served with Bass ale (even at the Old Bar) but we try to use local products whenever possible. I have used the portions from the original recipe, though you can adjust for your personal taste. You may also try using a spicy ginger beer for another fine rendition.

SHANGHAI TEA ∎ *Peacock Alley*

1½ oz. Pierre Ferrand Ambre cognac
½ oz. Sweet Vermouth Infusion (Noilly Prat; recipe follows)
¾ oz. Pama liqueur
¼ oz. fresh lime juice
1 oz. prepared green tea (chilled)

Add all ingredients to mixing glass. Add ice and stir for 30 seconds. Strain into Old Fashioned glass filled with large ice cubes or sphere. Garnish with orange peel.

Sweet Vermouth Infusion

Bring to boil one bottle sweet vermouth (750 ml.) with 6 cardamom pods, 6 cloves, and 1 cinnamon stick. Remove from heat and allow to cool, fine-strain, and funnel back into bottle. Lasts 6 weeks refrigerated.

Created by our opening assistant general manager and sommelier Evelyn Hsu Ciszak, this interesting *Punch* included an XO cognac in the decadent early days of the relaunching of Peacock Alley during the autumn and holiday season of 2005. Even with two ingredients that require prior preparation, it's not as complicated as it may seem to put together. Prior to testing it for this book, I had not tried it in many years and forgot how much I enjoyed it. The lime juice is there to add a bit of acidity. The green tea and spiced vermouth can be prepared the day before.

SHERIDAN PUNCH

4 oz. Lemonade (recipe follows)
1 oz. Michter's US 1 rye whiskey

Add ice to Collins glass. Add lemonade and stir briefly to integrate. Float rye whiskey on top. Garnish with lemon wheel.

Lemonade

2 oz. fresh lemon juice
1½ oz. Simple Syrup
5 oz. water (chilled)

▌ *(Yield: 2 servings)*

Add all ingredients to mixing glass and stir to integrate.

Mr. Crockett's entry in *Old Waldorf Bar Days* reads as follows:

> Some say this was named after General Philip Sheridan, famous
> Union cavalry officer during the Civil War. Some advance the
> claim of Richard Brinkley Sheridan, the Irish dramatist; and
> there are advocates of Pat Sheridan, long head houseman of the
> Waldorf, for the honor of being godfather to this Punch. Well,
> they were all Irishmen, or of Irish descent, and an Irish barman
> composed the drink.

This simple, enhanced lemonade can be adjusted for personal
taste on many levels. The original recipe had vague directions as to
how much spirit to add. I went with the ratio here, as I think a refreshing quencher like this should be light on the liquor. You will
likely be having more than one, as you would with a Punch. The
serving of lemonade is a basic rendition. You can pull back on the
syrup or add a quarter ounce if your tastes run on the sweet side.
There was another variation listed called the **Rum-Ade**. I would go
with a dark variety there. Whether you're using rum or rye whiskey, I would preserve the float effect by adding the spirit float just
before serving, and allow your guests to stir it in or not.

SIDECAR

2 oz. Courvoisier VSOP cognac
1 oz. Combier Liqueur d'Orange
¾ oz. fresh lemon juice

Rub lemon wedge around half of rim of chilled cocktail glass and
roll moistened portion in superfine sugar (optional). Add all
ingredients to mixing glass. Add ice and shake well. Fine-strain
into prepared cocktail glass. Garnish with orange peel.

2 oz. Boulard Grand Solage VSOP calvados
1 oz. Domaine de Canton ginger liqueur
¾ oz. fresh lemon juice

Rub lemon wedge around half of rim of chilled cocktail glass and roll rim in superfine sugar (optional). Add all ingredients to mixing glass. Add ice and shake well. Fine-strain into prepared cocktail glass. Garnish with lemon peel.

This descendant of the **Brandy Crusta** remains one of the most-requested classic cocktails. Possibly created in Paris prior to Prohibition, and popular throughout if you were lucky enough to know where to find such things, it didn't hit its stride until after Repeal Day. It's one of the few cocktails to have roots in the pre-Prohibition era and actually remain a commonly requested item.

I would not use your best brandy here, as it will be lost within the citrus and liqueur. Original recipes cite equal portions of the ingredients but the combination here will yield the most balanced result. Traditionally served without a garnish, the modern version includes an orange twist.

The *Southeast Sidecar* made its Peacock Alley debut in 2008 when Domaine de Canton liqueur was released. I was asked to create a cocktail for the event launch and this was our entry, adding some julienned fresh ginger to a bottle, just to ramp up the ginger identity a bit. Be sure to adjust when using in recipes calling for the unadorned liqueur. The apple brandy is a nice twist.

Finally, there was, of course, a **Cuban Sidecar**. I recommend a good dark rum for a more complex result.

SKIPPER

2 oz. G'Vine Floraison gin
½ oz. Luxardo maraschino liqueur
¼ oz. fresh lemon juice
¼ oz. fresh orange juice
¼ oz. house-made Grenadine

Add all ingredients to mixing glass. Add ice and shake well. Strain into chilled cocktail glass. Garnish with brandied cherry.

Mr. Crockett noted that bartender Johnnie Solan claimed the **Skipper** was named for a yacht captain who frequented the bar, but couldn't recall his name. Or it was the name he went by ("Hey, Skipper, would you like another?"). In any case, the touch of grenadine and orange bitters were not included in the original recipe but work for a more balanced and seaworthy result. Try both.

ſLING/TODDY (Cold)

ſLING

2 oz. spirit of choice (brandy, genever, rum, whiskey, etc.)
¼ oz. Simple Syrup

Add spirit of choice and simple syrup to Old Fashioned glass. Stir briefly to integrate. Add a couple of large ice cubes or sphere and stir again to integrate. Garnish with freshly grated nutmeg.

TODDY (COLD)

2 oz. spirit of choice (brandy, genever, rum, whiskey, etc.)
½ oz. Simple Syrup
2 oz. chilled water

Add spirit of choice, water, and simple syrup to Old Fashioned glass. Stir briefly to integrate. Add a couple of large ice cubes or sphere and stir again to integrate. Garnish with freshly grated nutmeg.

These are the first "multicelled organisms" of the cocktail world, and although the *Toddy* predates the *Sling*, I have listed these related recipes under the descendant rather than the forefather. The *Sling* is typically being served cold and the *Toddy* is primarily served hot. Though each can be prepared in both manners (and should be, as there are examples of more than a few in this book alone), for the sake of clarity, I erred on the side of simplicity.

Wearing its nutmeg garnish with pride, the once-popular *Sling* reached its apex of popularity at the turn of the eighteenth century. Its slight variation, the *Toddy*, is also closely related to the *Fix* and the *Sour*, in which one or two minor variations make all the difference. Here again, size and portion are factors, along with the final garnish of nutmeg, which is (almost) a necessity. The genever variation was seemingly the first and, like other potables of the day, would be called for by its lead ingredient. An entry-level Armagnac or rye whiskey works well, as they take to the added sugar quite nicely.

Old-time execution would have you combine a level teaspoon of superfine sugar with the water prior to adding the other ingredients. You can go that way for history's sake, but the syrup cuts to the chase and is more consistently adjusted for personal taste. It certainly makes for the slightly timelier preparation, especially if you're serving to a group. Either way, there should be just the hint of sugar, to avoid a syrupy cordial result.

Also worth noting is that the *Toddy* and the *Sling* are the direct predecessors of the **Cocktail**. Simply put, the *Cocktail* is a "bittered" *Sling*. Three of the four identifying ingredients of a *Cocktail* are represented here; bitters are the only holdout. The *Julep* is simply a "minted" *Sling*, but that's another story.

An integral part of these recipes is the water. With the *Sling*, any less water and you may as well not include it at all. You'll be better served by allowing the ice to melt for a few minutes before tasting. In the *Toddy*, it depends on your mood and if you're having more than one, but you shouldn't overthink it. I like to think that in the *Sling*, the water is there to temper the strength of the spirit component, whereas in the *Toddy*, the spirit is there to help make the water worth drinking.

The *Toddy* first appears in the Old Books in the form of an **Apple Toddy Cold** (Laird's bonded applejack or an entry-level calvados would be used at our bar). Again, though the *Toddy* is more famously served hot, there are four cold versions listed in the Old Books: **Brandy Toddy** (cognac), **Kentucky Toddy** (bourbon), **Bacardi Toddy** (white rum), and **Rum Toddy** (Jamaican rum). The **Pepsin Toddy** is unique enough for its own entry.

These drinks are all uncomplicated staples, but know that they dominated their era. In any case, with the almost limitless possible variations on these templates, you can easily enjoy a new version every night of the week.

∫NOW BALL FIZZ

> **2 oz. Boylan, Fever-Tree, or other cane-based ginger ale (chilled)**
> **2 oz. GrandTen Distilling Medford rum or Berkshire Mountain Distillers Ragged Mountain rum**
> **½ oz. Simple Syrup**
> **½ egg white**

Add chilled ginger ale to small Collins or Fizz glass. Add remaining ingredients to mixing glass. Dry-shake for 5 seconds. Add ice and shake for 10 seconds. Strain into Collins glass.

ʃNOW BALL FIZZ ▮ *Jacques Straub Rendition (a.k.a. Silver Bowl Fizz)*

1½ chilled club soda
1½ oz. Bombay Sapphire London dry gin
1 oz. Hermann J. Wiemer dry Riesling wine (Finger Lakes)
1 oz. grapefruit juice
2 drops orange flower water
¼ oz. Simple Syrup
½ egg white

Add chilled club soda to small Collins glass. Add remaining ingredients to mixing glass. Dry-shake for 5 seconds. Add ice and shake for 10 seconds. Strain into Collins or Fizz glass. Stir briefly with bar spoon to integrate. No garnish.

The Old Bar's recipe is basically a **Whiskey Fizz** (without a citrus element, by the way; feel free to add a half ounce of lemon juice for a traditional Fizz). If you can't procure one of these new versions of old rums, the standard Appleton dark Jamaican rum will do.

The *Drinks* version of the *Snow Ball Fizz* is quite the eye-opener. In his original recipe, Mr. Straub placed the grapefruit juice in the lead role and although it makes a fine Bracer, having the gin lead the way makes for a more balanced result. The high acidity, brought on by the dry white wine and the grapefruit juice, makes the orange flower water superfluous, though I kept it for tradition's sake. Use this recipe when in need of something lighter than a *Ramos Gin Fizz*. I think that if Fizzes make a true comeback, this one will surely be leading the way.

ʃOOTHER

1 oz. Pierre Ferrand Ambre cognac
1 oz. Appleton Estate Reserve rum
½ oz. Combier Liqueur d'Orange or Pierre Ferrand dry curaçao
½ oz. fresh lemon juice
¼ oz. Simple Syrup
¼ oz. fresh apple juice (apple cider, if unavailable)

Add all ingredients to mixing glass. Add ice and shake well. Strain into Hoffman House goblet or wineglass with large ice cubes or sphere. Garnish with fresh seasonal fruit.

I first discovered this Punch as we were reopening Peacock Alley in 2005. One of the more complex concoctions in the Old Books is represented here pretty much in its original state, though I wouldn't squawk at a touch more fresh apple juice or cider. Jacques Straub's 1914 version adds applejack and omits the apple juice. This could also have been a misinterpretation on someone's part, but at the end of the day, I don't think it really matters. The rum and cognac do the heavy lifting here anyway. Feel free to tinker with the ingredients to find a suitable version for your palate. Some grated nutmeg for the finish wouldn't be a bad thing here either.

This can also be served warm if you wish: just add all ingredients to ceramic mug and add 3 or 4 ounces of hot water. At that point the freshly grated nutmeg would become essential.

ſOUR

2 oz. spirit of choice (brandy, genever, gin, rum, whiskey, etc.)
¾ oz. fresh lemon juice
½ oz. Simple Syrup
½ oz. egg white (optional)

PREPARATION NO. 1 (MODERN)

Add all ingredients to mixing glass. Add ice and shake well. Strain into footed Sour glass or tumbler. Garnish with citrus twist (paired to base spirit) and brandied cherry.

PREPARATION NO. 2 (MODERN—WITH EGG WHITE)

Add ingredients to mixing glass. Dry-shake for 5 seconds. Add ice and shake for 10 seconds. Fine-strain into chilled cocktail glass. Garnish with citrus twist (paired to base spirit) and brandied cherry.

PREPARATION NO. 3 (MODERN—NEW YORK, BRUNSWICK, OR WALDORF SOUR—NO EGG WHITE)

Add all ingredients to mixing glass. Add ice and shake well. Strain into Old Fashioned Collins glass filled with large ice cubes. Pour a half ounce of dry red wine into jigger and slowly pour over back of spoon for float.

Serve with straw. No other garnish necessary.

Old Bar Variation

1 teaspoon superfine sugar
1 oz. water (chilled)
½ lemon
2 oz. spirit of choice (brandy, genever, gin, rum, whiskey, etc.)

Add sugar to chilled tumbler along with water. Squeeze lemon into glass, discard shell, and stir to integrate. Add spirit of choice and ice cubes. Stir briefly to integrate, though I would roll this once or twice from tumbler to shaker tin and back again for best results.

The classic **Sour** is an evolutionary offshoot of the **Punch** group, which came into prominence in the mid-nineteenth century. Traditionally built in the glass, as in the preceding *Old Bar Variation*, this recipe can claim more than a few variants. For the general build, I would try all versions at some point, as they are all simple enough to prepare. Though not strictly traditional, I personally find that a touch of egg white and its added bit of froth to be very pleasing, with the Old Bar's being the cleanest and fastest. After all, these are the templates for some of the most popular cocktails ever created. Fizzes, Sours, Collinses, and Daisies, among others, all show their lineage with simple substitutions or additions. Using bitters on the surface as an elaborate garnish has come in and out of vogue with these as well.

As for the Old Books, they had plenty of twists. There is the **Bacardi Sour**, with white rum at the base and lime juice in the citrus slot (that is your world-famous **Daiquiri**, folks!). Mr. Crockett name-checked the **Brandy Sour**, which I would use a simple VS cognac for best results.

The **Pequod Sour** is your classic **Whiskey Sour** with a few sprigs of mint included. It works especially well if you use the rolling technique during preparation. The barmen at the Old Bar apparently also labeled a version of a *Whiskey Sour* a **Santiago**, if served with a stuffed olive. I would not recommend it.

Another recorded recipe is the **Rum Sour**, which differs from the *Bacardi Sour* in that it features lemon juice in the citrus slot along with Jamaican rum. Use a rum originating from St. Croix and you'll have the **St. Croix Sour**. By simply floating a bit of dry red wine on top of that, you'll have what the Old Bar called a **Southern**.

You'll notice quite a few red wine floats, as this was a signature maneuver at the time of the Old Bar. There's the **Brunswick Sour**, created in the now-extinct Madison Avenue's Hotel Brunswick. As listed here, it is a rye whiskey–based *Sour* with a dry red wine float. *Sours* with red wine floats later came to be known as New York Sours, though it seems the Waldorf barmen had no problem claiming this simple adornment by naming it a **Waldorf Sour**. Either way, try it on as many variations as you like. Most work for me.

As for a garnish, the now-classic rendition is the skewered orange slice and brandied cherry "flag," with the cherry sitting between the two sides of a folded orange or lemon slice make for a bright and colorful topping.

I recommend keeping the base spirits on the weaker side, using flavorful but basic expressions that come in around 80 proof. Though these are diluted with water, that is the point: they are made for the long haul and enjoying more than one. Keep your overproof spirits for another time.

STEINWAY PUNCH

> 1½ oz. High West Rendezvous rye whiskey
> ½ oz. Pierre Ferrand dry curaçao
> ¾ oz. fresh lemon juice
> ¼ oz. Simple Syrup
> 2 oz. chilled club soda

Add all ingredients except club soda to mixing glass. Add ice and shake well. Strain into Old Fashioned glass or Hoffman House goblet filled with large ice cubes. Add club soda and stir to integrate. Garnish with lemon wheel and brandied cherry.

Mr. Crockett noted that this Punch was named for Charles Steinway, "a well-known gourmet of the day" who was also a son of the piano company Steinway & Sons. We can safely assume he whiled away his free time at the Old Bar. Mr. Crockett omitted its identifying ingredient, orange curaçao, which I found in Jacques Straub's *Drinks* (1914). In lieu of Ferrand's, Royal Combier or Grand Marnier orange liqueur would be the traditional call, though you may want to omit the simple syrup. I also tried this with an entry-level Armagnac in the rye slot to astounding results. Be sure to try it.

STEPHEN'S COCKTAIL

1 oz. Lustau Don Nuño oloroso or Lustau Puerto Fino Solera Reserva sherry
1 oz. Noilly Prat extra dry vermouth
1 oz. Bénédictine liqueur

Add all ingredients to mixing glass. Add ice and stir for 30 seconds. Strain into chilled cocktail glass. Garnish with lemon peel.

This trailblazing recipe of the Old Bar is due for a comeback. The flavor profile of this cocktail is exactly what is in vogue; it can be enjoyed either before or after dinner. From the moment I tasted it, I knew that it wouldn't be long before it would make an appearance on the Peacock Alley menu. I tried this cocktail with a couple of different bitters just for the sake of it, but they got in the way of the sherry, which should lead the way. One quick note: keep the sherry dry, as the Bénédictine is more than enough sweet. Who Stephen was may never be known, but what we do know is that he had great taste in cocktails. See **Tip Top** for variation.

STINGER

2¼ oz. Royer VSOP cognac
¾ oz. Tempus Fugit crème de menthe

Add ingredients to mixing glass. Add ice and shake well. Strain into chilled cocktail glass. No garnish.

Ray Milland, in the classic 1948 film noir *The Big Clock*, enjoyed these with authority, although by the third round he requested that they include "green mint," and although the color of the liqueur has no bearing on the taste profile, you can imagine the results. If you'd like to enjoy them in the manner of Mr. Milland and as they did at the Old Bar (though maybe not in such prodigious amounts), you would serve them up, as directed here. This preparation breaks from tradition, as a *Stinger* is typically shaken, even though it lacks citrus or cream.

Post-Prohibition, and certainly by the 1950s, these began to be served over crushed ice as they went from after-dinner drinks to anytime drinks. If going that way, you may want to use a straight 2:1 brandy-to-liqueur ratio. It's better on a summer night, perhaps, but I'll stick to the Old Bar's presentation.

There is also a **Brant** cocktail, which predates the Old Bar and gives the *Stinger* the true cocktail treatment by adding a couple of dashes of Angostura bitters, stirred and served up with a lemon twist. It's worth a try. See **Prince** for variation.

ƒTONE FENCE

> **5 oz. Doc's hard apple cider, chilled (NY) or**
> **Orchard Hill hard apple cider, chilled (NY)**
> **1½ oz. Laird's bonded applejack brandy or Boulard Grand Solage VSOP calvados**
>
> Add chilled cider to stemmed goblet or Bordeaux-style wineglass, then pour in chilled apple brandy. Garnish with freshly ground nutmeg (optional).

JERƒEY

> **2½ oz. Laird's 7½ Year Old apple brandy**
> **½ oz. Simple Syrup**
> **2 dashes Dr. Adam Elmegirab's Boker's bitters or Angostura bitters**
>
> Add all ingredients to mixing glass. Add ice and stir for 30 seconds. Strain into chilled cocktail glass. Garnish with lemon peel.

The Old Bar's *Jersey* is simply your standard applejack-based Cocktail. Though served up here, presenting it in an Old Fashioned glass works just as well. The original **Jersey Cocktail** (found in Jerry Thomas's book) was simply bitters, a touch of sugar, and local dry cider with a lemon twist. To make the Old Bar's version of a **Cider**, just omit the sugar and serve on ice in a Collins glass. Clearly, it led the way to the enduring *Stone Fence*.

This Revolutionary War–era quaff enhanced cider by using rum in the starring role, but the more than appropriate apple-based brandy works like a charm. You could add an ice cube or two, but if your cider is well chilled and you give a quick turn on ice to your spirit, you really don't have to dilute this autumnal classic. I do like to top it with one good scrape of nutmeg, but that's just me. If I had my way, this would be a sight on the Thanksgiving table as familiar as sweet potatoes and cranberry sauce. It is light enough for you to have more than one, but strong enough to allow you to survive the most trying of relatives.

STORMY MANHATTAN ISLAND ∎ *Peacock Alley*

2 oz. Don Q añejo rum
¾ oz. Domaine de Canton ginger liqueur
¾ oz. fresh lemon juice
1 rounded bar spoon of jalapeño jelly (Braswell's or Stonewall Kitchen) or
¼ grilled and seeded fresh jalapeño pepper

Add all ingredients to mixing glass. Add ice and shake well. Fine-strain into chilled cocktail glass. Garnish with lemon peel.

This cocktail was created for a promotional film showcasing Puerto Rican rum. The production company had asked for two cocktails to feature during a segment but needed a third because the shoot was moving along quickly enough to squeeze another in. I wound up running to the Peacock Alley kitchen and saw charred, grilled jalapeños being prepared for a service. I quartered and seeded one and added it to the recipe listed here. It was a huge hit. Our enhanced ginger liqueur (with julienned fresh ginger in the bottle) really sits nicely alongside the other ingredients. Though it may not be for everyone, this spicy and toasty cocktail is unique.

You can use hot pepper jelly for more consistent results. Another serving suggestion would be to pair it with Asian cuisine. See **Buck/Rickey** for variations.

STRAWBERRY

2 oz. Hine VSOP cognac

½ oz. house-made Strawberry Syrup

1 dash Luxardo maraschino liqueur

2 dashes house-made Cocoa Bitters or Fee Brothers Aztec Chocolate Bitters

Add all ingredients to mixing glass. Add ice and stir for 30 seconds. Strain into chilled cocktail glass. Garnish with small strawberry, slit and set on rim of glass.

I can see how this may have been popular at the Old Bar. The original recipe called for orange bitters but the chocolate variety made much more sense—once you try it, you'll see why. This makes for quite the after-dinner drink, paired most obviously with dark chocolate and fresh strawberries. The original recipe also suggests the juice of twelve strawberries, which yields a much drier result and does no particular service to either the brandy or the fruit. The syrup is the way to go here.

STRAWBERRY FIELDS ∎ *Peacock Alley*

2 ripe strawberries

2 basil leaves

6 mint leaves

1 bar spoon superfine sugar

¼ oz. fresh lemon juice or 2 dashes Horsford's acid phosphate

2½ oz. Hendricks gin

1 oz. fresh orange juice

Add strawberries, basil, mint, sugar, and lemon juice (or acid phosphate) to mixing glass. Muddle to release juice from strawberries. Add gin, orange juice, and ice. Shake well and fine-strain into Old Fashioned glass filled with large ice cubes or sphere. Garnish with mint sprig.

First appearing on Peacock Alley's cocktail list in the spring and summer of 2006, this was a huge success and favorite of Hotel guests. One quick note: as with most things muddled, the sugar is used not only to provide sweetness to the drink but, more important, as the abrasive element that helps break down the fruit and herbs. That's why most muddled drinks call for actual sugar and not syrup. If you have acid phosphate handy, use that to add acidity to this cocktail without imparting more citrus flavor. Either way, this will be a summertime staple.

SUBURBAN

1½ oz. Michter's US 1 rye whiskey
¾ oz. Appleton Estate Reserve rum
¾ oz. Quinta do Noval 10 Year Old tawny port wine
1 dash Angostura bitters
1 dash Regans' Orange Bitters No. 6

Add all ingredients to mixing glass. Add ice and stir for 30 seconds. Strain into chilled cocktail glass. Garnish with orange peel.

Yet another in honor of the Wall Street financier and horse stable owner James R. Keene (see **Futurity**), this one is named specifically for the Suburban Handicap race, which has been run in New York nearly every year since 1884.

Usually ruby port, sweeter with fewer barrel and spice notes, is the go-to when it comes to filling in a cocktail. The original recipe did not specify the type of port wine, but after I tried a ruby and a tawny, the tawny won out. It paired more suitably with the spirits and resulted in a much more complex finish. Either way, this is a strong steakhouse sipper. Break out the cigars.

SUISETTE FIZZ

1½ oz. chilled club soda
1½ oz. Hennessy VS cognac
¾ oz. Martini & Rossi sweet vermouth
¾ oz. fresh lemon juice
½ oz. Simple Syrup
1 whole egg (small)
3 dashes Kübler absinthe

Add chilled club soda to small Collins or Fizz glass. Add remaining ingredients to mixing glass. Dry-shake for 5 seconds. Add ice and shake for 10 seconds. Fine-strain into Collins glass. Stir quickly with bar spoon to integrate. Garnish with freshly grated nutmeg (optional).

This **Royal Fizz** (so called because it contains the entire egg) is a definite product of its time and subscribes to the "everything but the kitchen sink" theory of cocktail creation. Though I have to say, in the end, this is a fine representation of a wintertime Fizz. When preparing for yourself, you may want to adjust an ingredient or two. Go right ahead; this one can take a bit of tinkering. Though not included in the original recipe, a sprinkling of freshly grated nutmeg on the top would be a grand addition.

ſWAN

2 oz. Hayman's Old Tom gin *or* Bols genever
1 oz. Noilly Prat extra dry vermouth
¼ oz. fresh lime juice
2 dashes Pernod Original Recipe absinthe
2 dashes Angostura bitters

Add all ingredients to mixing glass. Add ice and stir for 30 seconds. Strain into chilled cocktail glass. Garnish with orange or lemon peel.

With its namesake ingredient now defunct, the gents at the Old Bar prepared this cocktail with genever at its base, while Jacques Straub, in *Drinks* (1914), made his with London dry gin (both using equal ratios to vermouth). Without the inclusion of some sort of sugaring agent or even a bianco vermouth to offset the bitters, absinthe, and lime juice, Old Tom gin is undoubtedly the way to go, especially if I want to abide by the recipes from the Old Books and still have something we all want to drink. The result is a few clouds on a sunny day away from outright success. Let me clarify: when combining such strong personalities, you just know an argument could break out, and I think that's what we have here. Some of your most dominating ingredients all take supporting roles for the betterment of the end result. That said, if using genever or London dry gin, a quarter ounce of gum or simple syrup will go a long way, or you may want to split the vermouth between a dry and bianco variety.

As previously mentioned, if you see citrus in a cocktail and the directions say to stir, it's a very small amount and usually in lieu of bitters. It's meant to balance the cocktail and give it a spine without the flavor profile that the bitters may bring to the equation. This recipe is an anomaly in that it includes both.

SYMPHONY OF MOIST JOY

½ oz. Combier Rose liqueur
½ oz. yellow Chartreuse
½ oz. Tempus Fugit crème de cacao
½ oz. Hennessy VS cognac

Add shaved ice to coupe or small wineglass. Pour ingredients in order. Garnish with seasonal berries and fresh mint (optional). Serve with small straw.

Most likely born as a Pousse Café, in *Old Waldorf Bar Days* (1931), Mr. Crockett exclaimed that this after-dinner drink "seems to have been a rhapsody in cordials." It certainly is. If your tastes lean toward the minty side of things, just replace the crème de cacao with crème de menthe (as the original did); either way you may have a new favorite dessert in a glass, one with a unique and eyebrow-raising name, to boot.

TANGO NO. 2

¾ oz. Appleton Estate white rum
¾ oz. Bénédictine
¾ oz. Noilly Prat extra dry vermouth
¾ oz. Cinzano Rosso sweet vermouth
¾ oz. orange juice
1 dash Regans' Orange Bitters No. 6

Add all ingredients to mixing glass. Add ice and shake well. Strain into chilled cocktail glass. Garnish with lemon peel.

Although different versions of the *Tango* appear in other books of the era, this one was ours. In fact, the Old Books contained two that shared the title.

This recipe was unbranded when it came to type and style of rum, and I tried more than a few. I finally landed on the one listed here because it had character but remained clean without adding extra sugar to the final mix. Bitters that were not included in the original are now integral for a balanced result. Although on paper this may look like a bit of a mishmash, it works surprisingly well. You could easily turn it into a large-format presentation and serve as a bowled Punch. See **Love** cocktail for **Tango**.

TEA COBBLER

2½ oz. black tea (chilled)
1 oz. Smith & Cross navy-strength rum
¼ oz. house-made Pineapple Syrup (or Cointreau, if unavailable)
¼ oz. Gum Syrup (or Simple Syrup, if unavailable)

Add ingredients to mixing glass. Add ice and stir briefly to integrate. Strain into Old Fashioned glass or Hoffman House goblet filled with crushed or pellet ice. Garnish with seasonal fruit. Serve with straw.

JAMAICAN COLD TEA

2 oz. black tea (chilled)
¼ oz. Smith & Cross navy-strength rum
¼ oz. Pierre Ferrand dry curaçao
¼ oz. Prune Syrup (recipe follows) (or house-made Demerara Syrup, if unavailable)

Add all ingredients to mixing glass. Stir briefly to integrate. Strain into teacup or Old Fashioned glass with one or two large ice cubes. Garnish with freshly grated nutmeg (optional).

Prune Syrup

1 c. water
1 c. sugar
½ c. chopped dried prunes

In a saucepan, bring water and sugar to boil over medium heat. Add chopped prunes and allow to cool. Refrigerate overnight and strain. Lasts up to one month.

TEA TIME

3 oz. black tea (chilled)
1½ oz. Appleton Estate Reserve rum
⅓ oz. fresh lemon juice
½ oz. house-made Demerara Syrup

Add all ingredients to Collins glass. Add ice and stir to integrate. Garnish with lemon wheel.

I've grouped all three of these recipes based on the fact that they share tea as their main ingredient. All of them demonstrate how important proportions are. What does separate them is their presentation. The *Tea Cobbler*, of course, is a *Cobbler* in spirit (although without its typical wine component). A helpful hint: if you want to prepare this cocktail with its hint of pineapple and you don't have the time to make a proper pineapple syrup, you can add a quarter ounce of pineapple juice to half an ounce of simple syrup (gum syrup adds viscosity and works better if you have it).

The *Jamaican Cold Tea* is of the delicate variety and is one of my favorites. You may also enjoy this with hot tea on cold winter nights. The prune syrup is not integral but it does add a unique figlike component to the finish. Just remember that if you go the extra yard and prepare an item such as this, it has other uses. This prune syrup is wonderful in oatmeal, for one, and can be used in other cocktails to surprising results (a **Sazerac** comes to mind).

Finally, we have a soon-to-be summertime favorite, *Tea Time*. What I like about this enhanced iced tea is that it is built in the glass with little fuss and can easily be prepared by the pitcher for gatherings. It's a sure winner that will have your family and friends offering you untold items of value for the recipe.

For the integral ingredient, we use a loose Russian black tea. The taste profile should be strong but not bitter; it has to retain its identity.

TENNIⅯ BALL ▮ *Peacock Alley*

1 oz. Żubrówka bison grass vodka
1 oz. Cocchi Americano bianco aperitif
1 oz. Midori melon liqueur
1 oz. fresh lemon juice

Add all ingredients to mixing glass. Add ice and shake well. Strain into chilled cocktail glass. Garnish with lemon peel.

Since 2006, The Waldorf Astoria has had the pleasure of hosting many of the media in town for the US Open Tennis Championships, including ESPN and the Tennis Channel. This easy quaff was created for their annual welcome each September.

When shaken together, the ingredients take on the color of a neon green tennis ball and they get along surprisingly well. The bison grass–infused vodka cuts through for a simple and fun mix that your guests can enjoy all summer long, even on ice.

TERENCE STAMP **I** *Peacock Alley*

2 oz. Russell Henry Malaysian lime gin or Tanqueray Rangpur Lime gin

1 oz. Cocchi Americano bianco aperitif

4 dashes house-made Cranberry Bitters (or Bittermens cranberry bitters)

Add gin and aperitif to Old Fashioned glass. Add ice and stir briefly to integrate. Top with bitters. Garnish with lime wheel.

Following the Old Bar and its tradition of naming cocktails for thespians, this one is for the British actor and more specifically his film *The Limey*. This subtle yet complex cocktail comes together for a unique trip across the palate. I will add that it is worth the effort to prepare your own cranberry bitters, as they are one of the more versatile types that you can have on your shelf—perfect with Champagne or even for elevating a simple gin and tonic to superior heights. Sometimes simple just works.

THOMPSON

1 pineapple wedge (small cut, about two inches)

1 lemon peel (about 1 inch by 3 inches)

1 orange peel (about 1 inch by 3 inches)

2 oz. Jack Daniel's Tennessee whiskey

1 oz. Martini & Rossi sweet vermouth

1 dash Regans' Orange Bitters No. 6

Add pineapple wedge and citrus peels to mixing glass. Muddle briefly to release essence. Add remaining ingredients. Add ice and stir for 30 seconds. Strain into chilled cocktail glass. Garnish with orange peel and brandied cherry.

This **Manhattan** alternate was named for Old Waldorf-Astoria resident and stage actor Denman Thompson. Mr. Crockett tells an endearing story about the time Mr. Thompson couldn't get one of his boots off and Hotel manager and owner George Boldt came to the rescue. This strange but satisfying cocktail probably eased the strain.

The original most likely contained rye whiskey at the base, but I like how the full-flavored yet still dry Tennessee whiskey is paired with the citrus, especially the orange. The use of a mild vermouth, something that will remain in the background while showcasing the fruit elements is imperative.

Although no bitters were mentioned in the original direction, a dash or two works wonders here. One final hint: if you don't have a fresh pineapple on hand, a quarter ounce of pineapple or orange juice will do the trick in a pinch.

Either Mr. Crockett's interpretation or the actual Old Bar book got the association wrong, but I think that this also can be listed as the **Honolulu No. 2**. The so-named cocktail in the Old Books is simply a "perfect" rye-based Manhattan, but the addition of pineapple would complete the titular connection and makes more than a bit of sense.

TIME AFTER THYME **▮ Peacock Alley**

2 oz. 86 Co. Caña Brava white rum
¾ oz. house-made Falernum Syrup
½ oz. fresh lemon juice
½ oz. fresh lime juice
5 sprigs fresh thyme (plus one for garnish)

Add all ingredients to mixing glass. Add ice and shake well. Fine-strain into chilled cocktail glass. Garnish with one sprig of thyme across top of glass.

Created in 2009 for our summer menu, this one is often requested by returning guests. The secret is our homemade Falernum, a spiced simple syrup originating in the Caribbean. This is one item that no commercially produced brand can come close to, and once you taste it (or even just smell it) you will know why. For the cocktail's base spirit, you'll want a dry rum with its own character but not an over-the-top identity, as the Falernum and thyme will take care of the flavor profile. If made correctly, this cocktail should leave a faux-salty finish on your palate, which makes it a surprisingly delicious pairing with charcoal grilled fish.

TIPPERARY ▪ *Adapted Hugo Ensslin Version*

2 oz. Bushmills Irish whiskey
1 oz. Martini & Rossi sweet vermouth
½ oz. green Chartreuse

Add all ingredients to mixing glass. Add ice and stir for 30 seconds. Strain into chilled cocktail glass. Garnish with lemon peel.

Mr. Crockett's transcription for the Old Bar's *Tipperary* (see **Ping Pong**) is very close to many other recipes found in this book. The original version of this entry called for equal portions of all ingredients, but save your booze; it's entirely too much. This adapted version from Hugo Ensslin's *Recipes for Mixed Drinks* (1917) more than does the job. It's best to keep the adjoining elements as tame as possible so the Chartreuse can properly play its part. Cocktail writer and barman, Gary Regan, simply rinses his glass with it. It's worth a try. The lemon twist works wonders. See **Woxum** for variation.

TIP TOP

2½ oz. Noilly Prat extra dry vermouth
⅓ oz. Bénédictine
1 dash Angostura bitters
1 dash Regans' Orange Bitters No. 6

Add all ingredients to mixing glass. Add ice and stir for 30 seconds. Strain into chilled cocktail glass. Garnish with lemon peel.

Although there are more than a few non-spirit-based cocktails in this book, it's always surprising how clearly they demonstrate that a little goes a long way. In this example, the dry vermouth is the star, so your choice here counts. Because the Bénédictine is also the sugar component, using a vermouth with floral qualities or that leans toward the bianco side will throw the final result off-kilter. Here, the drier, the better. The original recipe did not include orange bitters but Jacques Straub's *Drinks* included four dashes, so I thought it was worth trying. If anything, you could probably lose the Angostura bitters and go all orange for a cleaner trip across the palate. Another warm-weather predinner treat when it may be too warm for a stronger drink. See **Stephen's Cocktail** for variation.

TRILBY

2 oz. Tanqueray Old Tom gin
1 oz. Noilly Prat extra dry vermouth
¼ oz. crème Yvette
2 dashes Regans' Orange Bitters No. 6

Add all ingredients to mixing glass. Add ice and stir for 30 seconds. Strain into chilled cocktail glass. Garnish with lemon peel.

TRILBY NO. 2 ▮ *Harry Johnson Adaptation/Toots Shor*

▮ *Peacock Alley*

2 oz. Buchanan's DeLuxe 12 Year blended Scotch whisky
1 oz. Martini & Rossi sweet vermouth
¼ oz. Marie Brizard Parfait d'Amour
1 dash Pernod pastis
1 dash Regans' Orange Bitters No. 6

Add all ingredients to mixing glass. Add ice and stir for 30 seconds. Strain into chilled cocktail glass. Garnish with lemon peel.

Here is another cocktail that dates back to the nineteenth century and has enough variations to prove it. The Old Bar's take on the *Trilby* was a nod to the 1895 play of the same name, which showed at the nearby theater at the second Madison Square Garden (Twenty-sixth Street and Madison Avenue). As the Old Bar opened in 1897, the show's 208 performances (and its extremely popular companion novel) left quite the impression. The crème Yvette adds fruit to the Old Tom's sweet note here, while the dry vermouth and bitters keep the whole thing very well balanced. To my palate, it seems surprisingly modern.

Its "sweet" variation, which subs in sweet vermouth in the dry slot, the **Defender** is named for a famous America's Cup–winning yacht of the day and draws the recipe closer to the alternative **Martinez** cocktail it is. Just use a less imposing sweet vermouth, as you want the liqueur to shine through without having to adjust the amount. These are delicate cocktails; small moves in either direction yield extreme results. The original recipes call for dashes of the liqueur and you may want to add just a scant whisper of Crème Yvette, but a quarter ounce is your high mark in both of these cocktails. My rule of thumb: if it's in there, it has to have a purpose. As with the original *Martinez* recipe, equal parts of gin and vermouth were called for, but this gin-leaning version is the way to go. An even sturdier look would include a London dry gin at its base. If you did so, you would be enjoying a **Trilby No. 1**, from *The Savoy Cocktail Book* (1930). A worthy departure.

There is, of course, a **Trilby No. 2** in *The Savoy Cocktail Book* as well and it is actually (at least ingredient-wise) what Harry Johnson noted in his *Bartenders' Manual* (1900) as his *Trilby*. It includes identical ingredients but the portions differ immensely, with equal parts Scotch whisky, Italian vermouth, and Parfait d' Amour liqueur (a marshmallow, orange, and violet–leaning syrup, recently back in production), along with a couple of dashes of absinthe and orange bitters. It's extremely hard to get down.

Mr. Johnson's original Trilby tones down the Parfait d'Amour as an enhancement, making this quite the Robert Burns alternative and the cocktail that it was meant to be. It is also one that has direct ties to the creation of this book.

Toots Shor was a preeminent New York City bar owner—he would have said "saloon keeper"—of the mid-twentieth century. Host to celebrity clientele and workaday folk alike, the namesake Toots Shor bar was the place to be. As I was researching old cocktail books, I came across a 1960 *Calvert Party Encyclopedia* and in it was a cocktail named for Toots Shor. Unbeknownst to me at the time, it was the Savoy version of the Trilby No. 2, with its full-on dose of Parfait d'Amour. I doubt that this famous friend of Jackie Gleason and Frank Sinatra would ever have imbibed a mix that contained one-third Parfait d'Amour, but it did inspire me to come up with an adapted version befitting this legend. My ode possesses a siren-like drinkability, with all the ingredients playing a part, as with the finest of orchestras or, as Toots might have referred to it, a "sym-phony." I wished Toots were still around so I could have him try it. Do you know what all my tinkering basically resulted in?

Harry Johnson's original Trilby, with its reserved use of ingredients. Everything old is new again, or great minds think alike? I am starting to think all cocktails have already been created. Maybe they exist with a different name in some distant and unknown land, like the legend that everyone has a doppelgänger somewhere in the world.

TURF

2 oz. Bols genever
1 oz. Cinzano Rosso sweet vermouth
1 dash Angostura bitters

Add all ingredients to mixing glass. Add ice and stir for 30 seconds. Strain into chilled cocktail glass. Garnish with lemon peel.

TURF / TURF CLUB (ADAPTED FROM HARRY JOHNSON'S BARTENDERS' MANUAL)

2 oz. Anchor Distilling Co. Junipero gin
¾ oz. Noilly Prat extra dry vermouth
¼ oz. Luxardo maraschino liqueur
2 dashes Émile Pernot Vieux Pontarlier absinthe
2 dashes Regans' Orange Bitters No. 6

Add all ingredients to mixing glass. Add ice and stir for 30 seconds. Strain into chilled cocktail glass. Garnish with lemon peel.

Though first found in print in 1884 in *How to Mix Drinks: Bar Keepers' Handbook*, by George Winter, the *Turf Club* cocktail was, according to Mr. Crockett, a favorite of the Old Bar and was named for the horse-playing regulars there. This was "possibly two-thirds of the crowd." This is a first cousin of both the classic **Martinez** and **Martini** cocktails. The Old Bar's version is the genever-based model, while the 1884 *Turf Club* version was equal parts Old Tom gin and sweet vermouth (and used Peruvian bitters).

Nineteenth-century barman Harry Johnson's rendition is an enhanced dry *Martinez* with an absinthe adornment. (Mr. Johnson included a nearly identical recipe he referred to as the **Tuxedo**—but the sherry-enhanced version below is the recognized standard.) Both work marvelously if you ask me, but what I like best about this recipe is that the further you get from his recommended London dry–style gin in the starring role, the more interesting it becomes. For a guest's request for something special, I split the difference between Plymouth gin and genever. I also tried it with the saffron and rosewater–tinged Nolet's gin (again splitting the difference with the genever), and for something that is supposed to be difficult to pair with, I found it quite noteworthy. The moral of the story here is to be adventurous and trust what you like. Personally, I typically don't prefer vodka cocktails (I take mine from the freezer, neat) but in this mix, it makes a great vehicle for the supporting flavors. If going this way, use a full ounce of dry vermouth for best results. In any case, always keep an open mind and a daring palate. See *Martini—Amsterdam* for variation.

TUXEDO

2 oz. Plymouth gin
1 oz. Lustau Manzanilla or amontillado sherry
1 dash Regans' Orange Bitters No. 6

Add all ingredients to mixing glass. Add ice and stir for 30 seconds. Strain into chilled cocktail glass. Garnish with lemon peel.

Whether it was named for the Old Hotel's guests' upstate New York club in the town of Tuxedo or for its signature apparel, we may never know, but this almost perfect, bone-dry predinner tipple is one of the numerous must-tries in this book. Different types of sherry will all yield unique results. Many cocktails created today, using many more ingredients, strive to reach the balance and complexity that this one achieves with just three ingredients. Ninety-nine percent of the time, less is more. This one's a true classic and time traveler.

UNION LEAGUE

> **2 oz. Hayman's Old Tom gin**
> **1 oz. Graham's 10 Year tawny port wine**
> **2 dashes Regans' Orange Bitters No. 6**

> Add all ingredients to mixing glass. Add ice and stir for 30 seconds.
> Strain into chilled cocktail glass. Garnish with orange twist.

The Union League Club, one of the city's oldest high-society social clubs, still thrives today. This cocktail, pulled straight from the Old Books, needed very little tinkering. I did adapt it to lean on the base spirit, as the original includes equal portions of Old Tom gin and port. That version is a bit on the sweeter side, but it may be just right for some. This is yet another simple keeper that may be due for a comeback.

UNION SQUARE ▮ *Peacock Alley*

> **2 dashes Regans' Orange Bitters No. 6**
> **1 radish, thinly sliced**
> **3 cucumber slices, ¼ inch thick**
> **2½ oz. Russian Standard vodka**
> **½ oz. light agave nectar syrup (1:1 ratio agave and water)**
> **Paprika and kosher salt rim, optional (combine 2 parts paprika**
> **and 1 part kosher salt in saucer and mix thoroughly.**

Add bitters, radish, and cucumber slices to mixing glass. Muddle to break down and release flavors. Add vodka and syrup. Add ice and shake well. If presenting with rim, moisten half of cocktail glass with lemon wedge, then roll that side of glass into spice mixture. Fine-strain cocktail into prepared glass. Garnish with radish wheel (if not salting rim).

Named for the long-running Union Square Greenmarket, in New York City. Somehow these ingredients result in a watermelon-like flavor profile that will fool most of your guests and make for a fun afternoon of guessing the ingredients. The radish adds a spicy background while the agave syrup adds more than just sweetness. The rim is optional, though it does contribute another dimension. It's a slightly labor-intensive drink, but worth it.

VALENTINE'S DAY COCKTAIL
NO. 1 ▮ *Peacock Alley*

2 oz. Citadelle gin
½ oz. house-made Raspberry Syrup
½ oz. fresh lemon juice
¼ oz. Luxardo maraschino liqueur
2 dashes Abbott's bitters

Add all ingredients to mixing glass. Add ice and shake well. Strain into chilled cocktail glass. Garnish with fresh raspberry.

VALENTINE'S DAY COCKTAIL NO. 2 ▮ *Peacock Alley*

1¼ oz. Etter Zuger framboise eau-de-vie
1 oz. Combier Crème de Fruits Rouges liqueur
¾ oz. fresh lemon juice
½ egg white
2 dashes Regans' Orange Bitters No. 6

Add all ingredients to mixing glass and dry-shake without ice for 5 seconds. Add ice and shake for 10 seconds. Fine-strain into chilled cocktail glass. Garnish with lemon peel.

I usually try to feature two cocktails for a Valentine's Day dinner. If you're enjoying the *No.1* during the warmer months, feel free to muddle a few fresh raspberries if you have them or even shake with fresh mint (just be sure to fine-strain). It's also worth searching out Abbott's bitters, as they have a unique flavor profile that adds a nice snap to this sweet and tart cocktail. If you don't have some handy, a dash of Peychaud's also does the job.

The *No. 2* utilizes raspberry eau-de-vie as the base spirit. Similar to grappa but not grape based, the best ones, such as Etter Zuger, retain much of their natural fruit flavor. It is something not often found in crowd-pleasing cocktails, but I think we bridged the gap from challenging spirit to satisfying cocktail. I went with Combier's four-berry liqueur, but you could use a framboise liqueur for even more of a raspberry focus. Be sure to fine-strain to remove any ice chips from the final presentation, as you'll want a velvety trip across the palate.

VE∫PER ∎ *Classic*

2 oz. Plymouth gin
1 oz. Ketel One vodka
½ oz. Cocchi Americano aperitif

Add all ingredients to mixing glass. Add ice and stir for 30 seconds. Strain into chilled cocktail glass. Garnish with lemon peel.

This cocktail was pulled from the pages of Ian Fleming's first James Bond novel, *Casino Royale,* and Mr. Bond's directive to shake it and not stir it was at least partly responsible for drinkers demanding all of their cocktails be prepared in this way. Shaken, it becomes a watery mess, with the ingredients losing their identity. Stirred, this spirit-heavy concoction retains its leaden consistency, offering a complex and bracing trip across your palate.

If I do have an issue with this recipe, it's that it seems more natural to me that you would want to enhance your relatively blank-canvas vodka with the much more flavorful gin as opposed to the other way around, so I came up with the ***Reverse Vesper***. In a standard Vesper, I use the

FRANK'S CASINO

more neutral-flavored Plymouth gin to try to keep the vodka's identity, whereas in the adapted version, I've included the bolder London Dry gin to help lift its head over the fence. This is probably my favorite vodka-based cocktail.

For the aperitif element, the original called for Kina Lillet, which is no longer produced with the same bittersweet profile. Cocchi Americano, which has not only the sweet and fruit-forward aspects of Lillet but also the all-important bitter element, will get you closer to the intended result.

A dash of orange bitters would add yet another layer. Either way, it's one of the finest pre–steakhouse dinner cocktails ever created and I'm sure it would have been as popular in the Old Bar as it is today.

VICTORY SWIZZLE

¾ oz. Bols genever
¾ oz. Bushmills Irish whiskey
¾ oz. Appleton Estate Reserve rum
½ oz. fresh lemon juice
¼ oz. house-made Demerara Syrup
3 dashes Angostura aromatic or Dale DeGroff's pimento bitters

Add all ingredients except bitters to Collins glass. Fill with pellet ice. Swizzle or stir with bar spoon for 10 seconds, bringing the ice from the bottom of glass to the top, ensuring that ingredients are well integrated and cold. Top with bitters and serve with straw.

Mr. Crockett noted that the *Victory Swizzle* was named for one of Admiral George Dewey's significant victories (he attributed it to either Manila Bay or the Battle of Santiago de Cuba but leaned toward Santiago). Either way, it is a blueprint formula which can take some tinkering. Surprisingly, all ingredients keep their identity here, and although the bitters are not a typical ingredient, I took the liberty of adding them here. Another similar cocktail from the Old Books is the **Volcano Swizzle**, which uses Jamaican rum in the lead role. I would use Smith & Cross navy-strength Jamaican rum, doubling it in the spirits slots listed here and proceeding as directed. It's a fine alternative.

Swizzling is the act of stirring with a stick (or spoon) with two hands, as if you were trying to start a fire though without quite the same amount of vigor. Or, you can do what I sometimes do and just stir, bringing up the crushed ice from the bottom of the glass with a bar spoon. I've included the bitters that work for me, though you can use the style of your choice. Traditionally, a Swizzle would not have an abundance of fruit as garnish, but a snapped orange peel over the top of the drink will make for a fine bouquet and intoxicating first sip.

VIEUX CARRÉ ∎ *Classic*

1 oz. Knob Creek straight rye whiskey
1 oz. Frapin VSOP cognac
1 oz. Martini Gran Lusso sweet vermouth
¼ oz. Bénédictine
2 dashes Peychaud's bitters
1 dash Angostura bitters

Add all ingredients to mixing glass. Add ice and stir for 30 seconds. Strain into Old Fashioned glass with large ice cubes or sphere. Garnish with lemon peel.

This now-classic New Orleans sipper has been around since the 1930s, and was reportedly created at the landmark Hotel Monteleone and named for the French Quarter ("Old Square"). It has seen quite the resurgence in popularity. Part Old Fashioned, part Sazerac, this sipper takes to tinkering quite well. I used the brands listed here for a more robust version. Feel free to adjust for personal taste. In any case, this will certainly enter your repertoire if you enjoy classic cocktails that veer slightly off the beaten path.

VIVARY

1½ oz. Noilly Prat extra dry vermouth
1½ oz. Cinzano Rosso sweet vermouth
¼ oz. Emile Pernot Vieux Pontarlier absinthe
2 dashes Regans' Orange Bitters No. 6

Add all ingredients to mixing glass. Add ice and stir for 15 seconds. Strain into chilled cocktail glass. Garnish with lemon peel.

For decades, imbibing Americans did not enjoy the pleasures of vermouth. This once-banished necessity is now part of the conversation again. Be sure to prechill your vermouths as you don't want to over-dilute by over-stirring. The *Vivary* was a variation on the vermouth cocktails of the day that used both the dry and sweet variety and enhanced it with a touch of absinthe. Included in the Old Books were a **French Vermouth "Cocktail"** and an **Italian Vermouth "Cocktail,"** which are simply three ounces of either vermouth with a couple of dashes of orange bitters, stirred for a bit and strained. Do garnish with a lemon twist.

You can also use bianco vermouth or the newly popular amber vermouths at the base as well as nearly any combination in between. This is a great opportunity to utilize the new crop of artisanal vermouths. They remain practically unadorned so you can taste them for what they are.

Whatever your choice, these make fine summertime, predinner drinks, perfect on extremely warm days or when you feel like holding a cocktail glass in your hand without the usual walloping results.

WALDORF

2 oz. Rittenhouse bonded rye whiskey
1 oz. Martini & Rossi sweet vermouth
¼ oz. Pernod Original Recipe absinthe or Granier or Pernod pastis
2 dashes Angostura bitters

Add all ingredients to mixing glass. Add ice and stir for 30 seconds. Strain into chilled cocktail glass. Garnish with lemon peel.

SHERMAN (REVERSE WALDORF)

2 oz. Martini & Rossi sweet vermouth
1 oz. Rittenhouse bonded rye whiskey
2 dashes Pernod Original Recipe absinthe or Granier or Pernod pastis
1 dash Angostura bitters
1 dash Regans' Orange Bitters No. 6

Add all ingredients to mixing glass. Add ice and stir for 30 seconds. Strain into chilled cocktail glass. Garnish with lemon peel.

The original recipe of the Old Bar's *Waldorf* cocktail features equal portions of all ingredients. Prepared this way, it's just a muddy, absinthe-heavy mess. Tempered for today's palate, it becomes an enhanced **Manhattan**, while still getting its point across. You could forgo the use of the strong and dry absinthe here and sub in a pastis, which is lower in alcohol, softer, and has a touch of sugar. The Old Books also include an identical recipe to the *Waldorf* called **Hearn's**, using Irish whiskey at its base—I recommend using orange bitters and a pot-still Irish whiskey to prop it up for the vermouth and absinthe. If you do sub in orange bitters and replace the absinthe with anisette (I like the outstanding Varnelli's l'Anice Secco Speciale), you will have the **Narragansett**, named for the Rhode Island summer getaway of the regulars of the Old Bar.

The *Sherman* is simply a reverse *Waldorf*, with sweet vermouth in the lead role. Feel free to experiment in this slot to find your personal favorites. I do recommend keeping it on the tame side, as full-flavored vermouths run the risk of smothering the whiskey.

London's *Savoy Cocktail Book* (1930) lists its *Waldorf* with Swedish punch and gin taking the lead. This is listed as an **Astor** cocktail in this book and should be remembered as such.

WALDORF FIZZ ▮ *New Waldorf Astoria Adaptation*

2 oz. chilled club soda
1 oz. Evan Williams bonded bourbon whiskey
1 oz. fresh orange juice
¾ oz. fresh lemon juice
¾ oz. Simple Syrup
1 whole egg

Add chilled club soda to small Collins glass or tumbler. Add remaining ingredients to mixing glass. Dry-shake for 5 seconds. Add ice and shake for 10 seconds. Fine-strain into chilled Collins glass. Stir quickly with bar spoon to integrate. No garnish.

Although not listed in either of the Old Books, there is a *Waldorf Fizz* found in Jacques Straub's *Drinks* that contains no alcohol. For that version just omit the bourbon. The interesting thing here is that there's also a version in Jack Grohusko's 1933 edition of *Jack's Manual* that includes 100 proof bourbon, so I split the difference and combined both versions. At the end of the day, this is basically a whiskey-based **Royal Fizz**, as it includes the entire egg. See **Fizz** for variations.

WALDORF PUNCH

1 tsp. superfine sugar
¾ oz. water (chilled)
½ fresh lemon
2 oz. Rittenhouse bonded rye whiskey
¾ oz. dry red wine (Bordeaux Supérieur works well)

Add sugar to chilled Old Fashioned glass along with cold water. Squeeze lemon into glass. Discard shell and stir to integrate. Add whiskey and large ice cubes. Stir briefly to integrate, then float red wine, pouring slowly over back of spoon. Garnish with fresh mint sprig.

What separates this from a standard whiskey Punch is the float of red wine, which brings a dry first sip to the sweetened Whiskey Sour just below the layer of wine. The rustic preparation and added water also separate this from a **Brunswick Sour** (a.k.a. *New York Sour* or *Waldorf Sour*), though just barely. Although rye whiskey was traditionally the base sprit, feel free to use most any American whiskey if you wish. The time-honored methodology for the preparation is listed here, though you can omit the granulated sugar and add half an ounce of simple syrup, adjusting the water to taste. I would not garnish this with fruit, as you want the red wine float to be the star.

WALK IN THE WOODS *(Autumn Wedding Cocktail)* ▮ *Peacock Alley*

1 oz. Buffalo Trace bourbon
1 oz. Sandeman Fine Rich Madeira
1 oz. fresh apple cider
¾ oz. fresh lemon juice
¼ oz. grade A maple syrup
1 dash Angostura bitters

Add ice to mixing glass. Add ingredients and shake well. Strain into chilled cocktail glass. Garnish with freshly grated nutmeg.

I created this seasonal offering for friend and then-director of restaurants Jeff Krauthamer and his wife, Cara, for their wedding reception. Feel free to pull back to a half ounce of Madeira and cider and add a half ounce of bourbon if you are enjoying this one at night and would prefer something a bit stronger. It works both ways.

WARD EIGHT

2 oz. Jim Beam pre-Prohibition-style 90 proof rye whiskey
¾ oz. fresh lemon juice
¾ oz. fresh orange juice
¼ oz. house-made Grenadine

Add ingredients to mixing glass. Add ice and shake well. Strain into chilled cocktail glass. No garnish.

Dating back to the Boston politics of the nineteenth century, this Sour is still popular today. The Old Books described it as a Whiskey Sour with grenadine, but the recipes that predate the Hotel include orange juice, and this version has become the standard. Some recipes reduce the juice portion by a quarter ounce in each case, but I like the vibrancy of this version. The extra juice helps to keep it light. Try both variations and decide for yourself.

WEEK-END AT THE WALDORF

❚ *Ted Saucier's* Bottoms Up

2 oz. 86 Co. Caña Brava white rum
½ oz. fresh lime juice
⅓ oz. Luxardo Triplum triple sec
⅓ oz. house-made Strawberry Syrup

Add all ingredients to mixing glass. Add ice and shake well. Strain into chilled cocktail glass filled with pellet ice. Garnish with one slice of fresh strawberry.

This was a favorite of Ted Saucier's during his time in Hollywood during the production of the 1945 MGM film *Week-End at the Waldorf.* Originally served as a bone-dry blender drink, it's presented here over crushed ice. It's a great refresher either way.

Although not entirely shot on location, this motion picture was the first Hollywood production to feature location scenes, and you can see how little the Park Avenue entrance and lobby have changed over the years. A number of renovations restored it to its opening glory and specifications in 2013, and its elegance remains. I am fond of saying that you can sometimes feel the "ghosts" in the lobby (in a good way), and when you view this film, you can see them for yourself.

WHISPERS OF THE FROST

1 oz. George Dickel rye whiskey
1 oz. Quinta do Noval 10 Year Old tawny port or Graham's ruby port
1 oz. Lustau Don Nino oloroso sherry
⅓ oz. house-made Demerara Syrup
2 dashes Angostura bitters (optional)

Add all ingredients to mixing glass. Add ice and stir for 15 seconds to integrate. Strain into goblet or Old Fashioned glass filled with pellet ice. Garnish with seasonal fruit.

Due to the cryptic original instructions provided by the Old Books, this **Cobbler**-type concoction is often mistakenly served up. The frost in the title most likely refers to that on the outside of the well-chilled glass. Ruby would have probably been the port wine of choice at the Old Bar, but I prefer the more complex tawny. You can also adjust the sugar, experimenting with a simple syrup. In the end it's your preference that counts. Two alternate servings come to mind for this winner: you could present this as a *Punch* with a touch of water and large ice cubes, or you could warm it up for cold winter nights. Just add a half ounce of water and cinnamon stick if warming.

WHITTAKER

2 oz. Byrrh Grand quinquina or Maurin quina (chilled)
1 oz. Martini & Rossi sweet vermouth (chilled)
2 dashes Regans' Orange Bitters No. 6

Add all ingredients to mixing glass. Add ice and stir for 15 seconds. Strain into chilled cocktail glass. Garnish with lemon peel.

Named for Imperial Hotel owner Preston Whittaker, who Mr. Crockett claimed was seen more often at the Old Hotel than his own, this flavorful, low-impact, wine-based cocktail is a winning concept that is pliable enough to take to a bit of tinkering. As always, your vermouths and aromatized wines should be chilled for longevity and for recipe usage as well. Try an amber or extra dry vermouth for unique results.

WILD CHERRY

1½ oz. Hayman's Old Tom gin or Etter Zuger kirsch (optional)
1½ oz. Rothman & Winter cherry orchard liqueur or Heering cherry liqueur
1 dash Fee Brothers cherry bitters or Regans' Orange Bitters No. 6

Add all ingredients to mixing glass. Add ice and stir for 30 seconds. Strain into chilled cocktail glass. Garnish with brandied cherry.

I tried allowing the listed Old Tom gin to lead the way, but the result was too boozy for this sweet and easy sipper. What did work was placing kirschwasser eau-de-vie in the gin slot, as the dry cherry brandy paired nicely with the cherry liqueur. I could almost smell the Old Bar when I tasted this one. The original recipe did not include bitters, but I feel a touch earns its keep here, especially when going with an equal portion of spirit to liqueur.

WINTER

2 oz. Myers's Jamaican dark rum
½ oz. fresh lime juice
½ oz. Simple Syrup
¼ oz. The Bitter Truth pimento dram or St. Elizabeth allspice dram
1 dash Angostura bitters

Add all ingredients to mixing glass. Add ice and shake well. Strain into chilled cocktail glass. Garnish with orange peel.

> **2 oz. Avuá Amburana cachaça**
> **1 oz. Domaine de Canton ginger liqueur**
> **½ oz. fresh lime juice**
> **½ oz. fresh pineapple juice**
> **1 dash Dale Degroff's pimento bitters**
>
> Add all ingredients to mixing glass. Add ice and shake well. Strain into chilled cocktail glass. Garnish with orange peel.

This recipe of Mr. Crockett's, found in the "Jamaican Jollifiers" chapter of the Old Bar book, left room for interpretation. It listed choices in both types of juice and in enhancing liqueurs (lime or lemon, ginger or allspice). Since it's called "Winter," I chose the deeper-flavored ingredients and used the lighter ones for a completely different drink, the *Summer*. These are interesting **Daiquiri** alternatives to keep in your repertoire.

WORLD CUP ∎ *Peacock Alley*

> **1½ oz. Avuá Amburana cachaça**
> **1 oz. Château Petit Guiraud Sauternes wine**
> **¾ oz. fresh grapefruit juice**
> **¼ oz. Luxardo maraschino liqueur**
> **2 dashes Regans' Orange Bitters No. 6**
>
> Add all ingredients to mixing glass. Add ice and shake well. Strain into Old Fashioned glass filled with large ice cubes or sphere. Garnish with brandied cherry.

Created for the 2014 World Cup in Brazil, this complex cocktail features an artisanal, barrel-aged cachaça, which adds a significant depth of flavor. The spice notes imparted by the cachaça are quite memorable and pair nicely with the sweetness of the Sauternes (the famously delicious Bordeaux dessert wine) and helps give it an identity of its own. You could also add another half portion of wine and serve as a large **Cup**. (See "Large Cups and Punches" chapter).

1½ oz. Bols genever (Holland)
¾ oz. Noilly Prat extra dry vermouth (France)
½ oz. Fernet-Branca liqueur (Italy)
½ oz. Iris liqueur (United States)
2 dashes Regans' Orange Bitters

Add all ingredients to mixing glass. Add ice and stir for 30 seconds. Strain into chilled cocktail glass. Garnish with lemon peel.

Created for an event in 2012, this intriguing tipple turned out to be an unintentional nod to the Old Bar. Iris is a domestically produced liqueur with high floral notes and a hefty viscosity that stands up to the other ingredients, though the liqueur slot proved to be quite pliable and can be adjusted for personal taste. That said, the Italian Strega liqueur would probably come closest to achieving this profile if the small-production Iris is difficult to procure. Its sister product, Calisaya liqueur, would also work well, and although it may seem crazy, Chartreuse, maraschino, elderflower, and even a curaçao such as Grand Marnier would all bring different elements to the table. Either way, I think this ranks toward the top of the drinks we've created that take on the tone and soul of the Old Bar's offerings. If only Mr. O'Connor and Mr. Solan (among the other Old Bar bartenders) were around to tell us for sure.

WOXUM *(Improved)*

1½ oz. Boulard Grand Solage VSOP calvados (or Laird's bonded applejack, for original)
1½ oz. Noilly Prat extra dry vermouth (or sweet vermouth, for original)
½ oz. yellow Chartreuse

Add all ingredients to mixing glass. Add ice and stir for 30 seconds. Strain into chilled cocktail glass. Garnish with lemon peel.

Mr. Crockett himself admits that this drink's origin is obscure but then ascribes it, ever so politically incorrectly, to a "bunch of Indians who raised hell in the Bar when they could get away with it." What I find most interesting about that comment is that in one of the toniest hotels of the day, you had some good old-fashioned rabble-rousing going on. Now, I'd think that such mayhem was not tolerated for long, but it's good to know that the Old Bar was occasionally a bit rough around the edges.

The original recipe was equal parts applejack and sweet vermouth and is actually best served in that proportion, though using a more flavor-forward vermouth will allow you to go with a 2:1 ratio, which may be best after dinner. Our improved version above utilizes dry vermouth and makes for the better drink. Another interesting variation featured at Peacock Alley uses barrel-aged cachaça (Avuá Amburana) split with the calvados for an even more floral spin. Definitely worth a try. See **Tipperary** for variation.

X MARKS THE SPOT | *Peacock Alley*

1½ oz. Appleton Estate white rum
½ oz. Giffard Banane du Brésil liqueur
½ oz. Domaine de Canton ginger liqueur
½ oz. fresh lime juice
½ oz. fresh orange juice
½ egg white
1 dash Dale DeGroff's pimento bitters

Add all ingredients to mixing glass. Dry-shake for 5 seconds. Add ice and shake for 10 seconds. Fine-strain into chilled cocktail glass. Garnish with one star anise, floated on surface.

Inspired by trade winds and sunken treasure, this complex sipper was born. For a more detailed garnish, you could place three black peppercorns "leading" to the "X" star anise for more of the map motif. Another alternative is to place the star anise in the center of a crushed ice–filled Old Fashioned glass, to find a "sunken treasure." Floating a bar spoon or two of ruby port will add another unique and multi-dimensional twist (serve that one with a small metal straw).

YACHT CLUB

2 oz. Appleton Estate white rum or Don Q añejo rum
1 oz. Martini and Rossi sweet vermouth
¼ oz. Rothman & Winter apricot liqueur
1 dash Regans' Orange Bitters No. 6

Add all ingredients to mixing glass. Add ice and stir for 30 seconds. Strain into chilled cocktail glass. Garnish with lemon peel.

PARADISE

2 oz. Appleton Estate white rum
1 oz. Rothman & Winter apricot liqueur
2 dashes Regans' Orange Bitters No. 6

Add all ingredients to mixing glass. Add ice and stir for 30 seconds. Strain into Old Fashioned cocktail glass with large ice cubes or sphere. Garnish with lemon peel.

At first glance, these are very closely related recipes, but further investigation uncovers vast differences. No bitters were included in the Old Bar's *Yacht Club* and it originally featured the very popular Cuban Bacardi rum at the base, sidled with sweet vermouth and a "dash" of apricot liqueur. It has its moments but needs a stronger rum to stand up to even the most neutral of vermouths. For an alternate, go straight for an añejo (nothing too sweet) and you'll be fine. An aged agricole would also raise eyebrows.

In an effort to improve upon the original, I swapped out the sweet vermouth for dry in the Peacock Alley rendition. I suggest sticking to white rum here for an astounding result. Prepare to be surprised.

Lastly we have the *Paradise*, which excludes vermouth altogether. Originally served up, this may shine best as something to have after a summer barbecue dinner with an ice cube or two. See **Charlie Chaplin** and **Hop Toad** for variations.

YALE

1½ oz. Hayman's Old Tom gin
1½ oz. Cinzano Rosso sweet vermouth
2 dashes Regans' Orange Bitters No. 6
1 oz. chilled club soda

Add all ingredients except club soda to mixing glass. Add ice and stir for 30 seconds. Strain into chilled cocktail glass. Top with club soda. Garnish with orange peel.

As you would imagine, the Old Bar was quite the attraction for the Ivy League set, with nearly every school getting a commemorative cocktail named for it, and Yale was no different. What separates this from your standard **Martini** is the chilled club soda topper at the end. The first recipe in print, in *Modern American Drinks* (1895), did not include vermouth of any kind and added a dash of Peychaud's bitters. You can do that in the recipe here, if you like, for a slightly different twist. If you want to go all in and omit the vermouth, I would use only two or two and half ounces of gin and be sure to stir long enough for proper dilution. I did not adapt the portions to lean on the gin, as the intention of the soda is to lighten the drink.

Z

ZAZA

1½ oz. Plymouth gin or Spencerfield Spirit Edinburgh gin
1½ oz. Bonal quinquina aperitif or Dubonnet
2 dashes Regans' Orange Bitters No. 6

Add all ingredients to mixing glass. Add ice and stir for 30 seconds. Strain into chilled cocktail glass. Garnish with lemon peel.

Often referred to as a **Dubonnet Cocktail**, this one was named for a much-produced play whose title character is a prostitute who becomes a music hall entertainer, most famously played by Claudette Colbert in the 1939 film. I chose to mix this one up a bit to what I think are fabulous results. The original recipe leans on the aromatized wine with a 2:1 ratio. I felt this cocktail would be better served if both ingredients had equal billing, but if you do lean on the gin with a 2:1 ratio, you will be enjoying a **Colonial** or a **James**.

The Edinburgh gin is an 80 proof aromatic gin that straddles the line between the new and old-school styles and pairs well with the many botanicals of the aromatized wines. I prefer a lemon twist here, but orange works fine as well (try both!).

The **Daniel de Rouge**, **Dorlando**, and the **Zaza No. 2** are nearly identical recipes that utilized Old Tom gin and were poured in equal proportion with the aperitif wines. I would lean on the Old Tom here with a 2:1 ratio for best results. (The orange bitters are a constant with all of these recipes.)

5 ЅTAR ▪ Peacock Alley

2 oz. Pyrat XO rum
½ oz. grade A maple syrup
1 oz. half and half
1 pinch Chinese five-spice powder

Add first three ingredients to mixing glass. Add ice and shake well.
Fine-strain into chilled Old Fashioned glass. Add the pinch of five
spice in center, for garnish.

This interesting **Milk Punch** variation made its debut on the cocktail list for the reopening of Peacock Alley in 2005. A guest favorite,
we occasionally put it back on the list around the holidays. The
Chinese five-spice is the oddball here, of course, but that's what
makes this cocktail memorable. Some of the most common spices
included in this traditional spice mixture are
cassia (cinnamon), cloves, fennel seeds,
Sichuan pepper, and star anise, though
others may be subbed in. As for the
rum, the recipe is quite pliable.
Drier agricoles work (a personal
favorite), as well as variants that
lean toward the sweet side.
You could use whole milk if you
like, but we prefer the richness
of the half and half in this instance. I think you will too.

1915

1 oz. New York Distilling Company Dorothy Parker gin

1 oz. Pierre Ferrand dry curaçao or Combier l'Original Liqueur d'Orange

1 oz. half and half (or heavy cream, depending on the variation)

Add ingredients to mixing glass. Add ice and shake well. Fine-strain into chilled cocktail glass. Twist an orange peel to release oils, then discard.

This, according to Mr. Crockett, is so named in honor of the year. It's supposedly the last cocktail invented at the Old Bar, though I find that kind of hard to believe as the Old Bar closed at the beginning of Prohibition in January 1920. As for the drink itself, I kept the original recipe portions, but ramping up the gin a half an ounce will move this into the *Alexander* category and certainly have more of a bite. Use heavy cream if going this way. The brandy-enhanced dry curaçao will yield more complex results while the triple sec variety will allow the orange notes to shine. Use half and half in that case, as you will probably be having more than one. Either way, a great dessert alternative. Though not included in the original recipe, the orange peel twist brings it all home.

LARGE CUPS AND PUNCHES

Weaving their way through many cultures and eras, the large-format Punch and its relatives were staples in the era of the Old Bar. They're a lot less intimidating than you may think—just follow the basic format for your classic renditions and then modify with different spirits, wines, and spices.

Mr. Crockett famously included in his preface to the "Punch" section of *The Old Waldorf-Astoria Bar Book* his acknowledgment of the birth of Punch to seventeenth-century India, and more specifically the old British East India Company and its efforts to popularize tea. *Pancha*, the Sanskrit word meaning "five," represents the number of basic ingredients that defined it: spirit, water (or tea), sugar, lemon, and spice. Or, more specifically, strong, weak, sweet, and sour. Though by no means a hard-and-fast rule, it does begin to explain that a Punch can be viewed simply as a large, lower-impact cocktail, served either by the glass or from a bowl and meant to be enjoyed in a group setting—perfect for both the impromptu week-end home gathering and the special celebration. Certainly nothing to be afraid of.

Historically, Punches were made to be savored for long stretches of time, which is why there is plenty of water, cider, or tea included, as well as ice. Without these ingredients, you would have a big bowl of booze, a room full of intoxicated guests, and a party that would last for about an hour.

In the recent past, Punches were mostly associated with holiday and end-of-the-year celebrations, but they can and should be prepared all year long. Some of the easiest-drinking and seasonal versions are the lighter summertime offerings using wine, genever, gin, or rum as the base spirit.

Though not called by name in either of the Old Books, a pre-prepared oleo saccharum will properly authenticate your Punch. An oleo saccharum is a modified sugar base that has extracted the oils from citrus peels. Lemon is the one most used in traditional recipes, though when I prepare a Punch for a large event, I prefer to add the rind of an orange, grapefruit, or lime for depth of flavor. (I've found that one or two small lime rinds add a darker tone, especially in lighter Punches.)

The Old Bar book listed more than thirty Punches under that subtitle, another batch in the "Cups" subchapter, and another grouping in the "Brandy Potations" and "Jamaican Jollifiers" sections. Fewer than half of them were specifically large format, and only one was a hot Punch. The difference between some Cups and Punches is a bit ambiguous, though it's safe to agree with Mr. Crockett when he stated that Cups are "a beverage made with wine, generally ice, and with flavoring herbs and fruits. In olden times, vegetables were also included, particularly cucumbers." It would be convenient if it ended there, but Cup recipes also include spirits and Punch recipes often include wine. In my opinion, it is an antique argument. Cups simply place wine in the lead role and make little effort to cover the defining taste profiles of Punch, though I rarely find myself bogged down by such distinctions and neither should you. Cocktail historian David Wondrich's all-encompassing book on the subject, *Punch* (2010), would be the best place to fill in the historical gaps.

The by-the-glass Punches that are listed alphabetically throughout this book can easily be extrapolated to large format if so desired. In fact, the following recipes can be blueprints for more elaborate explorations. Just remember that Punches are not the forum to show off the best offerings that your cabinet or cellar has to offer. The idea is to have a good time for a (relatively) long time, and after a party or two where Punch plays the central role, you will be quite comfortable with serving them. I think that today's lower- and mid-range spirits are probably on a par with, if not better than, some of the best hooch available at the time of the Old Bar. They are most certainly better made.

Once the oleo saccharum is incorporated with spirit, juice, and water, you can leave the rinds in the bowl if you're going for a rustic finish. More often than not, you will want to remove them, as the Punch is better served with fresh fruit slices and/or spices as the garnish. To help incorporate the oleo saccharum into the rest of the Punch, add a cup of boiling water to the oleo saccharum to dissolve the granulated sugar prior to serving the Punch, especially for Punches that omit fresh juice. Just chill and reserve it for time of service; a simple stir or two will have you ready to go in no time. My direction for portioning off is strictly personal. You may add as much or as little as you prefer, but as with any culinary recipe, it's better to start with less and add more in small increments; otherwise you will undoubtedly over-booze these recipes. If they're made in advance, you can also use a bar spoon or so of the oleo saccharum base as the sugar component of some of your classic cocktails for a small but not insignificant variation.

As previously mentioned, the use of Champagne proper is optional, and although the Champagne at the time of the Old Bar was probably sweeter in taste, be sure to use a dry sparkling such as a Spanish cava if not using a brut Champagne, as the added sugar in the Punch's recipe will balance the final result. This also holds true for standard table wines. The sparkling water used at the Old Bar ranged from natural mineral water with small bubbles (imported from Europe) to siphoned seltzer with large bubbles, imported from Brooklyn and the Lower East Side. Use what you have handy. Ice blocks are much easier to make today than at the time of the Old Bar. Freeze a quart container or two (or Tupperware-type bowl) a day prior to your event, release from container, and place in center of your serving bowl. There are many beautifully decorated and elegant new punch bowl and glass sets available today, but there are also some appealing vintage and era-appropriate sets that can be found online and in antique shops. The choice, as always, is yours.

OLEO SACCHARUM (Waldorf Astoria)

Using a horizontal, Y-type vegetable peeler, separate the rind of the following, trying to avoid the white pith as much as possible:

4 lemons
1 lime
1 orange
1 grapefruit (or half if large)
(for traditional rendition, use 6 lemons only)
1 c. granulated sugar

Add all ingredients to nonreactive bowl and muddle well, incorporating the rinds and sugar (about 5 minutes). Cover, then let rest for at least 2 hours or overnight. At this point it is ready to use. You can also prepare it ahead of time and store in a resealable airtight container in the refrigerator for up to two weeks, using as needed. If you have one handy, a vacuum sealer would be perfect here. You can simply defrost overnight or in a hot water bath for a more "instant" use. In any case, for the sake of this book and the following recipes, this represents one full portion.

BASIC PUNCH RECIPE

1 bottle (up to 32 oz.) spirit of choice
32 oz. water (sparkling optional)
6–8 oz. fresh lemon juice
½ portion Oleo Saccharum (or more to taste, depending on lead spirit)
1-qt. block ice
Freshly grated nutmeg and/or citrus slices, for garnish

Think seasonally when it comes to the starring role here. For example, genever would be fantastic during the summer, while cognac would be better in the winter. I've intentionally left the amounts of fresh juice and sugar variable, so you can adjust based on the lead spirit. For instance, you may want less sugar if using sweeter, dark rum, or you may want more if using a dry rye whiskey. Once you actually prepare a few of these, you will know what works for you.

As with any cold Punch, I strongly recommend combining all ingredients at least a few hours prior to using and refrigerating them. When serving, add block ice from your mold and the pre-batched cold Punch to a bowl and you'll be all set. The ice block will do more for maintaining temperature than it will for dilution, which is fine, as the ingredients are already properly balanced.

■ ■ ■

The recipes in the Old Books were more or less listed as the following recipes are, though I've adapted where necessary:

WINE OR CIDER BASE

BISHOP PUNCH (Pitcher)

1 750 ml. bottle Bordeaux Supérieur red wine
3 oz. Smith & Cross navy-strength rum
2 oz. fresh lemon juice
3 oz. Simple Syrup
Large ice cubes
Fresh citrus slices for garnish; freshly grated nutmeg, optional

Not to be confused with the nearly opposite cocktail version (see alphabetical listing), this quickly assembled and pliable crowd-pleaser can be adjusted for personal taste or style of wine, since all of the ingredients are enhancements for the wine.

BRANDY CIDER NECTAR (Pitcher)

32 oz. Orchard Hill hard apple cider (NY) or Doc's hard apple cider (NY)
10 oz. sparkling water
3 oz. Hennessy VS cognac
2 oz. Lustau Don Nuño oloroso sherry
2 oz. fresh lemon juice
¼ portion Oleo Saccharum
Large ice cubes
Freshly grated nutmeg for garnish

This autumnal concoction also included a few dashes of the definitely not seasonal pineapple syrup or juice. I left it out, as it did not seem appropriate, but you can try it if you'd like. I also used a richer oloroso sherry here, but a fino-style such as Tio Pepe would yield a unique result. Use as dry a cider as possible. Although the Old Bar served this one from a pitcher, you could also double it and serve it from a bowl with dried apple slices for garnish.

CHAMPAGNE CUP *(Pitcher)*

1 750 ml. bottle brut Champagne (or Spanish cava)
1 10 oz. bottle sparkling water
3 oz. Hennessy VS cognac
2 oz. Luxardo maraschino liqueur
2 oz. Bénédictine liqueur
Large ice cubes
Fresh citrus slices and mint for garnish

Also known as the ***Brandy Champagne Punch***, this was seemingly the house recipe for a Cup by the pitcher. If you substituted an entry-level red Bordeaux (commonly referred to as "claret" at the time of the Old Bar) for the Champagne you would have a ***Waldorf Claret Cup***. In that rendition, if you substitute curaçao for the maraschino in the liqueur slot, you'll have a ***Claret No. 2***.

If you used a Riesling as your choice in the lead role (the Old Bar would've leaned on the sweeter styles, though I'd go with a drier trocken-style today), you would then have a ***Hobson's Kiss***. As with all of these types of recipes, the spirits and liqueurs were merely flavor enhancers. Keep that in mind and adjust as you see fit.

(WALDORF) CHAMPAGNE PUNCH

1 750 ml. bottle brut Champagne (or Spanish cava)
1 750 ml. bottle chardonnay (an entry-level white burgundy would be ideal)
¼ portion Oleo Saccharum (or to taste)
1-qt. block ice

Place all ingredients (except ice) in a container, stir to integrate, and refrigerate for at least 2 hours. If necessary, transfer to a bowl, stir to integrate, then add a block of ice. Garnish with fresh citrus slices.

A traditional *Champagne Punch* would not have included the chardonnay (just two bottles of sparkling wine). However, it would have added an ounce or two of fresh lemon juice and a couple ounces of standard sugar. It would've also used an ounce or so of fresh raspberry or strawberry syrup for decorative purposes. There was another variation called the **Champagne Kinsley**, which subbed in red burgundy (pinot noir) for the white. I would forgo the syrup if you're going this way.

CLARET CUP AUX CERISES PUNCH
(Red Wine and Cherry Punch)

2 (750 ml.) bottles Bordeaux Supérieur red wine
16 oz. Cherry-Infused Rum (Smith & Cross navy-strength; recipe follows)
¼ portion Oleo Saccharum (or to taste)
1 liter sparkling water
1-qt. block ice

Cherry-Infused Rum

8 oz. ripe and pitted sweet cherries
16 oz. Smith & Cross navy-strength rum

Add cherries to airtight glass container and muddle briefly to expose flesh. Add rum and infuse for at least 3 hours or overnight. Fine-strain prior to use.

Place wine, rum, and oleo saccharum into container, stir to integrate, and refrigerate for at least 2 hours. If necessary, transfer to bowl, then add sparkling water. Stir to integrate, and add block of ice. Garnish with fresh citrus slices and optional nutmeg.

This agreeable Punch has just the right amount of dark fruits while still remaining on the dry side. Remember, you want to have more than one serving of them. I boosted the amount of rum in order to add a bit more fizzy water at the end while still giving it some impact. Though no sugar was included in the original recipe, I added a small amount of oleo saccharum for a touch of citrus and sweet. Again, you can omit it or adjust accordingly for your own taste.

MOSELLE CUP (Pitcher)

1 bottle Riesling (trocken-style preferred)
4 oz. Lustau Don Nuño oloroso sherry
3 oz. Rémy Martin VS cognac
2 oz. Marie Brizard anisette
¼ portion Oleo Saccharum (to taste)
16 oz. sparkling water

Add all ingredients except sparkling water to pitcher. Stir to integrate, and refrigerate for at least 2 hours. Add sparkling water, stir to integrate, and serve in cups with 1 or 2 large ice cubes each. Garnish with fresh mint.

The oddball ingredient here is the anisette; you would think that it wouldn't work but it does. I left this recipe pretty much as is. Any adjusting that needs to be made, I will leave to the maker. A similar recipe, **Rhine Wine Cup**, calls for a sweeter Riesling and subs in curaçao for the cognac and maraschino for the anisette. It's worth a try if a second pitcher is required.

If you use the sweet, Bordeaux dessert wine Sauternes in the lead role, you'll of course have the **Sauternes Cup**. It's garnished with cucumber slices—no harm there either way.

PUNCH UNIVERSAL

1 bottle chardonnay (entry-level white burgundy)
6 oz. Appleton Estate extra rum
6 oz. Martell VS cognac
½ portion Oleo Saccharum
1 liter sparkling water
1-qt. block ice

Place all ingredients except sparkling water and ice in container, stir to integrate, and refrigerate for at least 2 hours. If necessary, transfer to bowl, and add sparkling water. Stir to integrate, then add block of ice. Garnish with fresh citrus slices and mint.

This one will be a go-to for your summer gatherings. The Old Bar cut the sparkling water by half in most of the wine-based Punches, but with the addition of the liquor enhancements, a whole bottle will be just fine.

SPIRIT BASE

CARIBBEAN FISH HOUSE PUNCH
(Waldorf Astoria Variation)

1 750 ml. bottle Appleton Estate extra rum
12 oz. Pierre Ferrand 1840 cognac
6 oz. Peach Brandy or house-made substitute (see "House-Made Recipes")
4 oz. Luxardo maraschino liqueur
6 oz. fresh lemon juice
¾ portion Oleo Saccharum (or to taste)
48 oz. water (chilled)
1-qt. block ice

Place all ingredients except water and ice in a container, stir to integrate, and refrigerate for at least 2 hours. If necessary, transfer to a bowl and add water. Stir to integrate, then add block of ice. Garnish with freshly grated nutmeg and fresh citrus slices.

Although this Punch is traditionally much more citrus-forward and served without maraschino liqueur, I've opted to let the Old Bar's hefty version stand. It's intriguing but not surprising that the by-the-glass recipe differs in both ratio of spirit and lack of maraschino but there you have it. As previously mentioned, David Wondrich's recipe for a doctored-up peach brandy is so good you can drink it as is. If at some point proper peach brandy becomes widely available, my recommendation would be to use that, especially if the cost of this small-production item becomes a non-issue.

An interesting variation from the Old Bar, called the **Old Navy Punch**, manages to ramp up the *Fish House* to yet another level of potency (something I wouldn't think possible). Simply use the overproof Smith & Cross navy-strength rum in the rum slot and add six ounces of fresh orange juice and a bottle of sparkling wine of your choice. Remove the maraschino and substitute one liter of sparkling water for the still water for a survivable result.

COLD BRANDY AND RUM PUNCH

12 oz. Pierre Ferrand 1840 cognac
4 oz. Appleton Estate Extra rum
4 oz. house-made Peach Brandy
4 oz. fresh lemon juice
½ portion oleo saccharum (or to taste)
32 oz. sparkling water (chilled)
1-qt. block ice

Place all ingredients except sparkling water and ice in a container, stir to integrate, and refrigerate for at least 2 hours. If necessary, transfer to a bowl, and add water. Stir to integrate, then add a block of ice. Garnish with freshly grated nutmeg and fresh citrus slices.

I've amended the title of this Punch, which originally had rum in the lead, to reflect the amount of spirits used in the recipe. Consider this the daytime version of the standard *Fish House Punch*.

JAMAICA ORANGE CUP *(Pitcher)*

8 oz. Smith & Cross navy-strength rum
8 oz. fresh orange juice
8 oz. water
⅓ portion oleo saccharum (orange-base preferred)
1 liter sparkling water

Add all ingredients except sparkling water to a pitcher. Stir to integrate, and refrigerate for at least 2 hours. Add sparkling water, stir to integrate, and serve. Add 1 or 2 large ice cubes to each cup and garnish with half an orange wheel.

I've opted for the stronger, navy-strength rum to help provide a backbone, but a standard-proof Jamaican rum will also work for a lighter result. The original recipe includes "orange essence," but the addition of even the strongest of orange flower water made little difference, though making an orange peel–based oleo saccharum did. Just be mindful to adjust the amount against the natural and variable sweetness of your freshly squeezed orange juice.

JAMAICA SWIZZLE (Pitcher)

8 oz. Appleton Extra rum
8 oz. Smith & Cross navy-strength rum
3 oz. fresh lemon juice
3 oz. fresh lime juice
2 oz. house-made Demerara Syrup (or house-made Falernum Syrup)

Add all ingredients to a pitcher (stainless steel preferred). Add crushed ice and swizzle for at least 30 seconds to ensure proper dilution. Add more crushed ice, then pour into a small wineglass. Serve with a straw. Garnish with fresh mint.

The original recipe somehow omits sugar of any kind. I highly recommend using Falernum syrup here to add another dimension, but if you don't have it, the demerara will be fine. I used two types of Jamaican rum, but you could go with one or the other. If it's a tad on the strong side, feel free to omit the navy-strength rum and double the standard-proof rum. Remember, swizzles are to be savored and sipped slowly. If you don't have a swizzle stick, plunging and stirring with your bar spoon will do just fine.

MYERS'S PLANTERS PUNCH

1 750 ml. bottle Myers's rum
3 oz. St. Elizabeth allspice dram or The Bitter Truth pimento dram
32 oz. water (sparkling optional)
6–8 oz. fresh lime juice
½ portion oleo saccharum (or more to taste)
1-qt. block ice

Place all ingredients except ice in a container, stir to integrate, and refrigerate for at least 2 hours. If necessary, transfer to a bowl, stir to integrate, then add a block of ice. Garnish with freshly grated nutmeg and fresh citrus slices.

This modified take on your basic Punch called for Angostura bitters. In order to help give this its own identity I've added allspice dram, which delivers the spice note and a little bit more. The result leaves an intriguing and decidedly cola note on the finish. A new favorite.

PING PONG PUNCH

16 oz. Old Overholt rye whiskey
16 oz. Martell VS cognac
¼ portion oleo saccharum (or more to taste)
1 750 ml. bottle sparkling water (flat, optional)
1-qt. block ice

Place all ingredients except sparkling water and ice in a container. Stir to integrate and refrigerate for at least 2 hours. If necessary, transfer to a bowl and add sparkling water. Stir to integrate, then add a block of ice. Garnish with fresh seasonal fruit slices and mint, and optional freshly grated nutmeg.

Splitting the lead role between two base spirits makes all the difference here. The original calls for the mint to be crushed but it's not necessary. Just top each cup of Punch with a freshly awakened sprig of mint; it makes for a much cleaner presentation.

The original recipe includes no citrus component but three or four ounces may add the bit of backbone that you desire. If you're going without, I would try this with noncarbonated water for a creamier finish.

HOT DRINKS

As with all the recipes in this book, my goal was to make them as approachable as possible. My hope was that readers would attempt what appeals to them and over time expand their palates and comfort level to include even those that initially did not. When preparing to tackle the hot drinks entries of the Old Books, I set out to make each of their methodologies as accessible as I could. If we could avoid whisking eggs and sugar by dry shaking, which we've practiced, then that's the way I chose to go, even if it bucked convention. I have prepared them in both manners and in the instances that it worked, there was no discernible difference between them. The only exception is probably the sugar cube versus syrup, as I kept the cube; the extra step of dissolving it as syrup always seems to result in a slightly sweeter outcome. So prepare yourself to expand your wintertime repertoire and move beyond the neat dram of whiskey or snifter of brandy. Your guests will most certainly notice your ever-broadening range of offerings. Oh, one last tip when it comes to hot drinks: you will want to warm your glassware with hot water to temper the serving glass and to help keep the temperature of the drink. You don't want to pour your warm Toddy into a cold cup.

BAKED APPLE TODDY

¼ warm baked apple (per serving)

1 demerara sugar cube

2 oz. Laird's bonded applejack or Boulard Grand Solage VSOP calvados

6 oz. hot water

Rinse, peel, and core apple(s). Wrap in parchment paper, place on baking sheet, and bake at 350 degrees for 30 to 40 minutes.

Add sugar cube to ceramic cup or mug. Add enough boiling water to dissolve. Snap lemon peel, rub around rim of cup, and drop in. Add spirit and stir to integrate. Add baked apple portion and top with boiling water. Stir, breaking down the apple. Garnish with freshly grated nutmeg.

A wintertime classic since the eighteenth century, this treat is very simple to prepare and also gives you another use for your bounty of fruit after a Saturday afternoon of apple picking.

Some personal touches can include using maple syrup for the sugar component, or you could sprinkle the apples with a hint of ground cinnamon prior to baking. Most important, this warming sipper gives you a reason to turn your oven on during a cold winter night.

BLACK STRIPE (BLACKSTRAP) TODDY

⅓ oz. Plantation blackstrap molasses

2 oz. Pusser's British Navy rum or Smith & Cross navy-strength rum

5 oz. hot water

Add molasses to ceramic cup or mug. Add a bit of hot water to integrate. Add rum and top with hot water. Stir again to integrate. Garnish with freshly grated nutmeg.

This traditional Toddy becomes much more enjoyable in this hot incarnation. Use funky and assertive rums only here. This is another time traveler. See **Black Stripe (Blackstrap)** for cold variation.

IRIʃH COFFEE ▮ *Peacock Alley*

1½ oz. Bushmills Black Bush Irish whiskey
1 oz. Baileys Irish cream (room temperature)
5 oz. freshly brewed French Roast coffee
Fresh whipped cream

Warm coffee glass with hot water. Let stand for a minute and pour out. Add all ingredients, in order listed. Stir to integrate and top with a small amount of the whipped cream. Garnish with freshly grated nutmeg (optional). Serve with spoon.

A traditional *Irish Coffee* would have white sugar cubes as the sweetening component and omit the Baileys Irish cream. Baileys adds sweetness and makes for a softer mouthfeel, which also allows you to omit the additional cream and sugar if you so choose. As for the cream, we go with the full-on sweetened whipped variety for a decadent treat. Float double or heavy cream over the back of a spoon for a traditional presentation. This is one of our guests' favorites as they are making their way back to their rooms after braving a cold NYC night on the town. It's just the thing to warm them up, inside and out.

(WALDORF) MILK PUNCH

5 oz. whole milk
1 tbsp. superfine sugar
1 egg yolk (optional)
2 oz. Bacardi añejo rum

Add milk to saucepan and heat to simmer (do not boil). Add sugar to ceramic cup or mug. Add egg yolk and rum to mixing glass and dry-shake for 5 seconds (this will temper the egg and help prevent scrambling). Add to cup, top with hot milk, and stir to integrate. Garnish with freshly grated nutmeg.

The original recipe listed in the Old Books was called **Bacardi Milk Punch** (of course it was) and is technically a hot Eggnog. You can forgo the egg to have your traditional Hot Milk Punch. The recipe directed building it in a bowl to whisk the egg yolk and sugar, then adding the remaining ingredients to a separate bowl, generally making the job harder than it had to be. Dry shaking the yolk to emulsify it more than does the job. You could also sub in any number of base spirits (think higher-proof cognacs and bourbons), but start with dark rum if only for the sake of the Old Bar's ritual. A blend of cognac and rum would also be historically correct and quite easy going down.

ʃLING/TODDY

1 demerara sugar cube
1 lemon peel
2 oz. spirit of choice

Add cube to ceramic cup or mug. Add some boiling water to dissolve cube. Snap lemon peel, rub around rim of cup, and drop in. Add spirit and stir to integrate. Add boiling water to fill, stir again to integrate, and serve. Garnish with freshly grated nutmeg (optional).

Dating back to the mid-1800s, this template recipe can also be used for other base spirits. The **Hot Gin Sling** (London dry) and **Hot Sherry** (I like an oloroso; a grated nutmeg garnish is essential) were made in exactly the same fashion. There was the famous **Hot Whisky Skin** (the skin being the lemon peel), which would also be listed as **Hot Scotch**. The **Columbia Skin** was listed in the Old Books and is no different from the other two. Your choice of whisky is entirely up to you, though I will say as these sippers are minimally adorned, you could use some of the good stuff here and still taste it. The **Hot Brandy** slotted in cognac, though any type will do here. Try an entry-level Armagnac for something a bit drier. Rye whiskey works to that end as well. This template also provides ample room for experimentation. Maple, grenadine, ginger syrup, and other sweeteners work great. Falernum can also be used to provide sweetness, spice, and additional flavors. And different spices can be incorporated for garnishes as well. Okay, you get the idea.

ʃPICED RUM

5 whole cloves

1 lemon wedge

1 demerara sugar cube

2 oz. Plantation Original Dark rum or house-made Spiced Rum Infusion (see *High Thread Count*)

5 oz. hot water

Poke the cloves into the fruit side of the lemon wedge. Add sugar cube to ceramic cup or mug. Add some boiling water to dissolve cube. Add prepared lemon wedge. Add rum and top with hot water. Stir to integrate and serve.

This recipe has changed very little over 150 years and we still make a good number of these each winter. A flavorful dark rum is what would have been traditionally used, though, when it's available, we use our house-made spiced rum for delicious results.

ʃPICED RUM NO. 2 *(Hot Buttered Rum)*

1 demerara sugar cube

1 lemon peel

2 oz. Smith & Cross navy-strength rum

1 small dollop unsalted butter (about the size of a sugar cube)

5 whole cloves

5 allspice berries

1 cinnamon stick

Add sugar cube to ceramic cup or mug. Add some boiling water to dissolve. Snap lemon peel, rub around rim of cup, and drop in. Add spirit and butter and stir to integrate. Add spices. Add boiling water to fill, stir again to integrate, and serve. Garnish with freshly grated nutmeg (optional).

The spice portion of the *Hot Buttered Rum* is strictly optional, though the original recipe does list it as such, as does *Jerry Thomas' Bartenders Guide* (1862). Basically you are adding a bit of unsalted butter to your standard Rum *Toddy* to yield a *Hot Buttered Rum*. You could also place the spices in a tea ball or strainer and let them steep for a few minutes to work their magic, then remove the strainer to avoid battling the loose cloves and allspice. Either way, this is a warming treat for a cold evening at home.

LARGE CUPS AND PUNCH

GROG

2 c. Don Q añejo, Bacardi dark, or other amber rum
¼ c. demerara sugar
6 c. Formosa oolong tea or other medium whole-leaf tea

Add all ingredients to heatproof container and stir to integrate. Serve in ceramic cups. Garnish with lemon peel.

This simple, tea-based *Grog* has roots in the seventeenth century. Water was first used to cut the rum to varying levels of potency; tea came later. The Old Bar's original recipe is an astounding 1:1 rendition. That's just not right. I would opt for the 3:1 or 4:1 variation of tea to rum, as you might want more than one of these on a cold winter night. As for the ingredients, be sure to pair the tea to the rum. The delicate oolong called for in the Old Books would get lost with an assertive rum. If you'd like to use one of those, go with a stronger black tea for best results.

HOT RUM PUNCH

½ portion Oleo Saccharum
8 oz. Myers's Jamaican rum
4 oz. Hennessy VS cognac
2 oz. Combier kümmel
2 oz. Bénédictine liqueur
48 oz. boiling water

Add oleo saccharum to a heatproof container. Add a cup of boiling water and stir to dissolve. Add spirits and stir to integrate, then add remaining hot water. Serve in ceramic cups. Garnish with fresh citrus slices.

There are a few ways to prepare a hot Punch. One alternate preparation is to prebatch the spirits and oleo saccharum and pour that into your guests' cups, then fill with hot water and add a lemon or orange peel. It may make things easier, depending on the number of guests. Just be sure to use at least a 3:1 water-to-spirit ratio. The enhancement liqueurs might be represented with relatively small amounts, but they have strong profiles and surely make their presence known. Adjust with caution.

LOCOMOTIVE *(Pitcher)*

12 cloves
2 cinnamon sticks
1 750 ml. bottle red wine
4 egg yolks
4 oz. house-made Honey Syrup
4 oz. Grand Marnier

Add spices and wine to saucepan over medium heat. Simmer for a few minutes (do not boil). Remove from heat and let rest. Add egg yolks and half of the honey syrup to mixing glass; dry-shake for at least 5 seconds. Add remaining honey syrup and Grand Marnier to mixing glass and roll between mixing glass and shaker a few times to integrate. Add to serving pitcher. Fine-strain wine into pitcher and stir to integrate. Serve in ceramic cups. Garnish with freshly grated nutmeg.

Named for the new mode of transportation in the nineteenth century, this unique serving goes back to *Jerry Thomas' Bartenders Guide* (1862). Other recipes of the day direct whisking the eggs, but dry shaking will more than do the job. This offering may seem complicated, but it's actually quite easy to put together. You can also wrap the spices in cheesecloth; however, because of the short warming time, I think you will get more flavor from the spices if they sit directly in the liquid rather than bunched tightly together. It's easy enough to fine-strain them out. Another tip is to prepare the wine portion of this recipe earlier in the day or the night before and cover it, leaving the spices in to integrate. You can then just reheat it and prepare the egg portion when the wine is ready. In the end, this enhanced *Mulled Wine* is another surprising recipe that will definitely come into heavy rotation in the winter months.

MULLED WINE

⅔ c. sugar
1 tbsp. whole cloves
4 cinnamon sticks
1 whole lemon rind
1 whole orange rind
2 750 ml. bottles red or port wine
8 oz. spirit of choice (optional)

Add all ingredients (except liquor, if using) to saucepan over medium heat. Simmer for a few minutes (do not boil). Remove from heat, cover, and let rest (overnight is best). When you're ready to serve, add liquor (if using) and heat to simmer. Fine-strain into ceramic cups. Garnish with freshly grated nutmeg.

This is probably the oldest category of drink in the entire book and also the most global. Nearly every society has some version of mulled wine, which dates back, in some form, to ancient Egypt and Rome. Now relegated to a wintertime tipple, this easily prepared spiced wine will surely bring the holiday spirit to any gathering. Just a couple of quick notes: You may want to pull back on the sugar if you are using port as your main ingredient (I also would not add a spirit if using port, but that's just me). For the spirit enhancement, thinking outside the box will be rewarded. Spanish brandy will pair naturally with the spices, as will dark rum, though the choice is entirely yours. I tried to keep the simplicity of the original recipe, but you can adorn this with additional spices as well. A few allspice berries or crushed cardamom pods will bring a unique twist to this tried-and-true classic.

TOM AND JERRY

FOR BATTER:

6 whole large eggs (separated)
1 oz. Smith & Cross navy-strength rum or Appleton Estate Extra rum
1½ c. sugar
½ tsp. ground cinnamon
¼ tsp. ground cloves
¼ tsp. ground allspice
¼ tsp. freshly ground nutmeg
1 tsp. organic vanilla extract
⅓ tsp. cream of tartar

2 oz. Prepared Tom and Jerry Batter
1½ oz. Martell VS cognac
½ oz. Smith & Cross navy-strength rum or Appleton Estate Extra rum
4 oz. whole milk (hot)
2 oz. water (hot)

STEP 1 (BATTER)

Separate the yolks and whites of eggs into two bowls. Add the rum to the yolks and beat until combined. Then add sugar, spices, and vanilla extract and whisk until completely combined and smooth in texture. If it's too thick, you can add another half ounce of rum.

STEP 2 (BATTER)

Add cream of tartar to whites and whisk until thickened and soft peaks are formed. Gently fold in the whites to the yolk mixture until combined and until there are no white streaks.

STEP 3 (SERVING)

Add batter, cognac, and rum to warm ceramic cup or mug. Top with hot milk and water mixture. Garnish with freshly grated nutmeg. Serves about 10.

Often credited to early nineteenth-century London writer Pierce Egan and popularized in the Northeast United States around that time, the *Tom and Jerry* nog has experienced both peaks and valleys of popularity. But it has steadfastly held its own through the ages, reaching its pinnacle every holiday season. The famous bowl and cups bearing "Tom and Jerry" in Old English font still reappear annually. They are especially popular in the northern Midwest United States but are becoming more visible every year.

This is another one that might be a bit of a challenge the first time around, but don't worry, it is for everyone. And if you make your first *Tom and Jerry* on Thanksgiving, I promise that by New Year's you won't need a recipe.

The recipe found in *Jerry Thomas' Bartenders Guide* was humbly made with only water as the thinning component. Later, in the post-Prohibition era of prosperity, whole milk was used, and while an all-milk T&J is decadent, you can really have only one. Cutting the milk with water meets in the middle and makes hardly a difference taste-wise, but it's noticeably less filling. You may fiddle with the ratio as you see fit. Traditional recipes also include up to and over a full pound of sugar. Trust me, the amount in the recipe here is more than enough. Preparing them à la minute does make for improved service, but you may batch it out in a punch bowl for best results while the batter is at its lightest. You can also serve another round the next morning. Just make sure to keep the batter refrigerated at all times. The split of hard stuff is yours, but the healthy dose not only warms you up, it makes the calories worth it.

Lastly, one of my favorite hacks includes using the prepared batter for a cold Egg Nog, for satisfying your guests who might prefer their Nog cold. Just add 2 ounces of batter to mixing glass along with 2 ounces of your favorite booze and 3 ounces or so of whole milk (or half and half). Add ice and shake well, then double strain for a smooth texture. Finish with some grated nutmeg and you're good to go. Serves two.

HISTORICAL CONCOCTIONS

I have opted not to include the following recipes in the main body of this book but to give them their own section here. These concoctions, though once popular in the Jazz Age (or prior), are typically no longer found on cocktail lists, even in the most adventurous establishments. This does not mean that they do not possess merit or are not worth trying (except the *Vin Mariani* and *Whiskey and Tansy*, which would be harmful to your health, as you will see in the coming pages). It just means that their style, methodology, and taste profile are no longer in favor. That's not to say that they won't make a comeback, but I thought it best to group them here instead on the off chance that they do.

Pousse-Cafés were featured only in the finest of hotels and restaurants at the turn of the twentieth century. They would typically be served with a cup of hot coffee or espresso, and great care had to be taken to execute them correctly. There is no way to quickly prepare one; only a patient and steady hand will yield the desired result. Mr. Crockett stated that if you shake a *Pousse-Café* and strain it (I'll assume that ice was involved), you will have a Peplo cocktail. All I can say is that although you can experiment with the ingredients in each combination and occasionally come across one that works in cocktail form, arbitrarily shaking every recipe that follows just will not work. The layering of a Pousse-Café allows the flavors to cross the palate in a particular sequence. That is why recipes are listed in the order poured, both for weight and density and for flavor profile, but most of all for looks. The professional bartenders who were the Pousse-Café specialists took much care to ensure that the layers were evenly spaced and the spirits did not mix. If they did, the result was more often than not a gray, murky mess. So much for the Peplo.

I recommend using a one- to two-ounce stemmed cordial or pony glass for Pousse-Cafés; some recipes call for a sherry glass. Use one on the small side. Using a narrow chrome pour spout on your bottle is essential. Slowly pour the ingredients in the order listed, almost dripping each down the back of a bar spoon and along the glass, being sure each new layer sits on the layer below it. Everyone should try to make one once, if only for laughs. I recommend trying the *Small Beer* first, as layering heavy cream onto the top of a shot of dark crème de cacao is easy enough. After that, you are on your own. Though it's only included in some of the following recipes, most can be served with what is more or less the standard garnish: a brandied or a Luxardo maraschino cherry placed in the center of a small skewer, then suspended across the rim of the small glass.

POUSSE-CAFÉS OF THE OLD BAR

Apologies in advance for the Old Bar's era of "creative" drink names. Rest assured, we use different titling practices today.

ANGEL'S BLUSH OR KISS (a.k.a. Martinique)

1 oz. Bénédictine
⅓ oz. heavy cream

ANGEL'S DREAM

⅓ oz. Luxardo maraschino liqueur
⅓ oz. heavy cream
⅓ oz. crème Yvette

Garnish with brandied cherry on a small skewer, placed across rim of glass.

ANGEL'S TIT

1 oz. Luxardo maraschino liqueur
⅓ oz. heavy cream

BABY TITTY *(Sherry Glass)*

½ oz. Marie Brizard anisette
¾ oz. crème Yvette

Top with whipped cream and serve with brandied cherry on top.

BRANDY CHAMPERELLE

⅓ oz. Grand Marnier
⅓ oz. Angostura bitters
⅓ oz. Royer VSOP cognac or Lustau Don Nuño oloroso sherry

BRANDY SCAFFA

½ oz. Luxardo maraschino liqueur
¾ oz. Royer VSOP cognac
2 drops Angostura bitters

COME UP SOME TIME ▮ *(Oscar)*

⅓ oz. Marie Brizard apricot liqueur
⅓ oz. Martell VS cognac
⅓ oz. heavy cream

GARDEN OF EDEN

½ oz. crème Yvette
½ oz. Giffard apricot liqueur

JOHN FRAZER

1 oz. Luxardo maraschino liqueur
5 drops Angostura bitters

JOKER *(Sherry Glass)*

⅓ oz. Marie Brizard anisette
⅓ oz. crème Yvette
⅓ oz. Bénédictine
⅓ oz. heavy cream

JONES LA POUSSE

1 oz. yellow Chartreuse
¼ oz. heavy cream

KING ALPHONSE

1 oz. Kahlúa coffee liqueur
¼ oz. heavy cream

LOENSKY

¾ oz. Combier kümmel
½ oz. Chivas Regal 12 Year Old Scotch whisky

(See *Loensky Cocktail* for variation)

MINCE PIE

¾ oz. white crème de menthe
½ oz. Hennessy VS cognac

RAINBOW *(Sherry Glass)*

¼ OZ. OF EACH INGREDIENT:
House-made Grenadine
Luxardo maraschino liqueur
Green crème de menthe
Yellow Chartreuse
Grand Marnier
Cognac

SMALL BEER

1 oz. dark crème de cacao
¼ oz. heavy cream

Made with coffee liqueur in place of the cacao, this becomes a *King Alphonse.*

THREE QUARTER
(Sherry Glass)

½ oz. yellow Chartreuse
½ oz. Grand Marnier
½ oz. Hennessy VS cognac

WALDORF *(Sherry Glass)*

¼ OZ. OF EACH INGREDIENT:
House-made Raspberry Syrup
Anisette
Parfait d'Amour
Crème Yvette
Yellow Chartreuse
Green Chartreuse
Martell cognac

WALDORF-ASTORIA
(Sherry Glass)

1½ oz. Bénédictine (chilled)

Topped with whipped cream.

WIDOW'S KISS
(Sherry Glass)

⅓ oz. Bols Parfait d'Amour
⅓ oz. yellow Chartreuse
⅓ oz. Bénédictine
1 egg white, whipped into a
    foam, then place a bit on
    top
1 strawberry slice (thin and
    placed on top of egg
    white)

UNIQUE SERVINGS WITH EGGS

Although there are many examples of recipes that include either all or part of an egg, the following recipes exhibit their egg component in a more, shall we say, pronounced way.

These were certainly all products of their time and yes, I tried them all (though not on the same day). I've also included Mr. Crockett's (or Oscar's Tschirky's) original recipes, as there was very little to modify with most of them. These were usually taken in the morning as a Bracer in one gulp or, at worst, two. If your constitution is such that you can get some of these down, in my opinion, you don't need a pick-me-up. These recipes should all be served in a sherry glass, with the ingredients slowly added in the order they are listed.

GOLDEN SLIPPER *(Sherry Glass)*

½ oz. yellow Chartreuse
1 egg yolk (small)
½ oz. Danziger Goldwasser

GOLDEN WEST ∎ *Oscar*

¼ oz. yellow Chartreuse
1 egg white (dry shaken for 5 seconds)
1 oz. Tio Pepe fino sherry

HONEYMOON
(a.k.a. Lune de Miel)

⅓ oz. Marie Brizard white crème de cacao
⅓ oz. Marie Brizard Parfait d'Amour
1 egg yolk (small)
⅓ oz. Combier kümmel

KNICKERBINE

⅓ oz. Combier crème de rose
1 egg yolk (small)
⅓ oz. Bénédictine
⅓ oz. Combier kümmel
3 drops Regans' Orange Bitters No. 6

L'AMOUR

⅓ oz. Luxardo maraschino liqueur
1 egg yolk (small)
2 drops organic vanilla extract
⅓ oz. Hennessy VS cognac

MOUNTAIN

2 oz. Doc's hard apple cider (NY)
1 egg yolk (small)
Salt and pepper to taste

The original recipe calls for the entire egg. That right there is a tall tale kind of performance, as in, "I saw him drink two 'Mountains.'" Maybe with just the yolk . . . maybe. Oh, and the salt and pepper actually help.

PRAIRIE OR PRAIRIE CHICKEN

1 egg yolk (small)
Salt and pepper to taste
½ oz. Hayman's Old Tom gin

In a sherry glass, slowly add the ingredients in the order that they are listed.

The original recipe calls for the entire egg here as well. Again, I've adapted it by using the yolk only. You can thank me now.

SHERRY AND EGG

⅓ oz. Lustau Don Nuño oloroso sherry
1 egg yolk (small)
⅓ oz. Lustau Don Nuño oloroso sherry

In a sherry glass, slowly add the ingredients in the order that they are listed.

HOT WITH FLAMES

The following recipes include the direct use of fire. I am not referring to the quick, lightning bug–type flaming of an innocuous orange
peel here; I am talking about actual flames. In one, the ignited spirit
moves from tankard to tankard, the barkeep throwing and catching
the stream in a growing arc. I am not including them within the
alphabetical portion of this book; I did not want them or their methodology to be taken lightly.

The *Blue Blazer* is a creation of the famous nineteenth-century
barman "Professor" Jerry Thomas, and it appears in his *Bartenders
Guide* (1862), recognized as the first published bar book. I have
personally prepared this simple hot Toddy in the showy tradition
that it calls for and believe me, it's dangerous even after you get the
hang of it. I am not going to list a play-by-play for performing this at
home because pouring ignited liquor from glass to glass is an act
whose worst-case scenario I have no interest in being responsible
for. I have included its basic recipe, minus the flying flames. Although
there is no real need to use a cask-strength whisky, as we are not
setting it alight, I wanted to keep Mr. Thomas's intention of curing
the common cold and flu and knocking the guest for a loop. If you
prefer, you may use other cask-strength spirits in lieu of the Scotch.
Smith & Cross navy-strength rum and Booker's bourbon both come
to mind as fine alternatives. If you use the New Jersey–made Laird's
bonded applejack and follow directions for the "stationary" *Blue
Blazer*, you will have the ***Jersey Flashlight***.

BLUE BLAZER TODDY/JERSEY FLASHLIGHT

1 tsp. demerara sugar
1 lemon peel
2–3 oz. hot water (just boiled)
1½ oz. Laphroaig cask-strength Scotch whisky

Place 1 tsp. sugar in small ceramic coffee mug. Twist freshly cut
lemon peel to release oils into cup; run along rim and drop in. Add
hot water and stir to dissolve sugar. Add whisky, stir, and serve.

CAFÉ BRÛLER

1 lemon wedge
3 oz. hot French roast coffee
1 oz. Royer Force 53 cognac

Rub lemon wedge along half rim of small wineglass, to about a half inch down from top of glass, then discard. Roll moistened side in superfine sugar, careful to only apply the sugar to the outside of the glass. Add coffee and then top with cognac. Set to flame and serve. Extinguish flame upon serving.

This is obviously served to delight your guests and should only be attempted, as with any flamed cocktail, by an experienced and, even more important, sober server. If you've already had a few, just omit the flame; it's a fine after-dinner drink with or without it.

As an alternate serving, you can present this in a standard coffee cup, omit the sugared rim, place a sugar cube in the cup, and proceed as directed in the recipe.

FLAMBEAU *(a.k.a. Orange Flambée Cognac)*

2 oz. Royer Force 53 cognac

Remove fruit from one small orange, keeping the peel, saving fruit for another use. Turn peel inside out and place in coupe glass. Add shaved or crushed ice around orange. Add cognac. Light orange with match and extinguish for aroma. Serve with small straw.

Although it seems a bit laborious, this presentation makes for quite the serving and most important, it tastes delicious. The orange notes and cognac are a great pairing. If you don't want to set it aflame, that is more than okay; they didn't set it on fire every time at the Old Bar either. They called that the **Orange Brandy Cup**.

ITEMS OF THE
PRE-PROHIBITION BAR

AMMONIA *(Old Bar Recipe)*

½ tsp. aromatic spirits of ammonia
4 oz. water or 8 oz. Coca-Cola (chilled)

Used as a hangover cure, you can still find the potable aromatic spirits of ammonia in pharmacies. It was also used as an antacid; according to Darcy O'Neil, author of *Fix the Pumps* (2009), it became somewhat popular as an addition to Coca-Cola and other flavored sodas. Although it's not the best tasting thing you will ever have, it is a true sample of the pre-Prohibition bar.

DELGARCIA

1 oz. Courvoisier VSOP cognac
1 small lemon peel
1 sugar cube

Fill pony glass with cognac, leaving room at top for sugar cube and peel. Place lemon peel on top of glass and balance sugar cube on it. Instruct guest to place cube in glass and twist peel, then place in glass as well.

This unique "glass service" cordial is all about the presentation. Very simply, it's a cognac that is served neat in a pony glass with the garnishes placed above the rim. This little "participation" exercise is a real throwback, best served after dinner.

HAPPY THOUGHT

½ oz. Varnelli anisette
½ oz. Tempus Fugit crème de cacao
½ oz. Combier crème de rose
½ oz. Tempus Fugit crème de menthe
½ oz. crème Yvette
½ oz. Hennessy VS cognac

Add all ingredients to mixing glass. Add ice and stir for 20 seconds. Strain into two cordial glasses. No garnish.

Mr. Crockett surmised that it was a "bartender's 'happy thought' to grab up every bottle within reach, one after another, and pour some of each into a glass." He also wondered what the aftermath of drinking this would be. The original recipe directs that the ingredients be poured in the order listed in a wineglass over ice. I tried so you won't have to, but if you must, only the serving suggestion listed here really works.

SAM WARD

2½ oz. yellow Chartreuse (or Combier Abricot apricot brandy)

Cut a lemon in half and hollow it out. Place in small tumbler and fill with shaved ice. Add liqueur. Serve with small straw.

Samuel Ward was the first president of the New York Temperance Society, but his son Samuel Cutler Ward married Emily Astor, sister of John Jacob Astor III, and was in regular rotation at the city's finest restaurants. Although he predated the Hotel, his reputation had apparently enough lasting power that not one but two drinks were named in his honor. Substituting apricot brandy for the Chartreuse gets you an ***Apricot Sam Ward***. Originally presented as the delivery device, the lemon cup takes some work, but it is quite the conversation starter. This is best served in a glass as a summertime dessert course.

VIN MARIANI (Old Bar Recipe)

2 oz. Vin Mariani (no longer produced)
1 oz. sweet vermouth
1 dash orange bitters

Add all ingredients to mixing glass. Add ice and stir for 30 seconds. Strain into chilled cocktail glass.

Angelo Mariani's "Vin Tonique Mariani à la Coca de Pérou," more popularly known as "Vin Mariani," was a red Bordeaux wine–based, coca leaf–enhanced tonic that was available from the 1860s to the mid-1910s. Supposedly, each ounce contained six milligrams of cocaine. It was fully endorsed by the celebrities of the day ranging from Ulysses S. Grant, writer Émile Zola, and actress Sarah Bernhardt to Pope Leo XIII. Obviously no longer produced today, this recipe is included for completion's sake.

WHISKEY AND TANSY (Old Bar Recipe)

3 leaves tansy, or pony of tansy mixture (do not purchase; see description)
1 jigger whiskey

Add ingredients directly to whiskey glass and stir to integrate.

When I began research on the then unknown-to-me tansy flower, I thought it would just be a matter of procuring the dried flower and proceeding with the recipe from there. Luckily, as part of my research I consulted the very detailed bartender's companion *The Drunken Botanist*, by Amy Stewart (2013). After I made her personally aware of my intention to not only try the recipe myself but include it in this book, she strongly advised against it. She wrote, "Tansy can be quite toxic (as with many poisonous plants, toxicity levels vary with age, part of the plant, weather, etc.) and some people are highly allergic. I'd suggest people read it for historical interest but steer clear of using it. Alcohol is a solvent that extracts chemicals from plants pretty indiscriminately, so you don't really know what you're doing when you drop a plant (which is nothing more than a green, living chemical factory) into alcohol." I always try to listen to those who know more than I do. I suggest that you do the same. Thanks, Amy!

ACKNOWLEDGMENTS

Joseph Taylor worked at the Old Hotel until its last day (May 3, 1929) and as Mr. Crockett notes, "His self-respect would not permit him to work in a speakeasy." Mr. Taylor was "looking forward eagerly to getting back behind a counter and plying the cocktail shaker in the old way, with 'real stuff' to pour into it from genuinely label bottles. But he did not live to see that day." Just as Joseph Taylor never stepped foot in the "new" Hotel, I wasn't around to see the Old Hotel, so I guess in this small way we are linked. Without his foresight we would not have a *Waldorf Astoria Bar Book* in any form, so this humble update and revision is dedicated to him. I would also like to think that Albert Stevens Crockett would have enjoyed sampling more than a few of these recipes, so a tip of the cap to the work of Mr. Crockett as well. I hope that they are both in their rightful places at each side of a big bar somewhere. Here's a round to Oscar Tschirky, Jacques Straub, and Ted Saucier, whose impact on the practice of drinking well in relation to this book lies at its foundation. A countless amount of cocktail books and manuals were consulted in the research of this book; I would like to thank those that came before whose influence is woven within the fabric of it.

For my comrade in arms in this whole endeavor, Matt Zolbe. Having the director of Sales and Marketing as your ally when dipping your toe into the murky waters of cocktail book writing cannot be understated. I was lucky beyond any expectation to have such a like-minded supporter.

To Orion Berge, Jon DeRosa, and Chef David Garcelon for their constant support (at all hours of the night) and for providing a proper sounding board from early on, when the lines on the map pointed in countless directions.

To Ed Costa, Bryan Woody, Eric Long, Stuart Foster, Chef John Doherty, Grady Colin, Diarmuid Dwyer, Thomas Long, Ronen Nissenbaum, Mark Ricci, and Brian Galligan, who each in their own way allowed me to get on this canoe in the first place and never once attempted to man the helm.

To the culinary staff that I learned so much from and whose assistance help make the beverage program something special: Chefs Charlie Romano, Peter Betz, Michael Ottomanelli, Cedric Tovar, Ryan Alday, and Nancy Olson. A special thank-you to Evelyn Hsu Ciszak, whose guidance and compass of the bar during the very early days of Peacock Alley cannot be understated.

For my coworkers and fellow managers both past and present. For my Waldorf Astoria colleagues who helped make my day-to-day that much smoother while undertaking this project and whose opinions also helped shape this book: Jeff Krauthamer, Jonathan Masel, George Pappas, Jessica Fusco, Abby Murtagh, Jasmin Howanietz, and especially Julien Pierlas. The helpful assistance of our archivists, Erin Allsop and Deidre Dinnigan, and our social media crusaders, Megan Towner and Melissa Howard, is also appreciated.

A sincere thank-you to the following leaders and influencers of the food and beverage industry who were integral to say the least: Gary "Gaz" Regan, whose support from early in my career predates Peacock Alley and whose mentorship I appreciate more than he probably knows. He was also the first on the canoe. To my friend Allen Katz, another early passenger whose opinion helped forge the pages to come. For the early conversations with David Wondrich. His books were also influential to me prior to this project but didn't really come to focus until I started it. Dale DeGroff, who also was an early supporter whose relationship and influence also predates Peacock Alley. Philip Duff and Martin Doudoroff for helping bottle some of the ends as I came down the stretch. Throughout the process, I solicited the perspective of some of the barmen and women whose opinions I respect and who I have also regarded as friends long before this book was ever a thought—I thank them for their time: Nathan Dumas, Michael Neff, Ms. Franky Marshall, Evan Thomas, and Brian Matthys. A New Orleans shout-out to Russ Bergeron and Chris Hannah for local recipe checks and a thank-you to Darryl Barthé as he is removed from the F&B industry but helped chime in at length with the "civilian" response. This role was also played by my decades-long NYC-based friend, Steven Brown.

I would also like to thank some of the writers who found space in their pages for me through the years: Kara Newman, Steve Reddicliffe, Rosie Schaap, and Robert O. Simonson. A huge thank-you to others whose books cleared up quirks and grey areas: Andrew Willett, Amy Stewart, Darcy O'Neil, and Brad Thomas Parsons. Lastly, for guiding me into the world of publishing with contacts and essential advisement, Karolina Waclawiak.

Thanks to the legal consult of my new pal, Karen Shatzkin.

Thanks to my editor at Penguin, Emily Murdock Baker, who was one of the few allowed on deck and never made a rush for the steering wheel. Her guidance (especially early on when it was needed most) is truly appreciated. A thank-you also goes out to the watchful eyes at team Penguin: my production editor, Katie Hurley, and Sabrina Bowers for the interior design (squeezing in three books' worth of text while making it readable was no easy task). I was also lucky to have such a talented artist in Josie Portillo, whose drawings not only helped lighten the look of this book but also did service to the spirit of the original drawings by Leighton Budd.

To my team of Peacock Alley bartenders, whose ability to remain onstage, in an arena that is open nearly twenty-four hours a day deserves decidedly more recognition than this industry gives to them. Their contributions go well beyond that of bartending. Some have been here longer than others but they all have worked for the success of this operation and each is integral to its ongoing influence: Darren Pelan, Michael Nowicki, Bledi Noka, Tom DeFrancesco, Sergey Nagorny, Noah Small, Frank Nolan, John Frey, Marie Duverger, and Luke Lin. Early teammates whose terms are not forgotten include Eric Dennis, Nick Psinakis, and Rebecca Schlossberg.

And last to my family and friends, who were able to understand that writing a book while running bars allows for little or no playtime. To my mother, Carmella, whose impact as a host not only influenced me but many of my friends as well. I am elated that she survived her battles to see this book. I am sad that my father did not. He would've gotten a kick out of it for sure. This section would not be complete without my son, Joseph, whose early foray into professional kitchens I was flattered to be a part of but happy he was able to find another calling; and my daughter, Alyssa, who I have proudly watched become a caring, wonderful mother herself and a best friend. But most of all, this book is for my wife, Margaret, who would get only slightly perturbed, as I would shake her awake with yet another "final" version of a recipe. It could not have been attempted, much less written, without her partnership and support, which along with my love, I strive to return daily.

INDEX